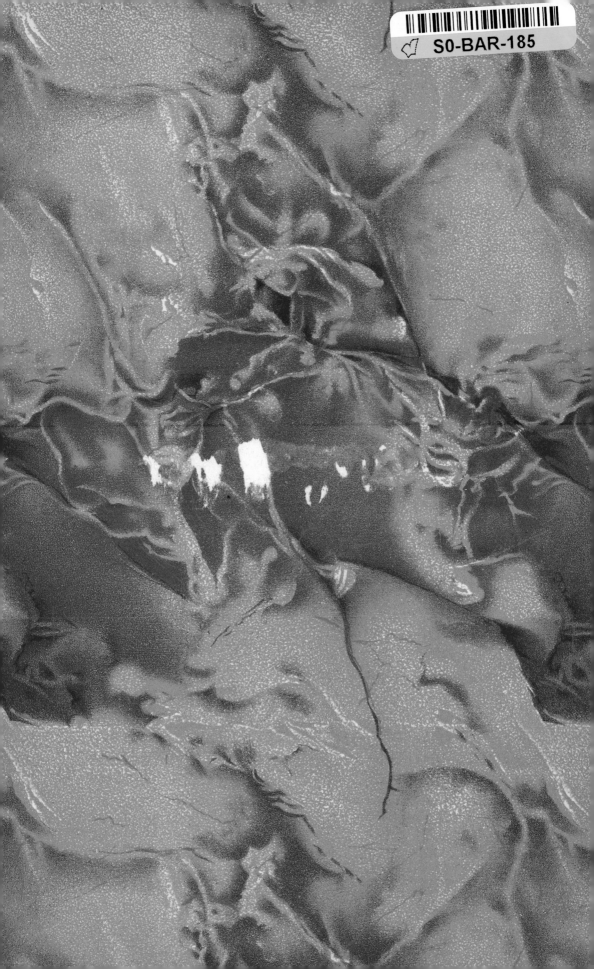

State Capitol of Virginia

VIRGINIA

REBIRTH OF THE OLD DOMINION

BY

PHILIP ALEXANDER BRUCE, LL. B., LL. D.,

Centennial Historian of University of Virginia
and
Late Corresponding Secretary of the
Virginia Historical Society

Virginia Biography
By Special Staff of Writers

Issued in Five Volumes
VOLUME II

ILLUSTRATED

THE LEWIS PUBLISHING COMPANY
CHICAGO AND NEW YORK

1929

V

SECESSION AND POST-BELLUM PERIODS, 1860-1876

CHAPTER 1

CAUSES OF VIRGINIA'S SECESSION

The debate in the Constitutional Convention of 1788, led, on one side, by Madison and Marshall, and on the other, by Henry and Mason, with backers hardly less able or less well-informed than themselves, disclosed the wide gulf which existed between those who favored the adoption of the great instrument drafted at Philadelphia in 1787 and those who opposed it. Some members, like George Mason, for instance, refused to sign the final resolution approving that instrument, on the ground that it failed to offer enough safeguards for the protection of the rights of the Southern Commonwealths. In the end, the ratification by the Virginia Convention only took place when important amendments had been submitted and accepted.

One of the most significant of these amendments contained the declaration that the State reserved the right to secede whenever the powers of the National Constitution should be perverted to the oppression and injury of the American people. Virginia was not the only State which expressly retained this right. South Carolina, New York, and Massachusetts adopted a similar provision. It is true that no such provision was imbedded permanently in the phraseology of the National Constitution, but the document distinctly affirmed that all rights not plainly delegated to the Central Government were reserved by the States, and among these rights, Virginia, along with the other Southern Commonwealths, claimed that the right of secession was the foremost.

It was the conviction of her people that the inhabitants of each State were the citizens of that State and not of the United

7

James Madison

States. In their view, there was no direct relation between the individual citizen, and the United States as a whole. The tie was with his own Commonwealth; to that Commonwealth, his primary allegiance was due; and if he was in the Federal Government's employment, he was at once to be relieved from the obligation of his oath, should his State adopt an ordinance of Secession. The view of the Constitution expressed in the celebrated Kentucky Resolutions of 1798-99, the fruit of Jefferson's pen, was the one generally entertained in Virginia. That view held that the Federal Constitution was a compact between the different States and the United States; that all violations of that compact on the part of the Federal Government, by assuming functions not intrusted to it, were illegal and without force; that the General Government was not made by this compact the exclusive or final arbiter of the powers delegated to itself; and that, as in all other cases of compact in which there was no common judge, each party had an equal right to determine whether an infraction had been committed, or not, and if so, the manner in which it should be redressed.

At one time, Jefferson, the author of these memorable words, was greatly alarmed by the encroachments of the National Government on the powers reserved to the States. A certain letter written by him, under the influence of this apprehension, clearly voiced the sentiments of most of his contemporaries in Virginia. "Are we to stand to arms?" he asked. "That must be the last resource," said he, in reply to his own question, "which is not to be thought of until much longer and greater sufferings. We must have fortitude and longer endurance with our brethren while under delusion * * * and separate from our companions only when the sole alternatives left are the dissolution of our Union with them, or submission to a government without limitation of powers. Between these two evils, when we must make a choice, there can be no hesitation."

When Virginia finally took up arms, were her people in that extreme situation, which, according to Jefferson, alone

John Marshall

would justify them in having recourse to rifle and cannon? Had the provocation by the North risen to such a height as to cause that situation to be no longer endurable? At more than one crisis in the affairs of the Nation between the Missouri Compromise and the election of Lincoln, it was the opinion of the Virginians in the mass that their safety within the Union was in jeopardy. What led them to reach such a conclusion? One of the principal reasons was the attitude of the North, regarded as a whole, towards the institution of slavery. During colonial times, and for a considerable period afterwards, the New England and Middle States were in the possession of numerous slaves. Moreover, New England's ships were profitably engaged in the importation of raw Africans for the use of the Southern plantations. This traffic ceased in 1808. By this time, New England had abolished the institution, and the middle states had also adopted measures which would ensure emancipation at an early date. There was no special pretense, on their part, of purely moral motives in pursuing this general course. As a matter of fact, no large estates were to be found in these communities on which slave labor could be made lucrative by the cultivation of great staples. The land, as a rule, was divided among small proprietors, who tilled their soil with their own hands. This interest was supplemented by the spread of local manufactures, and the rise of a vigorous artisan class. It has been very correctly said that, as the number of slaves had always been limited in the Northern States, "the stability of no great interest there was jeopardized by their emancipation; that no large amount of property was confiscated in liberating them; and that no dangerous population was admitted as freemen to a community with which it would be impossible for them to amalgamate."

Furthermore, the black population of the North had been diminished by sales to Southern planters before the day for their manumission had arrived. That part of the country was so free from the disadvantages of the African's presence at the end of the Revolution that a tide of immigration from Europe soon set in in that direction. Employment was quickly found by these foreigners, not only in the manufacturing centers of the northeastern and middle states, but also on the wide plains of the fertile regions of the West, situated within the confines of the territories. Their settlement tended to strengthen the importance of the National Government. Communities arose in that quarter which looked upon themselves, not as a part of the State to which they really belonged, but as a part of the United States. Their point of view was national, not local; not only because these Western States were too young to have any history, but also because so many of their people had been born in European lands, which were in the habit of exalting the central government over the local. There was in such communities but little stimulant for local pride, and hence their public sentiment was acutely conscious of the capitol at Washington.

On the other hand, in the commonwealth of Virginia, the attitude of the public mind, as the result of one hundred and eighty years of a separate and practically independent existence before the United States was ever thought of, was naturally not one that was disposed to acknowledge inferiority to a newly created central power. There were few factories of importance in the communities of the State to create a leaning in favor of the tariff, and thus foster a disposition to rely upon that central power for the promotion of the State's financial and economic welfare. The National Government was not in the Virginians' eyes a cow to be perennially milked for the advancement of local manufactures, and the construction of public highways and long canals. In reality, there were no selfish local interests to shake their loyalty to the Doctrine of States Rights. The pursuit of agriculture was the employment of the great mass of the Virginian people; and this pursuit was, not only not assisted by the operation of the tariff, but was actually damaged by that tariff's increasing the cost of all the farm supplies which the landed proprietors had to buy. This was especially true in the case of agricultural implements and clothing for the slaves. Beyond offering the Virginians protection from foreign invasion, and simplifying their commercial intercourse with the other States, the existence of the National Government was the source of no conspicuous advantage to them as a community, from a purely practical point of view.

Nothing arose in the long interval which followed the close of the Revolution to alter this condition. During that interval, the absorption in agriculture only grew more intense, and thus the economic interests remained the same. No great cities sprang up; such manufactures as existed expanded but slowly; and there was hardly any addition to the population from immigration. In short, all the influences in actual operation tended simply to confirm the Virginians' original attitude towards the National Government. The Doctrine of States Rights, as formulated by Jefferson and Madison, continued without any really substantial change in the popular mind. If any change did take place, it was to be found in the increased rigidity of the Virginians' loyalty to the principles of that doctrine. This was because they, along with the people of the South in general, had reached the conclusion that the maintenance of States Rights was the only bulwark that was likely to resist the assaults which were directed against slave institutions. Why was the strength of this bulwark so long overrated? Why did not the Southern States, with Virginia at their head, adopt the policy of emancipation as the only certain means of removing the most formidable of the political dangers which confronted them so increasingly?

There was during, and after the close of, the Revolution, a perceptible public sentiment in Virginia in favor of manumission of the slaves. But it was not strong enough to overcome the practical obstacles to such a consummation. In the first place, land, negroes, and livestock made up the three really important forms of property in the state, as they had also done in the colony. It was a community of farmers and planters alone, as we have already stated. While it is true that the great majority of the small proprietors cultivated their own soil with their own hands, yet the entire body of the larger landowners were absolutely dependent on slave labor for the production of crops. To abolish the institution of slavery without compensation, as the Abolitionists proposed, was to destroy at a stroke about one-third of the capital of the slaveholders. There have been in history few people who were either willing or able to make such a sacrifice.

Great Britain had fully recognized the injustice of uncompensated abolition in the West Indies. She modified the destructive force of the stroke by paying for all the slaves in the islands which were under her dominion. But no such proposal was ever made seriously by the American National Government. The loss was expected to fall on the people of Virginia, and her sister states of the South alone, although it was chiefly through the instrumentality of Northern ships and Northern slave-dealers that the slaves had been brought into the Southern ports.

But the loss of slave capital was not the only form of damage which would ensue from emancipation. Where were substitutes to be obtained to fill the places of the freedmen? Would these freedmen be willing to work in the ground as they had done before their bonds were loosed? The story of Jamaica after the liberation of its slaves did not encourage such a belief. If the freedmen should desert the hoe and the plough, and the fields should be left to the growth of weeds, the land would quickly sink in value, and all other farming interests would fall off in sympathy with this decline. In other words, bankruptcy in part at least appeared to be the fate of Virginia, should she quietly submit to the dictation of the Northern Abolitionists. One generation of her people at least would be ruined; and this would probably have ensued even had she adopted the policy of gradual emancipation recommended by Jefferson and urged by

so many of her public men in the great debate in the General
Assembly in the winter of 1832-33.

It should not be forgotten that the institution of slavery, as
it existed in Virginia, offered a social as well as an economic
side.   There were, in fact, numerous social reasons why the
owners of slaves shrank from the deliberate destruction of the
tie.   There had been African slaves in the community from a
time as early in its history as 1619, when the Dutch man-of-war
had landed a small company of that race on the wharf at Jamestown.   But no remarkable increase in the number introduced
had taken place until after the opening of the eighteenth
century.   From that date, however, down until the beginning
of the War in 1861, the black population had steadily augmented.

Previous to 1700, with rare exceptions, the household servants had been drawn from the ranks of the indentured white
women.   But even in the time of the first William Byrd, as we
know from his own disposition, as recorded in his letter-books,
many planters showed a preference for black servants over
white.   During the period that preceded the Revolution, the
employment of negro slaves had become practically universal
under the domestic roof; and this condition continued without
any change so long as the institution of slavery lasted.   Indeed,
it became almost impossible for Virginians of means to conceive
of their domestic hearths as devoid of the presence of black
servants.   These servants were as much a part of the family
circle as the white members themselves.   There was not a family
event from season to season in which they did not have their
share.   They received the new-born infant into their arms; they
nursed the young child with maternal fondness; they gathered
in a beaming throng behind the assembled guests at the family
weddings; at gay entertainments, they looked on unrebuked at
the dancers in the drawing-room; they watched through the
night with patient solicitude at the bedside of the sick; they
shrouded the dead for that breathless slumber which shall never

be broken; and crowded about the grave when the body was committed to the earth.

The planters who owned slaves were perfectly aware that, should the tie of their proprietorship be broken, this close and sympathetic association would cease, since it was inconsistent with a state of freedom on both sides. No such attitude of absolute devotion like this had ever existed in the relations with white servants as a class, however conscientiously they might perform their duties. Was it unnatural that the slaveholders should shrink from the destruction of the social bonds that united them to the faithful black people who had a part in every social experience of their lives?

But there was still another aspect of emancipation which might well have caused them to pause when urged to begin it. Between no two races on earth was there a wider physical and moral gulf than the one which separated the white people of Virginia from its black people. The white were descended from pure European strains which had enjoyed the benefits of the highest civilization for centuries. These strains had been the leaders of mankind throughout the modern era. They were influenced in their lives by the spirit of an invincible pride of race. Especially was this true of the descendants of the original English settlers. They had occupied the great plain east of the Blue Ridge since the foundation of Jamestown. They had reduced it to tillage; had erected homes on its face; had established everywhere a strong framework of local government, and through all, had been warmly loyal to that government; and when necessary, had fought for its protection against the Indians, the French, and the British in turn.

What would be the social effect on this community should the slaves be liberated? Could it continue to stand without serious alteration if the negroes were allowed to share in its destiny as freedmen? Would it survive at all in the form which alone would make it tolerable to the white inhabitants? Was there not danger that the whites, under the influence of the new

JAMESTOWN CHURCH TOWER IN 1890

system, would gradually sink to the social level of the former slaves? Would not social equality between the races become as universal as, in our day, it has become in some of the South American countries? What would be the inevitable result? Miscegenation with the approval of the law! A mongrel race, neither African nor Anglo Saxon! Or it might be a venomous political and economic rivalry would spring up between the two races, even should amalagamation be avoided,—a struggle really for existence on the same soil. Only the pistol and rifle could settle such an issue; and in that conflict for mastery, the negro was the one who was the most likely to go to the wall.

Such anticipations as these were not favorable to the adoption of emancipation by the whites as a voluntary act on their part.

With all these substantial reasons for hesitation to take that momentous step, was it at all remarkable that the people of Virginia, like the rest of the Southern people, should have been further influenced to retain the institution of slavery by the intemperate conduct of so many of the conspicuous Abolitionists of the North? The self-reliant life of the plantation had made them peculiarly proud and independent in spirit and keenly resentful of intrusion into their intimate domestic affairs. But above all, the anti-slavery propaganda was exactly calculated to stir up slave revolts, which had always been looked upon in the South as the most terrifying calamity that could fall upon any community. The history of the Gabriel and Turner insurrections lingered more vividly in the Virginians' remembrance than the bloodiest of the Indian massacres of the Colonial age. The most atrocious of all crimes in their view was to encourage a repetition of these catastrophes. And yet apparently this was the purpose which, not only the professional agitators of the Garrison stripe had in view, but also the circle of the great writers of New England, who employed their pens unceasingly to influence public opinion against the slaveholders.

Naturally, the Virginians recoiled from the prospect of the economic blight, domestic degradation, and political confusion which might ensue from the liberation of hundreds of thousands of bondsmen. They also knew that they had no reason to reproach themselves for a failure to make the necessary sacrifices to improve the general condition of their slaves; and it was with indignant warmth that they rejected the falsehood that they were, in their conduct, less humane or less conscientious than the Northern people. With these inflamed feelings, was it strange that the people of Virginia, like the Southern people at large, should have protested against the dark implications directed against their social framework in Mrs. Stowe's *Uncle Tom's Cabin?* This book drew a picture of slavery which expressed with peculiar vividness all the detestation of that institution which had been gradually forming in the minds of the outside world under the influence of the violent denunciations of it by the fanatical school of northern orators and poets. Mrs. Stowe's novel, in the course of the first year, found millions of readers in all civilized lands, for it was soon translated into the principal foreign languages. The stage took up the story, and its scenes were reenacted with the poignancy of real life before numberless sympathetic audiences who had never beheld a slave, and had only vaguely heard of the existence of the Southern States.

Even those Virginians who had no toleration for the institution, and would have gladly seen it abolished, resented this aspersion on the social life of their section, and, in consequence, were led to nurse a feeling of bitterness against the Northern people, among whom the attack had originated. It seemed even to this moderate section that it was hardly just that the Southern people should be held up to universal reprobation for the retention of a social and economic system which had prevailed among all the branches of the English peoples only a few decades before; and which had been discarded in the end by certain of these branches, not because it was decided to be immoral, but because it was found to be unprofitable.

But the shock to the Virginians caused by the publication of *Uncle Tom's Cabin* was trivial in comparison with the sense of horror aroused by the raid of John Brown and his followers on the quiet and remote town of Harper's Ferry. In the midst of the peace which prevailed in the state, the announcement of this event fell upon the ears of its citizens like the sound of fire-bells at night from every quarter of a great city. The hour of universal conflagration seemed to be at hand; and that hour was not the less dreadful because it had been expected by many as the logical result of the campaign of relentless vigor which had been so long in progress against the South among the most violent Northern advocates of emancipation by force. There were influences behind the act of Brown which made it appear to be something more than the deed of a fanatic or madman. It was soon learned that the invasion had had at its back the moral, and in some cases, the pecuniary support of representatives of the best culture of the North,—men of destinction and influence like Gerrit Smith, Theodore Parker, Samuel G. Howe, and Thomas W. Higginson.

It was not probable that a high-spirited, yet conservative, people like the Virginians would regard with equanimity such an attack upon the safety of every man, woman and child, and of every home, within the confines of their commonwealth. And yet they put a sharp restraint upon any disposition to break away from the Union which this consummation of all the aggressions from which they had suffered already was so aptly calculated to arouse in their breasts. It was not long before the states lying further south were passing ordinances of secession under the influence of the conviction that Mr. Lincoln's election had terminated all hope of safety within the fold of the Union. But Virginia refused to accept that event in this pessimistic light. She considered the course of the seceding states to be unwise in spite of all provocations; and she continued to urge

a spirit of moderation as long as there was any hope of a compromise. It was due to her influence that a Peace Conference
assembled, in the hope of discovering a basis for the permanent
settlement of the great controversy which divided the two sections of the country. And it was not until the call for troops to
scotch the movement for a lasting separation was issued by
Mr. Lincoln that her Secession Convention followed the example
which South Carolina had been the first to set.

However much Virginia might regret that action of her
sister state, she felt that it was not possible for her to array
her physical and moral forces against the people to whom she
was bound by far closer ties than the ones which united her to
the people of the North. Her action was both unselfish and
chivalrous, for she had nothing to gain from the upshot of
the impending conflict whichever way the scales of fortune
might turn. Her people were not ardently in favor of secession.
Freed from all extraneous influences, the Virginians would not
have withdrawn from the Union, although they had become
keenly aware of the antagonisms that had raised a barrier
between the North and the South.

As a matter of fact, Virginia had, of all the states, the most
justifiable reason, from a purely historical point of view, to
cherish the bond that joined her to the United States. Was it
not her Washington who had assured the nation's existence by
his sword and planted its government on a lasting foundation by
his wisdom and unselfish devotion? Was it not her Jefferson
who had declared America's right to take an equal position
among the nations of the world? Was it not her Madison who
had been chiefly instrumental in shaping the fundamental law
of the country? Was it not her Marshall who had consolidated
the powers of the central administration and made those powers
supreme? Was it not her Monroe who had created a lasting
shield against foreign intrusion? Was it not her Jefferson and
Monroe again who had doubled the area of the Republic by the
addition of Louisiana and Florida? Was it not her Lewis and

Clark who had laid the basis of the claim to the Oregon territory? Was it not her Houston who had secured the national possession of the Empire of Texas, and her Scott and Taylor, the national possession of California?

These were sentimental recollections, it is true, but they alone might well have created an emotion of reluctance to take the plunge when withdrawal from the Union was contemplated.

CHAPTER II

DIFFICULTIES CONFRONTING THE CONFEDERATES

In describing the obstacles which had to be surmounted by the Confederate States before they could hope to win their independence, it should be remembered that these obstacles were common to them all. It will be necessary to discuss these disadvantages in their relation to the whole South, but the fate of Virginia was as intimately involved in the fact that they existed as if she alone was concerned. There was one feature of her situation which made her more vulnerable than most of her sister Southern States. She abutted on the North in the very quarter from which attacks were most certain to come. It was positively necessary that the Federal capital should be vigorously protected from capture. How could this be most successfully done? By an offensive campaign, or series of campaigns, against the country lying south of the Potomac. Nothing would be accomplished by allowing the Confederates to besiege Washington. The first step required imperatively of the Federal armies was to cross the Potomac and advance into Virginia.

On the other hand, it was equally imperative that the Confederates should defend Richmond, their capital, from assault.

The space lying between the two national centers was so narrow comparatively that it was inevitable that the intervening terrain should become the scene of many battles in succession, and the ground be torn up by shot and shell. Want would follow in the train of the devastation, and, in consequence, the last vestige of prosperity would be wiped out for the time-

23

JOHN LETCHER
Governor 1860-1864

being. All this had been fully expected by the people of Virginia when they decided to withdraw from the Union. They did not shrink from the terrible penalty which they had to pay for their support of a great principle; but not even their most extreme conception of what they would suffer surpassed the actual condition in which the state was left at the close of the war. And yet not one murmur of regret was heard from the vast majority of the people as the armies of both sides swayed to and fro between the banks of the Potomac and the banks of the Appomattox. All the losses and horrors of invasion were borne by them with unwavering patience and heroic fortitude.

From start to finish, the advantages preponderated in favor of the Northern side. At the beginning, the greatest of these advantages consisted of the possession by the Federals of a framework of government which had been organized at the beginning of the Nation's history; which had already been in active operation for seventy-five years; and which was served by a host of trained and experienced employees. Most important of all, its Treasury Department was immediately capable of raising any fund which might be needed to finance the Federal prosecution of the war. The credit of the Federal Government was of the highest character, not only among the people of the North, but also among the people of all the foreign countries which were in possession of money to loan. The possibility of the dismemberment of the Union did not, in the long run, lower this credit in the eyes of Northern lenders at least, for even should the South succeed, the United States,—curtailed it is true,—would remain. The South, on the other hand, even after it had organized a government, could offer no certain guarantee to foreign lenders for the return of their money; and the best security which she could give to creditors among her own citizens was a promise to pay at the end of a definite number of years, after independence had been won. Only very patriotic, or very sanguine, minds could be expected to consider such security to be really satisfactory.

But what was probably an equal advantage in favor of the North was the existence at Washington, long before the first gun was fired, of a War Department that was prepared, from the first hour of hostilities, to equip and forward thousands of troops to the field. This Department possessed every material appliance for the vigorous prosecution of war. It had under its orders many hundred officers who had enjoyed the training and discipline of the West Point Military Academy; it possessed already an accumulation of arms and ammunition; and additional stores could be easily and quickly furnished by numerous establishments already in operation, or by purchases in European markets. Its recruiting system had been perfected by years of actual practice. Its means of transportation, both by land and water, had been rapidly increasing with the extension of steamboat and railway lines in all parts of the North, which made possible a rapid concentration of troops at Washington, or at any other point where might be considered to be desirable. By the same means, food for these troops might be rushed forward without serious delay.

On the other hand, what was the situation of the South in these vital details? She had to create a war department, and to set it to functioning at once in spite of its imperfect state. There was no little army of regulars, such as the Federal War Department possessed, to form a nucleus for the large forces which had to be organized for the actual fighting. There were even lacking, at first, the necessary number of drillmasters to whip the raw soldiers into military shape; and there was available only a small quantity of guns and ammunition, as the South did not possess the factories for their manufacture. Acquisition of such materials abroad was soon cut off by the stringency of the Federal blockade.

Moreover, the Southern States had not made the same progress in railroad building as the Northern; and for this reason, the transportation of troops and supplies was not carried out, in proportion to bulk, with the same ease and rapidity as was so

noticeable in the same operations on the Federal side. It was
seen towards the end of the war, when the Confederate soldiers
in the trenches were suffering so severely from scanty food, that
no special want prevailed in those districts of the lower South
which had either escaped from invasion altogether, or had been
rarely visited by contending armies. The means for collecting
such food as was available in these districts had been shortened
by the inability to maintain the railways in the state of repair
required by the constant demand for facilities for a heavy passing traffic.

The Federal Naval Department was organized as efficiently
as the War. The number of ships at the Department's command was not curtailed by secession. Every vessel of war,
which, before hostilities began, was in the active service of the
Federal Government, remained in its possession when that
event took place. Most of these warships were the products
of the highest constructive skill that could be employed at that
time; they were fully equipped for battle; they carried the necessary quota of trained officers; and they could be moved at once
to any part of the coastal waters where their presence was
needed. Here was a sea-arm that was immediately supplementary to the land arm; and it was in even better shape than the
latter to deliver a blow, to the damage of the Confederates.

The newly recruited Federal troops could only be of use after
they had been drilled. This would take up considerable time.
But the crews of the warships were ready at the firing of the
first shot to advance into the center of the conflict. It is true
that the vessels which were first engaged in that conflict had to
meet the terrible impact of the ironclad *Merrimac*, but this
formidable vessel, after doing severe damage, ran aground, was
blown up, and was not replaced, as the invention of the *Monitor*
class of warships and the use of torpedoes had put an end to the
domination of the *Merrimac* type. From the hour that this
famous vessel disappeared, the Confederacy possessed, for all
practical purposes, few vessels ready for war. Every one of its

shipyards on the sea-coast was too much exposed to attack by water to make the building of warships there advisable. The Confederates were compelled to rely chiefly on submarine explosives for defense against the incursions of the Federal gun-

Courtesy of Virginia Chamber of Commerce

STRATFORD, BIRTHPLACE OF GENERAL ROBERT E. LEE

boats; but this means of warding off invasion was not, in the end, generally successful.

The South was singularly vulnerable in the length of its coast line; and also in the extraordinary number of openings which existed in that line in the form of estuaries and sounds that narrowed into navigable streams reaching far into the country back of the sea. With the exception of Tennessee and Arkansas, the interior could be penetrated just so soon as the Mississippi could be cleared of the Confederate land and floating batteries to be found all the way from Vicksburg to the mouths of the river below New Orleans.

The great streams, beginning with the Potomac on the north, and running down to the Rio Grande itself, were soon in the possession of the Federal fleets. They were useful to the Federal cause by rendering the changes of strategic base in military operations quickly feasible, and by making easy the transportation of supplies and troops for the armies. But for the Federal seizure of the waterway of the Mississippi, the Southern cause would not have been cut off from the three States of Texas, Arkansas, and Louisiana, which had formed a productive recruiting and provisioning field for the different forces defending the eastern regions of the Confederacy. Practically, the States west of that stream were as isolated from these eastern regions as if they had been a part of California, and, in reality, a section of the hostile North.

The opening of the Tennessee River enabled the Federal fleets to destroy forts situated far within that territory, and thus strengthen the Federal army that was contending for the possession of the very heart of the Confederacy. The mastery of the Potomac hastened the supplies of food and recruits for the troops at Fredericksburg by allowing a port of debarkation to be erected at Acquia Creek. In the same way, the mastery of James River saved McClellan from destruction after his defeat on the Peninsula; and later enabled Grant to cross the stream without opposition and plant himself at the very back door of Richmond, with no interruption whatever of his communications, although a Confederate army stood between him and Washington by land.

But there were two other advantages which the possession of fleets of ocean-vessels and flotillas of river-boats gave the North almost from the start. These offensive instruments not only prevented the exportation by the Confederacy of cotton and other products for exchange for European munitions of all sorts, but they also interposed to put a stop to the importation of such

supplies as would have found their way into the country for
sale from foreign ports. A free exportation of cotton would
have given the Confederate Government a broad basis on which
to purchase all the guns and ammunition which it needed; and
it would also have created a gateway through which large numbers of foreign recruits would have poured in to augment the
Confederate armies. While the Federal blockade was not entirely effective, it was sufficiently so to shut off all but a comparatively insignificant trickle. Practically, it was successful
from an early day, and grew more and more so as the constrict-
ing power of the United States increased in force.

It is no overstatement to say that, had the Confederacy possessed fleets of her own able to overcome the Federal fleets, or at
least to keep them away from her coasts at all points, her conquest would never have been accomplished. Indeed, with the
resources of Europe to complement her own, her strength would
have been invincible. So far from the vast seaboard of the
South offering any serious obstacle to the overrunning of her
different States, it really made their invasion easier by the number of back doors which it presented for the penetration of the
interior. It has been justly said that it was the Federal naval
power which enabled the Federal military power to vanquish
the Confederacy.

One of the most effective factors of superiority which the
North enjoyed over the South at the beginning of the conflict
was the existence in all parts of the Federal domain of a great
number of manufactures of all kinds. The North was a well-
balanced combination of shop, factory, and farm.[1] The South
was a vast series of large and small plantations, which produced
certain great staples, but depended upon the purchase of its
manufactured supplies from communities beyond its borders.
The North could count its trained mechanics and artisans by
the half million; the South only by the thousands. The number
in the North rapidly increased with the progress of the War, in

[1] Bruce's Life of General Robert E. Lee, p. 100.

order to keep step with the augmentation of the manufactures. In the South, on the other hand, both manufacturers and artisans began perceptibly to decline in number from the beginning of hostilities, except in the province that supplied the cannon, small-arms, and ammunition needed by the troops.

The comparative dearth of business men of great natural capacity and long training in the Southern States was another fact that favored the North at the start.   From the close of the Revolution, the manufacturing and mercantile interests of Pennsylvania, New York, and New England, had been expanding, and as they did so, there sprang up an ever-increasing band of men who had been employed from their majority in the management of business affairs of the highest importance.   They were zealous, untiring, and resourceful.   When war was declared, they were ready, not only to put their expert skill at the service of the various Departments of the Federal Government, in the prosecution of the War, but they exerted themselves to the utmost to supply the Federal armies with all the articles needed by the soldiers, whether in the form of food, clothing, guns, or ammunition.   Their factories were increased in number, and every deficiency which existed at the start was promptly remedied by additions to machinery and working-men.   If their own shops could not make this deficiency good at once, they imported what was lacking from Europe and turned it over to the Federal authorities.   Perhaps, no country in history in an emergency of life or death, was served by abler men of business than the North during the War of 1861-65.

But it would be a mistake to suppose that the South was, to all practical intent, devoid of men of great business capacity. Unfortunately for its cause, their training had not, as a rule, been in the province of manufactures.   Indeed, their principal knowledge of business affairs had been restricted to the management of large plantations, and the production and marketing of staple crops.   It required uncommon administrative talent to direct these estates with success.   This talent took the form as

MAJOR-GENERAL WINFIELD SCOTT

much of an ability to control men as of an ability to keep straight an infinite number of small details. There was little room, however, to increase profits by the exercise of shrewdness in dealing with competitors, and in utilizing the trend of commercial events. Most Southerners had small information about complex forms of business in the ordinary run of their transactions. Indeed, outside of a few towns like Richmond, Savannah, Charleston, Mobile, and New Orleans, the South did not pretend to much knowledge of mercantile life and manufacturing processes. The practical pursuits of its people as a whole were rural, and, therefore, simple and uncomplicated.

To be plunged into a great war, that extended its operations over a thousand miles or more, imposed a sudden and unexpected draft on the powers of even the most capable Southerners; and it cannot be said that the emergency was met with the promptness and skill exhibited by the Northerners, simply because they had not enjoyed the same training. Nor did actual participation in the War make good in time all the deficiencies which existed at first. The transportation service of the Confederacy practically broke down near the end of hostilities. The commissary department, at a time when the South still remained in possession of large quantities of food, functioned so poorly that the Confederate troops in the trenches of Petersburg were frequently on the edge of starvation. The management of the Confederate Treasury did not indicate any genius in that province, which alone could have counteracted the financial drawbacks of the South's constricted situation.

Another point in favor of the North from the start was her ability to accredit her diplomatic representatives to all the great foreign Powers. This gave her a standing abroad which the unrecognized Confederacy could not aspire to. The influence of these representatives was necessarily extensive. The envoys of the South, in such capitals, for instance, as Paris and London, had to enter important political circles by the backdoor and the backstairs, as it were. Everything they were able to do for the assistance of the Confederacy could only be done indirectly and undiscovered, as if their character was no higher than that of conspirators. They were unable to purchase supplies for the Southern armies, since the independence of the South had not been recognized. Ships which they obtained for the concealed design of preying on the commerce of the United States, had to steal away from English harbors under false charter parties. With the single exception of securing a few marauding vessels, like the *Alabama*, these Confederate envoys accomplished nothing, even at the hour that the fortunes of the Confederate armies were at the zenith. As these fortunes declined, the private influence of men like Mason and Slidell perceptibly shrank even in those circles where the Confederate cause was regarded with sincere good-will and sympathy.

But the most important factor of superiority which the North possessed was its ability to put the largest forces in the field. Numerically, the two opponents were far from standing on a footing of equality. The twenty-two Northern States contained twenty-two million inhabitants; the eleven Southern States contained only nine millions; and of these latter nine, about three and one-half were slaves, while of the inhabitants of the North, only five hundred thousand were such. But the supporters of the Federal Cause were not restricted to troops recruited in the North. A very large contingent for the upholding of that Cause was obtained from the mountain districts of Western Virginia and Eastern Tennessee, where, owing, to the absence of negroes, there were many thousand persons entirely disaffected to the Confederacy. There had never been any sympathy between these highland populations and the inhabitants of the neighboring lowlands, and they entered the War on the Northern side with all the greater ardor for that reason.

Furthermore, the Federal armies were increased by the addition of large bodies of black troops. These troops had been gathered up either from the ranks of refugees, or from the hordes of idle blacks, who were found in those portions of the

South which had been overrun by the Federal forces. A third accession was made by the enrollment of German and Irish volunteers, who had been drawn to the United States, after hostilities began, by the prospect of bounties and pensions, which were to be extended to all who would enlist.

We have described briefly the various advantages which the North enjoyed over its antagonist, the South, at the outbreak of hostilities. What, on the other hand, were the points of superiority, at that time, in favor of the latter? Previous to the War, the life led by the Southern people in the mass was fundamentally different from that pursued by the Northern people as a mass. It is true that, in the North, there was a large population actively engaged in the calling of agriculture; but the most important division of the great body of its inhabitants was employed in the factories. This element resided in villages, towns, and cities. There was no influence in their surroundings that prepared them for the fatigue of the march, the privations of the camp, the bloody conflict of the battle-field. In fact, not many of this section of the general population had ever beheld a weapon more formidable than a pistol; and still fewer had tested the vigor of their legs in any excursion more strenuous than a picnic. Their only experience of the horse was when he hauled the products of the factories to the railway station and brought back the supplies of raw cotton and wool for the looms.

There was not much personal independence in the life of these factory towns. Men were herded together in tenements and under factory roofs. They resembled the inhabitants of an ant-hill,—always busy with their work, but possessed of little to differentiate one from another. The condition of the people in the great cotton and tobacco regions of the South was entirely the opposite in its character. The whole face of that country was covered with a vast net-work of plantations, both large and small. The owner of the small plantation was as independent on his estate as the owner of the large was on his. He looked

around him, and whether he cultivated his land with his own
strong arm or not, he was master of every thing in his immediate environment. The very seclusion of that environment increased his utility to stand and live by the strength of his own
character alone. Humble might be the background of his social
existence, but he was master of his own time, and he listened to
orders from no man. By necessity, he grew to be sturdy and
self-reliant. The lives of the people of this Middle West resembled closest the plantation life of the South.[2]

The same traits were developed to an even higher degree in
the individuality of the wealthy landowner. His situation was
equally independent, while the sphere in which he moved was
far wider and more imposing. He was not only the master of
his own life, but also of the lives of his dependent bondsmen.
Unlike the small landowner, he enjoyed an opportunity to learn
how to guide and manage men. By the mere force of his ownership of his plantation and his slaves, he was a leader who was
always loyally obeyed within his own domain.

It seemed natural enough that the men who had occupied
this position on the large estates should be elected the lieutenants
and captains of the companies recruited in their neighborhoods
for an active share in the War. Many of them had already
served in high rank in the militia, and had acquired skill in military maneuvers. Not a few of them, when hostilities began,
raised companies at their own expense and led their soldiers into
battle.

It was said of these Southern planters, large or small, that the
life which they had followed in the country had cultivated in
them "quick and accurate sight, firm nerves, constant watchfulness, and the ability in emergencies to decide upon the instant."
Throughout the greater part of the year, they were in the habit
of making excursions in the fields and woods in the pursuit of
game. It might be the bear, the deer, the fox, the wild-cat, the

<hr>

[2] The lives of the people of the Middle West resembled closest the
plantation life of the South.

raccoon, or the otter; or it might be the wild turkey, the duck, the Canada goose, the partridge, the pheasant, or the woodcock. Or the ponds and rivers might be sought for the numerous varieties of fish which they had to offer the angler.

No attention was paid by these adventurous hunters and fishermen to the vicissitudes of the weather. Rain or sunshine in spring, summer, and autumn, and ice and snow in winter, did not deter their feet in these tramps over hill and valley. They took every change of the atmosphere with equanimity as it came in the order of nature. Was it likely that a man who could shoot with unerring aim the whirling partridge or woodcock as it rose, or the deer as it crashed through the underbrush, would miss his target when he fired his rifle at the blue-coated enemy? Was it probable that one who had been hardened by cold and heat in the open air, would shrink from the hardships of the bivouac or the privations of the camp?

Moreover, there was hardly a man to be found among them who had not been trained in horsemanship from boyhood. The cavalry was an arm of the service for which all had a natural aptitude, perfected by long experience. The Southern horseman was born a scout, with an eye for the lay of the land, a quick vision that detected at once the approach of danger, and when that danger arrived, a spirit that met it with coolness and intelligence. A cavalry charge was for the Confederate soldier the greatest of all adventures, and it was not without some precedence in his hot pursuit of wild animals in the forest.

There was another advantage which the Confederates possessed throughout the course of hostilities. They felt all this time that they were resisting an inhuman attack on their native soil. Every man, as he struck a blow at the enemy, did not forget that there was a mother, wife, and child under the home-roof far away, who were to be protected from the incursion of a foreign soldiery carrying devastation and ruin and insult in their steps. They did not consider themselves in the light of aggressors. In their own eyes, they were merely defenders of their own hearths and those around it who were dear to them. Gladly at any moment they would have laid aside their arms had the assault on the South been discontinued and peace restored, with permanent independence for their States.

Indeed, it was not the conquest, it was not the destruction of others, which they had in view in the campaigns in Virginia, and Georgia, and Tennessee, and the Carolinas. It was simply the right to establish their own government and found their own separate nationality. Such was the feeling that nerved their arms and inspired their breasts from start to finish.

CHAPTER III

THE CONFLICT AND ITS RESULTS

There were to be two conspicuous results of the war which was now casting its shadow over Virginia. The one was physical; the other, social and political combined. The physical and social result was to be a degree of destruction in diverse ways such as the world, in our modern age at least, has rarely seen duplicated. Fortunately, time was to efface the vestiges of devastation which were so deeply stamped on the whole area of the State for so many years. But the political and social result was so radical that it gave an entirely different character to the community, such as not even time itself could ever modify. In fact, the abolition of slavery alone, one of the lasting consequences of the surrender of the Confederate armies at Appomattox, has worked a revolution in the nature of Virginian social and political life that only tends to spread wider and strike deeper as the years recede. Doubtless, many far-seeing minds among the Virginian people anticipated this upshot of the threatened conflict. Indeed, this may have been one element at least in the reluctance which the State at large showed so plainly to cast off its allegiance to the Union.

But whatever may have been the motive behind that attitude of delay, the energies of the population in the mass became deeply enlisted in the practical prosecution of the war so soon as it broke out. The call for troops by Mr. Lincoln was the signal for the consolidation of public sentiment in favor of resistance to the invasion which was now so clearly impending. Removal of the capitol from Montgomery to Richmond made it inevitable that the soil of Virginia would become the cockpit, within the limits of which the issue of the mighty contest would be decided. Now began a series of campaigns which, like an engulfing wave, was to sweep backwards and forwards across this arena during an agonizing period of four years. Most frequently the victory was with the Confederate army, but defeat did not serve to weaken the Federal Cause permanently. Indeed, the North came back at its antagonist with undiminished courage, and with an ever-increasing numerical superiority. As the conflict drew to a close, the defenders of Richmond dwindled until there were not sufficient troops to man the trenches, or the required amount of food and supplies of guns and ammunition to sustain the military strength of those who remained in the ranks.

It would not be appropriate in a work of the present kind to give a detailed description of the events that occurred in the course of the war. We shall be satisfied to offer an outline of those that were of the principal moment in their effect on the fortunes of the Confederacy.

The most important, in the beginning, was the appointment of Robert E. Lee, who had resigned from the United States army, to the position of Commander-in-Chief of the Virginia forces. Colonel Lee had, previous to this promotion, acquired a high reputation for military skill and personal intrepidity in the war with Mexico. It was anticipated that he would succeed General Winfield Scott when this officer should retire from the chief command of the United States regular army. So great was the confidence which General Scott placed in the ability of his distinguished subordinate that he earnestly recommended Colonel Lee to Mr. Lincoln and the Secretary of the Federal War Department as the fittest officer to take charge of the army which was then rapidly forming at Washington for the invasion of Northern Virginia. But Lee declined to accept this honor when it was offered to him indirectly by an emissary of the Federal Government. In other words, he reserved his services

GENERAL ROBERT E. LEE

General Lee on His Horse Traveler

for his native State, although he made no public or private profession of being a secessionist.

His first important duties, after receiving his commission for
the Virginia Convention, were (1) to supervise, in a general
way, the drilling of the large mass of recruits who had assembled
in the camps around the City of Richmond; (2) to take steps
for the manufacture of small arms, cannon, and ammunition;
and (3) to organize company after company, regiment after
regiment, for active participation at the front. Within a few
weeks, he had dispatched sixty infantry and cavalry regiments
to the assistance of the forces now entrenched in Northern Virginia and awaiting the threatened attack of the Federal army
descending from the Potomac. It was due largely to his energy
in hastening reinforcements that the Confederate army concentrated at Manassas was strong enough to repel the attack of the
Federal forces, and drive them back in confusion to the defenses of Washington. This battle occurred in July, 1861.

Unfortunately for the Confederate Cause, the victory was not
followed up by a rapid advance upon the Federal capital. The
Federal Administration soon recovered from its panic, and began to take the most active measures to organize another powerful army for another campaign. In the meanwhile, General
Lee had been engaged in a military incursion into the mountain
districts of Western Virginia, which had been overrun at an
early day by a small army commanded by General McClellan.
McClellan, successful in his energetic offensive, had been rewarded by promotion to the command of the new army, now
assembled in the vicinity of Washington. Lee was appointed to
halt any further penetration of the Western Virginian districts,
and if possible, to recapture the ground which the enemy had
seized. A variety of circumstances, however, such as heavy
and continuous rains, the rugged terrain, and an epidemic of
sickness among his soldiers, brought his advance to an end;
and he was ultimately compelled to withdraw from the country,
with the enemy still in possession.

The practical result of this abortive campaign was the establishment of the State of West Virginia, which was made permanent by the destruction of the Confederacy in the end.   The
original State was thus deprived of thirty thousand square miles
of territory, rich in a great variety of mineral and forest
products.

The army under Johnston, in the long interval between July,
1861, and March, 1862, had remained quietly encamped, while
McClellan was employed behind the fortifications of Washington in forging a mighty instrument for the destruction of the
Confederacy.   He had assembled 150,000 troops for drill and
equipment.   At the same time, 30,000 had been collected in
Western Virginia, and an additional 30,000 in the Shenandoah
Valley.   General Johnston had enrolled only 60,000 to oppose
this formidable host.

In anticipation of investment, should he remain in the
neighborhood of Manassas, the Confederate Commander slowly
withdrew behind the line of the Rappahannock River.   His
position here was so strong that McClellan decided to transport
his great army to Fortress Monroe, and from that place, launch
a powerful offensive against the City of Richmond.   To a certain extent, this movement jeopardized the safety of Washington, and in order to protect it, McDowell was stationed between
that city and Fredericksburg, while Federal troops were dispatched to the Valley to close the gateway to the North at
Harper's Ferry.   General Jackson was soon ordered to that
quarter by the Confederate Government for the purpose of driving the Federals there across the Potomac, and in a series of
masterly maneuvers, he was finally successful in doing this.   But
before he could press on to the fortifications of the Federal capitol, he was instructed to march to the scene of the fighting
which was now going on along the Chickahominy.

After McClellan disembarked his troops at Fortress Monroe,
he advanced to the line of intrenchments which Johnston, who
had shifted his army to the Peninsula, had thrown up in the

GENERAL J. E. JOHNSTON

vicinity of Yorktown. The Confederate Commander slowly fell back before the enemy towards Richmond. A battle was fought at Williamsburg; without, however, halting the Federal progress in the direction of the Confederate capitol. Two other battles took place, further on,—one at Seven Pines; the other at Fair Oaks. Still McClellan held his ground. He was now posted almost in sight of Richmond, and in the sound of its church bells and steeple clocks.

Johnston was wounded in the course of the latter battle, and General Lee was appointed to take the place thus made vacant in the command. His first act was to throw up a long line of breastworks; his second, to order General Jackson to march down from the Valley and post himself on the Confederate left. At this time, the Federal army stood astride of the Chickahominy River. One part of it was encamped on the south bank; the remainder on the north.

Having sent General Stuart to reconnoiter the rear of General McClellan's forces, and to ascertain McDowell's exact position near Fredericksburg, Lee quietly awaited the sound of General Jackson's approach. When informed of that officer's arrival in the vicinity of Hanover Court-House on the left, he undertook to carry out the plan of battle which he had formed. Under the provisions of this plan, Jackson was to attack General Porter's corps occupying the right wing of the enemy. As he should drive the Federals down the eastern bank of the river, a part of the Confederate army, under A. P. Hill, was to cross the stream by the upper bridge, and join Jackson in the rush; and when the second bridge was uncovered, D. H. Hill and Longstreet were also to cross and to unite their forces with Jackson's and A. P. Hill's.

Lee was hopeful that, by this maneuver, he would cut the Federal right wing off from its base of supplies on the Pamunkey, and thus compel it to fall back on the Federal center and left, with the final result of forcing the Federal commander to retreat in confusion to Fortress Monroe.

GENERAL STONEWALL JACKSON

The consummation of the plan was delayed by Jackson's failure to carry out the part assigned to him with the required degree of promptness. On the day that he was expected to arrive in front of Meadow Bridge, he was so dilatory that A. P. Hill, fearing the complete rupture of the original plan, crossed the stream and attacked the enemy without waiting for support. He was repulsed, but in the night Porter fell back to the plateau of Gaines Mill, where he was in close touch with the rest of the Federal army. Here he was routed by the combination of Confederate troops under Jackson, Longstreet and the two Hills; but the remnant of his corps succeeded in joining their comrades on the south side of the river. McClellan promptly retreated to the protection of his gunboats lying in the James River near Harrison's Landing; but before he could reach this point, he was compelled to fight several battles, which impeded but did not stop his progress.

While these events were happening, a second large army under General Pope was in the course of organization at Washington. In July (1862) this army was ready to invade Piedmont, Virginia. A portion of it was soon encamped at Culpeper. To halt its further advance, Jackson was dispatched to that quarter with 24,000 troops. Although greatly out numbered, he attacked the enemy at Cedar Mountain and defeated them. A few weeks later, Lee and Longstreet, accompanied by the rest of the Confederate forces, joined him.

The united Federal troops under Pope's command now faced the entire Confederate army. Taking alarm, the Federal commander drew back to the line of the Rappahannock, where it would not be safe to attack him from in front. Could the Confederate troops be hurried around to his rear? This maneuver was soon undertaken by Lee. Jackson, with his corps, was dispatched to the far left, in the direction of Thoroughfare Gap. Through this Gap, his adventurous troops passed, and then descended to the plains of Manassas, lying many miles behind the position occupied by the Federal army. So soon as Pope heard of Jackson's presence there, he drew his army back a second time, with the hope of intercepting him. In the meanwhile, Lee had set the remainder of his soldiers in motion, and at quick step followed in the path which Jackson had blazed. Before he could unite with that officer, a battle had begun at Groveton, in which only Jackson's corps was engaged. The fight was resumed at Manassas, and was in progress when Lee and Longstreet deployed on the ground. It was not until the ensuing day that the conflict ended in the precipitate retreat of the Federal forces behind the fortifications of Alexandria.

Encouraged by this victory, Lee determined to invade the North, since he was hopeful that, should he succeed in winning a great battle on that soil, the independence of the Confederacy would be acknowledged both by the Federal Government and by Foreign Powers. At this time, its fortunes were declining in the West. This signified that the room for recruits and army supplies was steadily growing more narrow. The campaign that followed ended in the drawn battle of Sharpsburg. After prodigies of valor, the Confederate army withdrew from the field and retired to Northern Virginia. Here Lee posted his troops and quietly awaited the development of McClellan's opposing plans. While stationed at Warrenton, this Commander was superseded by General Burnside.

While these events were taking place on land, a naval engagement had been fought in Hampton Roads which was to revolutionize the entire manner of naval warfare. When the Federal authorities abandoned the Norfolk Navy Yard in 1861, they scuttled the forty-gun frigate, *Merrimac,* then lying in the harbor. But the Confederates soon raised her to the surface, and changed her outer equipment into that of an iron-clad. When she was ready to venture out, the Federal wooden men-of-war, the *Congress* and the *Cumberland,* were anchored near Newport News. Making her way to that point, the newly christened *Virginia* rammed the *Cumberland* and burnt the

Congress to the water's edge. A third vessel had escaped by shying off into shallow water.

Returning next day to destroy this last vessel in her turn, the Virginia found herself confronted by a small low lying iron-clad shaped like a cheese-box, with a revolving turret. This was the *Monitor,* which had been constructed by Ericson, a Scandinavian inventor. It did not possess a ram, but was armed with two powerful guns. A battle began between the two strange sea-monsters, and in the end, the *Monitor* drew off into water not sufficiently deep to float her enemy. Balked by this fact, the *Virginia* withdrew to Norfolk. A few days afterwards, she returned in the hope of alluring her former antagonist into a second conflict. But the challenge was not accepted.

When Norfolk was evacuated by the Confederates, an attempt was made to remove the *Virginia* to the waters of James River below Richmond, but owing to her heavy draught, she ran aground of Craney Island and had to be blown up.

By December, 1862, Burnside, who had, as we stated, succeeded McClellan, had concentrated a large army on the Stafford Heights opposite the city of Fredericksburg. Here he planted a great mass of artillery, the fire of which was expected to sweep the broad plain south of the Rappahannock River, over which the Federal infantry would have to pass before they would be able to reach the Confederate position on the line of the southern hills. On this line, Lee was present in person, with his lieutenants, Jackson and Longstreet.

Having first made a determined effort with a detachment to force a passage of the river opposite the town, Burnside marshalled his great army for the assault on the enemy further south. The Rappahannock was crossed without opposition. As the troops, rank upon rank, began the march over the plain, a heavy mist wrapped the whole landscape in an impenetrable blanket; but the mounting sun, after awhile, dispelled this thick veil, and the entire force, with a magnificent battle front, were seen advancing. A single battery only ventured to dispute their

A Confederate Private

path as they drew near to the foot of the hills. One section
of the Federal army swerved to the right, and in vain endeavored to drive the Confederates from their position on Marye's
Hill. The other section, by creeping through a wooded angle
in the Confederate line on the left, snatched a momentary success; but, in the end, were compelled to fall back to the plain.
Repulsed in every quarter, the Federal army slowly retreated
unmolested to their entrenchments across the river.

Both of the opposing armies now withdrew into winter
quarters. In the Spring (1863), the new commander of the
Federal forces, General Hooker, who had succeeded General
Burnside, advanced along the north bank of the Rappahannock
to a point where the fords above Fredericksburg made it practicable for him to cross the stream and post himself at a hamlet
in the Spotsylvania wilderness known as Chancellorsville. This
was the center of a wide district overgrown with bushes and
stunted trees that had sprung up after the removal of the original growth for the purpose of supplying fuel for the neighboring iron-furnaces. Hooker, as soon as he halted in the midst of
this tangled brake, dispatched the leader of his cavalry arm in
a raid towards the west and south.

Leaving a large detachment opposite Fredericksburg to hold
back the Federal forces still remaining there, Lee advanced his
army to a position that confronted Hooker's breastworks. Per-
ceiving the difficulty of carrying these works by a forward
assault, Lee, in concert with Jackson, determined to despatch
one-half of his army along Hooker's front to a point where he
would be able to turn and overwhelm the unsuspecting Federal
right wing. This dangerous maneuver was carried out with
success, until Jackson, who was in immediate command, fell
wounded by a volley from his own men, who failed to recognize
him and his escort in the falling darkness.

During the night, Hooker drew back towards the fords and
threw up a second line of strong entrenchments.

A fierce battle began the next day, and fortune going against the Federal side, Hooker under cover of night, fell back to the river. The fords were soon crossed, and the Federal army, which had been in a corner of extraordinary peril, found itself safe from further pursuit. The Confederates had won a splendid victory, but a dear payment was made for it in the death of Jackson. "You have lost your left arm," Lee wrote to him as he lay on his last bed, "but I have lost my right." From that time, the Confederate commander never ventured on those great turning movements which previously had been carried out, with Jackson's cooperation, so successfully, on more than one occasion.

It was now clear to Lee that the cause of the South was not likely to be substantially advanced by defensive victories alone. Apparently, the North remained as resolute as ever in spirit, and as abounding in material recources. The Confederacy could not hold out permanently against the existing odds, for even its triumphs must gradually lead to its exhaustion. Apparently, there was no disposition among Foreign Powers to recognize the Government at Richmond. Fredericksburg and Chancellorsville had been won in rapid succession, and yet no authoritative voice was heard on the other side of the Atlantic that offered either verbal encouragement or active assistance. Silence prevailed in European Cabinets, although there were many evidences of private sympathy with the cause of the Confederacy and its intrepid defenders on the battle-fields of Virginia and the states further south.

At this hour, Vicksburg was in imminent danger of falling into the hands of its besiegers. This would mean that the Confederacy would at once be severed, and, in consequence, the region west of the Mississippi River would be able to furnish no further substantial aid to the Cause. Lee's only hope for the success of that Cause lay in the discouragement which a victory on Northern soil would almost certainly raise in the hearts of the Northern people. And, moreover, such an invasion, whether

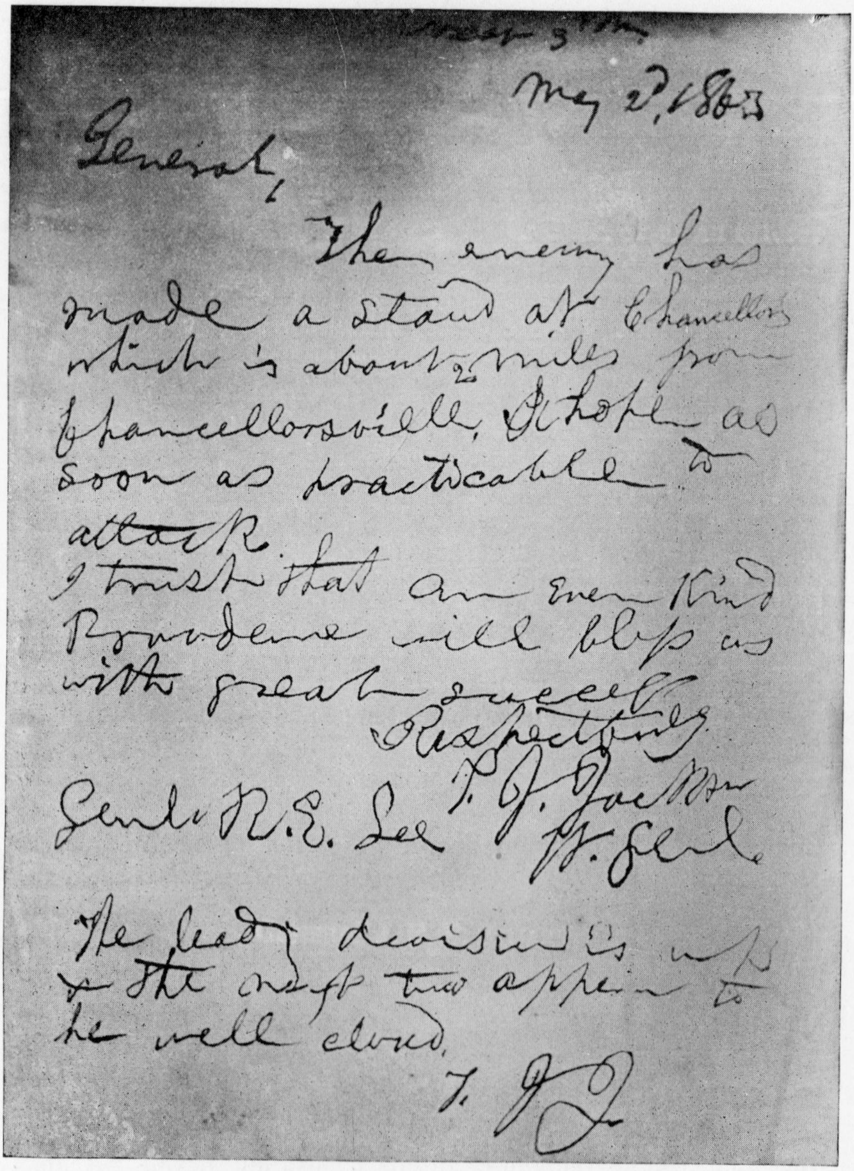

May 2, 1863

General,

The enemy has made a stand at Chancellors which is about 2 miles from Chancellorsville. I hope as soon as practicable to attack.

I trust that an ever Kind Providence will bless us with great success.

Respectfully,
T. J. Jackson
Lt. Genl.

Genl. R. E. Lee

The leading division is up & the next two appear to be well closed.

T. J. J.

JACKSON'S LAST MESSAGE TO LEE

ultimately successful or not, would draw the Federal army from the devastated fields of Virginia.

In June, the advance towards Middle Pennsylvania began. As the march proceeded, the Federal forces hovered between their enemy and Washington without making any additional attempt to stop their progress. Stuart was ordered by Lee to keep well to the right of his army, and to act both as a screen and as a band of scouts, but, unfortunately, this distinguished cavalry officer allowed himself to be drawn too far away to carry out the real purpose of the movement in which he was engaged. When he halted, he found himself as far north as Carlisle, and it was only on the night of the second day of the Battle of Gettysburg that he was near enough to participate in it.

Previous to that battle, the Confederate army had posted itself at Cashtown on the east side of the South Mountain. This was about twenty miles from the position occupied by the Federal army. While stationed here waiting for the complete concentration of all his forces, Lee had given orders that no encounter with the enemy should be invited until he was ready to move forward in full strength; but one of his brigades, anxious to procure supplies, and not aware that a detachment of the enemy was encamped a few miles off at Gettysburg, advanced to that town, and on reaching it, had a brush with this isolated force.

The next day, a fight began with a division of the Federal First Corps, which had come up in the night. An important section of the Confederate army, having hurried up in time, was engaged in this conflict, and it was successful in driving its opponents back upon Gettysburg in confusion. A general battle would have been precipitated before night-fall had the two hostile hosts now been present in full strength. But Longstreet, on the Confederate side, was still four miles off, and the large part of the Federal army was at a still greater distance away. During the night, the Federal Commander began hastening forward the remainder of his corps; but it was not until mid-day that the last of them reached the ground. In the meanwhile, Longstreet had advanced leisurely towards Gettysburg, which he reached at eight o'clock in the morning. Instead of beginning the fight at this time, when all the Federal forces were not yet on the ground, he argued with Lee in favor of a flank movement, always a difficult step to take in the presence of the enemy. By the hour he was willing to strike, which was four in the afternoon, the entire Federal army had concentrated on the Heights and was ready to resist attack.

The Confederate assault on the second day was sufficiently successful to justify Lee in renewing the fight on the third. His plan was to send a heavy force against the Federal entrenchments on the Ridge, in the hope that, by splitting the defending forces into two fragments, he would be able to throw both of these disrupted wings into such confusion as to cause an immediate withdrawal from the field of the entire Federal army in a condition of irrevocable defeat.

The charge of the Confederate division which was assigned to this maneuver is one of the most famous in history. Unsupported by reinforcements either in the rear or on the flank, they rushed up the slope of the hill in the midst of a galling fusillade, and even succeeded in entering the Federal first line, but overwhelmed by superior numbers, and decimated by the continuous fire, they were compelled to abandon what they had partly won and retreat to their starting point. The Federal Commander deemed it prudent to refrain from a counter-stroke. During the rest of that day, and all the following, the two antagonists stood upon their arms. On the second night, Lee set his troops in motion and retired towards the Potomac. Crossing that river without serious molestation from the enemy, now hovering behind him, he fell back slowly towards the Rapidan. Meade posted himself at Culpeper Court-House not far away.

A campaign of maneuvers now began. The Federal army at one time, retreated as far as Chantilly before the Confederates. "I could have thrown them further back" said Lee, "but I saw no chance of bringing them to battle, and it would have only served to fatigue our troops by advancing further." The winter of 1863-64 was now approaching and Meade decided to make an attack before the season set fully in; but, on approaching the Confederate position at Mine Run, he found it too strong to be assaulted. Military operations soon ceased, and the two armies went into permanent winter-quarters.

In the meanwhile, the fortunes of the Confederacy in the West had fallen under a dark cloud. Vicksburg had surrendered; the battle of Missionary Ridge had been lost; and the southern forces had retreated into Georgia. Two great military hosts were soon organized by the Federal Government. The one was designed to destroy the Confederate army stationed at Dalton, under the command of Johnston; the other, to destroy the Confederate army in Virginia, under the command of Lee. General Grant was placed in military control in the latter scene. He assumed charge in the spring (1864) at the head of 120,000 men, supported by 316 pieces of artillery. Lee could marshal only 60,000 men in opposition, supported by only 224 pieces of artillery.

Grant was the most formidable leader whom Lee had yet faced. He was remarkable for tenacity, resolution, vigor, and energy, although he made little pretension to original military genius. He announced his policy to be "to hammer continuously against the armed force of the enemy and his resources, until, by mere attrition, if by nothing else, there would be nothing left of him but to submit." He was perfectly aware of the fact that the Federals could better afford to lose ten men and five cannon in battle than the Confederates could lose one man and one cannon; and he did not scruple to use the Federal superiority in resources to a degree which almost exhausted the patience of the North. "I will strike Lee," he declared at the beginning of his campaign, "if he will stand." Instead of Grant "going where Lee was," to use his own words, it was Lee who

RECUMBENT LEE AT LEXINGTON

was following close at Grant's heels, and in the end always interposing between him and the Confederate capital.

The conflict between the two armies began with the battle of the Wilderness. In vain, Grant assailed the Confederate lines, almost hidden from sight by the underbrush. Repulse met him at every point of attack, with an aggregate loss of over 17,000 men. Moving eastward, the Federal commander found himself again face to face with Lee when he arrived at Spotsylvania Court-House. Here a terrific fight ensued; but again the Federal frontal assaults were unsuccessful in breaking through. Once more Grant set his army in motion eastward. He had, by this time, received reinforcements to the number of 40,000 troops. Lee had received from the beginning of the campaign only 14,000.

Again at the North Anna, Grant strove to penetrate the line of steel and muskets before him. Again he failed. At Cold Harbor, still further eastward, he threw himself on the Confederates with a fierceness and a vigor that surpassed even his previous efforts. The only result was that, at the end of the battle, over 13,000 Federal dead and wounded were strewn over the ground. The casualties of his antagonist were trifling in comparison.

Grant had made four great flank movements, only to find at the end that he had lost one in every three of his soldiers, a number equal to the entire force with which Lee had opposed him. His only gain had been that his policy of attrition had succeeded in diminishing the size of the Confederate army, without that army being in a position to replace the depletion to the degree necessary for the maintenance of its strength. The northern people were deeply discouraged by the upshot of this campaign; and but for the Federal victories in the South would probably have consented to a peace favorable to the southern cause.

By the summer of 1864, Grant had crossed the James River, and the siege of Petersburg had begun. This continued down

to the spring of the following year. In the meanwhile, Early
had been sent by Lee to the Valley, and he had been successful
in penetrating as far as the fortifications of Washington. By
the end of his campaign, however, his troops had dwindled away
under the attacks of an overwhelming force commanded by
Sheridan.

Grant continued to extend his lines westward of Petersburg
in the hope of hewing his way around the Confederate right
wing. Frontal assaults were also made, and, in one instance,
these movements were assisted by the explosion of a mine.
Federal raiders in force were also dispatched southward to cut
off the supplies of the Confederate army by burning the railway
bridges. The limit of Confederate conscription had, by this
time, been reached, and the defenders in the trenches were
suffering from the lack of food. Steadily, the Confederate troops
were decreasing in number; and they were further discouraged
by their knowledge that Sherman was rapidly approaching Virginia with a victorious army. The defeat of a detachment at
Five Forks, on the Federal left, made it impossible for the Confederates to protect themselves in the rear on that side, and
Lee reluctantly decided to abandon his position.

The retreat began, which ended at Appomattox, where the
Confederate forces, about 8,000 only with arms in their hands,
surrendered. Thus closed the great war, which had been sustained by the South until she had reached a condition of complete exhaustion.

CHAPTER IV

PLANTATION LIFE BEHIND THE LINES

We have described the campaigns in Virginia during the war, not so much for the purpose of picturing their respective movements in rapid succession, as of demonstrating how completely these campaigns extended over the surface of the state, and, inferentially, how destructive they were, in reality, to the material interests of every community penetrated. There was not a single division of the commonwealth which escaped the devastation that accompanied every advance and retreat. First, as we have seen, the Federal army poured into the region that spread from the Blue Ridge, by way of Warrenton and Manassas, to Washington. Subsequently, the same ground was fought over by the armies of Pope and Lee, after the wave of invasion had rolled as far as Gordonsville. The Valley had been the scene of as many as three campaigns at different periods of the war. Jackson and his opponents had contended for its possession; so had Sheridan and Early; so had Siegel and Breckinridge; and so had Hunter and McCausland.

The region surrounding Fredericksburg and Chancellorsville, as far as Orange, had been a cockpit of struggling armies. So had the region that lay between Orange and Cold Harbor. Not a foot of ground but showed the track of a soldier, too often steeped in blood; and this was equally true of the Peninsula from Hanover Court-House to Malvern Hill, and from Malvern Hill, through Williamsburg, to the intrenchments of Yorktown. On the south side of the James, Grant and Lee had locked horns in a desperate contest for mastery. Raiding parties

61

had been thrown out from Petersburg by the Federals, which swept southward towards Weldon and southwestward towards Danville. When the Confederate retreat began, the country extending from Amelia Court-House almost as far as Lynchburg felt, for the first time, the tramp of the invader; but the hostile occupation was long enough to consume the last remnant of food and forage.

When the war ended, practically the whole face of the country was so desolate that the ruin was perceptible to the most unobservant eye. With armies swaying backwards and forwards, the condition of the people who remained in the homes was only too frequently one of acute want. It is not our purpose, however, to draw a general picture of the dearth which followed in the lives of those who were too old or too young to take part in hostilities, or who were prevented by their sex from sharing in the hardships and perils of the field.

Behind the lines, during the first three and a half years of the war, there were some neighborhoods in the state which had not known the intrusion of the enemy. This was particularly the case in that part of Virginia which lay between the Middle James River and the Carolina border. This was the most important slave and tobacco section of the commonwealth. We propose to take a typical plantation in this section and show what was the effect on its inhabitants of that desperate struggle which was going on beyond the northern horizon. The merely constrictive, as compared with the brutally destructive, impression on the economic interests of the community resulting from the struggle was more perceptible on an isolated estate like this than it was in the Valley of Virginia, for instance, which was so often invaded and swept clean of supplies for man and beast. We shall designate the estate selected simply as the plantation. The account which we shall give of it was characteristic of all the like undevastated properties in that part of Virginia at that time. The general condition of all was substantially the same.

One of the incidents that occurred on the plantation chosen for a brief description was distinctly suggestive of rural superstition under the influence of the warlike rumors. There was a great flight of locusts in the summer of 1860, and it was noticed that, on the wings of each insect, there was printed in the membrane, in a conspicuous form, the letter W. To the minds of the common people, this indicated that hostilities were certain to begin at no distant date. The nervous barometer already pointed to war, and this ominous letter confirmed the worst apprehensions. Those learned in the history of Virginia recalled the fact that the great Rebellion of 1676, under Nathaniel Bacon, was heralded by a similar invasion of locusts.

A far more tangible proof of actual warfare was to be seen, a few months later, in the drilling of an artillery company in an old field of the plantation. This company had been fully equipped by the owner of the estate, at his own expense. Numerous tents whitened the surface of the field; there were each day charges of cavalry in carrying out the different maneuvers; and also a prolonged training in the use of the guns. Many negro servants were visible in the background where they filled the parts of valets and cooks. The company was composed of the foremost young men in the community, who were entering into the war with as much zest as if it was a tournament in which they were about to participate. The sound of music, whether of the banjo or the voice, enlivened the air at night, when the youthful soldiers gathered around their campfires; and many a story of devotion in love and of gallantry in battle were told by members of the resting groups, or a tale of Scott, or Cooper, or Simms was read aloud to attentive ears. The food was prepared in the great kettles of the plantation, and, at mid-day, consisted in part of the richest Brunswick stew made up of several varieties of meats and vegetables, mixed to a turn by the veteran cooks of the encampment.

Later, this troop saw active service in the war; many of its members were killed; and several rose to distinguished rank as military officers.

No single troop of cavalry or company of infantry was afterwards drilled on the plantation with the same formality; but, throughout the war, the older boys of the neighborhood, who were still too young to be enrolled in the army, met at the plantation store on Saturday afternoon and were there grounded in simple maneuvers by some old planter who had enjoyed in his youth the training of a military school, and who had not forgotten all the lessons which he had learned there. In several instances, these boys stole quietly away from their homes, and making their way on horseback to the outposts of the nearest Confederate army, endeavored, not always with success, to join the ranks as private soldiers.

A band of these youths, who had learned to handle guns in the hunting field, were liable, along with men too old to be called into more active service, to be summoned, at any hour, in their character as a home guard, to a rendezvous for the performance of some special duty growing out of the local exigencies of the times. Although the community had been stripped of every person of military age and capacity, there was never any evidence of revolt among the slaves in the neighborhood. They seemed to be more thoughtlessly and sincerely submissive and loyal than before the war; and yet there was always a subconscious impression in the minds of the white people remaining behind on the plantation that all the black men and women were not entirely to be trusted—a mere suspicion, which, by all the conditions appearing on the surface, at least, was unwarranted. It was this feeling, which was never acknowledged at all, that had, perhaps, something to do with the formation of this home guard of boys under military age and men over military age.

Their periodical drill in the field adjacent to the plantation store, the most public spot on the estate, and their occasional

WILLIAM SMITH
Governor 1864-1865

traversal in a body of the country roads in the vicinity, carried a significance that was palpable to all, and especially to the negroes, who shrank by nature from the sight of muskets and swords, even in the hands of persons of small military training.

It was towards the end of the war that the services of a patrol in force was most desirable. As the siege of Petersburg dragged itself along, the men in the trenches became more and more susceptible to the discouraging influences of their situation. They were poorly clothed; they were scantily fed; and they were exposed to the harsh changes of the weather, without any real protection. All these drawbacks they could have borne without discontent had there been in the background any reason for hopefulness for the cause which they were supporting; but as the winter of 1864-65 drew to an end, they only saw their own ranks growing thinner and the Federal investment becoming more successful. Still, the great majority were not shaken; but a small proportion did yield to the impulse to abandon the trenches unobserved, and steal away through the woods, with the intention of reaching their homes on foot. Many of these deserters lived in the region which the army of Sherman was devastating; and they keenly feared for the safety of their families without the presence of any male member.

Especially during the months preceding the surrender at Appomattox, the forests of the plantation were haunted by many of these disheartened soldiers. They were frequently seen by the people there, both black and white, and their presence naturally excited alarm. In reality, however, their depredations did not go beyond the killing of a hog or the robbing of a hen-roost, for the purpose of procuring food. The patrolling by the home guard, perhaps, prevented the committal of more serious offenses against portable property. A short time after the surrender, these fugitives disappeared from the woods as silently as they had come. The home guard was disbanded, and its members turned once more to the pursuits of peace exclusively.

The mistress of the plantation was the sister of the Confederate secretary of war, a fact that was well known to the families of the small farmers in that part of the state. There were few of these families who did not number a father, husband, or son in the ranks of the Confederate armies. Many of the wives had been left without any strong arm and industrious hand to support them and their children. At times, the situation of some of them was that of almost complete destitution. Under the impression that the mistress of the plantation could, by a favorable word, influence the War Office to issue a furlough to the absent bread-winner, some forlorn woman and her brood, with every sign of poverty in their aspect, would appear in a rickety mule or ox cart, and submit her whining prayer, accompanied by the eager promise that the son or husband would return to the army just as soon as the corn had been planted or garnered, according to the season. Sometimes the children, brown from long exposure to the sun in the fields, and thin from lack of nourishing food, would bring an illiterate and tear-stained letter from a mother too ill to come and make her request in person.

The mistress had her own reasons for anxiety. She had a husband, brother, and numerous nephews in the army constantly exposed to the peril of shot and shell, and the diseases of the camps. In that remote corner of the state, the mail was always belated, and sometimes failed to be delivered at all. A great battle would occur, and days would pass before the list of casualties would become known to her. In the meanwhile, she had to go about her daily duties with all the patience that she could muster to sustain her strength. Ultimately, she had to console herself for the loss of several nephews of extraordinary promise, who perished on the battlefield, and of a brother who died of fever caught in the trenches.

Almost equally poignant to her feelings was the burning of homes which had been familiar to her from childhood as the inherited domiciles of friends or kinsmen; the devastation of

GENERAL J. E. B. STUART

their farms; and the dispersion of their slaves. Nor was the presence of herself and her young children on the plantation by themselves, in the midst of a large circle of negroes, a situation free from causes of apprehension in times so full of turbulence and uncertainty. Moreover, she looked on herself as responsible for the proper management of the most important business of the estate; and the constant and vigilant supervision which this self-imposed duty demanded of her was well calculated to cause her additional harassment.

No adequate tribute has yet been paid to those women of Virginia who, during the absence of their husbands in the Confederate armies, voluntarily and bravely assumed the care of the plantations on which they had been residing before the war began. What was true of the women of Virginia was also true of the women of the whole South. It required tact, self-control, sound judgment, and firmness, to fill the place of their natural protectors, now exposed to all the perils of the field. That the supplies of food which were received by the Confederate armies was as large as they were, was due, in no small measure, to the ability in the management of plantation affairs which these women displayed.

Occasionally, the particular plantation which we have been describing became the asylum of wounded Confederate officers, whose presence tended to support the mistress' authority; and they also personally aided her to the extent of their power in facilitating the plantation operations. In spite of the gloomy and uncertain times, they kept up the customary brightness of their spirits, for most of them were young, and endeavored thus to lighten the anxieties of their hostess. In those years, the most popular songs were *In the Good Old Colony Days,* and *The Bonnie Blue Flag,* and the sounds of these stirring tunes were often heard from the lips of these youthful heroes as the family lingered at night in the drawing-room or on the verandas. So soon as they had made a recovery from their wounds, they went back to the front; in some instances, to perish in the field.

What was the ability of the plantation to furnish nourishing food for these officers as well as for its own people? The cultivation of tobacco had ceased at an early day, and the greater part of the arable lands was devoted to the production of corn, wheat, and hay. These crops were designed primarily for the sustenance of the Confederate armies, but they also served to satisfy the needs of the plantation itself. As the locality was not invaded by a hostile force while the war was in actual progress, and as the slaves remained faithful to their work until the hour of emancipation, no real lack of food, in the coarser forms, was ever experienced. There was always an ample quantity of cornbread, cooked in the different ways so commonly noticed in both cabin and mansion before the war opened. Beef was a rare luxury for the table even of the mistress. Mutton was more frequently seen there; but the principal flesh was obtained from the hog-pen and poultry-yard. This source of supply remained down to the last hour of the Confederacy. It was supplemented in season by fish captured by hook and line or in the seine.

Wild game, like hares and squirrels, were usually plentiful, while partridges, turkeys, and other wild fowl were always abundant, because they were not so often hunted now that the young men of the family had been drawn away to the army. A negro fisherman and huntsman was kept closely occupied in furnishing such additions to the larder during a large part of the year. The orchards continued to bear in season their different varieties of fruit, while the vegetable garden produced an undiminished profusion of tomatoes, potatoes, onions, celery, beets, sweet-corn, artichokes, beans, peas, and the like. There was, in fact, no real dearth of any of the articles of food which the plantation had furnished immemorially. An attempt was even made to add to these products for domestic use a few others which had never before been seen. A striking instance of such a novelty was the sorghum plant, which was now cultivated on a considerable acreage in the low-grounds. The purpose of this was to obtain a supply of molasses.

The most acute scarcity lay in those articles which, in happier times, had been bought from the grocers in town, who had imported them from foreign countries. Preeminently such were coffee and tea. These, during the latter part of the war, entirely disappeared from the table. A substitute for coffee was sought in toasted wheat, and for tea in the highly flavored root of the sassafras shrub, which was found growing luxuriantly in every abandoned field on the upland. Plum puddings, mince pies, raisins, almonds, oranges, bananas, cocoanuts, which garnished the table formerly, were not now procurable. Candies of foreign manufacture were no longer to be seen. The place of all these foreign nuts and sweetmeats was taken by black walnuts and hickory nuts, gathered from the plantation trees; by sweet potatoes, baked in the skin in the kitchen oven; or by apples, baked on the hot open hearth; or by homemade cakes, sweetened with sorghum; or by popcorn, heated to the bursting point in the skillet.

During the years before the war, the plantation had counted on its roll of slaves a respectable number of trained handicraftsmen, who supplied the mechanical skill needed in the course of the plantation operations. There was a blacksmith, shoemaker, spinner, weaver, tailor, tanner, mason, and carpenter. In more than one instance, there were two of a kind. These men enabled the master to meet every demand for special *finesse* of hand as it arose. The estate itself furnished most of the raw materials which were required for manipulation. There was no need, as a rule, of purchasing such materials in town or country store.

The mistress had the use of these skilful slaves after the departure of the master, and they became more and more indispensable as the war went on. But they were often hampered, after the first year of hostilities, by the difficulty of procuring the materials which they needed for conversion. The blacksmith began to complain of the dearth of iron called for in his work, while the tanner was unable to furnish all the leather demanded, owing to the impressment of beeves by the Confederate Commissary Department; and what he did supply was often imperfectly cured because of the lack of the right ingredients. Towards the end of the war, all the slaves and even the children of the mistress wore shoes bottomed with wood; and the leather uppers retained their original texture and coloring as raw-hides.

Courtesy of Virginia State Chamber of Commerce

MODERN METHOD OF
HAULING COTTON, NORFOLK

Before the war, the slaves had been in the habit of cultivating small patches of cotton in the gardens which they were permitted to lay off in the immediate vicinity of their cabins. These gardens, after hostilities began, were enlarged for the production of a greater quantity of the cotton fibre. In the absence of a supply from the fields of Georgia, Alabama, and Mississippi, this domestic output became of increased importance as furnishing the only material for the cabin looms. The quantity of plantation wool which had once been consumed in the manufacture of cloth, had, with each year of the war, fallen off with the gradual destruction of the flocks of sheep by their conversion into mutton for the plantation household. The production of flax in greater abundance was also a characteristic of these constricted times. The finished stuff, in the instance of each of these staples, was ordinarily of a coarse texture; but it sufficed to clothe decently the bodies of the slaves and protect them from the vicissitudes of the weather.

During the hot days of midsummer, one of the most distinct sounds to be heard vibrating drowsily in the stagnant air was the soft whir of the spinning-wheel or the shuffle of the bars of the loom. To this work, a man, with an assistant or two, was assigned as his exclusive occupation; but many of the elderly women were also skilful in handling these domestic implements; and their services, particularly at the beginning of winter, were called into requisition.

The older members of the planter's family managed to supplement their hoarded supply of clothes, purchased before the war, with garments manufactured in the mills that furnished the uniforms for the soldiers. But, as the conflict progressed, that source proved to be less and less productive, and this fact increased the necessity of extreme care on their part in the preservation of the old suits and dresses in their possession. The children of the Mansion were, towards the end, provided with clothes entirely by the domestic weavers and seamstresses; and in this respect, enjoyed hardly an advantage over the youthful slaves with whom they played and hunted. The summer hats which the boys of the family wore were plaited of straw by the hands of the slave-women, who formed the main part of the staff of the Great House. In the winter, the fur of rabbit, squirrel, and raccoon was used for the same purpose; and these skins were also converted into warm gloves, which defied the nipping air of the frosty fields.

Candles were made of tallow, in moulds which had descended, perhaps, from a remote date in the past. The great fires kindled upon the principal hearths in winter played no small part in lighting up the sitting and bedrooms of the planters' homes. No article in common use was more abundant than wood. The forests spread away for many miles in every direction; and in the winter season, the plantation hands had ample time to cut and store away a large supply for consumption in cabin and mansion.

It was fortunate for the recreation of the mistress and her older children that a large number of books had been purchased for the mansion before the war. This contained all the most highly esteemed classics of the language, both English and American. A taste for reading, in addition to the love of life in the open air, had been cultivated in both the boys and the girls; and in stormy weather, during the mild seasons of the year, and in the cold of snowy winter days, the library became the most popular room in the house. There was little increase in the size of this collection in the course of the war. Such as was made was in the form of certain novels which had been printed on coarse paper, and in blurred type, on Confederate presses. In some cases, the backs of these editions were composed of wallpaper. There were three contemporary novelists represented; namely, Victor Hugo, Miss Augusta Evans, and Miss Mulbach. Perhaps no works of fiction were better known to the Confederates in general than the *Toilers of the Sea, Macaria,* and *Joseph the Second and His Court.*

In spite of the narrowness of the times, a daily journal continued to be issued in the capital of the state. The news recorded in its columns was scant in quantity; but it was the only means by which the mistress of the plantation could obtain, with a fair degree of promptness, such information as she possessed of the movements of the Confederate armies.

All the social entertainments, which, before the war, had given so much charm and vivacity to the life of the neighborhood, were soon dropped. The young men were absent in the army, and many of the young women were engaged in some form of work in the plantation homes which was designed to advance the cause of their country. Only on the occasion of

the recurring Sunday services at church did the mistress leave
her own roof.   The church edifice was situated several miles
away; and to this spot, she drove through the forests in her
carriage, in the company of her children.   The congregation consisted entirely of superannuated men, women, and boys and
girls.   Several times towards the end of the war, the solemnity
of the hour had been disturbed by the muffled roar of cannon
towards the North; and on one occasion, at least, the services
had been brokèn up by the rumored approach of Federal
raiders.

Epidemics on the plantation were not unknown.   These
sprang from the diseases contracted by slaves, who had been
drawn from the cabins and fields to work on the Confederate
fortifications.   Such a draft was made for the defenses of Petersburg.   This resulted in the death of several of the negroes
in the camps, while others had returned home deeply infected,
only to perish there after their arrival.   A large number of
the youngest and most vigorous mules and horses were also impressed by the Confederate Government for the use of the army,
and were never seen in their old quarters again.   They too gave
their lives for the Cause, or passed into the possession of the
enemy, to be finally distributed in the cities of the North.[2]

---

[2] A more detailed description of this plantation in war times will be
found in an article written by the author and contributed to the pages of
the January, 1915, number of the *South Atlantic Quarterly*.

CHAPTER V

CREATION OF WEST VIRGINIA

If one were asked to name the two most conspicuous, and also most permanent, results of the War of 1861-65, so far as the public welfare of Virginia was involved, the answer, undoubtedly, would be: (1) the abolition of slavery; and (2) the establishment of the State of West Virginia. Both events were irrevocable from the beginning, and both were equally profound in the impression which they have made already on the destinies of the original commonwealth. The abolition of slavery, as we shall see in a later chapter, disorganized a system of labor which had been in active and unbroken operation from the middle of the seventeenth century; moreover, it radically altered a social framework which had been inherited,—in spirit at least,—from colonial times; and it also undermined an individualistic civilization by creating the amplest room for the encouragement of cooperative and community effort. This signified the expansion of manufactures in every form, and the increase in the number and size of cities.

The creation of the State of West Virginia, which occurred, as we shall soon see, before the final settlement at Appomattox, disrupted the original territory of Virginia at the very hour that the tide of battle was tending to remove forever all those causes which had so long nourished a feeling of hostility between the Eastern and Western inhabitants of the old commonwealth. Had no step been taken before the close of the war to bring about the formal secession of Western from Eastern Virginia, no single adverse influence of importance at work before that

76

event would have survived to keep in existence the antipathies and antagonisms that had burned so hotly during so long a period prior to the opening of the War for Southern Independence.

There was nothing really permanent in the nature of the reasons for this sharp division between the peoples of the Eastern and Western counties. Had Virginia continued intact, like Georgia, Mississippi, or Texas, a traveler today, passing from Norfolk to Wheeling, or from Bristol to Harper's Ferry, would observe no such difference in the public and private life of the people residing in these wide spaces as would be sufficient to hold them apart in interest or sentiment. Indeed, he would find them,—whether their homes were situated west of the Alleghanies or east of the Blue Ridge,—identified with each other in their loyalty to a common state government, and closely affiliated on every other side of their social, economic, and political welfare. And yet, during several generations before the final separation of Western and Eastern Virginia actually took place, the opposition that alienated their respective inhabitants from each other was so acute, and, apparently, so incapable of radical removal, that the final formation of West Virginia as a new state seemed now to have been inevitable, whenever an opportunity should arise for its consummation. It was only during a period of violence that such an opportunity was likely to occur. When it did occur, immediate and almost ruthless advantage was taken of it.

What were the causes of difference between the Eastern and Western sections of the original Virginia? In the first place, there was a distinct difference in the social character, if not social origin, of the people of the two divisions of the Commonwealth. This difference would not have been so great had the population of Eastern Virginia resembled the population of the Valley; namely, the Scotch-Irish and the Germans. The social spirit of Western Virginia was nearer to the spirit of these communities than to the spirit of the communities situated east of the Blue Ridge, as far as Tidewater; but there was a considerable gap even here. Unlike the Western Virginians, the Scotch-Irish and the Germans grew gradually to be in substantial sympathy with the people of Eastern Virginia. They never displayed any desire for separation. They never really antagonized their Eastern neighbors. They were faithful citizens of the Commonwealth from start to finish, and came forward with alacrity to fight its battles when the War of 1861-65 was precipitated.

A large proportion of the inhabitants west of the Alleghany Range had come in from the Northern States, and unlike the Scotch-Irish and the Germans of the Valley, never lost their touch with the communities of Pennsylvania and Ohio, from which so many of them had sprung. They had nothing originally in common with the people of Eastern Virginia; and the existence of the mighty barrier of the Alleghanies had, no doubt, a very powerful influence in preserving this spirit of social independence.

But another fact, besides social origin, existed to create an attitude on their part of opposition to the East. There were, in reality, few slaves in the possession of the people west of the Alleghanies. Their communities were to all purposes communities of freedmen alone. The great staple, tobacco, was not seen in the fields of the proprietors of the soil. They did not own estates embracing many acres. On the contrary, their lands were limited in acreage. Indeed, a large proportion of the farms occupied sites on the slopes of the mountains or in the coves of the foothills.

There was no room in a region like this for the prosperous working of the institution of slavery. But even if there had been, regarding it simply as a system of labor, there were no great natural highways by which the products of the soil could be transported to the seaboard. The only important rivers west of the Alleghanies flowed towards the Ohio. These were all streams full of dangerous falls, which seriously impeded navigation by making canalization expensive as well as difficult. There were, it is true, numerous turnpikes, but the distances were great, and the only means of transportation and conveyance were the wagon and the carriage. There was no railway in all that region before the Baltimore and Ohio line was built, and no canal until the completion of the Chesapeake and Ohio, near the Potomac. Both of these public improvements, however, lay on the far northern boundary.

But it was not due to mere sentiment and convenience that the question of slavery and internal improvements excited so much antagonism in the minds of the people of the Trans-Alleghany. The section of the state east of the Blue Ridge insisted in convention that the number of slaves in a community should be made a part of the basis of representation in the General Assembly. This gave the East a majority in that body out of proportion to the size of the white population. To this difference, the people west of the Alleghanies never became reconciled, although an attempt was made to settle it by compromise. The advantages of internal improvements on a national scale were indefinitely postponed by this inequality, for it conferred the preponderating political power of the state on the people of the East, who were opposed to the acceptance of national aid in carrying out such improvements. It is true that the General Assembly, as time advanced, used its financial resources to build and maintain a system of internal improvements that would satisfy the just complaints of the Western Virginians. But, in the long run, these improvements never reached the proportions of either a canal or a railroad. Neither the James River and Kanawha Canal nor the Central Railway had crossed the borders of Western Virginia by the time the War of Secession had begun. The turnpike constituted practically the only highway, although there had been an attempt to improve the navigation of the Kanawha and the other large rivers in the Trans-Alleghany region.

On many occasions previous to the actual withdrawal of
Western Virginia, predictions had been made that the original
State of Virginia would, in time, be divided into two commonwealths. Webster had, many years before the War of 1861-65
broke out, warned the people of Eastern Virginia that they
must expect this consummation, should they venture to enroll
their state on the side of a new nationality. The question of
separation had often been boldly brought up in the course of
the meetings of the state legislatures and Constitutional conventions.

When the ordinance of secession was adopted in April, 1861,
by the convention then in session, the number of delegates from
Western Virginia who signed it did not exceed two or three in
all. The rest of the representatives from that quarter had, by
this time, retired to their homes beyond the mountains. Thirteen of these men had been expelled from the convention, on the
sole ground, as they claimed, that they had cast their votes in
opposition to the passage of the ordinance. No reason was given
in the resolution which declared their seats vacant.

The most prominent and determined persons among them
were John S. Carlile and Waitman T. Willey. They and their
followers were received on their arrival west of the Alleghanies
with some confusion of feeling, which they endeavored to
crystalize in favor of loyalty to the Union by a series of public
meetings, in which secession was denounced as a monstrous
crime. Willey opened the attack at Morgantown. It was unanimously declared at the large assemblage on this occasion that
Secession was treason, and that, if it was carried as far as
actual practice, Western Virginia would break off all connection with Eastern and erect a state government of its own.

A second meeting was held at Clarksburg, under the counsel
and active direction of Carlile, and the participants in it took
a position as advanced as that assumed by Willey and his followers at Morgantown. The ordinance of secession was emphatically repudiated, and a convention was urged to assemble in

May at Wheeling to decide upon the course to be pursued by the people of Northwestern Virginia in the existing crisis. There had been no legal authority for the summoning of this convention; nor were the members clear in their own minds at first as to what policy should be adopted. It was a purely revolutionary movement.

However much the men present in the convention might differ about matters of subordinate importance, they seemed to have been united in favor of destroying the bonds which had so long joined them to the State Government of the Old Dominion. The influence of Carlile was strenuously and persistently exerted to inflame this sentiment. That of Willey was used in opposition, as he considered it impossible for mere revolutionary measures to be capable of breaking the tie. He pointed out that the provisions of the Federal Constitution expressly forbade the establishment of a new state within an old state without the consent of the latter's Legislature. The convention was proposing to act unconstitutionally. Its course would be declared to be null and void. In short, its own edict in favor of a new state would be necessarily invalid.

Gradually the convention became convinced of the correctness of the view so forcibly expressed by Willey. How was its ardent wish for separate statehood to be realized? At this moment, a resolution was submitted by Francis H. Pierpont, which called for the assemblage of a convention on the eleventh of the ensuing June. It was provided that its membership should be restricted to delegates chosen by the counties which had refused to leave the Union after the passage of the Ordinance of Secession. Shrewdness was shown in omitting to prescribe what the proposed convention should consider and discuss. By this means, the question of the manner in which the division of the state should be carried out was left open for final decision. There was no doubt, however, as to the general determination to erect a new commonwealth.

When the projected convention met in June, thirty-five counties situated in the Northwestern region of Virginia were represented among the delegates, who numbered seventy-seven in
all. A marked difference of opinion came to the surface so soon
as the business of the session formally began. One section of
the members were in favor of at once establishing a new state
by combining for that purpose the "loyal" counties which were
represented on the floor. This was the impetuous plan originally advocated by Carlile. The other section, seeking to find a
constitutional method, direct or indirect, urged that the delegates, as soon as seated, should be taken as the delegates from
the entire State of Virginia. If it was essential, as it was, in
reality, under the Constitution, that the consent of Virginia
should be obtained before the formation of a new state could
become valid, then this was the only possible way in which the
pretension, however hollow, could be put forward that this consent had been secured. But this bold feint was not at once
attempted. The first step was to adopt a resolution affirming
that the delegates present represented the whole State of Virginia; that the "loyal" counties alone formed that state; that
the principal offices of its government, in consequence of the
"rebellion," were vacant; and that their place should be filled by
the election of a new governor, lieutenant-governor, and attorney-general. The convention then chose Francis H. Pierpont to
occupy the first of these posts, Daniel Polsley, the second, and
James G. Wheat, the third. When that body, having completed
its work, adjourned, it was with the understanding that it should
reassemble in August.

Under an ordinance of this second convention, a Legislature
met in Wheeling in July. It received, through Pierpont, the
announcement that the new administration had been recognized
by the Federal Government as that of the whole State of Virginia. Waitman T. Willey and John S. Carlile were elected to
the seats in the Senate which had been vacated by R. M. T. Hunter and James M. Mason, and on appearing in Washington, they

were promptly sworn in as holding perfectly valid, legitimate credentials. On May 13, 1862, this Legislature formally consented to the erection of the new State of West Virginia.

It is no unjust reflection on the origin of this new state to say that it drew its initial breath in an atmosphere of unscrupulous sophistry. Bald subterfuge was unquestionably the only means available of getting around the constitutional provision forbidding the establishment of the new commonwealth without the consent of the old State of Virginia; and such subterfuge was used to an extreme. To assert seriously that the Legislature which met at Wheeling in May, 1862, was, from any point of view, the legitimate General Assembly of the whole commonwealth of the Old Dominion, when it was composed only of delegates from the Trans-Alleghany region, was a mere travesty upon the truth, which was perfectly well-known to all who took part in its hypocritical deliberations. The Rump Parliament of Cromwell was no more the English Parliament than the Rump Assembly of Wheeling was the General Assembly of the ancient State of Virginia. No solemn thimble-rigging could make it different; and no persons were more conscious of the farce than Carlile and Willey, who were to benefit by it so signally.

The mere fact that Eastern Virginia at that hour was engaged in a conflict with the National Power was no justification, under any impartial interpretation of the Constitution, for action so illegal and arbitrary as that of these Western Virginia representatives. Nor is the accuracy of this statement lessened by the fact that the region west of the Alleghanies did have sound practical reasons for desiring to erect an independent state. We have already pointed out the grounds of controversy between the Western and Eastern sections. The respective interests of the two were radically repugnant. It was no advantage to Western Virginia to be bound to Eastern. In the origin of the bulk of her people; in their need of extensive internal improvements, which were only practicable through the aid of the National Government; in their hatred of slavery; in their

enforced subservience to the interests of Eastern Virginia,—all
these points, so conducive to antagonism, were sufficient in
themselves to create a plausible claim to a separate political
existence. Had that claim been openly, vigorously, and unanimously pressed before the War of 1861-65 broke out, and flatly
denied by Eastern Virginia, the inhabitants of Trans-Alleghany
would have possessed sound reason for complaining that they
had been treated with very grave injustice, although the action
of the Eastern Virginians would have been natural enough, in
the light of the magnificent mountain domain which they would
have been asked to give up.

If Western Virginia was firmly opposed to secession,—as
certainly her most influential citizens appear to have been, if an
inference can be drawn from the votes of her delegates to the
Secessionist Convention, which met in Richmond in the spring
of 1861,—did she not have the moral right to break off from
her connection with old Virginia? It was a most critical situation in which her people were placed by the issue before them.
Had they remained a part of Virginia, and secession had ultimately succeeded, then they would have found themselves irrevo-
cably bound to a community, the main interest of which,
slavery, would have continued to raise the same causes of friction which it had previously done during so many years. Not
the smallest hope of getting rid of the detested system would
have survived. The old doctrine of internal improvements, by
means of the state alone, would also have remained; and the
prospect of national aid would have vanished permanently. In
short, those grounds of reasonable complaint which the people
of Western Virginia had so long urged would never have been
rooted up had they found themselves, at the end of the war, a
division of a triumphant South.

On the other hand, cooperation with the North held out the
hope of the complete removal in the future of all those influences
which had been blighting their material welfare and irritating
their public sentiment. Slavery, for instance, would disappear

as a system to be reckoned with by the Western Virginians, for, if they remained a permanent part of the Union, that institution would no longer have an existence west of the Alleghanies, whether the North failed or succeeded in conquering the Confederacy. With themselves in absolute possession of their own independent commonwealth, they could pursue any national policy that should seem best calculated to advance their material interests. In consequence of this liberty, they could confidently anticipate, like the rest of the Northern States, the practical realization for their benefit of the doctrine of internal improvements at the expense of the National Government.

In brief, it was natural enough, in the light of their physical situation and economic interests, that the people of Western Virginia should prefer to remain in the Union. And this fact justifies a certain degree of condonation of the irregular, and altogether tortuous, manner in which their infant commonwealth obtained entrance into the circle of the States of the Union.

It should not be forgotten, too, that the hour was one in which the violent spirit that accompanies all wars,—and no war so completely as a civil war,—was running at its highest tide. Mr. Lincoln himself recognized that there was but one defense for Western Virginia's admission to statehood in such an anomalous manner which stood any chance of acceptance by the public sentiment of the world. This defense was that the creation of the new commonwealth was a war measure; and that, as a war measure, its creation was justifiable, because it sensibly aided the Federal Government in its struggle to prevent the permanent establishment of the Confederacy. It will be recalled that, in issuing the Emancipation Proclamation, the Federal President had sought to validate that unconstitutional act by the same course of reasoning. It was tantamount to admitting that, in law, there was no substantial ground for claiming that either act was entitled to be considered really legal. Necessity, the old proverb runs, knows no law, and this assertion was again verified in these two acts, as it had been verified ten thousand times during earlier periods of violence. In war, we are told, all laws are silent. The admission of West Virginia to statehood was only another proof of the pertinency of this saying. But the Western Virginians at least paid some degree of homage to law by throwing a thin deceptive veil of correctness over their action by pretending that they were conforming to the provisions of the Constitution.

Was the sentiment of the people west of the Trans-Alleghany generally in favor of the course which had led up to the creation of the new state? It has been asserted by at least one of its historians, Dr. James C. McGregor, that the popular sanction was limited in extent. "Just as the large body of Western Virginians were neutral in the conflict (the war) that was pending," he declared, "so were they indifferent as to the actions of the Wheeling Government, showing their disapproval by staying away from the polls. There was a general feeling that the new commonwealth, if formed, would be the result of a secret, restless desire on the part of aspiring politicians to obtain offices. The people were suspicious of a ruling clique which destroyed old constitutions and enacted new ones with such ease, and with so little regard to public sentiment. The same group of men organized the May Convention; summoned the June Convention; called together and sat as members in the rump legislature; met one day as the General Assembly of Virginia, and gave their consent to the very acts which they had agreed to the day before; created offices and fixed their own salaries. Then, to cap the climax, a free vote was made impossible, and none but known adherents of the New State were permitted to go to the polls. It was admitted that, even in the Panhandle, there was no enthusiasm for the new State."

It is quite certain, as Doctor McGregor asserts, that the movement in favor of the erection of a new commonwealth was carried through by a comparatively small body of able and determined men. But it should be remembered in at least partial explanation of this fact that Western Virginia was inhabited in a large division of its area by a peculiarly isolated and provincial population. Much of its surface was covered by mountains, with little connection of any kind with the lowlands. It was hardly to be expected that the citizens of such remote and secluded districts would have responded quickly, and as one body, to leadership, no matter how acute the crisis was, in reality. There were few newspapers in circulation; the people in the mass were illiterate; and the means of rapid communication from county to county were restricted. At the same time, had there been, as intimated by the historian quoted, a strong sentiment among the inhabitants at large in opposition to the program so vigorously and openly pushed forward by Carlile and Willey, that sentiment would have had sufficient opportunity to reveal itself.

Apparently, there was no man,—certainly no set of men,— who were courageous enough to come forward as a champion or champions for the preservation of the tie which united Western with Eastern Virginia. No evidence rose to light that there was even a smouldering sentiment in favor of secession.

The clearest proof that the action of the Western Virginian political leaders really reflected the leaning of the people at large is disclosed by the popular attitude towards the Confederate military forces, which, at first, under Garnett, and, afterwards, under Lee, endeavored to drive McClellan and Rosecranz in turn across the Ohio. Did either of these Confederate officers receive any assistance of importance in their respective campaigns through those distant regions? Was there any manifestation of sympathy for them on the part of the inhabitants? As little, in fact, as was extended to General Lee, in the course of his subsequent invasion of Pennsylvania. The reason was the same: the people were not only unwilling to take up arms in support of the Confederate cause, but they showed their real hostility to its success by maintaining an attitude of coldness and inertia that practically declined to risk life or property by swelling either Garnett's or Lee's army with recruits.

During many generations, the feeling of the bulk of the Western Virginians toward the Eastern had been one of sharp and, on the whole, justifiable antagonism. It would have been unnatural, indeed, had they now come forward to uphold and advance a cause which was essentially repugnant to the material interests of their very different communities, and to every tradition of their social and domestic life.

VI

POLITICAL RECONSTRUCTION AND ITS AFTERMATH

CHAPTER I

FIRST STAGE—PRESIDENTIAL RECONSTRUCTION,
1865-1867

Tennessee was more fortunate than Virginia in the retention of its original boundaries. The Western Virginians, in the mass, were not more hostile to the Confederacy than the Eastern Tennesseeans; and yet, today, Tennessee continues intact, while Virginia remains in a condition of mutilation, which is certain to last indefinitely.

When the State of West Virginia was carved out of old Virginia, with all the finality of the Adamic operation which produced Mother Eve, the remarkable feat was performed by the State Government at Wheeling of creating a new administration under a new governor, and yet not stripping the old governor of any of those executive functions which, in theory, at least, he had been performing east of that Trans-Alleghany region which made up the terrain of the infant commonwealth. Was not Pierpont the governor presumably of the entire State of Virginia before the new state assumed an independent existence? Was he not still governor of that remaining part which was situated east of the Alleghanies, with the exception of Jefferson and Berkeley counties? All that he and his associates, therefore, had to do, was to withdraw to the surviving section of his original jurisdiction.

Pierpont might very naturally, at this hour, have regarded the prospect before him with a high degree of ruefulness, however firm might have been his confidence in the ultimate success of the Union cause. He saw before his eyes, in the area of his

91

Francis H. Pierpont
Governor 1865-1868

supposed commonwealth, a wide stretch of country, which was, alternately, under the control of the Federal and the Confederate armies. From a political point of view, Eastern Virginia was a No Man's Land. Now a part of the great Valley would be restored to the possession of the Federal forces, and then General Early would advance up the whole length of it to the fortifications of Washington itself. General Lee would press the Army of Potomac back from Orange to the old battlefields of Manassas. Thus, from day to day, down to the last few months of the war, no one could say with perfect confidence in whose hands the control of a very large part of the state was really established. Nearly to the very end, the whole of Southside Virginia proper refused to acknowledge the increasing mastery of the armies of Grant and Sheridan.

In the midst of the swaying fortunes of war, in what corner of Virginia was Pierpont likely to find a spot stable enough to afford him and his peripatetic official companions a really permanent place of stoppage? The hour had arrived for him to depart from West Virginia. Where, on the other side of the mountains, should he halt? There was but one locality in old Virginia where he was certain of protection from the incursions of the terrible rebels. This was at Alexandria, which lay within the circle of the forts that had been erected in defense of the Federal Capital. This small town was really a part of Washington. Pierpont was as safe in its City Hall as Lincoln was in the White House. There he could quietly take his seat and nurse his patience until the Confederacy should fall exhausted. Every month he could hope to see the line marking the actual jurisdiction of the Confederate Government at Richmond recede southward until it should disappear beyond the border of Carolina.

When that desired hour should arrive,—as he was convinced it would do,— he would have excellent reason to congratulate himself that all the plans of his political associates in Wheeling had not been carried out to the extreme degree proposed. For instance, at the meeting in that city of the so-called Legislature of December, 1862, it was enacted that the new state, to which that Legislature was supposed to have granted a legal incorporation, should embrace, not only the counties of Frederick, Berkeley, Clarke, and Jefferson east of the Alleghanies, but also Tazewell, Bland, Giles, Craig, Buchanan, Wise, Russell, Scott, Lee, Highland, and Bath in the southwest; Shenandoah, Warren, Page, and Rockingham in the Middle Valley; and Loudoun, Fairfax, Prince William, and Alexandria east of the Blue Ridge. This measure, fortunately, proved abortive.

When, in 1863, the so-called "Restored Government" of Pierpont seated itself at Alexandria, he was confronted with the fact that his proclamations had no force beyond the limits of the County of Fairfax, the two counties of Norfolk and Princess Anne,—with the City of Norfolk added,—and the two counties of the Eastern Shore; namely, Accomac and Northampton. The position was one of little dignity and still less authority. There was, indeed, a certain degree of personal idiosyncrasy in his retention of this naked post, for he had been offered, and had declined, election to the office of governor of West Virginia. Had he retained that office, he would have enjoyed the assurance that he was respected as a man by the large majority of the people of his new commonwealth; and he would also have found himself in practical accord with that majority at every turn in the course of his administration. In addition, he would have known that the tide would never run so adversely to the fortunes of the Federal armies that his situation would become precarious by a successful Confederate invasion of the region lying on the western side of the Alleghanies.

On the other hand, in preferring to continue to be the so-called governor of old Virginia, and to remove to Alexandria under the protection of the Federal guns, he was clearly aware that the people of the contracted territory which would fall at once under his actual jurisdiction, would regard him personally with hatred, and his cause with loathing. Furthermore, as

Edmund Pendleton

the Confederate armies should retire further and further southward, the country left behind under his control, as the Federal
governor of Virginia, would be found occupied by a people animated by still greater bitterness against the usurping official.
No matter how conciliatory and kindly he might be, there was
not the smallest chance that he could bring local order out of
local confusion until the last soldier of the Army of Northern
Virginia had surrendered. All this hostile feeling, all these administrative difficulties, he was willing to face rather than remain in a safe and normal berth at Wheeling.

The Pierpont government established its offices at Alexandria in the summer of 1863. It was one of the characteristics
of the local duplication of authority that at least one district
supposed to be in its jurisdiction, namely, Fairfax County, was
represented both in the real General Assembly at Richmond,
and in the self-designated Legislature that convened at Alexandria. One of the first steps of the Pierpont government, after
taking possession of its new capital, was to summon a convention. This met in May, and promptly renominated Pierpont for
governor. The two men selected as lieutenant-governor and
attorney-general,—one of whom bore a name of high distinction, Edmund Pendleton,—refused to serve, and were replaced
by substitutes of extraordinary obscurity from both a social and
a political point of view, a proof of the very poor personal material upon which the cribbed and cabined administration at Alexandria had to draw. The second nominee for the lieutenant-
governorship, known by the singular name of Wunder, failed
to secure a majority of the small number of votes cast. But
one congressional district,—that in which Fairfax County was
included,—undertook to go through the farce of an election.
There was also a ballot for the members of the new General
Assembly which had been summoned to meet by Pierpont.

It was one of the strange contradictions of the hour that
Berkeley and Jefferson counties, at the very moment that they
declared at the polls that they were in favor of annexation to

West Virginia, elected the customary number of delegates to represent them in the next General Assembly to meet in Richmond. Berkeley County became a part of West Virginia in August, 1863, and Jefferson, in November, of the same year. But it required an Act of Congress in 1866, and a decision of the Supreme Court in 1870, to validate this action. After the close of the war, the General Assembly of Virginia, it appears, endeavored to nullify the vote in these counties for annexation authorized by the Alexandria Legislature in 1863; but, as just mentioned, the Federal political and judicial powers intervened to block that effort.

It was a fact of significance that three of the ablest justices of the Supreme Court,—Davis, Field, and Clifford,—affirmed, in a dissenting opinion, that the act of the original Legislature, in pronouncing the consent of the Alexandria Legislature,—passing as the Virginia General Assembly,—to be invalid, was not too late, as Congress had not yet ratified the transfer. Both Congress and the majority of the Supreme Court, however, were determined to enforce the transfer, and, like all the subterfuges that had characterized the admission of the new state, as a whole, this proceeding relating to a part was pushed through without regard to perfectly valid and rational objections. By this ruthlessness, old Virginia was permanently deprived of two of its fairest and most historic counties, which were closely identified, in their social and economic interests, with all that beautiful domain that lay in the vicinity of the lower Shenandoah River, which still remains a part of the original state.

The first Assembly of the Pierpont administration, which called itself, with a stretch of ironical imagination, the "Restored Government of Virginia," convened at Alexandria in December, 1863. This was only a few month subsequent to Pierpont's arrival in his temporary capitol. The Upper Chamber consisted of an imposing body of six senators. The districts supposed by a fiction to be represented by these men were Alexandria, Accomac, Fairfax, Loudoun, Norfolk County, and Norfolk City. The

Lower Chamber could count only one member more on its roll. Altogether, there were thirteen representatives in this legislature, which, although not as large as a town council, had the conscious effrontery,—which must have been a cause of sly amusement even to themselves,—to hold themselves out as the General Assembly of Virginia.

The fact that their numerical proportions were extremely attenuated, and that they were the actual spokesmen for a few counties alone, and these by means of the bayonet only, did not prevent Governor Pierpont's legislature from undertaking to adopt measures that would affect the vital welfare of the whole state, should the Federal arms ultimately triumph. Pierpont himself gave the cue. He was particularly interested in driving one more nail in the coffin of the institution of slavery. It was tacitly acknowledged at this time by most persons, whatever their affiliations in the war, that the institution stood little chance of survival in any event. It was also well-known to all that President Lincoln's Emancipation Proclamation had, by its impression on the sentiment of the World, weakened the chains of the bondsmen even behind the Confederate lines, although it did not immediately break those chains. Pierpont, however, was not satisfied with this situation. He urged the little body of men sitting in the Alexandria City Hall to summon a Convention to authorize the adoption of a constitutional provision for the permanent abolition of slavery in the State of Virginia. This momentous suggestion was sustained. Twelve of the delegates and senators, forming the majority, voted in its favor.

In selecting members of the proposed Convention, it was laid down that no one should be permitted to cast a ballot who had given assistance to the Confederacy. The number of voters, in consequence, was small. In Fairfax, the number was only two hundred and eight, and in Alexandria only ninety-four for the senatorial delegates and ninety-two for the county delegate. The ballots cast in Loudoun, Norfolk, and the Eastern Shore were still fewer, and they were from the hands of men who, as a rule, were unidentified with the welfare of these communities.

Only twenty counties were represented in the Convention which assembled at Alexandria in February, 1864, and the number of members did not exceed fifteen. Among the important changes which it made in the Constitution of 1850-51 were the following; it reduced the number of judges of the State Supreme Court to three; declared a residence of one year to be sufficient for the enjoyment of the local suffrage; disfranchised all Confederate office-holders; abolished the institution of slavery; laid a levy by the poll for the benefit of free schools; and pronounced in favor of equal and uniform taxation.

The Constitution adopted by the Convention was ratified by the few citizens who voted. The balloting took place in the spring of 1864. In the course of the ensuing summer, the precarious authority of the Pierpont administration was disclosed in the conflict with General Butler, the military commander of the Norfolk district. Butler, with characteristic abruptness and bluntness, submitted to the people the question whether they would prefer military rule to the existing civil. The vote was almost unanimously in favor of military rule. The jurisdiction of the Alexandria civil administration thus came, in the City of Norfolk at least, to a complete termination. And the effect was not confined to one locality. Before the war ended, that jurisdiction found itself limited to the counties of Alexandria and Fairfax. The taxes collected in these communities were unable to furnish a sufficient revenue for the disconcerted and bedraggled government.

The second General Assembly of the Pierpont Government met in December, 1864. There were no additions to the counties represented in the previous body, although the Confederate armies had, by this time, abandoned to the enemy's control the larger part of the territory of the state situated north of the James. The subject which enlisted the principal interest of the Assembly related to the status of the negro. What measure should be adopted to assure him the right to testify as a witness in court? What to enable him to enjoy the privileges of education? The Assembly acted conservatively on both questions by deferring their decision, since it was concluded that the hour was still unripe for such extreme steps. Congress showed its unwillingness to approve one of the Assembly's most important Acts when it refused to seat the two senators who had been chosen by that body to represent Virginia. The closing measure of the Assembly was the ratification of the Thirteenth Amendment. This occurred in February, 1865, only a few weeks before the surrender of the Confederate army at Appomattox.

The next Assembly which convened was still the Rump of Alexandria, but a body which had the right, by the triumph of force, to speak for the whole of the conquered state. In other words, the farce of the "Restored Government of Virginia" was not again, to the same degree, at least, required to be played.

Before the last gun was fired, President Lincoln had visited Richmond, and agreed to permit the legitimate Virginia Legislature, which had been sitting under the Confederate Government, to withdraw the Virginian troops from the field, should that body think it expedient to do so. Lincoln's terms were submitted to a meeting of the citizens of Richmond held some days after the closing scene at Appomattox. Already a call had been issued for the assembling of the Legislature to pass on these terms. In the short interval, opposition to Lincoln's overtures had been expressed in his cabinet, and what ever chance they had stood of acceptance was destroyed by the President's assassination.

In May, President Johnson, by proclamation, declared the general State Government under the Confederacy to be null and void, and instructed Pierpont to take charge of the civil administration of Virginia at once. He arrived in Richmond in May, and, in June, he summoned the Alexandria Legislature for the last time to convene. There were only twelve senators and delegates altogether present. The Alexandria Constitution of 1864

had deprived the largest number of Virginia's voters of the right
to cast a ballot by excluding those who had been in active sympathy with the Confederacy.   Pierpont recommended the repeal
of this clause.   "It is folly," he said, with remarkable moderation for the times, "to suppose that a State can be governed under a Republican form of Government, when, in a large part of
the State, nineteen-twentieths of the people are disfranchised
and cannot hold office."

Another utterance of significance was an address by the
Speaker of the House, in which he exclaimed with fervor:
"Whatever they (Congress) may do to the other States of the
South, thank God, they cannot now saddle negro suffrage upon
Virginia."   His audience consisted of the nine delegates who
composed the House at this hour.

Both governor and speaker, to their honor, were strongly
in favor of a policy that would allay bitterness and restore
peace.   In this, they were simply imitating the example which
had been set by both Lincoln and Johnson.   As long, however,
as the military arm of the National Government was present in
the state, there was no hope of any freedom of the ballot.   Thus
in the municipal election in Richmond in July, 1865, the three
highest offices were filled by the choice of old Confederate soldiers; but an order from the nearest Federal brigadier quickly
displaced them.   Pierpont was compelled to follow this cue.   He
forbade the election to any office in Virginia of any man who
had previously served the Confederacy in office.

Pierpont endeavored by all the means in his reach to establish permanent order, but in some of the steps which he took to
bring this about, he found himself in conflict with the extreme
Republicans, who were anxious to monopolize the political power.
This could not be accomplished as long as the former supporters
of the Confederacy were at liberty to cast a ballot.   This they
were now able to do by the act of the Legislature, with Pierpont's
consent.   The Union Association of Alexandria, not only condemned universal enfranchisement, but also recommended the

grant of suffrage to the negroes. This double policy, if carried out, would, they knew, make the supremacy of the Radicals immune to successful attack. Their chagrin and indignation were soon further inflamed by the evident intention of President Johnson to readmit the states of the South to the Union, with all their rights under the Constitution fully restored. He expressed his approval of the election for a new General Assembly and for the next session of Congress, which was now under consideration. Under the influence of this conciliatory attitude on his part, candidates for these offices came forward, not by formal nomination, but on their own motion.

Some imprudence was shown by several prominent newspapers, which led to their suppression by the Federal officer in local command, but, on the whole, the spirit of the Virginians at large was faithfully expressed in the resolution drafted at a public meeting held at Staunton in May, 1865, in which it was asserted that the people of Augusta County were sincerely determined to conform to the laws of the United States and to comply with all the requirements of the National Government.

In the Congressional and State elections which were held in October, 1865, only forty thousand ballots were cast; but these belonged to the conservative element in each community. The General Assembly were authorized by this vote to repeal the amendment to the Alexandria Constitution which had so seriously curtailed the right of suffrage. There can be no question that, had the congressmen elected on this occasion been seated, the state would have been saved from the period of confusion, injustice, and folly, which quickly followed their rejection in Washington. Presidential Reconstruction, the only wise policy to have pursued, ended in failure. Now ensued an interval of nearly two years,—December 4, 1865, to March 2, 1867,—in which the people of Virginia were left in a doubtful frame of mind as to their status both from a state and a national point of view. A considerable proportion of the younger negroes were now indisposed to labor any longer in the fields, and the General

Assembly was influenced by the losses and dangers which that fact created to pass a vagrant Act, which was eagerly seized upon by the Republican Party of the North as evidence of a determination to reinslave the former bondsmen by an indirect method. The military officer in command of the district somewhat abruptly forbade its enforcement.

There were few men in this Assembly who had been closely identified with any branch of the Confederate Goverment. This, perhaps, explains the fact that the only overture which was ever made to the State of West Virginia to recall her act of secession from the mother commonwealth was offered by this Assembly, and, as might have been expected, met with no success. In the meanwhile, the Reconstruction Committee of Congress had undertaken to inquire into the conditions at that time prevailing in the Southern states. The object of this investigation was to lay the foundation for the introduction of the drastic Reconstruction Policy, which the Republican majority in Congress intended to put in force. This sinister committee convened early in January, 1866, and accepted with satisfaction testimony to show that the Virginians were still disloyal to the National Government, and that neither Unionists nor negroes were able to obtain just treatment in the state courts. The harshest witnesses were, with few exceptions, of Northern birth.

The committee's decision was precisely in harmony with what might have been predicted. It declared that the Southern states, —Virginia included,—were unfitted for self-government; and that, therefore, they possessed no right to be readmitted to the Union. This was highly agreeable to that section of the Republican party in Virginia which was led by Judge John C. Underwood. These men had already condemned Governor Pierson for ultra conservatism, and had pronounced in favor of a territorial government. In May, a convention was held and the Union Republican Party of Virginia organized. The two principles which its platform supported with most emphasis were: (1) the disfranchisement of all voters who had acted with the Confederate

Government; and (2) the partial enfranchisement of the freedmen. In the following September, a National Republican Convention assembled in Philadelphia and recommended the adoption of manhood suffrage in the Southern States. This became, from this time, the policy of the National Republican Party. In the meanwhile, the Civil Rights Bill and the Freedmen's Bureau Bill had been passed by Congress.

Bitterness of feeling between the people of the South and the people of the North from this hour increased in acuteness. Several riots now occurred between the negroes and the whites in different parts of Virginia; and the personal hostility between the members of the two races grew rapidly in strength. In December, the General Assembly, by a majority of one hundred and one ballots, in a vote of one hundred and two, refused to ratify the Fourteenth Amendment. Pierpont was still filling the office of Governor, but his advice was too conservative to be acceptable at that moment of overwhelming irritation. On March 4, (1867), he communicated to the Assembly, then sitting in extra session, the news of the passage of the Reconstruction Act by Congress. But it was now too late to adopt the conciliatory measures which he had so earnestly recommended under the influence of a less passionate view of the situation.

Up to this time, in spite of the evil of vagrancy, which prevailed to a considerable degree, the general relations between the former master and the former slave had continued mutually friendly and helpful, with little interruption. There was, it is true, a disposition on the part of some of the young freedmen to wander away from the original scenes of their lives; a few of the older men also were inclined to test the actuality of their freedom by abandoning their native plantations; but in the mass, the black population of mature years remained in the cabins where they had spent their previous lives.

If we consider the kindly feeling which had always existed between the members of the two races in the era of slavery, there is no reason to think that freedom in itself would have aroused emotions of hatred and antagonism towards the whites in the breasts of the blacks. Throughout the long war which had just closed, there had not been in Virginia a single instance of open revolt by the slaves; and hardly an instance even of offensive conduct had occurred on the loneliest plantations. It is possible that, at this time, on these remote estates, the mistress, left alone with her children, with no real protection except what was afforded by a black overseer, felt an occasional apprehension, but it was never to a degree that caused her to remove to a safer place. The slaves had a thousand opportunities to resent with murderous blows the supposed wrongs inflicted on them in the past and the present by the dominant race. They not only did not take advantage of these opportunities, but they frequently refused to use a chance to escape to the armies of the invader when marching through their region.

Had the farsighted plans of Lincoln and Johnson been carried into force and Virginia restored, along with the other States of the South, on a footing of conciliation, forbearance, and non-interference, the relations of the two races would have moved along, without any permanent friction, in the ancient groove of friendship and good-will; and all the sorrows and humiliations of Reconstruction would never have occurred, to leave behind indelible memories of vindictive oppression.

CHAPTER II

SECOND STAGE—CONGRESSIONAL RECONSTRUCTION

The two organizations that were most useful to the Republican Party of Virginia in alienating the negroes from their former masters, even before they had acquired the right of suffrage, were the Freedmen's Bureau and the Union League. Had the former slaves been left to act on their own impulse, the mere reception of that right would not necessarily have led to serious antagonism with the white people, although it would have increased the chance of friction between the two races. It was these two powerful agencies, composed chiefly of unscrupulous adventurers from the North, that were mainly responsible for the alienation which so soon began to arise between the freedmen and their original owners. The Freedmen's Bureau and the Union League, which were supported by all the power of the Government in Washington, and the concentrated energy of the so-called "scalawags" and "carpet-baggers" on the ground, were the bodies to which the negroes, frightened by the possibility of restored slavery, which was held up before them as an ogre by their new friends, rallied with the liveliest loyalty.

The Freedmen's Bureau held itself out as the guardian of the former slaves, and claimed that its jurisdiction was practically unlimited. It was presumed to protect the negroes from every form of white oppression, even in the most ordinary walks of life. There was no instance of a supposed offense, indeed, however small, or however purely domestic, which it did not investigate.

The Bureau was established in Virginia within two months after the surrender at Appomattox. It had command over eight

106

districts, each of which was subject to a superintendent who was answerable to the central authority. Every district was divided into a subdistrict under the control of military officers. In the beginning, the bureau had possession of nearly one hundred thousand acres of confiscated or escheated land, which it rented to negro tenants. Many persons of the race, however, were supported by the distribution of daily rations. An effort was also made to erect schools for the use of the freedmen's children.

Even before Congressional Reconstruction began, the exercise by the Bureau of these benevolent, protective, and educational functions very naturally tended to give it great power over the minds of the negroes. From its first appearance in the State, the main object of the organization was to keep the blacks as far as possible in a condition of complete independence of their former masters. This, in itself, would have been sufficient to aroused hatred of the Bureau in the hearts of the white people, and sharp antagonism towards the negro also; and this feeling was further inflamed by the oppressive attitude which the Bureau so often exhibited in the exercise of its general jurisdiction.

A close and sympathetic coadjutor of the Bureau was the Union League, which had been organized at first at the North, but which spread into the South after the fall of the Confederacy. In Virginia, as elsewhere in the conquered States, the only persons eligible were the negroes and their radical leaders. Its sinister character was revealed by the fact that its sessions were held always during the hours of night. Practically, its only purpose, after Reconstruction began, was to form the negro voters into compact ranks, and to inculcate the duty of their remaining inflexibly loyal to the Republican Party in local as well as in national elections. In this purpose, these alien leaders were, for a time, eminently successful. It was considered, at that period, to be ominously significant that, in a total of ninety-four thousand ballots cast in the State election of 1867 by black voters,

Chief-Justice Chase.   President Davis.   Judge Underwood.

The First Mixed Jury in Virginia, 1866

only six hundred and thirty-eight were found recorded against the summoning of a Convention. Even if the discipline of the Union League over himself had not been extreme, every freedman would have feared assault from members of his own race, or at least social ostracism, had he disregarded the order which he had received to obey his white radical leaders.

If these leaders could have maintained their supremacy indefinitely, all hope of cooperation between whites and blacks would have been permanently destroyed. It was finally broken down largely by the influence of a secret organization which was far more determined in character than the League, as it was an issue now of the survival of the white community at all. This was the Ku Klux Klan. This association was not so extensive in Virginia as it was in the States situated further towards the South; but the shadow of it, when at the zenith of its strength in those more distant States, was projected warningly across the peaks of the Alleghanies and the Blue Ridge.

How completely null was the service which these two organizations of League and Bureau performed in restoring concord and prosperity to the distracted State was revealed in the condition which arose after March, 1867, throughout its area.

In the first place, the labor system had become gravely disorganized by the promises held out to the negroes by the leaders of the National Republican Party at Washington, and by the men who had flocked into Virginia from the North, in the hope of obtaining office through the new negro voters. The most popular of these promises was the subdivision of the lands among the freedmen by a formal Act of confiscation. A vague rumor ran from negro community to negro community that every head of a black family was to receive forty acres and a mule. The freedmen went so far as to divide up secretly many of the large plantations of the State, and, in some instances, quarrels arose over the appropriation of fertile corners that led to bloodshed.

The political turmoil in Virginia began from the moment the negroes made their first attempt to vote.   This occurred at Alexdria only three days after the passage of the Reconstruction Act of March 2 (1867).   An early order of General Schofield, who was in military command of Virginia, prohibited the holding of any local election until the registration of the voters, under the provisions of the second Act of Reconstruction March 23, had been completed.   The men appointed to compose the Board in charge were instructed to select, as local registers, Federal military officers, honorably discharged Federal soldiers, and native citizens of Union affiliations.

A campaign began in the Summer of 1867 in which the blackest passions were aroused in all who participated in it.   The sinister adventurers from the North, the keenly embittered native Union men, the frightened negroes, and the hangers-on of the Federal troops stationed in Virginia to maintain order, were arrayed in one solid mass against the conservative element in each community, which was represented there by the great majority of the whites.   The leader of the mongrel radicals was James W. Hunnicutt, who had, at one time, followed the calling of a minister of the Gospel, and later, that of an editor of a religious journal.   It was one of the contradictory features of his varied life that he had actually served as a member of the Secession Convention of 1861, and thrown the weight of his ballot in favor of Virginia's withdrawal from the Union.   Little importance was attached to his assertion, at a later date, that he had been coerced, against his convictions, into approving this extreme step.   But he had allayed all suspicions aroused in the minds of his radical associates by this incident by showing a violence of opinion that carried him even further than they in support of all the radical measures of the hour.   His views found their chief voice at first in the publication of a journal which obtained, at an early date, a wide circulation among the freedmen and the whites affiliated with them.

A Republican Convention assembled in Richmond in the Spring of 1867. Nearly one half of the delegates in attendance belonged to the negro race. The resolutions adopted by this Convention reflected with great clearness the aspirations of that race at this initial hour of their political freedom. These resolutions demanded protection for the blacks in the dispensation of justice in the Courts, and also asserted their right to hold office in the administration of the political affairs of each community. Above all, there was a call for the establishment of free schools, in the advantages of which the blacks would share on a footing of equality .with the whites. Another notable clause would have relieved the negroes even of a poll tax, for it demanded the limitation of taxation to property.

So extreme was the position taken by Hunnicutt that native Republicans like John Minor Botts, a local leader of a moderate spirit, endeavored, with the assistance of prominent men of the North, to establish a political organization that would win the support of a large number of the whites. It was seen by every one who made any pretense to political sagacity that no Republican Party, with an element of permanency in it, could be built up in Virginia, unless it could make an appeal to the respectable portion of the white population. There were now very many persons in this population who had come to the conclusion that the only means which the State could use to recover its former rights as a commonwealth was through the Republican Party; and that, if a new wing to that Party could be created by the adherence of representative Virginians, it would be likely to exercise great influence in the right direction at Washington. The men who favored the establishment of a purged organization advocated the acceptance of negro suffrage, and several other requirements equally hateful to the majority of the Virginian people, but considered indispensable by the North, if the State was to be restored to the Union.

The platform, which the supporters of the new party thought expedient, consisted of the following three clauses: "(1) We yield an unreserved submission to the demands of Congress; (2) the political power of the State, which has heretofore been wielded by white men alone, shall, henceforth, be possessed and exercised by whites and blacks together; (3) a new constitution shall be framed which shall establish perfect equality before the law between the races, civilly as well as politically."

It was openly announced by the men who were seeking to found this new party, composed of persons drawn from both the Republican and Democratic ranks, whether black or white, that Union men would alone be considered in the choice of a candidate for Governor.

But the hour was not really ripe for the movement to erect a white conservative Republican Party in Virginia, wise as it would have been at that juncture, and the attempt received no approval from any quarter. Its most ardent supporters turned for leadership to John Minor Botts, who soon issued a call for a convention. The situation at this moment indicated that the original Republican Party in Virginia was about to divide into two factions; one, substantially conservative, supported by many native citizens, who had formerly been Whigs in their political affiliations; the other, extremely radical, supported by the freedmen and their white leaders. The question of difference between the two wings was finally referred to prominent Northern mediators. The result of this step was favorable to the Radical wing, which was still under the control of Hunnicutt.

A call was next issued for a Convention to assemble at Richmond. In the meanwhile, the Conservative wing continued to exert itself to allure over the freedmen as the quickest way of crippling the Radical wing. It was also active in seeking to draw to itself a larger element of the better class of white people, in which course it was, to some degree, successful. A Convention favorable to supporting the Conservative Republican wing was held, first in Charlottesville, and, afterwards, in at least nine counties in turn. The members of these Conventions accepted negro suffrage as a principle established by the Constitution, and too late now to be disputed. No impression was, however, made by this attitude on the negro voters themselves or on their radical leaders. The blacks were now demanding something more than a free exercise of the suffrage. New spokesmen of their own race were calling for the fullest social equality as well as for absolute civil. Their white leaders encouraged this spirit of violence, for they perceived clearly that, if the respectable white people of the State should obtain control of the actions of their former slaves, the white radicals would have to give up all prospect of political predominance and official preferment.

The Convention was called to order on the first day of August. It was confidently expected that the contest between the two opposing leaders of the local Republican Party, Botts and Hunnicutt, would now be fought to a finish. One political cock or the other had to die in the pit. While Botts was somewhat vehement in his denunciations of Secession as "treason," he nevertheless favored the enfranchisement of the former Confederates outside of a small group of leaders. He also advocated the payment of the public debt so far as it had not been incurred in support of the war. Appropriately, the Convention came together under the roof of a capacious negro church; and such an overwhelming multitude of black faces were conspicuous to view in the assemblage that it might easily have been taken for a ordinary African congregation. Indeed, on the crowded floor, there were only fifty white delegates present. A heaving concourse of negroes, unable to pass the door, followed Botts to the Capitol Square, while Hunnicutt harangued the throng packed in the church. The white delegates at both meetings occupied precarious seats on the outskirts. They were picturesquely described by one of the local newspapers "as a white fringe on a black blanket."

The upshot of this split Convention was that the negroes were strengthened in their already emphatic determination to favor the extreme policy advocated by Hunnicutt. They positively refused, under his influence, to cooperate with the conservative white members of the Republican Party, or with those independent white citizens who would have acted with their former slaves, had they exhibited a conciliatory spirit. The great majority of these citizens were soon found in the ranks of the white conservatives of the State. The Richmond *Enquirer* voiced the revolt of the white people in the mass at this hour when it said: "The disgusting and loathsome exhibition of the past week, demonstrates to the plainest intellect that the fate of Hayti awaits Virginia, if, through apathy and indifference, the Caucasian majority in this commonwealth permit the African minority to obtain control of the Government."

Remarkable as it may seem, at the moment when the negroes were bringing out their full numerical strength in the registration,—which was now in progress under military supervision,— the white people were neglecting to meet the crisis by imitating the energetic example of their black opponents. It was as if the failure of the War and the odious political conditions which followed, had left them in a state of insensibility to anything that fate could impose on them further. In the meanwhile, the military power, under command of General Schofield, interfered whenever it saw proper. That power reduced to a travesty the operations of the civil government by often quietly annulling a decision of the courts, and displacing the civil authorities by the appointment of military commissioners. The number of former Confederates permitted to vote was materially curtailed, and no one was suffered to become a candidate for an official position unless he could show that he had not held office under the Confederate Administration.

Probably never before in the history of the Anglo-Saxon race had civil government sunk to such a state of impotence as this; or had been brought into such a condition of absolute contempt. The spectacle of thousands of full-blooded, corn-field negroes, as grossly ignorant, superstitious, and bestial, as their contemporaries in Hayti and Dahomey, rushing to the registration booths to have their names recorded on the books, so as to acquire the right to vote for the Constitutional Convention, was aptly calculated to impress their former masters as being indicative of a change in their lives that was calculated to make life intolerable. It seemed especially incredible that this sight should occur in Virginia, so closely identified as it was with the foundation of the Republic; so illustrious for the great names of Washington, Jefferson, Madison and Marshall, in one era, and of Lee and Jackson in another; and so famous for its refined and cultivated social life during several centuries. Was it unnatural that these scenes should have been seared into the memories of the Virginian people who witnessed them; and that they should bear fruit in the form of that political solidarity which remained unbroken at the end of sixty years?

The upshot of the election for the Constitutional Convention was a radical victory. In a total delegation that numbered one hundred and five, there were to be found only thirty-three Conservatives. Twenty-five negroes were chosen to seats. About one hundred and seventy thousand ballots were cast in all. It was noticed afterwards that at least forty-five thousand white registered voters failed to appear at the polls. In consequence of this remarkable fact, the blacks were able to win a majority of seventeen thousand in the election. Those voters who favored the holding of the Convention exceeded those who opposed it, by forty-five thousand. Of the persons who approved, about fifteen thousand were white; and of the persons who disapproved, six hundred and thirty-eight were black. So violent became the conduct of some of the radical leaders, under the fever of their triumph, that at least one of the most prominent, Hunnicutt himself, was arrested by a Conservative civil justice for words calculated to arouse the negroes to a general assassination of the whites. He was quickly released by the military power.

When, for the outcome of the Constitutional Convention at least, it was too late for action to be taken, the Conservative

Party began to shake off the strange garment of apathy which seems, so far, to have paralyzed the spirit of so many of its members. A Convention was now summoned to meet in Richmond in December (1867) ; and when it assembled, it was found to be composed of the most memorable body of men then alive in the Commonwealth,—a singular contrast to the throng of ignorant negroes who had come together a few months before, under the roof of the African church. In his address as president, Alexander H. H. Stuart summed up the determined attitude of the white people when he said : "Our rights may be wrested from us, but we will never submit to the rule of an alien and inferior race. We prefer the rule of the bayonet." The resolutions adopted disclaimed any purpose, or even wish to reenslave the negro. Virginia, it was declared, should resume its place in the Union, and all the rights guaranteed by the Constitution should again become the possession of its people. It was boldly asserted that "to subject the whites, in their local administration, to the absolute supremacy of the black race, just emerged from personal servitude, was abhorrent to the civilization of mankind." All who desired the restoration and preservation of a white man's government were urged to support the Conservative Party, and by one vigorous and united effort, save themselves from ruin and disgrace.

The Constitutional Convention began its sessions in Richmond in the month appointed. It was the first body of the kind to assemble in Virginia since the Convention of 1850, which was the most radical known in the history of the State up to that date, as it broadened the basis of the suffrage to manhood. This was considered, in those times, to be a measure that was attended with definite possibilities of danger to the community. What would the members of that Convention, liberal as they were in their views of the increasing rights of democracy, have thought had they been able to foresee the membership and principles of the next Constitutional Convention? Could they have rolled the future back to their own age and entered that hall and glanced around, what would their startled eyes have lighted upon? A band of twenty-five negroes, recently slaves, sitting in the midst of forty-five white men, on a footing of political, if not social, equality, and taking a verbose share in the discussions! Of the white men, only fourteen altogether were natives of Virginia. The remainder were unsavory adventurers from the North and Europe. There were thirteen who had come originally from New York; two from England; and one from Ireland, Scotland, Nova Scotia, and Canada, respectively.

The radical leaders, supported by their noisy but obedient negro followers, found no difficulty in overriding the wishes and recommendations of the impotent Conservatives. The white people of Virginia were practically not represented at all in the framing of an instrument which was to touch them more nearly than it did the freedmen, since the latter were, at that time, without property, and without any tie of local responsibility.

The President of the Convention was John C. Underwood, a native of New York, who had been appointed by the Federal Government to the office of District Judge of the State at a time when his actual jurisdiction was limited to the few counties under Federal control. He was a man of moderate ability, who was deeply envenomed by the harsh partisanship of the hour. The work of the Convention, as finally consummated, reflected the opinions of men of his type, which were really the convictions of the radicals who were now in possession of the National Government.

It was significant of the negro members' feeling that they unanimously opposed the insertion in the Constitution of any clause which could be interpreted as a reference to race distinctions, although such a clause would have helped to preserve their freedom, and also strengthened their newly received privileges as citizens. A declaration in favor of the supremacy of the National Government, regardless of any State ordinance to the contrary, caused a debate of considerable bitterness, as the Conservatives, in spite of the upshot of the recent War, were unwilling to acknowledge that the States were practically powerless in law, whether so in actual fact or not, when their authority conflicted with that of the United States. The object of the radicals was to stigmatize secession as treason in the Constitution of the Commonwealth. A more moderate tone, however, prevailed, which accomplished the same purpose, without the use of such an extreme expression.

In the discussion of measures relating to the affairs peculiar to the State, many days were spent in deciding upon the right provision to be adopted for the rates of taxation. These rates, it was declared, should be equal and uniform in every community of Virginia. There was now great diversity in the amount of the poll tax levied in different counties. The radicals successfully endeavored to lower this tax, as it fell so directly on the negroes. At the same moment, they increased the tax on real and personal property,—little of which was held by the blacks,—by requiring that such property should be assessed at its full value. A further imposition on the owners of such estates was a tax on all incomes in excess of one thousand dollars. Every measure submitted which would tend to break the hold of the owners of land was received with favor by the radical element in the Convention, as it would increase the negro's chance of securing an interest in the soil.

Apart from this question of taxation, the most important subject that came up for decision involved the establishment of the free school. This system of education had long prevailed at the North; it was, from the beginning, close to the hearts of the radicals from that quarter in the Convention; and there would have arisen no disagreement among the controlling element as a whole, in that body, had the negroes been willing to accept the separation of the two races in the school-house. An amendment which called for such separation was at first voted down by this Northern element, out of consideration for the feelings of the black members. Ultimately, however, the more conservative of these alien Republicans joined with the native Virginians in declining to insert in the Constitution a clause in favor of mixed schools. The principle of public education was, nevertheless, adopted.

A vigorous attempt was made to declare the right of suffrage to be a natural right, and Underwood even favored its recognition as such in the case of women as well as of men. It was finally resolved that all male citizens above twenty-one years of age should possess the right to vote, provided that they had not been proven to be lunatics, or had not been convicted of felony, treason, bribery or duelling, or had not been disfranchised by the Reconstruction Acts or the Fourteenth Amendment.

CHAPTER III

THIRD STAGE—RESTORATION OF WHITE CONTROL

Pierpont's term as Governor expired abruptly through the publication of a military order, issued by General Schofield, which directed Henry H. Wells, the former provost-marshal of Alexandria, to take possession of the office. Pierpont had pursued a middle course in his administration, and like all of a compromising turn of mind, in revolutionary times, had failed to satisfy the wishes either of the Radicals or of the Conservatives. He fell between two stools,—he was too conservative to suit the views of the Radicals, and too radical to suit the views of the Conservatives; but after his displacement, the white people were more inclined to respect his conduct and to acknowledge the uprightness of his purposes. His light burnt sanely in the midst of that fantastic and darkened confusion, but it was not influential enough to serve as a guide for persons of either extreme. The white people at first could not make up their minds to follow his advice; but had they done so, it would have resulted in their earlier extrication from the bog into which they had been plunged by the bestowal of the suffrage on the negro. If that unnatural spirit of apathy which led forty-four thousand white men to refrain from voting one way or the other in the polling for the Convention had continued, it would have been fatal to the future of Virginia for an indefinite period. The outlook, indeed, would have been hopeless. But the hour was now approaching when, with firm determination, this apathy would be cast aside and a policy adopted which would lead to deliverance. In the meanwhile, the course of events was preparing the way for the hastening of this consummation.

The appointment of Wells to the Governorship was a step really favorable to the best interests of the whites. Hunnicutt, the grotesquely unscrupulous head of the Radical Party, had announced his candidacy for that office, and backed by the compact mass of the negro voters, he would, if he had been nominated, have stood a very fair chance of winning it. His incumbency of the post, had he succeeded, would have signified the sharp aggravation of all those evils which had already sprung from the domination of the blacks in the late Convention. The whole programme of the majority in that body, which was practically designed to make of local society and government a mongrel combination of the most monstrous character, would, under his administration, have been carried out, so far as the new executive and his followers in the General Assembly would have had the power to do so. That power would at least have been sufficient to keep the relation of the races in a state of permanent turmoil.

General Scofield had little sympathy with the radical programme which was formulated in the Convention. He expressed the belief that, without the cooperation of the whites almost as a body, no policy, radical or conservative, could be made effective; and that the radical proposals, since they were destined to gain no support from the ranks of property and intelligence in the State, would only terminate in failure. His appointment of Wells was intended to balk as far as possible Hunnicutt's designs, which would have shown increased vitality had he been successful in capturing the office of Governor.

The opinion had been growing among the Republican members of Congress that their party in Virginia was not likely to remain in control there if reliance should be placed on the negro vote alone. This conviction, as we have just stated, coincided with that of General Scofield. It was hoped that Wells would prove himself to be capable of winning a more general support at the polls than his predecessors had done. Hunnicutt was discredited by Wells's advancement; the same fate befell all those native radicals, locally known contemptuously as "scalawags," who were his chief coadjutors; and the control was shifted to the carpet-baggers, who, in the spirit of Wells himself, had settled upon the body of the prostrate State like a flock of ill-omened birds. These sinister immigrants, however, were not sufficient in number to fill all the offices which had been emptied by military order because the white incumbents had been found unable to take the test oath imposed by Act of Congress in July, 1862. In 1869, after Stoneman had succeeded Scofield, there were over twenty-six hundred vacancies, and in some parts of the State, the functions of local government were either seriously hampered or ceased altogether to operate.

The struggle for supremacy between the white people of Virginia and the horde of negroes and their radical white allies began with deadly energy in 1868. Two Conventions were held at Richmond in the spring of this year, which represented respectively these determined opponents, now grappling for the mastery in a spirit which refused to give or take any quarter. The Republican Convention, by a majority of one hundred and forty-two votes, nominated Wells for the governorship over Hunnicutt, who received only eleven in a total of one hundred and fifty-three. To this paltry dimensions had the strength of the Virginia Marat been reduced! A creature of turbulent times, a piece of temporary froth thrown up on the surface of the boiling contents of the political pot, he, from this time forward, sank into the obscurity from which he had been originally projected, practically deserted by his former negro followers, and discarded even by the national leaders of his own party.

In the autumn, General Grant was chosen to the office of President. The white Virginians had been hoping that negro suffrage would be defeated by the election of his opponent, Horatio Seymour, but the Republican victory was so complete that it seemed now almost impossible for such suffrage to be avoided. We have seen that every previous movement by any considerable body of white citizens in favor of accepting negro suffrage as an established fact had not succeeded in modifying the opposition among the whites to the blacks' possession of the ballot. They had kept on trusting that this evil hour would be ultimately staved off by a turn in events either local or national. This always more or less obscure prospect was now destroyed. Negro suffrage had to be faced as a positive certainty. But many whites continued to refuse to accept this outlook. The more thoughtful element, however, were not to be deceived by such a delusion.

A bill was introduced in Congress in December, 1868, that appointed May, 1869, as the date for holding the election for the adoption or rejection of the Underwood Constitution. The measure went over in the Senate for the Christmas recess. Before that body could concur with the House in accepting the Constitution, there was published simultaneously in the *Whig* and the *Dispatch,*—two journals that were less uncomprising than the *Enquirer,* the main organ of the rigid Conservatives,—a communication signed *Senex,* which was soon known to have been written by Alexander H. H. Stuart of Staunton.

It will be recalled that Mr. Stuart had, as president of the Conservative Convention which assembled in Richmond in December, 1867, expressed himself with great vigor in opposition to any course that would place the white race under the control of the black. "We prefer the rule of the bayonet," he had exclaimed. Only one year had passed since he had uttered these words, which had found such a sympathetic response in the minds of the white people of the State. He now came forward and boldly advocated a policy which would consent to the full enjoyment of the suffrage by the negro as the only hope of obtaining a nullification of those clauses of the new Constitution which disfranchised so large a proportion of the white voters. Negro suffrage, he said, was inevitable. The sentiment of the North was practically unanimous in support of it, and, ultimately, that sentiment would prevail, no matter what position the South should take. Was it not the part of true statesmanship to recognize this fact, accept it, and endeavor to obtain something of importance to the welfare of the white people in return?

Mr. Stuart predicted,—and time has shown him to have been entirely correct,—that, in spite of negro suffrage, the property and intelligence of the State, which, he said, must continue to be concentrated in the hands of the white people, would maintain its natural irresistible supremacy. His advice was undoubtedly sound, unpalatable as it necessarily was to men who had been slaveholders so recently. Mr. Stuart was very much respected, but, having been a Whig throughout his career, and identified as such with measures that were not approved by the large majority of the Virginians under the old regime,—he had, for instance, like so many other patriotic Whigs, opposed Secession,—he had now no fund of popularity to draw upon as a long trusted political leader; and, in consequence, his counsel, in spite of its practical good sense, made little impression, at the moment, on the rank and file of those to whom it was so earnestly addressed. The *Enquirer* was especially sharp in censuring the author for what was described as his "inopportune" suggestion.

But Stuart was not to be discouraged by the criticism which was now leveled at him. He quickly followed up his letter to the *Whig* and *Dispatch* respectively by obtaining the cooperation of a number of prominent and influential men in the Conservative Party. Judge Sheffey and John B. Baldwin were the most conspicuous at first. A meeting composed of twenty-eight persons of the same representative type was held in Richmond within a week, and before Congress reassembled after the Christmas recess, a committee of nine had been chosen for the mission of visiting Washington, and holding a conference with that body,—which had the ultimate decision,—for the specific purpose of securing some valuable concession in return for quiet acceptance of negro suffrage as an established fact. This concession was expected to be the rejection of the Underwood Constitution in its present form. The Committee numbered in its membership, not only Mr. Stuart and Mr. Baldwin, two of the ablest, most experienced, and most patriotic public men in Virginia, but also John L. Marye, who had won a high reputation during the discussions in the recent Constitutional Convention; W. T. Sutherlin, a man of affairs; James Neeson, a distinguished lawyer; and Wyndham Robertson, who had filled a state official position of importance.

The Committee's chances of success were materially increased by the support which it received from General Stoneman, who was in command of the Virginia Military District. It was also openly approved by citizens of such high standing in the Conservative ranks as James A. Seddon, formerly Secretary of War in the Confederate Cabinet; Thomas S. Flournoy, the unsuccessful candidate for the governorship in the famous Know-Nothing Campaign; Allan T. Caperton, afterwards a member of the Senate; and Frank Ruffin, subsequently State Auditor. Governors Wise and Smith threw their influence in opposition.

The Committee was received with favor on its arrival in Washington. Some of the most powerful senators on the Republican side approved the purpose which it had in view. So did the entire body of the Democratic members of that body. The *New York Tribune,* the most influential of all the Republican journals, gave the mission an outspoken and vigorous support. In the meanwhile, the Radical Party in Virginia had been following the committee's actions with suspicious intentness. A delegation, headed by Governor Wells, was appointed to visit Washington and combat the purpose which its members had in view. It was not until the end of January that the Reconstruction Committee was ready to grant a hearing to both delegations. John B. Baldwin came forward as the spokesman of the Committee of Nine, and Wells as the spokesman of the opposing body. Testimony was introduced by the Radicals to demonstrate that the state of society in Virginia had sunk to the border line of anarchy; that Republicans were subject to constant outrages; and that the negro could expect no justice in the courts presided over by the Conservatives, nor any real liberty during the existence of the vagrant and contract laws. These statements were vigorously controverted by the testimony of Conservative witnesses.

The Committee of Nine also appeared before the Judiciary Committee of Congress. Above all, they were successful in enlisting the support of General Grant, the President-elect, in their favor. Grant expressed strong disapproval of the test oath, and the consequent disfranchisement of so many of the whites.

Beyond producing a more conciliatory attitude in Washington towards the Conservative Party, the upshot of the Committee's mission appeared unimportant at first; but, as we shall see hereafter, the train was laid for the attainment of the purpose which they had in view; namely, the submission of the Underwood Constitution to a vote without the provisions as to the test oath and disfranchisement. Had that Constitution been ratified as it originally stood, about ninety-five per cent of the adult white males of the State, it was estimated at the time, would have been deprived, not only of the right to hold office, and to sit on juries, but also of the right to cast a ballot, which the most ignorant and stupid negro in the corn and tobacco fields would now enjoy.

The Conservative Republicans in Virginia themselves revolted at such a prospect. An unofficial committee, counting in its membership such men as Franklin Stearns and Edgar Allan, appeared in Washington simultaneously with the Committee of Nine; presented themselves at the same time before the Reconstruction and Judiciary Committees of Congress; and used their influence with their national political associates to persuade them to consent to a separate vote on the disfranchising and test oath articles of the Underwood Constitution. It was due largely to the patriotic efforts of these men that that body was ultimately led to act favorably on the petition of the Committee of Nine.

Naturally, the Republicans in Congress lent a peculiarly attentive ear to the convictions of men of their own partisan affiliations.

But the Conservative Republican leaders in Virginia, in taking so advanced and so decisive a step, were sowing the seeds of schism in their own ranks. The wing led by Wells were fully determined to carry the impending election for Governor, whether the State should be saddled with negro supremacy or not. Wells himself had not been successful in winning a large personal following among the whites even of his own party, and at this juncture, many of its members turned emphatically against him, and issued a call for a Convention, which was expected to nominate a candidate in opposition to him. In the meanwhile, the Executive Committee of the Republican Party had deliberately set aside his nomination.

Among the enemies whom Wells had made was William Mahone, who, by his presidency of certain railways of the State, had acquired considerable power with the Republican leaders. Wells had offended Mahone by consenting to sell the Commonwealth's interest in the Virginia and Tennessee Railroad and its allied lines,—of which, Mahone was the chief officer,—to the Baltimore and Ohio Railway. This railway was unfavorable to Mahone's reelection to his old post, as it feared that, under his energetic management, these various lines,—which he was now proposing to consolidate,—would curtail the traffic that the Baltimore and Ohio at this time monopolized in the West. Mahone had kept in close association with Edgar Allan, and, through him, quietly exerted a strong influence with many members of the Convention which had assembled in Petersburg to replace the nomination of Wells. Nevertheless, Wells, by his command of the ballots of the negro members, again carried off the nomination for Governor; but his victory was seriously diminished in effect by the choice of a negro for the second place on the ticket.

The Governor's enemies were not to be permanently disconcerted by his success in the Convention. After the adjourn-

GILBERT C. WALKER

ment of that body, they, under the leadership of Mahone, brought forward the name of Gilbert C. Walker as a substitute for the name of Wells; and in an address which they soon issued, they recommended him without reserve to the favorable consideration of the Conservative Republicans. This address was signed by one hundred and fifty men who represented the most respectable element in that Party.

A more admirable nomination at that hour could hardly have been made. Walker was a former citizen of New York, who had settled in Norfolk after the close of the War, and identified himself closely with the business interests of that city. He was conservative in his political views, though affiliated with the Republican Party in national politics. So earnest was he in his desire to rescue the State from the evils of negro rule, which he knew would follow the ratification of the Underwood Constitution without amendment, that he visited Washington in order to use his influence with relatives in the Senate to persuade them to favor the petition of the Committee of Nine. He was a man of popular manners, excellent talents, and of impressive personal appearance. On the new ticket proposed by the seceders from the Petersburg Convention he stood alone, as no nominations were made for the subordinate offices.

Wells, by March (1869), had become so discredited by the attacks of his influential enemies,—who even charged him, unjustly, it seems, with purloining a private letter for his own political advancement,—that General Stoneman, still in military command of the district, displaced him from office for a short time, but finally restored him to his post; without, however, offering any explanation of his action in either case. The tide was now running strongly against the Radical wing of the Party. President Grant, in harmony with the opinion which he had privately expressed to the Committee of Nine, advised Congress, in his first message, to submit the Underwood Constitution to a vote of the people of Virginia, with permission to reject or adopt, by a separate ballot, the test oath and disfranchisement clauses. Congress, as we have already stated, assented to the recommendation; and a day in the ensuing May was selected by Grant for the holding of the election.

Three tickets were now seeking popular approval. The Conservative Party, composed almost entirely of native whites, which had nominated Colonel Robert E. Withers for the governorship, was in favor of the rejection of the Constitution from the first to the last letter. The Radical Republicans, on the other hand, favored the adoption of that instrument without the change of a sentence. This wing was headed by Governor Wells. The Conservative Republicans, under the leadership of Gilbert C. Walker, favored the ratification of the Constitution with amendments that would eliminate the clauses that called for the introduction of the test oath and disfranchisement. The Conservative white party was known to embrace a majority of the persons entitled to vote; but this fact did not cause them to feel confident of success in the election, even should their full strength be concentrated at the polls. It was the day when the military commander of the District did not hesitate to remove the governor himself from office without giving any reason for his action. What was there to prevent him from declaring a Conservative majority to be the fruit of electoral fraud, and throwing out the successful candidate and replacing him with the candidate of the Radical negro party? This contingency made the Conservative leaders disposed to act with calculated prudence and wariness.

The most astute and powerful of these was William Mahone, who, as we have seen, had already shown a willingness to ally himself on occasions with the Conservative Republicans, if the cause of the Conservative whites could be thereby promoted. He thought that the hour had now arrived when that cause imperatively demanded the pursuit of such a course, and he urged the chairman of the Executive Sub-Committee of the General Conservative Committee to recommend it to his associates. This sagacious advice was warmly seconded by the Committee of

Nine, which was still in existence, with its prestige very much enhanced by Congress' action in approving their petition asking for a modification of the Underwood Constitution by amendment. The most influential member of that Committee, John B. Baldwin, was particularly earnest in counselling a fusion with the Conservative Republicans, who had nominated Gilbert C. Walker.

Responding to the general wish in their party for such cooperation, the Conservative Executive Committee summoned a Convention to assemble in Richmond for the purpose of giving the stamp of their political associates' formal approval of the proposed step. So soon as this body met, the nominees of the white Conservatives, Withers, James A. Walker, and Marye, withdrew their candidacy, and after a vigorous debate, showing a diversity of opinion among those present, these resignations were accepted by a majority vote. It was decided to be expedient to make no nominations in their place.

Had the candidates of the Conservative Republicans been substituted by name, the sentiment of many of the delegates would have been offended, as the act would have appeared to be a surrender to their Republican opponents. In intentionally failing to swallow the Conservative Republican ticket by adopting it by name, the majority of the Convention felt that they were preserving their party allegiance, and, at the same time, creating an opportunity, without formal compromise of their principles, by which the strength of their party could be thrown in support of Gilbert C. Walker and those associated with him on the Conservative Republican ticket. Later on, the Conservative Executive Committee issued an address approving the Conservative Republican nominees, and recommending that they should be supported by the whites. The contestants for the honor of the governorship were, in this practical way, reduced to Wells and Walker. There could be no question in the minds of the white Conservatives as to which of the two was to be preferred. It was felt by the bulk of the party that, should nothing more be accomplished than the elimination of the highly objectionable radical politician Wells, the gain would be of a substantial character. His influence would certainly be destroyed by defeat, and his radical associates, in their turn, could not escape the effect of the same blow. It was, in reality, the first long step towards the permanent emancipation of the white people from the radical yoke.

In the campaign which followed, no charge of apathy could be brought against the white people. The stolid despair that had crippled their strength in the election for the Underwood Convention had, by this time, passed away. A crisis was known to be at hand, and unless it was met with the firmest resolution and the keenest energy, Virginia, it was foreseen, could not hope for a generation, perhaps, to shake off the galling domination of the white and black radicals. The landowners did not scruple to warn their negro laborers that they would be discharged if they remained members of the Union League, or if they voted, in the election, in opposition to their employers' wishes and interests. The white leaders, indeed, went so far as to nominate several negroes to the membership of the House of Delegates. This was the most convincing proof of their fixed purpose to win at the polls. In some districts, where the numerical strength of the Conservative Republicans preponderated, the white Conservative ballots were cast unanimously in support of their candidates.

The zeal of white Conservatives was quickened by the spectacle of Wells appearing at courthouse after courthouse and delivering heated and abusive speeches, amid crowds of applauding and menacing negroes. The Conservative auditors, most of whom could recall the patriotic political addresses, on similar occasions, in slavery times, were, by these revolutionary harangues, only strengthened in their determination to drive, by an overwhelming adverse vote, these alien parasites from the State, which they were seeking to strangle by subjecting every community to the rule of the most ignorant and venal element of its population.

When the issue of the election was published, it was found that Walker had triumphed by a majority of eighteen thousand votes. What was still more noteworthy, the amendments relating to the test oath and disfranchisement had been defeated by an even larger margin. The Constitution, with these amendments omitted, had been adopted.

Of the one hundred and eighty members of the new General Assembly, seventy belonged to the white Conservative Party. This apparently ensured possession of the State for that party, but, at this moment, General Canby, who was in command of the Military District, required all State officers to submit to the test oath, in spite of the upshot of the election on this point; and he persisted in this position until commanded by President Grant to withdraw the order. When the General Assembly convened in October, an attempt, which also ended in failure, was made to administer the test oath to its members. That body now adopted the two amendments to the National Constitution, and Virginia was soon restored to all her former rights as a State of the Union. Thus ended the Period of Reconstruction within her borders.

CHAPTER IV

THE DEBT CONTROVERSY

In our description of the period intervening between the close of the Revolution and the beginning of the War for Southern Independence, we dwelt at some length on the policy which the people of Virginia had adopted in favor of the construction of public improvements, on an important scale, at the expense of the State. We pointed out the fact that the majority of the population that resided east of the Blue Ridge were strongly opposed to receiving the National Government's assistance in the erection of such improvements. The result of this attitude was that the extent of these improvements was curtailed, but not to a degree that prevented the accumulation of a large debt. Before the War between the States opened, there was no difficulty in carrying the weight of the interest which had to be paid on this liability, since the people of the Commonwealth were, during the years that immediately preceded that event, in a high state of prosperity.

Among the earliest public ventures in which the public money was expended was the creation of facilities for the navigation of the Potomac and James Rivers. At that time, the State considered that these investments for the benefits of easy transportation were made positively secure by the bonds and stocks which it received for advancements from its treasury. In 1816, these securities were consolidated into one fund, the interest from which was to be reserved for public improvements. The fund was placed in the custody of a Board of Public Works, which was to exercise their cooperate judgment in its disposition.

About twenty-two years afterwards, the demands on the fund were so much greater than the Board was able to satisfy that the General Assembly decided to support the various public enterprises, now so frequently coming up, by the negotiation of State bonds. This was practically a new policy, that would, perhaps, never have been adopted had not Western Virginia been so eager to remove its isolation by the construction of railways, waterways, and roadways through its rugged mountains. The cost of such highways, owing to this terrain, was peculiarly great, and this cost could only be met by floating bonds. Such was the first important step in the creation of the State debt, which was to raise such a schism among the people of Virginia when their lot had fallen upon impoverished times.

When the war-cloud burst in 1861, Virginia, by these borrowings, had built or aided in building, a system of canals, railways, and turnpikes, that furnished her eastern region certainly, and her western also to some degree, with fair facilities for the transportation of crops to market, and the conveyance of travellers. By 1861, she had invested, in round figures, about thirty-five million dollars in public improvements for this purpose. Nor, in making this investment, had she acted imprudently in the light of all that was to be foreseen at that time. Had no war broken out, the interest which she held in the various railway, canal, and turnpike stock companies would have secured, not only the return of the sums thus laid out, but, in some cases, a large addition to the original amounts. She had as much as twenty millions invested in railroads alone, which, in the last decade before the war, had begun to shadow forth the prosperity which they would have enjoyed, in abundant measure, but for the cataclysm of that terrible event.

The volume of bonded debt for which the State was liable was estimated in 1860 at thirty-three million dollars, but it possessed assets, calculated to be worth forty-three millions, which could be used to counter-balance its obligations. It is true that only the smaller part of these assets were returning interest at that time; but the future held forth a reliable promise that each investment would ultimately prove remunerative. Those that, so far, had not yielded any revenue were restricted to newly launched enterprises that required time to develop. A precautionary Act had been passed which forbade the State from guaranteeing the liabilities of the transportation corporations in which it held stock; and the accumulation of a sinking fund was made imperative.

The income of Virginia at this time amounted annually to a figure in excess of four million dollars, which left an ample surplus, after payment of all that was due by the State in meeting its current expenses. The private property in the people's possession exceeded a billion dollars in value.

In making the cause of the seceding States of the South her own, Virginia pursued a course which was directly in the teeth of the best interests of her own citizens. There is not on record in history a more unselfish, and, in the end, a more destructive act. Every thoughtful man within her borders was fully aware that her surface would become the principal battle-ground of the impending war, and that, in consequence of this fact, her material prosperity would suffer a complete blight, which a generation of peace probably could not remove. There was not a single kind of property in which she possessed an interest, and on which her ability to pay her debts depended, that would escape this blight. No simoom from the arid sands of Sahara could have carried a more withering breath in its bosom.

When the war ended, the following was substantially the condition of the State's most important assets. There was not a railway within its borders which could show iron rails that had not been worn almost down to their wooden sills. The bridges, when standing at all, were often too rickety to be trusted for a crossing. The culverts were in the same dangerous shape. The rolling stock was in the last stage of dilapidation. The James River Canal also had been steadily falling out of repair, until it was barely navigable even in sections. The turnpikes had been torn up by the wheels of artillery and army wagons, and further damaged by the rains and snow of several winters. Practically, there was no line of transportation that was not in a state of bankruptcy. Where was the money to come from to be used for their restoration?

The people themselves had been stripped for the moment of every basis of credit by the destruction of their old labor system. All bank stocks had shriveled up to mere waste paper. Horses, mules, and cattle had disappeared in every district which had been the scene of a campaign. Many head elsewhere had been impressed for the use of the Confederate army. County and city alike disclosed the scars left by the torch. Richmond, the capital, was in ruins.

In short, it was as if a tornado had swept over the surface of the whole land, leaving the impression of its impact, not only on the ground itself, but also in the hearts of the people. There was, indeed, nothing surviving but the bare soil to offer up on the altar of further sacrifice.

After an interval of suspense, a feeling of less hopelessness began to prevail. This impression was encouraged by the inflation of prices that followed the war. This advance was especially observable in the case of the crops which were grown in the soil of Virginia. Fortunately, the State was made up almost entirely of agricultural communities, and while labor had been disorganized by emancipation to a degree that was never before known in the local history, nevertheless there lingered in the rural districts thousand of negroes who had not yet lost their habits of industry; and there was still to be found in those districts a great number of white men who were able to till the ground with their own hands. At least there was no prospect of starvation, in spite of the enormous depletion in the resources of the people. At the same time, the need of money for rehabilitation was never so acute, as the farms had sunk into a condition of general disrepair.

What hope could there exist of the payment of the public debt, now standing at thirty-eight million dollars, with overdue interest, when the tax-payers were so impoverished that they were barely able to meet their private expenses even by the exercise of extreme frugality and economy? Moreover, the high returns from the sale of farm products might at any time turn out to be wholly transient. Where, under these circumstances, could the means be obtained to keep the landowners solvent?

But the prevailing poverty and the possibility of hard agricultural times, always present in their minds, did not lower the moral tone of the Virginian people. They had been accustomed from the beginning of their independence to hold the financial standing of their State as a sacred charge. Their heroic record in the recent war, which had won the admiration of the civilized world, only made them more fixed in their determination to preserve their financial honor in spite of adversity. Impoverishment could not undermine and weaken this resolution. When the last General Assembly of a purely antebellum character in the personality of its membership, convened in December, 1865, the old spirit of fidelity to public obligations was as strong as ever. The principal of the public debt, swollen by the unpaid interest accruing during the war, was ordered to be funded, and the whole burden was then formally and quietly assumed as a matter of course. It was very properly anticipated that West Virginia would recognize her liability for one-third of the amount; and an overture was even made to induce that State to return to the Mother State, and again form a part of its area.

The destruction of the institution of slavery alone would have morally justified the representatives of Virginia in seeking a compromise of the debt. That institution had been struck down by a power which the State had tried in vain to resist. Every other surviving interest was in a condition either of actual ruin or languishing vitality. Now was the hour for an equitable adjustment, when all men could not fail to perceive that Virginia was really too prostrate to meet her liabilities in full. Indeed, there were not lacking signs that the creditors themselves would have been willing to forego their claims to a degree that would have made it more easy to endure the burden.

The stubborn sense of honor shown by this first General Assembly raised up a series of difficulties, of which advantage was taken later on by astute and unscrupulous politicians in pushing their own schemes for personal aggrandizement. Had there been no negro suffrage, these schemes would never have been successful. It was the former bondsman who was chiefly instrumental in making their realization practicable.

Like the old slavery question in national politics, the debt question from the beginning of the second General Assembly could no more be repressed than Banquo's ghost. In this second Assembly, the growing feeling of restiveness among the people under the load of the public liabilities, was reflected in that body's formal refusal to assume the share of the debt which belonged to West Virginia; and it also brought about a reduction of the interest on Virginia's share to four per cent from the original six. The holders of bonds could still collect their coupons at the latter rate. A willingness to make substantial sacrifices to provide the means to pay the interest was shown by the increase in the taxes at this time, although this addition could not be borne without augmented hardship. Some relief was obtained by the State by granting the roads in which it owned stock permission to purchase these securities.

There began to expand in a few years an institution that was destined to exercise a strong influence in encouraging a modification of the first rigid attitude towards the payment of the public debt in full. This was the public school system, which had been authorized by the Underwood Constitution. This system was not popular in the beginning, but it gradually overcame all opposition. The call which it made upon the public funds steadily grew; and this fact raised up a new set of opponents to an uncompromised debt. The establishment of the public schools was one of the new conditions, actual or threatened, which the first and second General Assemblies had been unwilling to face.

As we have already pointed out, the changes in many vital directions which the adoption of the Underwood Constitution introduced, swept away, for all practical purposes, nearly all those traditions and rules of administration which had survived down to the meeting of the Convention. It was as if a flood of muddy water had passed over the ancient landmarks of Virginia, altering all that it did not actually destroy. Never again could a legislative body with all the ideas that prevailed in the General Assembly of December, 1865, meet in Virginia. It was now clearly perceived that the conditions in existence had to be confronted in a straight-forward way, without regard to personal preferences or the influences of the past. This spirit, now for the first time, began to touch the public debt. The Convention, which was composed of the most impecunious section of the population, started that debate. How could all the pecuniary demands of a popular administration, the radicals asked, be made compatible with the absorption of public money in the payment of a debt that had been contracted during the existence of the hateful regime of slavery?

The Radical Party was defeated ultimately by a combination of the Conservative Republicans and the white Conservatives. Moderation, in fact, won the day; but the minds of the Virginians at large were more disposed now to yield to changes which they could not alter. There was no longer a blind loyalty to the principles of the past. The spirit of expediency was now in the ascendancy, as the only means of escaping from greater evils.

When the first General Assembly to meet under the regime of Reconstruction convened, it was found that twenty-seven negroes occupied seats in the body; and that there were few well-known faces among the white members. It was, indeed, a motley legislature which took up the business of the State; but.

it soon exhibited a disposition to look at the question of the public debt from that conservative point of view which had characterized the attitude of its predecessors. The debt had now swollen to forty-five million dollars. In the meanwhile, although the value of realty in the cities had grown, that of two-thirds in the counties had fallen off. Moreover, the prices of farm products were slowly shrinking.

On Governor Walker's recommendation, the General Assembly made provision for funding Virginia's two-third's share of the debt in bonds, with interest payable in coupons at the original rate of six per cent. The one-third share of West Virginia was funded in coupons alone. The coupons of Virginia were to be receivable as legal tender in the payment of taxes, and all other obligations due the State. This provision was destined at an early day to become a cause of violent contention in the history of local parties.

A second Act of the same Assembly that was to enter deeply into State politics and increase the existing agitation, was the grant of permission to consolidate the three railways that united Norfolk with Bristol. Mahone was the president of these combined lines, which fact, with his talent for political organization, invested him with great political influence. He was convinced that the interests of these lines and his own personal power would be damaged by the policy of "free railroads," which Governor Walker advocated, in his desire to enlarge the railway facilities of the State, even if it should involve the sale of all the railway securities which the State now owned.

It argued discouragingly for the success of the Funding Act that the remaining income under the operation of the new tax law would be entirely absorbed in meeting the interest on the debt, after an appropriation had been made for the support of the public schools. There would be nothing left for any other public purpose. The only hope of an increase of revenue to cover the contingent expenses of the State Government lay in the bare practicability of a growth in prosperity. It was not clearly perceived at the time the Act was passed that it was not really approved by a great majority of the people taken in the mass. In a short while, it was intimated that the Funding Act could not have been adopted had not the negro members been bribed; and that other improper means had been employed to the same end by the lobbyists.

There soon sprang up two influences that were either indirectly or directly repugnant to the Conservative Party's policy about the State debt: first, men, like Mahone, connected with established railway lines, foresaw in the "free railroad legislation," which meant private ownership, a power hostile to their own supremacy. This made them radical in spirit politically. Second, men interested in the public schools or in State assistance in other forms, favored the modification of the Funding Act because it diminished, if it did not destroy, the Commonwealth's ability to give material financial aid to the school' system.

The first balloting that took place after the adjournment of the legislature which adopted the Funding Act was not decisive in bringing out the popular feeling in regard to that measure. The Conservatives carried the election, it is true, but by a majority little in excess of two thousand votes. In August, 1871, a State Convention was summoned by the executive committee of that party to meet in Richmond. This body was content with simply recommending a single rallying cry: "Conservative or Radical rule," and in the election that followed, succeeded in increasing the number of their representatives in the next General Assembly.

In the course of the preceding campaign, the Funding Act came in for a considerable measure of adverse comment. No voice apparently was raised in favor of augmenting the taxes so as to afford ample revenue for the support of the public schools and other new public policies of equal importance. In the teeth of a suggestion by Governor Walker, who was endeavoring to uphold the credit of the State as essential to its future prosperity, the General Assembly instructed the Auditor to suspend the operation of the Funding Act.   Walker vetoed this bill. The Assembly next tried to destroy the validity of the coupon as a means of paying taxes and other dues.   The Supreme Court of the State blocked this measure by declaring it to be in opposition to the clause of the National Constitution which forbade the impairment of a contract.   Then followed a series of legislative Acts which had in view the recall of numerous measures which had been passed at a time when the disposition towards the debt was firmer and more decided in its favor.   The tendency was now stronger to relieve the people at large of every form of taxation as far as not needed for the actual maintenance of the local and State governments.   This policy was incompatible with the payment of the interest on the State debt, but was called for by the depressed economic condition of the population at this time.   The situation was rendered more alarming in 1874 by the disclosure of the fact that the deficit in the State Treasury amounted, in one form or another, to at least two million dollars.

Under the influence of Governor Kemper, who succeeded Walker, the General Assembly consented to authorize a conference with the holders of the State debt, many of whom were foreigners.   A compromise was proposed; but it ended in failure.   The Conservatives, who still controlled the legislature, now came to the conclusion that the payment of interest on the debt was unescapable.   The only possible practical means of effecting payment was by cutting the public expenses to the bone; discovering additional objects of taxation; and placing the sinking fund on a different footing.   The result of adopting this policy was a saving of two hundred thousand dollars annually; but this sum did not do away with the deficit as a whole.

The antagonism between the treasury and the public school system, in consequence of the repeated failure by the former to pay the latter the entire amount to which it was entitled, became acute.   The State superintendent of the system, with a spirit

JAMES LAWSON KEMPER
Governor 1874-1878

that refused to compromise, insisted upon his department's legal
right to receive the funds held back.   The increasing popularity
of the public school aroused a new opposition to the severe drain
created by the debt on the revenues of the State.   The existing
sentiment in favor of the readjustment of that liability grew
in earnestness and determination. -There was now heard more
openly than formerly the assertion that, as all men acknowledged
the justice of assigning to West Virginia one-third of the principal and accumulated interest for loss of territory, so there
would be equal equity in reducing the remaining portion to fifteen million dollars for the loss of property within the borders
of the Mother State during the course of the war.   This sum
was the share for which the mutilated Commonwealth was liable
at the beginning of that conflict.   The men who assumed this
position felt themselves further warranted in their view by the
State Government's increasing inability to provide for some of
the most essential needs of the community in consequence of the
deficit caused by the payment of interest on the accumulated
debt.

A new legislative attempt was soon made to outlaw the
coupon by placing an enormous tax upon it; but this device also
failed. So strong was the rising tide of adverse sentiment,
however, that some of the foremost Conservatives in Virginia,
like R. M. T. Hunter and Alexander H. H. Stuart, thought that
it would be wise to make overtures to the creditors in order to
persuade them to compromise their claims.   This was the atmosphere in which Readjustment was born, and those who honestly
deemed that policy just and reasonable, regretted all the more
the fact that it had been delayed, instead of its being taken up
promptly by the first white Assembly which met almost immediately after the close of the war.   But it is to the lasting honor
of the members of that assembly that they refused to take into
account their losses in the settlement of the State debt, whether
it was inevitable that they would have to do so in the end or not.
It was not really considered to be unavoidable until the question

had become a football in the arena of politics, thus jeopardizing the retention of all the political and racial advantages which the Conservative Party had won after so many sacrifices.

It was now that Mahone, who had been conspicuous in the presidency of several important railways, afterwards consolidated, came forward more actively, though at first more or less secretively into political life. His consolidated railroads had passed into the hands of a receiver, and he was, therefore, more free to gratify the political aspirations which he had so far repressed. Personally, he was of respectable but obscure social origin; and although highly distinguished as an officer in the course of the war, had afterwards acquired a reputation for constant scheming in favor of his railway interest, and in spite of his acknowledged services, also for doubtful loyalty to the Conservative Party, both of which imputations caused him to be regarded with distrust. It was reported that he employed for the promotion of his various ambitions an active lobby during the sessions of the Assembly; that he had acquired at least one influential organ without being willing to acknowledge his proprietorship; and that he had recourse to other methods that were calculated to create a popular prejudice against him as a man of remarkable adroitness, but of a very determined spirit.

In 1877, when an election was to be held for a new Governor and General Assembly, Mahone presented his own name, before the convention met, as a candidate for the nomination to the first office, but the lack of political confidence in him in the Conservative Party was so great that he found himself confronted by a particularly resolute opposition from the other candidates. Apparently, he abandoned after this all hope of success if he should continue to pursue his original course. This fact led him to write two public letters, in which he condemned the policy of paying the public debt to the last dollar; and he also urged the recognition of the supposed prior claim which the public schools possessed to the funds in the State Treasury. That this position had now become a popular one is proven by its adoption by nearly all the other candidates, but none showed any disposition to stand back in his favor when the balloting in the convention began. Finally, by throwing his followers on the side of the representative of the Valley, Colonel Holliday, Mahone succeeded in nominating him over his rivals. He thus played the part of a Warwick, who was not likely to forget the claim which that circumstance created. The platform was expressed in vague terms so far as it touched on the public debt.

One of the first proceedings in the General Assembly which convened after Holliday's election was the submission by the Finance Committee of the House of a bill, supported by all the Republican and Independent members, and such of the Conservative as voted, which declared that the payment of the present rate of interest on the debt must be subordinated to the payment of the expenses of the State Government, and, also, of the appropriations for the public schools. The Governor vetoed this bill as soon as it was laid before him, and the Supreme Court of the State reaffirmed the validity of the Funding Act.

The *Whig*, which represented Mahone and his followers, now openly announced that it was in favor of "forcible readjustment." The prevalence of the rapidly growing sentiment in support of the *Whig's* position probably had a decided influence in alarming the bondholders, and making them more disposed to listen to overtures for a reasonable compromise. The proposition took the form of the McCulloch Bill, which was passed in March, 1879. The Independents in the General Assembly cast their votes against its adoption; and one half of the Republicans followed their example. Accompanying the McCulloch Act was the Henkle Act, which provided that the collectors of taxes should reserve out of all cash payments received by them, three-fourths of the funds appropriated by the State each year to the public schools.

The question again presented itself: could the State count upon sufficient income, without any increase of taxation, to pay even the reduced interest charge which was the most important feature of the McCulloch Act? If the Treasury could find the revenue for this purpose, would the financial needs of the public schools be also promptly met? Apparently, the Henkle Act had at least protected the schools by giving them a priority. If the two should absorb all the income, where was the money to be obtained for the institutions of higher learning, the State hospitals, and the like? The uncertainty was so patent as to justify the Readjusters,—in their own opinion at least,—in continuing the policy embodied in the Barbour Bill, which, endeavored to place the payment of the interest on the debt the last in the scale of the State's obligations.

CHAPTER V

THE READJUSTER PARTY

The operation of the Barbour Bill in actual practice, had it been passed, would, perhaps, have amounted to repudiation, since, after a liberal reservation of funds for the payment of the State's expenses, and the sum required for the support of the public schools, there would quite probably have been little surplus left to defray the interest on the State debt. This probability was perfectly well known to those who advocated the measure. Among these men, who had now come to be known as Readjusters, this bill, and not the McCulloch Act, expressed the policy which they wished to see carried out; and steps were soon taken by them to embody it in a formal public platform by an independent party. John Paul, of the Valley, took the lead. He proposed that a convention should be held for that purpose; this suggestion was sustained by numerous mass meetings; and a printed address was issued to the people of Virginia by the chief promoters of the new movement. In this document, a date was fixed for a representative conference of the new party to formulate its principles.

At the back of the movement lurked, in voluntary obscurity at first, the shrewd and thoroughly experienced leader of the new party, Mahone, whose influence was, perhaps, all the greater because his skilful manipulations were, for a time, kept under cover. His supposed organ, the *Whig,* blew the trumpet, and was untiring, both in denouncing those who favored the McCulloch Act, with its honorable provisions for the settlement of the debt, and in organizing the opposition to its acceptance as final.

149

When the Readjuster Convention assembled, it was found that only three cities and fifty-nine counties were represented by the one hundred and seventy-five delegates present. These were sufficiently identified in sentiment, in spite of their motley character, to join practically unanimously in approval of the address which had been drafted by the leaders. Among the voluminous clauses in this document was one which asserted that three per cent was the highest rate of interest which the State would be able to pay on the debt, without encroaching on the revenues needed to sustain all its necessary activities. A second clause condemned the McCulloch Act as entirely delusive in the remedy which it offered for a settlement. A third refused to recognize Virginia's liability for the share of the debt assigned to West Virginia. A fourth called for coupons, for the interest charge, which would not be receivable for taxes. A fifth condemned the funding of the debt by any foreign agency. And a sixth demanded that no settlement should be valid unless it had been ratified by a popular vote.

From a political point of view, one of the most significant clauses of all was that which censured the advocates of the McCulloch Act for showing no concern for the improvement of the negro, "though now invested with all the rights, privileges, and immunities of citizenship." This was the first sop thrown to the blacks, who were to be so far propitiated as to induce them to support the new party. Equally significant was the appointment of Mahone as chairman of the Executive Committee which had been named to effect a permanent organization. Mahone had, at the start, been the *deus ex machina* in the near background. He now stepped out from this cover into the light and became the frankly and openly acknowledged leader of the new movement.

A conflict, in the precise array of a great line of battle, now began between the party known as the Readjusters and the party known as Funders, each with a clearly defined principle that was antagonistic to the principle of the other. The Readjusters were in favor of partial repudiation, if that course should be necessary for the retention of sufficient revenue to meet all the new governmental wants of the State; and in their own minds, they were convinced that the State could not pay the present rate of interest on the debt, and also pay the now swollen expenses of the State administration. Many members of the party were mere agitators and demagogues as deserving of as little respect as the Hunnicutts, who sought to rise to power in Reconstruction times through the exploitation of the negro. There were many, however, who belonged to a more honest category.

Mahone, disappointed by his failure to bend the Conservative Party to his own business and political purposes, was now using the Readjuster Party to accomplish his personal ends. It is possible that many members of the Funder Party were actuated by a regard for the preservation of their own financial interests, but the bulk of that party were unselfishly anxious to uphold the good name of the State by the maintenance of its pecuniary credit, which could only be effected by the creditors entering voluntarily into any settlement of the debt which might be proposed by the debtor. They thought very properly that it was wrong for the debtor to adopt any policy looking to that consummation which had originated entirely with himself, and which also revealed a spirit suggestive of the attitude of the highwayman when he exclaims, "stand and deliver."

There was, perhaps, some reason to think that the State could not carry on its regular administration, settle the dues of the public schools, contribute to the support of the higher institutions of learning, provide for the enlargement of the hospitals for the insane, the deaf and dumb, and increase the usefulness of its agricultural department, if six per cent had to be paid on the debt. It was admitted by all that the levy of new additional taxes would not be consented to by any section of the community. A resolute effort to enforce the provisions of the McCulloch Act was the only honorable course to follow, and this would have been pursued without hesitation by the representative citizens of the State, had not the question become mixed up with the muddy stream of political ambition, backed up by a low standard of public principle, tempered to no small degree by an honest conviction that the State was too impoverished to pay its debt in full.

Mahone soon found himself seconded by a number of lieutenants as astute, resolute, and ambitious as himself. Such were John E. Massey, James Barbour, William E. Cameron, and John S. Wise. Massey, like Mahone, was of obscure social origin, but he was a man of great native force. He was always imperturbable, no matter how great the provocation to lose his temper. Both he and his chief were of ungainly appearance, with little personal magnetism. Mahone was a man of a small, wiry frame, with the long straggling beard of the old-fashioned itinerant preacher, and a bloodless complexion and a shallow eye that were distinctly suggestive of the impoverished whites of slavery times. He was now placed in the situation that was best calculated to bring out his remarkable talent for organization, his skill in political manipulation, and his turn for commanding a mixed following that represented the least respected element in the community.

The fateful question was: which group of partisans should control the General Assembly of 1879-1880, the Funders or the Readjusters? By July, 1879, Mahone had welded the Readjusters into a compact aggressive body, by means of mass meetings, at first; and afterwards by a shrewd selection of candidates. All this time, he had refused to acknowledge that the Readjusters had abandoned the Conservative Party. His followers, taking the cue from him with practical unanimity, defied the Conservative State Committee to read them out of the fold. That committee met this hypocritical protest by declaring the McCulloch Act to be the only issue that was to be accepted or rejected by popular sentiment in the pending campaign, and demanding that its support should be the test of party fealty in the election. By the middle of the summer, the public discussion had been carried to all the court-house greens. The ablest and most experienced speakers whom the Funders could summon were enlisted to take the platform there; and there they were met by the most skilful speakers whom the Readjusters possessed.

The latter showed political shrewdness in concentrating their attention at first on the electorate of the Southwest and the Valley, in which divisions of the State there were few negroes to confuse the debt issue by arousing fear of black domination. The strength which the Readjusters developed in these counties was proclaimed far and wide through the State for the purpose of creating the impression everywhere that opposition to the Funders' plans was much greater than was imagined in the districts in which the negroes had the majority. This idea was subsequently driven home in these districts,—which, for the most part, were made up of Tidewater and Southside counties,—by a vigorous restatement of the position which the Readjusters had elsewhere taken on the public debate. Was the debt a just one as it stood? If not, should the McCulloch settlement be sustained? Was not the various schemes which the Readjusters had in view for the improvement of conditions generally in the State superior to any which the Funders advocated? Such was the line of argument that they pressed on the hustings, while their leader worked indefatigably behind the lines, and most often below the surface, to strengthen his organization.

The Funders, on the other hand, dwelt on the honorable origin of the debt, the necessity, for sake of Virginia's reputation for good faith, that it should be paid, and the damage that would be inflicted on the State's credit should it be repudiated, even in part. The McCulloch Act was a settlement, they said, that was satisfactory to the creditors as shown by the degree to which the funding under its terms had already gone. It was not harsh in its provisions, either to the State or to the bondholders, and there was good reason to anticipate that the charge on the public revenues would be easily borne without detriment to the other demands upon the Treasury. The rate of interest, at first, would be only three per cent, and by the time the higher rate would become payable, the prosperity of the Commonwealth would have grown so substantially that the additional drain would not be seriously felt. The Henkel Act, in any event, protected the appropriations reserved for the public school.

The feeling aroused by the public discussions was often extremely bitter. Personalties, and charges, and counter-charges, were exchanged by the speakers on the platform in the court-room and on the courthouse greens. Blows were passed. Duels were threatened. The strong partisanship of the ante-bellum days of Whigs and Democrats was renewed; and the whole scene was one of a divided white population fighting over an issue apparently involving life and death.

In all this contention, the negroes were, at first, somewhat apathetic. The situation was really one calculated to confuse them. The political rule which had governed members of this race hitherto no longer applied. In the first place, the Republican administration at Washington threw its influence, in the beginning, more or less openly on the side of the Funders, because they were seeking to sustain a sound financial policy which had been always one of the Republican Party's principal claims to public confidence. In the second place, there were among the Readjusters many men who bore some of the oldest and most honorable names in their respective districts. Previously, this fact had been enough to cause the negroes to be suspicious of any party so distinguished. With them, the habit had been to find out how the bulk of the white people were going to cast their ballots, and then to vote directly to the contrary.

In the situation now confronting them, both parties were controlled by white leaders, who, unlike their previous leaders, were not drawn chiefly from the North, but from the same soil as themselves. Still there were enough local Republicans supporting the Readjuster Party to attract the negroes' attention, and make them more favorable to that party than to the Funder Party. Later on, the Readjuster campaign managers gradually disseminated the report among them that the success of the Funder cause would mean the closing of most of their schools by curtailing the revenue hitherto reserved for public instruction. A more uncertain rumor also spread that a Funder victory would be quickly followed by an increase in the tax on whiskey.

At the beginning of the campaign, the Readjusters were cautious in making open overtures to the negro voters, as they were afraid that this would arouse the old race prejudice, to their political detriment. This attitude of prudent reticence in time radically changed. The desire for a party triumph became so strong, with the progress of the canvassing, that the reluctance to approach freely the negro voters disappeared. They were now promised the gift of new political rights. And the additional assurance was extended to them, through their preachers, that the most energetic pains would be taken to balk all effort of the Funders to deprive them of the rights which they already enjoyed. To prove the reliability of their word, the Readjusters supported many negro candidates, and the Funders were forced to follow their example in more than one district.

So wrought up was the feeling on both sides when the campaign closed that the *Whig* expressed the resolution of each party when it advised the Readjusters "to vote or die, and have your vote counted or give short shift to those who seek to prevent." In the election which followed, the Funders were defeated by a majority of twenty thousand ballots in favor of their opponents. Without the negro voter, the cause of the Readjusters would not have won. It was a fact of significance that the cities and towns, and even the villages, supported the Funders, while the opposition came from rural districts, in most of which the white population far exceeded the black. It was for this reason that the fear of negro domination played no part in some sections of the State in swelling the vote of the Funders.

For a time, the legislative programme of the Readjusters was blocked by Governor Holliday, who was not in sympathy with the principles of that party. In the meanwhile, the policy of Mahone and his followers became involved in the play of national Republican politics. In spite of the fact that fifteen years had passed since the close of the war, the feeling of the majority of the whites towards the National Republican Party had shown little tendency towards mollification. It is true that, in those regions of the State where there were few negroes, this feeling was not so strong; but it is a notable fact that, even in the course of the embittered campaign of 1879, vigorous resentment was expressed by the Readjusters when accused of coquetting with the National Republicans. They denied emphatically, as we have seen, that they had deserted the Democratic Party.

There would have been no reason for their taking this position had they not been aware that the abhorrence of the National Republican Party was still as keen as ever in Virginian hearts; and that coalescence with that organization by open proclamation would be the end of any political body in the State which made it. As a matter of fact, the Virginian voters, whether favorable to readjustment or settlement of the debt, had, in casting their ballots, given no serious thought to Federal politics. State politics alone were considered. The controversy was within the circle of a single family. Not national offices but state offices were borne in mind.

But the hour was now approaching when the Readjusters would be caught up in the sweep of the National Republican Party's interests, and their point of view, in consequence, would be materially altered. While, so far as Virginia was concerned, the Republican National Party had in recent years made no attempt of any real importance to interfere in the affairs of Virginia, there being no occasion for it owing to the prudence of the white people, the persistency with which the State remained aloof from national political influences was a cause of irritation at the North. All the commonwealths of the South which had thrown off the domination of the negroes and the radicals imi-

FREDERICK W. M. HOLLIDAY
Governor 1878-1882

tated Virginia's example, and this only served to increase the distrust felt by their former enemies.

In vain President Hayes endeavored to break the spell of Southern "Bourbonism," as it was called by those out of sympathy with that conservative attitude of mind. The only open susceptibility to his overtures was shown by a few men, who hoped to be nominated to a seat in the cabinet or to a diplomatic post. It was also thought that Mahone and his principal followers lent a furtive ear to the song of the tempter. There was evidence of the justness of this suspicion some time afterwards, when Senator Don Cameron, of Pennsylvania, was able to make a secret arrangement with Mahone, under which, in return for supporting Grant for a third term, Mahone was to receive the aid of the Republican members of the General Assembly when his name should be brought forward in that body as a candidate for the United States Senatorship. He carried out his part of the bargain by advising the Readjusters and local Republicans to cast their votes for a fusion ticket pledged to Grant, to be composed of six Readjusters and five Republican electors. The proposal failed, by a narrow margin, to obtain the required number of votes in the Republican State Convention.

Mahone, disconcerted by the miscarriage of his plan, persuaded the Readjuster Convention, that met soon afterwards, to nominate an independent ticket of electors favorable to General Hancock for the Presidency but the Conservatives declined to accept this ticket, and nominated one of their own, which was successful in defeating that of Mahone. Thus it will be perceived that, as late as 1880, he continued to wear the mask of the Democratic Party, behind which his winking at the Republican was but poorly concealed.

In March, 1881, he took his seat in the Senate, where he was to find it impossible long to ride the Democratic horse alone. Indeed, it was due to his casting vote that the Republicans were enabled to organize that body. But he still held himself out as a Democrat, although asserting his right as a Readjuster to act independently of its dictations. That he was considered one of themselves by his Republican colleagues was indicated by their ardor in defending him when attacked by the Southern Democratic members.

The Republican Party of the North soon gave many signs of their readiness to aid the men whom the next Readjuster Convention nominated for the Governorship and the General Assembly. This Convention was held in June, 1881. Federal appointments to office were made with a view of increasing the Readjuster's chances of success, and every other influence available was employed by their Northern allies to the same end. The result was the triumph of the coalitionists. William E. Cameron was chosen Governor, and a majority favorable to the policy of the Readjuster Party on the question of the public debt was elected to the General Assembly. Practically, the Readjusters had already merged with the Republicans when they began to enact the debt legislation which was so repugnant to the best political and moral sentiment of the State. The supremacy of the party remained unbroken for a period of two years. They controlled the Legislature; they controlled the Governor; they controlled the State Supreme Court.

When the General Assembly convened in December, 1879, at which time a Funder occupied the Executive Mansion, the Readjuster majority seated in that body passed what was known, from the name of its sponsor, as the Riddleberger Bill. This Bill was vetoed by Governor Holliday, but later on, was signed by Governor Cameron in a somewhat altered form. The Act, as it stood subsequent to this formality, reduced the public debt of the State,—after deducting a one-third share of the principal and interest for payment by West Virginia,—to the total sum of twenty-one million dollars in round figures. The interest rate was fixed at three per cent. The old bonds were required to be exchanged for the new. This settlement was accompanied by a measure known as the Coupon Killer, by which, without violating the National Constitution's provision against the impairment of a contract, the settlement of taxes by means of the existing coupons would be made so cumbrous and inconvenient that few holders,—especially if residents of Europe,—would have recourse to them. It was anticipated that, in this way, the depletion of the Treasury would be permanently halted.

Having passed the Bill, which repudiated a very substantial proportion of the State debt, the Readjusters undertook to enact legislation of almost equal importance touching other aspects of public affairs. This legislation had, in most instances, a decided partisan bent. The prepayment of the poll tax, as a requisite in voting, was repealed, because it had seriously diminished the number of negro ballots cast in previous elections. The former liquor license was restored, as it fell more lightly than the Moffett regulation, and was, therefore, more popular, though less remunerative to the State, and less easy to enforce with strictness. The rate of taxation on land was indirectly reduced by a more liberal assessment, and taxes in general were cut to the extent of ten per cent.

All these measures were designed to curtail the expenses of the small property-holders, and those persons, who, like the majority of the negroes, owned no property at all. On the other hand, a much heavier burden was imposed upon all corporations. In this course, the railways were the chief sufferers, as their valuation was increased to a point rarely justified. This hounding of corporate wealth was especially inconsistent at the moment when the necessity of encouraging all means of advancing the industrial wealth of the State had become a slogan of the Readjusters.

Extraordinary favor, on the other hand, was shown to the system of public schools in the distribution of the revenues which these new measures brought into the Treasury in unprecedented abundance. A special tax for the support of that system was required to be paid by the railroad and telephone companies; and a further advantage was granted by reserving for the same purpose a larger proportion of the volume of gen-

eral taxes. The sum which was supposed to represent the un-
settled amount of what was due the public schools under the
previous Conservative Administration was ordered to be paid,—
in part, by the delivery to them of a round sum of four hundred
thousand dollars; and, in part, by quarterly instalments of
twenty-five thousand thereafter. The negro Readjusters were
rewarded by the erection of a normal and collegiate institution
at Petersburg. For their benefit especially, the poll tax was
ultimately abolished entirely; and their good will too was chiefly
considered in the repeal of the law which punished petty offenses
by the public whipping-post. Measures of genuine public usefulness were introduced to protect farmers in the purchase of fertilizers, and to improve their modes of tillage by the establishment of agricultural experiment stations. A stricter set of
regulations was also adopted to assure a more reliable method in
storing and sampling tobacco in the public ware-houses.

The bitterness of the recent campaign, so far as it was felt
by the Readjusters, vented itself promptly in the displacement
of the incumbents who had occupied the State offices by the
Conservatives' appointment. The first nominees of the Readjuster caucus were men like Massey, for the first auditorship,
and C. M. Reynolds and T. T. Fauntlery, for the treasuryship
and secretaryship of the commonwealth respectively. Perhaps,
the most ruthless act was the refusal to reelect William H. Ruffner to the office of Superintendent of Public Instruction, which he
had administered with extraordinary ability and fidelity, during
so many years. The various boards of the different State institutions were soon filled with Readjuster partisans, often as in-
competent as they were obscure. Especially was this so in the
instance of the University of Virginia, whose Visitors had previously numbered some of the most distinguished citizens of the
State. The Court of Appeals, the highest tribunal in the Commonwealth, did not escape. The members of that bench, exalted
in public esteem by their high character, long experience, and
great learning, were all dropped, and their seats taken by men

who, in some cases, had no claim personally or professionally
to much popular consideration.   Most of the county judges, who
had long enjoyed universal respect, were rooted up with the
same cynical roughness.   Several of their successors were subsequently removed for their share in malodorous transactions.

In the midst of this profuse distribution of public offices, the
negro was not often recognized, and when he was, his appointment was restricted to a justiceship of the peace, or some position of a still more obscure character.   The Readjusters understood the sentiment of the Virginian people at large sufficiently
well to be aware that the advancement of the blacks to political
honors would react upon the stability of their party.   The
"faithful allies," as they were termed in the moment of victory,
had to content themselves with the political crusts and husks
when they received any reward at all, except valueless words.

Mahone, after his election to the Senate, obtained a still
greater ascendancy over the leaders of his party.   He even
dominated Massey, whose gubernatorial ambition he had disconcerted, and rigidly required that every Readjuster member
of the Legislature should, in writing, bind himself to submit to
the decision of the party caucus.   Four Readjusters of the
Senate refused to do this, and for that reason, they were known
in the history of the general movement as the Big Four.   Subsequent events were to show that they initiated a revolt which
was to end in the destruction of their party.   But the remainder
of that organization were kept loyal by the distribution, not only
of State offices, as already pointed out, but also of Federal, since
President Arthur was anxious to use every means in his power
to maintain and strengthen Mahone's hold on the State.   This
attitude of the national administration confirmed the fidelity
of the negroes, already disposed to follow the Readjuster leaders
obediently.   Many of the influential members of the race were
practically bribed by the gift of large sums of money.

A powerful machine, controlled by Mahone, resulted; and
it was employed with a degree of arrogant ruthlessness that ulti-

mately was to have an important influence in undermining his power. In the meanwhile, he did not conceal his determination to convert the Readjuster Party into the local Republican Party, without any Readjuster spots. It was this fact that soon encouraged the Conservative voters of the State to unhorse him. In this movement, they had the powerful assistance of Massey, who asserted that there was no longer any need for a Readjuster Party; and that there was no more need now, than formerly, for a Republican Party in Virginia. The Conservatives supported him for the office of Congressman-at-large. Ultimately, they accepted the legislative results of the Readjuster movement as irrevocable, and in the next campaign made a battle cry of "Mahoneism and Republicanism" alone. They dropped the name of "Conservatives," and assumed that of Democrats. Their cause was helped by a race riot which occurred in Danville in the course of the canvassing for the State Legislature. In the ensuing election, the Democratic majority exceeded eighteen thousand of the popular vote, and the party was able to count in the General Assembly a majority of two-thirds of the members. The grip of the Mahone machine was in time broken; a liberal policy was adopted; and the State remained permanently in the Democratic camp. The Constitutional Convention of 1902 made all the changes in the fundamental law necessary after a lapse of nearly twenty years. Some of the most important of these were not adopted earlier, as it was regarded as impolitic and unsafe to do so.

VII

REBIRTH OF THE OLD DOMINION—
DEVELOPMENT AFTER 1876

CHAPTER I

EDUCATION—SEATS OF ADVANCED LEARNING

In the chapter descriptive of the condition of education during the Federal period, we dwelt at some length on the work performed in this province by the principal colleges and the State University of that day. The chief educational energy of the Virginian people at that time was directed towards the improvement of these higher institutions and the various academies which supplied them with pupils. While the instruction of indigent children reached a far greater number than has been generally known, there was little in the spirit at the back of this tuition to give it a high degree of usefulness. This was not the case with the lessons imparted in the institutions established by private gift, denominational zeal, or the public purse, for the benefit of students who were able to pay a fee for their instruction. These institutions continued to grow in importance down to the opening of the war for Southern Independence. Several of those with small finanical resources were compelled to close their doors while the conflict was in progress. But hardly had the sound of the last gun fired at Appomattox died away among the surrounding hills when the locked doors were reopened and solicitation was made for pupils.

There is nothing finer in the history of Virginia than the ardor with which the young men, many of whom bore on their persons the scars of battle, turned to education as practically their only means of advancement in those desperate times. There was no sacrifice which their parents were not willing to make to provide the means of obtaining for these earnest and eager

167

spirits advantages of a year or more in academic halls. And many young Virginians, who were without parental backing, energetically worked their way with their own hands through the different class-rooms.

The gravity of the students during the first years after the war was a subject of public comment. It was as if they knew that on themselves depended not only their own future success in life, but also the full recovery from ruin of that beloved country for which so many of them had recently fought. The usual frivolities of college seemed to be abandoned for the time-being. All thought was concentrated on study, whether inside or outside the class-room. It would be hard to overstate the importance of this spirit in hastening the restoration of the prostrated land. Many of these young men became the leaders of their respective communities, and set an example which carried far in the lives of the people at large.

The noble manner in which the colleges met the call made on their slender resources by these eager bands of students constitutes one of the most inspiring chapters in the history of Virginian education. The lecture-halls were generally bare and uncomfortable; the scientific apparatus was frequently scant and imperfect; and the treasuries were constantly in need of funds for the most urgent purposes. But the lack, the deficit, made no real difference. There were the old text-books still ready for service. Above all, there were the professors, men who represented the ripest scholarship of the South, and its finest social spirit, to impress their lessons on the minds of their youthful auditors. The striking character of most of these men, particularly those who had passed through the furnace of war, left its stamp upon the ideals of the young men both as to personal bearing and moral and intellectual outlook.

The period just before the conflict of 1861-65 began, and for several decades afterwards, revealed a high quality in the men who selected the profession of teaching as their vocation in life. In those times, the rewards of few occupations were so great as to draw all the best talent to their pursuit. Law, no doubt, offered the most assured prospect of an abundant return from the exercise of skill, learning and industry, but not even law was held in higher esteem than the calling of the collegiate professor. The question of money did not enter into it any more than it entered into the calling of the clergymen or the naval or

WILLIAM AND MARY COLLEGE

military officer. The position carried its own distinction; and throughout the State, in those times, there were numerous incumbents of the professorial chairs who were almost as well-known as the most conspicuous barristers or public men. It was a reputation which they deserved, not only from their wealth of scholarship and skill in teaching, but also from their unselfish devotion to their duties.

At the end of the war, the College of William and Mary was in ruins. Like the Virginia Military Institute, it had suffered from Northern invasion, and it was not until seven years had passed that its suspension was broken and its activities resumed, with the limited aid of the State. It began again to pursue the career of usefulness which had, at one time, made it the foremost institution of America. It was especially successful in reviving interest in the colonial history of Virginia, with which it was so closely identified in its early years. But in the other provinces of knowledge, it also maintained its old reputation for thoroughness and breadth of scholarship. We shall refer in a later chapter to its connection with the public school system of the present age.

Hampden Sidney College after the war, was so fortunate as to escape the interval of atrophy which fell on the College at Williamsburg. It was not long before its former prosperity was restored. This was because it continued faithful to the same high principles which had distinguished its administration from the beginning. It offered the same solid standards of learning; it encouraged still that patriotic spirit which had made its typical graduate an exemplar of bravery and integrity in all the great periods of commotion recorded in the history of the State; and it remained as loyal as ever to the purely religious influences which had so powerfully in the past impressed the minds and hearts of its students. It was, and it still is, this combination which has given the institution so fine a reputation, in spite of the fact that its annual lists of pupils have, until recent years, been comparatively limited in their length. It is still one of the most remarkable instances to be found in the United States of the small college which has, in so many cases, exerted an influence not the less profound and extensive because lacking in great endowments and possessing no long roll of students. It is *character* which this seat of learning has illustrated; and it has done this, not only in its work within its immediate precincts, but also in the careers of its graduates, who are still to be numbered among the most useful citizens of the State and the South. The effect of a religious education is still as conspicuous in the lives of those whom it is now teaching as it was in the days when it supplied so many incumbents to Presbyterian pulpits.

It was the fortunate lot of Washington College, after the close of the war, to find its new career in the beginning identified with the last and not the smallest service which General Lee

HAMPDEN SIDNEY COLLEGE
Building Completed in 1835

performed for the welfare of the Southern people. Before his election to the Presidency of the College, it had exercised a deep moral and intellectual influence in the various communities of the sturdy Covenanter population occupying the Upper Valley, but it had not enjoyed any wide degree of distinction. Situated as it was in an isolated corner of that beautiful region, which possessed a connection with the outside world only by means of the canal-boat and the stage-coach, it did not stamp itself very deeply on the educational history of the State at large.

It was because the College's early growth was associated with the illustrious name of Washington, and also because its location removed it from the most active currents of the country as a whole,—then so agitated by the suspicion and hatred springing from the recent war,—that General Lee decided to make his permanent home there by accepting the invitation to become the President of the institution. But he was not satisfied to fill the office in the conventional way. He was profoundly convinced that it was only through the spread of education that the South could fully recover from the wounds whch she had received, and retake her former place in the highest councils of the Nation. He preached this doctrine with an earnestness that was all the more effective because so absolutely free from any taint of personal aggrandizement. He preached it with a force that carried all the further because his name was the most honored within the borders of the Southern States.

There was something profoundly moving in the spectacle of the great soldier, so long associated with the implements and achievements of war,—the man of Second Manassas, Fredericksburg, Chancellorsville, Spotsylvania, and Appomattox,—turning his whole heart and mind towards the rehabilitation of his own stricken people by proclaiming in his official acts, as much as in his private words, the gospel of education. In his quiet way, General Lee was the first in time, as he was the foremost in fame of those wise educational statesmen of the modern South, who have done such invaluable service in raising its people to a new level of civil betterment, industrial expansion, and intellectual accomplishment, through the influence of education. Washington College, in the shadow of its great President, became the center of this splendid propaganda; it appropriately, after his death, broadened its name to Washington and Lee University; and it has, as the years have passed, grown in power and distinction by its fidelity to the traditions of its past, and at the same time, by its ability to learn and carry out all the practical lessons taught by the new age. Nor has it forgotten that early religious leaning which gave such an austere, but such a lofty, spirit to its teachings. The old Covenanter faith has been softened, but its stalwart benison remains.

Randolph-Macon College was so much crippled by the breaking out of the War of 1861-65 that its students quietly dispersed;

RICHMOND UNIVERSITY, RICHMOND

and when the doors were thrown open after the close of the conflict, the institution had been removed to Ashland, a village situated not far from Richmond. Small as the College was in its attendance of students immediately after this transfer, it set an example in the study of English which gave it a reputation with scholars that soon left a mark on that province of teaching throughout the South; and this reputation has survived to our own times. The initiation of this great work was due to Thomas R. Price, who, afterwards, filled the same chair in Columbia University subsequent to his retirement from the chair of Greek at the University of Virginia. Another scholar of almost equal ripeness in the same field, James A. Harrison, was associated with the same College during that period after the war when the call of education was apparently as strong as the call of religion itself.

Richmond College also suspended its lectures when the first gun was fired in 1861; but it was reorganized after the close of hostilities; an endowment fund was raised; and the halls and dormitories were opened to students. Owing to the zealous and energetic spirit of the great religious denomination which has always controlled it, namely, the Baptists, every year has become marked by an advance in its academic courses, an increase in the number of its students, and a broadening in the scope of its general influence. In recent years, its site has been removed to a locality in the vicinity of the city; a beautiful group of buildings has been erected; and the institution converted into a University.

Emory and Henry College, situated not far from Abingdon, was designed originally to serve as a manual labor school, in which the students were to be taught without charge in consideration of their tilling the College fields in the course of each afternoon. It attained to such prosperity in time, that, when the War of 1861-65 began, nearly three hundred young men were embraced in the attendance. This number was reduced to great slimness during the first years that followed the war; but the list gradually swelled until the students equaled in number the attendance of an earlier day. The college remains under the control of the denomination which founded it, namely, the Methodists.

Roanoke College, established in 1842, was a Lutheran seat of learning, and it long reflected the influence of its denominational origin by the religious courses which made up such an important part of its regular tuition. This formed a conspicuous feature of the curriculum at a time when Jefferson's example in omitting such instruction at the University of Virginia was regarded by many people of liberal minds as the one which should be followed by all colleges. Roanoke College has always shown a keen sympathy with the working of the public school system. As early as 1872, it organized a normal department, and has since, through its president and faculty, lent its aid to enlarge the usefulness of the teachers' institutes. It has been very active and successful in adding to its various facilities for higher instruction, and it exerts an increasing influence in the province of education.

Among the institutions to which we have referred, William and Mary College alone,—and this only in recent years,—possessed any connection with the State government. They have remained, as they began, private or denominational seats of learning. Apparently, with the exception of William and Mary College and Richmond University, they have restricted their tuition to men. Before taking up the work of the State institutions, like the University of Virginia and the Virginia Military Institute, it will be pertinent to consider the private and denominational colleges which have been founded for the higher education of women.

Hollins College and Mary Baldwin Seminary were both established before the War of 1861-65, and they both have survived to our own times with constantly increasing usefulness and distinction. Their original characteristic has been preserved. Instead of following the customary line of study pursued in young ladies' schools of their natal period, they adopted the system of instruction which had been introduced into all the colleges for male students. Hollins was the earliest institution in Virginia to be chartered for the purpose of educating girls in the most advanced courses of learning. The ancient languages, higher mathematics, and moral and natural philosophy, were all included in its range. Not even the obstructive years of the War of 1861-65 interrupted its career. In response to the demand for instructors in the public schools, it established a normal department, which prepared young ladies for the profession of teaching. Its reputation extended so rapidly that it was soon drawing students from other States to increase its volume of attendance. Its buildings, equipped with all the appliances of modern science, in time formed a large and imposing group of structures; its courses of study were broadened; the elective system was adopted in the province of art, music, and elocution; and a high standard for academic degrees was rigidly enforced. Up to about the year 1913, only two hundred and fifty-six of its seven thousand students had received the diplomas of bachelor of arts.

HOLLINS COLLEGE, HOLLINS

The record of the Mary Baldwin Seminary has been equally honorable. It resembled Hollins College in the fact that it was founded by a clergyman from the North; and a second characteristic was that both were denominational in sympathy at the start,—the one, Baptist; the other, Presbyterian. Originally known as the Augusta Female Seminary, this institution ultimately changed its name to that of Miss Mary Baldwin, who was among its first pupils, and who, afterwards, served as its principal, with an efficiency that raised her to the position of the first head-mistress in Virginia. The religious spirit of the school was shown by the deposit in the foundation stone of the main building of a Bible, with the legend: "The first text-book of the Augusta Female Seminary." Equally significant was the requirement, at a later date, that every pupil on Sunday morning should be present in the church and repeat to the principal the Westminster Catechism.

It was not until 1863 that Miss Baldwin assumed control of the school. She disclosed her strong Presbyterian faith and shrewd common-sense by obtaining the assistance of that pillar of her denomination, Professor McGuffey of the University of Virginia, in arranging the round of studies. So high were her moral and intellectual ideals, so thorough her standards of instruction, so practical her management, that the reputation of the school spread throughout the United States. She was further rewarded by the accumulation of a handsome fortune, which was largely employed, after her death, in accord with her directions by will, in raising the school to a still higher platform of usefulness.

Among the seats of learning controlled by the Randolph-Macon Board of Trustees was the Randolph-Macon Woman's College at Lynchburg. It was established upon the same foundation as the foremost colleges in the State for young men. Its courses of study were as broad, its standards of graduation as high, and its requirements for degrees as strict, whether it be the bachelor's or the master's diploma. The college took such an advanced position almost from the start, that it was the first institution for Southern women to obtain admission to the first class in the enrollment of the United States Bureau of Education.

A companion seat of learning of very high distinction is Sweetbriar College, which owes its existence to a bequest of a large estate for that object by its founder, Mrs. Fletcher Williams. Like Hollins College, and the Mary Baldwin Seminary also, it is situated in sight of a lofty mountain range, and is surrounded by scenery of extraordinary beauty. The scholastic purpose which the institution has pursued has been to combine a thorough intellectual collegiate training with a training which would fit its students for the practical work of their future lives, —more especially in the provinces of art and industry. The course of study is arranged for regular college students, and also for special students, who are left to adopt the field which they prefer.

Westhampton College is coordinate with the University of Richmond, but has a separate faculty and separate buildings and equipments. It confers the degrees of bachelor of arts and master of arts.

Scattered about different parts of Virginia are numerous schools for girls which do not pretend to the high standards of learning which distinguish those which have been just mentioned, but which nevertheless are entitled to high consideration from an academic as well as from a moral point of view. With hardly an exception, these local schools are under the control of the leading denominations: Methodist, Baptist, Presbyterian, Episcopalian, and Lutheran; but while they draw their principal patronage, each from its own sect, they are open to the admission of all in the broadest catholic spirit.

We have so far referred only to the Colleges which have been founded or administered under the direction of private interests or religious organizations. Our next step will be to describe briefly those which are connected with the State, and are partly supported out of the public treasury. The number of such institutions is small, but they stand at the head of the educational system of the Commonwealth.

It will be remembered that Jefferson, while he was building the University of Virginia, pointed out the advantage of extending higher education to several provinces which had not received the attention, which, in his opinion, they deserved. One of these was military science. It was to cover this local want that the Virginia Military Institute was founded. It owed much of its early inspiration to Captain Crozet, formerly an engineer officer in the service of the great Napoleon. He was, at this time, employed in engineering work for the State. But this did not prevent him from accepting the invitation to become the chairman of the first Board of Trustees. Probably the predominant military bent of the school from the start was due largely to him. It made a specialty of military science and the art of engineering, and this characteristic has been maintained to the present day, although still seasoned by the pursuit of such studies, among others, as history and the modern languages.

The high reputation which the Institute had attained before the War of 1861-65 was confirmed by the distinction which so many of its graduates won as officers of high rank during that great conflict. A halo of romance was thrown over it by the participation of its cadets in the Campaign of New Market, in the course of which they displayed the spirit of veteran soldiers, and by their skill and courage, contributed to its success. During hostilities, the buildings were destroyed by the enemy, but the revival of the Institute was not long delayed after the battles were over. The record which it had made in the field through the distinction of its graduates, but especially of one of its professors, Stonewall Jackson, helped it to recover rapidly from the losses which it had incurred. Its heightened reputation soon drew students in large numbers from other States as well as from Virginia. After a long interval, it was compensated in full by Congress for the destruction of its buildings during the war. This sum increased its ability to widen the scope of its usefulness. It has taken a position in the esteem of the Federal military authorities second only to that of the Military Academy at West Point. Its military training has steadily grown broader, and its general instruction more comprenhensive and more thorough.

The Virginia Polytechnic Institute owed its origin to a gift of landscript made by the United States Government. The pur-

pose which it has had in view has been to impart technical
training to farmers and mechanics. The first chairs that were
established were limited to the subjects of natural philosophy,
chemistry, mechanics, technical agriculture, and English. Not
long afterwards this course was enlarged by the addition of
farm management and natural history. The students have also
always received the benefit of military drill and discipline. The
Polytechnic Institute in time developed into the leading agricultural and industrial school of the Upper South.

The principal seat of learning in the State under the control
of the Commonwealth has been the University of Virginia,
which came out of the War of 1861-65 without any serious damage to its buildings. Indeed, lectures did not cease in its halls
even when the sound of the enemies' guns was audible to the
inhabitants of its precincts. In spite of the impoverishment
which had fallen upon every interest of Virginia and the South,
this institution showed such remarkable resiliency, that, even
during the first session of peace, it was able to lean for support
on a large attendance of students. The old number of profes-
sorships was quickly restored. The new incumbents of several
of the chairs had won a high reputation as soldiers or scientific
experts in the recent conflict.

Never before or since has there gathered in a Southern seat
of learning so memorable a faculty as the one which taught in
the university during the first decade that followed 1865. They
were memorable for their learning as scholars, their efficiency
as instructors, their high character as citizens, their personal
impressiveness as men. It is questionable whether the students
of that day derived more benefit from the tuition in the lecture-
halls than from personal intercourse with the members of this
distinguished group. In a sense, that period was as heroic as
the period of the war. It was the poignant time of recovery
from confusion and ruin; and splendid was the privilege of the
young men of that day to have sat at the feet of teachers, who,
taken as a body, possessed all those great qualities of mind

which defy the slings of adversity through fidelity to duty, loyalty to principle, and a serene courage in defense of convictions which nothing could shake or daunt.

During a period of several years, the University of Virginia was almost the only institution of higher learning in the South. The others had been so stricken by the calamities of war that they did not recover with promptness. Great as had been the university's influence under the old regime, that influence was increased, not lessened, in the course of these first postbellum years. An example of scholarship and discipline was set by it then that left a deep impression on the new careers of all the Southern colleges. If the university in time lost something in attendance, in consequence of the revived activities of these rivals, it was never tempted to lower its standards. It remained true to the principles which had given it so much distinction in the past. At the same time, it revealed a quick responsiveness to the requirements of the new age.

This was shown conspicuously in two events in its postbellum history. First, it recognized the need of enlarging its instruction so as to take in all those scientific subjects which had become such an influential part of contemporary thought. The ground covered by the new chairs was only limited by the amount of money available. Second, when it seemed expedient to drop the old system of faculty administration, that step was taken, in spite of the fact that it was in conflict with the Jeffersonian provision in the beginning. The presidency promised a higher degree of efficiency, and a more intimate touch with the educational tendencies of the age. It was, therefore, adopted. A more active sympathy with popular education was shown in the new form of administration. The university became, what Jefferson intended it to be, the capstone of the state public school system. It developed a keener interest in the general welfare of the community at large. It grew less individualistic, and much more democratic in the spirit of its academic work. Nevertheless, it remained true to those traditions of personal conduct, independent choice of studies, and thorough training, which had always distinguished its scholastic life.

The University enjoyed, during many years, the support of the finest private schools that have ever existed in Virginia. Many of these schools were models of what such schools should be in their courses of study, in the spirit of their teachers and pupils, and in the lessons of social and moral culture which they inculcated. The headmasters were among the most important citizens of their respective communities. Probably they were the most influential indirectly, for, under their vigilant eyes, passed the flower of those Virginian youths of the days which intervened between the close of the war in 1865 and the opening of the twentieth century. It was their high sense of honor, their enforcement among their pupils of the rules of the loftiest conduct, and their insistence upon the most thorough standards of scholarship, that left an indelible stamp upon the minds and hearts of thousands of young men destined to guide the public affairs of the state, and give tone to its private life as well.

Later on, the public high schools took the place of most of these postbellum academies, the suspension of which inflicted heavy intellectual and spiritual loss on the community.

CHAPTER II

FOUNDATION OF THE PUBLIC SCHOOL

The introduction of the modern public school system in Virginia was made completely and quickly practicable by the new environment which was created by the abolition of slavery. Had that institution remained intact after the close of the war in 1865, the influences which had militated against the spread of such a system in the state would not have been materially altered. When slavery was destroyed, the plantation economic order, and the social order dependent upon it, received what was to prove to be a fatal blow. The logical consequence of these radical changes was the creation of a community life which was no longer to be governed by the individualistic spirit to the same extent as the one which preceded it. It was this spirit which the independence of the old isolated and slave-cultivated plantations fostered. Each family in the rural neighborhoods, which contained the bulk of the population, stood, not only physically, but in all domestic and personal affairs also, practically withdrawn, to a large degree, from contact with the community as a whole. It was only on the spiritual side that the interdependence of the occupants of these rural districts was clearly recognized; and this was because they met weekly under the roof of the same church edifice.

A sentiment sprang up from this independent existence which encouraged families to rely almost exclusively on themselves, and to that extent, dwarfed the spirit of cooperation among them. The separate citizen expected far more of himself than of the community. It was one result of this self-reliant attitude that it did not occur to him to look to the community when the question of educating his children arose. This, in his view, was a matter as personal to himself as the procurement of food and clothes or any other thing necessary for their support.

But the very importance which the well-to-do Virginian under the slave regime attached to education for his own children at his own expense, must have made him at least sensible of the evil consequences of allowing the great mass of the lowest class of white people to remain in a state of unmitigated illiteracy. How far was he influenced by this feeling to aid this class in removing this condition? We have pointed out in our account of the Federal period how, from time to time, the General Assembly made specific provision for the instruction at public expense of those children whose parents were ready to take oath that they were too indigent to pay for such instruction. There were thousands of pupils in the secondary local private schools who were taught the rudiments in this way, and a far larger proportion would have obtained tuition to this degree at least had it not been for their parents' very natural indisposition to acknowledge their own poverty in such a formal way. Education acquired by public contributions, under such peculiar circumstances, could never have been invested with dignity. Nevertheless, the opportunity of securing it was far from neglected. Indeed, it was used to a degree not generally known even at the time, as the recipients of such instruction were, doubtless, disinclined to admit their dependent position.

It is certainly correct to say that the modern public school system of Virginia had at least its germ in the numerous charity schools which existed in the state previous to the war of 1861-65. It is quite possible that these schools, had they continued, would, in time, have brought about the system of free schools as we find it in Virginia in our own age. The adoption of manhood suffrage by the Constitutional Convention of 1850 was a distinct step in that direction, because it increased the political power of the class that was least able to educate their children at their own charge; and in thus augmenting the power of this class, it made the politicians the more disposed to listen to their appeal for a more honorable system than the charity schools. The effect was clearly perceived by 1860. In that year, not less than fifty thousand children were receiving instruction at the cost of the state. It is true that the length of time each year over which this was extended was necessarily short; but there were one hundred and thirty counties in which the annual session was held; and there were altogether thirty-one hundred schools.

As early as 1846, an act had been passed which granted to the children of all classes an education by the state without charge; and there were public schools of this kind in nine counties and four towns. These were known as district free schools, and they closely resembled the public schools of our own day. They were nearer the latter in spirit than the charity schools, and might in time well have developed into a universal system. During the twelve years between 1846 and 1860, the extent of the spread of the district schools outside of the towns had been very impressive.

The existence of both the indigent and the district free schools in such numbers fully justifies the assertion that the introduction of the modern system did not find a purely virgin soil in which to grow. It was in 1871 that this system was adopted by a constitutional provision. The men who were most instrumental in founding it were Republican strangers from the North, who had always been accustomed to the public school in the free communities of that section. They were influenced, first, by the desire to pattern the new state on the polity of those communities as far as practicable; and secondly, by the wish to give the negroes an opportunity to obtain an education. This could not be effected by themselves, owing to the poverty of the race. It could only be accomplished with the aid of the public treasury.

Although, as we have seen, there had been before 1860 a drift in Virginia towards the adoption of a system that approximated the modern public school system of the state, the public sentiment in favor of this system, when it was finally introduced by the ratification of the Underwood Constitution, was not at all general in the beginning. The reasons for the existence of this inimical feeling were: first, the most influential class in the community, having been in the habit of educating their own children at their own expense, was not disposed to alter their view of the propriety of this course simply because they had been defeated in war; on the contrary, many of these men detested the system proposed all the more keenly because it was supposed to be an invention of New England; second, there was a strong opposition among them to the suggestion that the negro, the cause of so many calamities, should be instructed at their charge; and, third, they objected to the costliness of building schoolhouses and employing teachers at a time when they could ill afford to contribute to such a step. It was urged that this expense would fall with unprecedented heaviness, now that the people of the state had become so much impoverished by the destruction of property in every form. There was but one aspect of the public school which commended itself to this class at the start; it would furnish the means of educating their children, which they themselves were now so often too poor to afford.

The new educational system was fortunate in the choice which was made of the first superintendent to be selected, after the claims of fifteen competitors had been thoughtfully weighed. The name of the successful candidate was William H. Ruffner. He was by inheritance, as well as by profound conviction, an advocate of the state free school, for he was the son of Henry Ruffner, at one time president of Washington College, who was so well-known for his earnestness and ability in urging the

WILLIAM H. RUFFNER

adoption of a public school system in Virginia long before it went into actual operation. The liberality and courage of his outlook were further revealed in his open opposition to the institution of slavery.

It was under such parental influence as this that William H. Ruffner grew to manhood, and the broad vision thus early instilled into his mind was now to find an appropriate field for its exercise in laying the foundation of the new system of public education in Virginia. From the very beginning, he breathed into the performance of his duties the exalted religious spirit of a crusader. He had been a clergyman by profession, and he carried into his new mission the enthusiastic zeal of a great preacher, the unselfish devotion of a practical philanthropist, and the sagacity of a ripe statesman. So long and so carefully had he been meditating on the subject of public education, so clearly had he framed in his own mind a scheme for establishing and supporting it, that, within three weeks after his appointment, he was ready to submit to the General Assembly his conclusions in the form of a report, which proved to be so comprehensive that it was accepted as the bill for the incorporation of the public school. This bill became a permanent law without any radical revision.

It is not too much to say that what the great financial reports of Alexander Hamilton were to the whole country at the beginning of our national history, such to Virginia was this first report on the threshold of the establishment of its system of public schools. It opened up a broad and clearly marked path to be followed from the start. It laid down the fundamental principles that were to guide for an indefinite period. It is true that the existence of the same system in the New England States, with all the various lessons which had been taught there by practical experience, was of extraordinary service to the new superintendent; but there were problems in reproducing this system in Virginia which had not been encountered north of the Potomac, and which had now to be solved for the first

advance of the public school system in the favor of the people at large than this local willingness to assume a new burden at a time of almost universal impoverishment. There was less need now,—if there had ever been any at all,—of the clause in the Constitution of 1869, which provided that each city or county should be held liable for the distruction of any school-house that had been erected within its boundaries, whether that destruction was attributable to the incendiary's torch or to the hands of a mob.

At the close of the first year, there were about three thousand schoolhouses in use, but their primitive character, as a rule, was revealed by the fact that over one half of the number were constructed of more or less roughly hewn logs. A considerable proportion even of these were unfit for permanent occupation. The pupils enrolled ranged from five years of age to twenty-one. At the beginning, the daily attendance embraced only 27.8 percentage of the white children eligible for public instruction, and 16.1 percentage of the colored.

At first, the smallness of the salary offered the teachers did not form a very serious obstacle to the acquisition of persons fitted for the position. The upshot of the war had brought an extraordinary degree of poverty into a large circle of both men and women who had enjoyed unusual advantages of education in the academies that had existed before hostilities began. After the close of the conflict, the opportunities for employment had narrowed so greatly that many members of this circle were compelled to turn to the first opening that arose for earning a bare livelihood. The school term extended over so few months at the start that some of the teachers were able, during the larger part of the year, to follow some other pursuit in addition; and while the remuneration which they had received for their brief annual service as teachers was absurdly meager, nevertheless it had a distinct value in increasing the means at their disposal. The fact that, at first, three-fourths of the teachers of both races were of the male sex, and that some of the white

were employed in the schools for colored pupils, is a proof of
the desperate circumstances which so many persons of culture
had to contend with during these first years in the history of
the public school system.

As we shall find later on, the number of male teachers
steadily dwindled as the community drew further away from
the end of the war, and gradually recovered some degree of
its old prosperity, which gave other openings for more profitable employment. The number of female teachers rapidly increased as the number of the male grew smaller, simply because
the opportunities for self-support enjoyed by women were not
in proportion to those possessed by men, even when some of
the wealth of an earlier day had been restored. The young men
of the families which still remained in the old rural communities found it to their interest to emigrate in large numbers so
soon as they came of age. They perceived that little was to be
gained by lingering in the old haunts; and this led the majority
of them to seek their fortunes in the nearest towns, or in distant states in the West or Southwest.

The women could not follow their example. What were they
to do before they settled down as wives and housekeepers? Many
of them turned to teaching as their only way of accumulating
something in anticipation of entering that condition; and others
besides were led, either by necessity or by natural inclination,
to adopt it as a permanent means of earning a livelihood.

The history of the public school system was not one of conspicuous advancement from the close of the first year. It was
now that the indomitable courage, the practical wisdom, and
the inspiring enthusiasm of Dr. Ruffner came fully into action.
There were many influences still at work to retard the success
of the schools. One reason which had discouraged their introduction before the war was the sparseness of the population
in the rural districts. Another was the badness of the roads
throughout the greater part of the year. These hostile conditions were even more in evidence after 1871 than they had been

before 1861. Indeed, few schools outside of the towns were so situated that they could depend upon a large attendance drawn from their immediate vicinity. They had to gather their pupils from a circuit which spread out many miles in area; and when the season was very wet or very cold, the highways were so bogged by mud or blocked by snow, that it was difficult for children to pass over them except on foot; and even in this way, the traversal was no easy accomplishment.

But it was not simply physical obstacles like those which we have just named that stood in the forward path. Political interference with the social status of the races in their relation to each other was attempted. The Civil Rights Bill debated in Congress during the session of 1873-74 seriously threatened the complete destruction of the system by apparently foreshadowing the adoption of mixed schools as the next important step. It is estimated that, during this critical period, more than two-thirds of the entire body of county superintendents threw up their commissions in depression or disgust over the prospect.

Before this cloud had passed away entirely, another arose to take its place. In our description of the controversy over the state debt, we referred to the diversion by the treasury to other purposes of the fund which had been reserved, by the provision of the Underwood Constitution, for the maintenance of the public schools. The revenues collected by the commonwealth were strained to the vanishing point at this hour by the payment of the interest accruing on its bonds. The impression in the minds of the majority of the Virginians then was, that an obligation of honor, like the state debt, had a superior claim over an obligation of expediency, like the need for popular education. This was the view of the courts also; and the schools, for the time being, seemed to be in imminent risk of going to the wall.

By 1878, the amount still due the teachers had swelled to two hundred and fifty thousand dollars. The closing of the door of every public school in the state appeared to be unavoidable unless local taxation, voluntarily imposed on themselves by the citizens of each district, should be used to save the situation. As a matter of fact, in some of the counties there was not a single school open to receive pupils. From over two hundred thousand children previously enrolled, the number sank to about one hundred thousand in 1879. How injurious was the default in the teachers' salaries was shown by the number on whom it fell. There were at this time in the state about two thousand white teachers and about four hundred colored. The former were entitled to $30.05 a month, if men, and $24.73, if women.

Under the influence of Dr. Ruffner's vigorous and persistent protests, supported by a very general public sentiment, the first step was taken to restore the revenue which was required by the public schools. This was done by the passage of the Henkel Act, which gave these schools a claim on the public taxes prior to that of the interest on the public debt. The public school system was further benefited by the appropriation to its use of four hundred thousand dollars acquired by the state through its sale of its share in the stocks and bonds of the Atlantic, Mississippi, and Ohio Railway. It was estimated that a million and a half dollars had been withheld from the public schools in order to meet other obligations of the state. The General Assembly expressed its intention to return the whole of this sum; and it made the first reduction in the amount due by the transfer, just mentioned, of the proceeds of the railway sale. Ultimately, the entire deficit was covered.

In spite of the determination to sustain the public school system, so plainly shown in these measures of the Legislature in its favor, that system was suffering from deficiencies which arose primarily from the absence of sufficient funds to ensure its increased usefulness. In the first place, there was now a pressing need of the consolidation of many of the existing schools. As the population in the majority of the country districts was widely scattered, the attempt to furnish each neighborhood with a teacher and schoolhouse, for which only a few pupils could be enrolled, resulted in a division of the already scanty funds set aside for public instruction. By erecting one school building and supplying one teacher where there were now two school buildings and two teachers, the chance of engaging a higher type of the latter was at once increased, as it made possible a larger salary.

In time, the policy of consolidated schools was carried out, and the difficulty of the greater distance to be traversed by the pupils in reaching the schoolhouse was met by providing for them a vehicle at the public expense.

In the meanwhile, the necessity of securing a thoroughly trained class of teachers grew more and more imperative. How could the children be expected to improve when so many of their teachers, however conscientious, were ignorant of the proper methods of imparting instruction to them? The normal school was the most obvious instrument to bring about the required change. Provision had been made for such schools by the terms of the Underwood Constitution, and only limited funds had prevented that provision from being carried out from the very start. As a substitute, the teachers' institutes had been introduced. These were local associations, which held formal sessions during several weeks in the course of each summer. They were useful, not only in inculcating the best methods of teaching, but also in raising an *esprit de corps* among the teachers, which gave a new dignity to their calling. They served to make teaching in the public schools a genuine profession, and not simply a temporary make-shift employment.

But Dr. Ruffner was not satisfied to confide the means of improvement to these local conferences. As early as 1880, he obtained the permission of the authorities of the State University to hold the sessions of a summer school within its precincts, which should be open to all the public school teachers of Virginia. The men engaged to overlook the management of this summer school were of the highest standing in their common calling. That the school had the countenance of the commonwealth as a whole was revealed by the governor's presence and participation in the proceedings. The entire section of each working day was taken up by those in attendance in listening to lectures by acknowledged experts, who touched on every aspect of the art of teaching from the most practical point of view. Four hundred and sixty-seven male and female teachers made up the audiences. Although this number was comparatively small, the benefit of the school was clearly recognized at the time and afterwards. The failure to repeat it at an early date arose from the fact that the state was unwilling to make an appropriation for its support. This niggardliness had also hampered the county institutes.

It was due to the pecuniary assistance of the trustees of the Peabody Fund that normal institutes for the benefit of both the white and colored teachers were subsequently held at various places in the state. It was the policy of this body thus to promote the improvement of those in charge of the instruction in the public schools as they considered this, and not contributions of funds to these schools directly, the most certain way of raising their efficiency.

It was left to Ruffner's successor, R. R. Farr, an appointee of the Readjuster Party, to aid in the establishment of two permanent normal schools. The one was the Farmville Female Normal School for whites. The other was the Normal and Industrial Institute for negroes erected at Petersburg. The negroes already possessed in the Hampton Normal and Agricultural School, a seat of education which, besides its purely industrial features, was active in preparing persons of the race for the duties of the public school-room. This great institution had opened its doors as early as 1868. In addition to a business course, a trade course, and an agricultural course, it provided an academical normal course, which served, in the beginning, a specially useful purpose in the absence of other normal schools for negroes.

WILLIAM EVAN CAMERON
Governor 1882-1886

Superintendent Farr seems to have followed more or less closely in Ruffner's foot-steps. Ruffner had set the example in summoning the first Conference of County and City Superintendents of Public Free Schools. This was not repeated during his administration; but, in 1883, a similar conference was organized by Farr into a permanent institution, which proved especially valuable, like the local county conferences, in invigorating the professional spirit of the teachers.

At the close of Mr. Farr's administration, there were over six thousand teachers employed in the public schools, both white and black. The number of women among them outran the number of men, although only four years earlier there had been seven hundred and fifty-one men in excess of women so engaged. Many of the teachers were not natives of Virginia. About twenty-five hundred only had been trained in the public schools of the state, and about fourteen hundred in its colleges and private academies. The average age of the white teachers ranged between eighteen and thirty. The average salary for men was thirty-one dollars, and for women about twenty-seven.

CHAPTER III

EXPANSION OF THE PUBLIC SCHOOL

By the time that the Readjuster Party had lost control of the State Government, the public school system had become so firmly intrenched that all danger of any permanent decline in its usefulness, or any relaxation in its grip on popular good will, had disappeared. It was one of the most convincing proofs of its vitality that, however antagonistic to each other the two political parties in the state might be, both vied in further buttressing the stability of the system, as an assured means of winning the people's favor. The Readjusters had shown a disposition to go even further than the Conservatives in promoting its welfare. To its interests, indeed, they subordinated every claim on the revenues of the commonwealth, after the actual expenses of local and state administration had been paid. This was not simply because they valued popular education for its enlightening influence, but as much, perhaps, because, in advancing it, they were taking the most effective step to increase their political power.

A system which could pass safely through the period of Mahone's almost ruthless ascendancy,—nay, which could thrive under it as it had never prospered before,—had little reason to regard the future with any misgiving as to the inherent strength of its position. It might continue for a time impeded by the lack of sufficient means to perfect its operation in every detail; but its deficiencies were certain to be ultimately modified, if not entirely removed, as the resources of the commonwealth should grow in volume, and every advantage which it already possessed should be confirmed and enlarged.

The first superintendent to be elected by the General Assembly after the restoration of Conservative control was John L. Buchanan, whose administration began in 1885, and lasted during a period of four years. One of its most significant features was the effort made to improve the condition of the schools for negroes. There still lingered sufficient prejudice against the education of the freedmen to retard the extension of equal facilities of tuition to the members of that race. As a rule, their schoolhouses were inferior to those of the whites; and they suffered to some degree from other drawbacks perhaps more serious. Their teachers were now of their own color, which increased the effectiveness of the lessons owing to a more intuitive, sympathetic, and confidential contact between pupil and instructor. These teachers had, in most cases, enjoyed the advantage of a fair equipment for their calling, since the negroes possessed, in the colleges at Petersburg and Hampton, two schools which were fully capable of giving a fair normal training. Other institutions existed, both within and without the state, which imparted a similar instruction for their benefit.

There was a disposition at this time among the various agencies,—like the Peabody Board, for instance,—interested in the welfare of the negro schools, to encourage, through them, the acquisition of an industrial training, which would have a direct relation to the employment to be followed by the pupils in after life.

One of the outstanding measures of the Buchanan superintendency was the adoption of a uniform series of text books. From the beginning of the system, some of the most valuable of the books in its use had been written by Virginians. Especially notable among these were Maury's geographies, Venable's arithmetics, McGuffey's readers, and Holmes's histories. The authors of these works were men of extraordinary attainments in general, and ripe experience in their special calling.

FITZHUGH LEE
Governor 1886-1890

John E. Massey, who succeeded Buchanan, had been a conspicuous figure in the Readjuster Party. Imperturbable, shrewd,
and well-informed, he carried out the functions of his office with
unusual efficiency. He concerned himself during his term particularly with increasing the number of children attending the
schools, and with improving the quality of the teachers. In
order to accomplish the first purpose, he made many excursions
through the state, in the course of which he displayed his remarkable powers of persuasion in a series of addresses directed
to the people at large. These speeches had, as their burden, the
benefits of education; the expanding requirement for a more
liberal rate of local taxation for the support of the schools; the
advantages of a superior type of schoolhouse over the log-house
then so generally to be seen; the demand for a better trained
teacher and more normal schools; but above all, the need for
a higher average in the daily attendance of children of the
school age. These were the most crying wants of the schools
at this time.

In order to increase the competency of the teachers, Massey
was extremely active in encouraging the holding of institutes.
During the first year of his administration, it was reported to
him by the different local superintendents that fifty-three of
the counties had failed to organize any institute at all. As these
institutes lasted for some time, and were unsupported by the
state, it was to be expected that many of the teachers would
be often unwilling or unable to bear the personal expense of
attending them. Under the leadership of E. C. Glass, the city
superintendent of Lynchburg, a more important means of training than the county institute had by this time been adopted.
This was the School of Methods, which assembled in successive
years in different places in the state; and with such excellent
results, as to draw to them the close attention of the public.
They were at first, however, entirely self-dependent. Under
Superintendent Massey's influence, the General Assembly consented to appropriate annually twenty-five hundred dollars for

their support. To this sum, the Peabody fund generously made a considerable addition. The dignity and stability of the School of Methods was later further advanced by the permanent choice of the University of Virginia as its place of meeting.

Another step forward was the organization of the Virginia State Teachers Association. This body has since held its sessions regularly once a year, and it practically embraces the entire number of teachers in the state. It has exercised a conspicuous influence in raising the status of the profession by increasing its usefulness and protecting its interests.

Two other features of Superintendent Massey's fertile administration were, first, the successful endeavor to gain for women the privilege of admission to the University of Virginia; and, second, a recommendation,—which was later on adopted,— that manual labor should be introduced as a part of the course in the public schools. Too many restrictions were thrown by the university authorities around the grant of female enrolment to make it acceptable to female students, and the opportunity for the moment passed unutilized. Ultimately, manual labor was permitted in the public schools in a modified form. This was considered especially desirable for the negro pupils. The Hampton Institute had already proved its employment to be entirely practicable.

At this time, there were in the state about one hundred and seventeen thousand colored children of the school age who were unable to read or write, as compared with one hundred and fifteen thousand white children of the same age, in the same condition. Virginia, unhappily, now occupied the unenviable position of being the seventh commonwealth in degree of illiteracy.

Massey was succeeded in the office of superintendent by Joseph W. Southall. Mr. Southall exhibited from the start a keen interest in the improvement of the rural schools. Their inferiority was, in his judgment, chiefly due to the meager salaries paid to the teachers; and to remedy the defect, to some extent, he recommended the consolidation of schools wherever this was practicable. By this means, the fund for disposition could be employed to a larger degree in increasing the remuneration of the instructors. There had, in reality, been no substantial addition to these salaries since the beginning of the system. In 1871, at the start, the payment made to male teachers was thirty-two dollars and thirty-six cents, and to female, twenty-six dollars and thirty-three cents. The corresponding figures for 1903 were thirty-four dollars and fifty-six cents for the one, and thirty-four dollars and fifty-six cents for the other. The total expenditures for the benefit of the public schools, had, in thirty years, swelled four hundred per cent, and yet the teachers' salaries had increased only a few dollars.

There had been a distinct improvement in the character of the buildings set apart for the public schools. This grew out of the fact that no new structure for this purpose was permissible unless its plan had been approved by the superintendent.

Mr. Southall urged that the graded school should be universally established in the rural districts; and that a high school should be erected in each county. By this means, a perfect articulation could be created between the primary school at the bottom of the system, and the University at the top. A promising pupil could thus advance, step by step, from the lowest to the highest rung of the ladder. The superintendent also repeated the recommendation of his predecessor in favor of the appointment of a Board of Examiners for the entire State. This was considered to be a certain means of improving the qualifications of the teachers. This reform was subsequently adopted. There was associated with it a system of inspection of the physical condition of the school-houses and the health of the school children.

A few years after the beginning of the next century, the number of children enrolled was 361,772, while the number in daily attendance was only 215,204. This represented an increase from 18.4 per cent to 40 per cent. The length of the session had grown from approximately five months to six and a half. The augmentation of the number of students was still more encouraging. There were now many thousand men and women, white or black, engaged in performing the duties of the schools. The commonwealth at this time made an annual grant of one million and a quarter dollars to defray the charges of the system. But most remarkable of all, the value of the property in one form or another belonging to it had risen from one hundred and eighty-eight thousand dollars to four millions and a half.

During the interval, the disproportion between the number of male teachers and the number of female had steadily enlarged. In 1905, for every white male instructor in the public schools there were four female. On the other hand, the disproportion was not so great in the case of the colored teachers. There were six hundred and thirty-eight male and fifteen hundred and forty-two female. This represented about one man to three women. The difference between the two races in the proportions just mentioned was attributable to the fact that the profession of teaching in the public schools was a more satisfactory calling for negro men than for white, as their aspirations were pitched in a lower key.

The physical character of the school-house at this time throws light on the general condition of the system. There were about seven thousand of these houses altogether. Of this number, two hundred and thirty were constructed of brick; eight hundred and seventy-eight of logs; over six thousand of frame; and about thirteen of stone.

The Constitutional Convention which assembled in 1902 reflected, in the various provisions for public education which it adopted, the high popular appreciation in which the system was now held. One of these provisions enlarged the membership of the State Board from three persons to eight. Three of these additions were to represent the group of State institutions of higher learning. Two were chosen from the ranks of the county superintendents. A more important provision still authorized the imposition of a State capitation tax on every male citizen, not to exceed one dollar and a half, for the benefit of the schools alone. Every board of supervisors in the counties, and every council in the cities, were also impowered to levy an additional capitation tax of one dollar for the same purpose.

There was observable about this time a disposition to encourage the formation of libraries as adjuncts to the public schools. In a few years, the travelling libraries sent out by the State Library were to become a very useful addition to the existing facilities for advancing the prosperity of the public schools. Many thousands of well-selected volumes were in this way put in reach of the families served by these schools, which, otherwise, would have been cut off from opportunities of reading the best modern literature.

From the beginning, the public school system had occupied a more advantageous, and also a more fruitful, position in the cities than it had done in the rural districts. This followed naturally from the larger amount of wealth which the urban centers of population possessed, since this made possible the collection, by local taxation, of a greater sum for the support of their local schools. This meant an ability to obtain a better class of teachers; to adopt more complete courses of studies; and to erect a more spacious and modern kind of school building.

Nearly all the important towns in the State had organized numerous public schools before the general system was launched in 1870-71. Thus Norfolk, as early as 1850, was subdivided into school districts supervised by school commissioners, and sustained by a public levy amounting to as respectable a sum as four dollars for every male adult residing in the city. A schoolhouse, with four commodious rooms, was set apart in each of these districts for occupation by teacher and pupils. Here was to be observed, in the beginning, the separation of the sexes in both study and recitation; but this rule was revoked in the elementary classes after the original schools had become a part of the public school system put in operation in 1871. Public instruction had, during many years, formed an important side of the civic life of Norfolk before that event occurred. No very radical change in the character of the public schools of that city took place after 1871, except that school-houses and teachers were provided for all negro children of the prescribed age. Naturally, the ripe experience acquired in the management of the ante-bellum schools and the schools in operation just before 1871, exerted a beneficial influence on the character of Norfolk's public schools from the beginning of their association with the State system. There were already as many as sixteen teachers at work, and close to one thousand pupils in attendance. Norfolk was in advance of most of the cities in this province.

Petersburg founded its system of public schools only three years before the adoption of the State system; Richmond only two; Lynchburg and Fredericksburg, only one.

The public schools of Petersburg were made possible before 1871 by the appropriation of a large sum for their benefit by the agent of the Peabody Fund. The attendance reached a total of fifteen hundred from the first year they were opened. By the beginning of the second year, the enrollment had nearly doubled, but at the end of ten years more, when the same schools had become a part of the State system, both the enrollment and the attendance revealed a decline in number. Petersburg could, before the State system went into effect, correctly boast that it had been the first town to build and dedicate a large school-house for the promotion of free instruction under the new regime.

The inauguration of free schools, independent of charity, did not take place in Richmond until four years had gone by after the close of the war. Even then, they were compelled to rely to some extent on the use of funds advanced by the Peabody Board of Trustees and the Freedmen's Bureau. One year later, the city appropriated a sufficient sum for their support, and appointed a superintendent to direct and control their operation. A large amount was, at the same time, reserved for the erection of school buildings. Only two years after the city system was merged in the State system, its courses were divided into grades running from the primary school to the high school. In the high school, the city possessed an advanced curriculum of studies which was not to be duplicated in the rural districts until many years had passed. So good were the public schools of Richmond, that, from the beginning, they were patronized by many parents enjoying the highest social position. It was estimated that not less than two-thirds of the entire enrollment of children of the right age in the city were in daily attendance upon the sessions of the public schools.

Between 1870-71 and 1906, the number of school-houses increased from seventy-three to two hundred and thirty-six; the number of teachers from seventy-three to two hundred and thirty-two; and the enrollment from about three thousand to nearly twelve thousand.

As early as 1871, a large sum was appropriated by the City of Lynchburg for the erection of public school buildings and for the payment of current expenses of administration. Within a few years, several high schools were set up, and the entire system of studies was gradually broadened under the direction and supervision of E. C. Glass, who still occupies the position of superintendent after over half a century has elapsed since his first election. The full play of his wisdom and experience has not been confined to the schools of his own city, but has shed its fruitful influence upon the operations of the State system at large. To no one connected with that system can be attributed a more useful work in the training of teachers than to this noble and venerable figure in the contemporary history of public education in his native State.

It was not until 1885 that Fredricksburg adopted a distinct system of city schools, independent of any adjacent rural district, like Richmond, Norfolk, Lynchburg, and Petersburg. Its first high school does not seem to have been inaugurated until 1885. Staunton followed the example of its sister cities at an earlier date. In 1873, it too became a unit for school administration. It already possessed a public school system when the State system was launched in 1871. Seven years afterwards, it introduced a complete system of graded schools modeled on the plan which had been adopted in Richmond. During some time, the instruction in its colored schools was given by the white race, but, subsequently, their places were taken by colored teachers.

At first, the Cities of Williamsburg, Danville, and Winchester shared the system of public schools with the respective rural districts in which they were situated; but this was accompanied by so many inconveniences that, finally, these towns were erected into separate units, after the pattern of the large cities. This was also the history of Portsmouth. The three important centers of population which had sprung up in more recent years; namely, Roanoke, Bristol, and Newport News, adopted an independent organization of their school system from the threshold of their first incorporation.

With the opening of the new century, the greater energy and alertness, and the wider outlook and more practical intelligence, which were revealing themselves so plainly in the industrial development of Virginia, also became equally perceptible in the province of education. There had been an impression from the beginning that it was through public education chiefly that the rehabilitation of the different communities of the State, especially the rural, was to be sought. The advance of the system of public schools had reached such a point before the end of the first ten years after 1900, that its acceleration assumed almost a double momentum within a comparatively short time. The Southern Educational Conference, first held in 1898, which embraced in its attendance some of the most prominent men residing in the South, was succeeded, year after year, by a similar assemblage, which produced a very stimulative and informative impression on the spirit of popular instruction. The educational propaganda which it spread abroad throughout the Southern States was soon duplicated by the work of the Southern Education Board.

14—Vol. 2

Under the general influence of these various agencies, a more fruitful day now dawned, which extended its beneficence to the remotest schoolhouse of Virginia. The minds of the people responded quickly to the possibilities of the new movement.

One of the most remarkable proofs of this growth in interest among the citizens as a whole was the existence of the Cooperative Education Association, which was organized in 1904. Its motto summed up in a general way the object which it had in view: "Every public school in Virginia must be made a community center where the people may unite for the improvement of their educational, social, moral, physical, civic, and economic interests." Its working aims were much more specific. It endeavored to assure for every child in the State public tuition for a period of nine months. This was at least one-third longer than the term which was actually enjoyed at this time. A second purpose was to encourage the erection of so many high schools that one would be accessible to every advanced pupil; a third, to improve the training of the teachers; a fourth, to introduce agricultural and industrial courses into the public school curriculum; a fourth, to increase the number of public school collections of books; and finally, a fifth, to establish a large number of traveling libraries.

But the scope of the Association's labors was not designed to be limited to the schools. A league was organized in every community with its work carefully assigned to numerous committees,—in addition to the one having supervision of the subject of education,—such as Health and Sanitation, Child Welfare, Roads and Streets, Agriculture, Civic and Home Department, Social and Recreation, Citizenship, Church and Character Building, Publicity, and Membership.

In 1905, the interest in the improvement of the public schools assumed such keenness that a campaign began that was only comparable in the intensity of its fervor to a religious revival. Preachers, editors, professors, and politicians joined their influence to advance the common cause. It is estimated that, in the course of this remarkable crusade, as many as one hundred meetings were held in the different counties; and that at least three hundred addresses by the foremost men of the State were delivered on these occasions in the aggregate. The deficiencies of the public school system were not minced in the smallest degree. The burning desire of all was to place that system on a new and far higher platform of usefulness.

It was in this prospective task that the Cooperative Education Association was destined to play so great a part; and that part was made more productive by the aid granted to the schools by the Southern Education Board and the then recently created General Education Board.

In this educational revival, which partook so largely, as we have said of the nature of a religious revival, there were among the many able and conspicuous promoters of the public school's expansion two men, Bruce R. Payne and Joseph D. Eggleston, chosen State Superintendent in 1906, who can be justly referred to as preeminent. Eggleston was the first to hold the office of Superintendent by popular election. He was, in the highest degree, vigorous, zealous, and sagacious in his administration of its duties. Indeed, it is not saying too much to assert of him that he was as distinguished for constructive force and vision as his most famous predecessor, William H. Ruffner,—a man in short of original power, with clear, definite, aggressive conceptions of the proper means to be used for the improvement of the schools under his charge.

When first elected, he found a central Board of Examiners in existence, and this he utilized in the management of the schools of the five divisions of the State. Under his guidance, its members were able to introduce a number of reforms, which, as we have already mentioned, had been long desired,—such as the establishment of additional summer schools; the erection of many new school-houses on improved models; the further consolidation of schools in thinly inhabited communities; the procurement of more regular conveyances for the children's use in

JOSEPH D. EGGLESTON

One of the most active Superintendents of
Public Instruction

going to or returning from school; and the acquisition of larger funds through local taxation with which to increase the salaries of the teachers.

A further step in this same direction was the passage, largely through the influence of the Superintendent and his associates, of a bill which appropriated fifty thousand dollars for the improvement of the school-houses and the further enlargement of the teachers' remuneration. A similar measure was the loan of considerable sums by the Literary Fund to the district board for the erection of school buildings. Under the Strode Bill, a subsidy of $25,000 was granted by the State for the benefit of the elementary graded schools. The generous action of the General Assembly, in making these appropriations, stimulated the different communities of the Commonwealth to emulate it by levying a higher rate of local taxes for the advancement of public education.

Another achievement of the Eggleston administration was the very successful promotion of the high school. Between 1905 and 1910, the number increased from fifty to three hundred and eighty-eight. The course in these schools extended, in some instances, to four years, and in none to less than two. There were many thousand pupils enrolled in them, under the instruction of eight hundred and thirty-seven teachers. The counties contributed three hundred and twenty-five thousand dollars to their support, and the State, one hundred and thirty-three thousand.

More important even than the establishment of so many high schools was the erection of a great normal school for women at Harrisonburg, of a similar school at Fredericksburg, and of a third school of the same kind at Radford. By this time, William and Mary College had fully demonstrated its usefulness as an institution for the pedagogic training of men.

Among numerous other achievements of Superintendent Eggleston's administration were the establishment and maintenance of normal training high schools and also agricultural high schools. A retirement fund was also set apart for the

teachers. The Superintendent was especially solicitous to raise
the sanitary and hygienic condition of the schools; and he was
equally earnest in demanding constant medical inspection for all
the pupils.

CHAPTER IV

PRODUCTS OF THE SOIL

In our description of the agricultural conditions that prevailed in Virginia before 1860, we pointed out the fact that more advanced methods of tillage were in use at that time than have been generally known or recorded. The purely agricultural region lying in the Eastern and Piedmont divisions of the State still suffered, however, from the effects of a system which had descended from the earliest settlement of the country. The extensive manner of culture had, from the start, been universal, since the chief crops were bulky staples, like maize, wheat and tobacco.

At first, tobacco had been practically the only crop. In the absence of artificial manures for its production, it had been necessary to possess as much virgin forest as the landowner was able to acquire. The clearance of new grounds was one of the most important annual operations of himself alone, if he was a small proprietor, or of his working force, if he was a large one. The new field was cultivated to exhaustion, and then abandoned, first to broomstraw and afterwards to pines. The tobacco crop, not only required minute and protracted attention, but also constant changes of ground, unless the old soil was persistently improved. In modern times, this fertility is obtained by manures. In an earlier age, it was assured by removal to a new surface. This was made possible even during the Federal Period by the abundance of land available for the hoe and the plough.

215

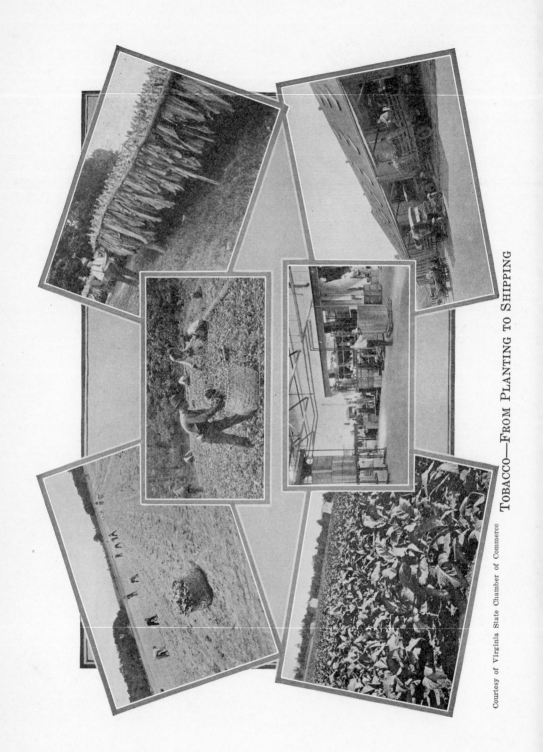

TOBACCO—FROM PLANTING TO SHIPPING

Courtesy of Virginia State Chamber of Commerce

The most conspicuous result of this system of culture was the impartment of an appearance of neglect to the face of the country. The old fields presented a ragged and deserted aspect, owing to the irrepressible tendency of the soil to put forth with remarkable quickness a thick covering of weeds and dwarfed shoots. Even the look of the woods was often unattractive, for they had, to a large extent, been gashed by the need of fuel for the tobacco barns. A traveller, passing through the counties east of the Piedmont region, would have formed a very mixed impression of the country as a whole. First, he would traverse a number of neighborhoods distinguished by a very limited area of fertile land. Afterwards, he would reach a section that was composed, in largest part,—especially along the banks of the streams,—of a soil of excellent quality. But wherever he went, although he may not have been always aware of it from the road, there were farms and plantations which were cultivated with scientific care, and also with no small productive success.

It should be remembered that Virginia, even during the decade preceding the War of 1861-65, was almost entirely an agricultural state. It was, in fact, throughout, a community of planters and farmers. There was not to be found in the United States a body of citizens more devoted to their calling or better trained to carry it on efficiently than the highest class of land-owners of Virginia at that time. This can be said with accuracy, in spite of the inexact methods which were too often followed, and in spite also of the apparent extravagance in the use of the soil by abandoning so much of it, year after year, to nature. The most creditable of the landed estates were situated in the valleys of the principal streams.

Under the influence of capable supervision by highly educated masters, and through lessons handed down from the past, slaves were found every where who were fully informed about all the simpler processes of agriculture. There was also a great number of planters and farmers who tilled their lands with their own hands. Many of these men were very skilful in the use of their soil; but there was no point of superiority in the field possessed by them over the most experienced slaves. Slave labor, in fact, was quite as productive as free labor. It is true that there were sections of Virginia without many slaves,—like the Middle Valley of the Shenandoah River, for instance,—which presented a much more valuable and attractive appearance than the counties in Eastern and Southside Virginia, where there were many slaves; but this was due chiefly to the extraordinary fertility of the ground, which permitted of an intensive cultivation by the owners.

When the War of 1861-65 began, the condition of the State was one of great agricultural prosperity, although its aspect in many of its parts compared very unfavorably with the aspect of such countries as England, France, and Holland, and even with the aspect of Southern Pennsylvania and Middle New York. It was occupied by a population which relied upon the cultivation of the ground for their livelihood, and it contained a body of men who had become experts in the management of large or, small landed estates. It was tilled principally by thousands of slaves, who had been trained to be skilful in their handling of all the staple crops. Naturally enough, the devastation and disorganization caused by the war had a tendency to throw the whole system, which had prevailed in the state for two centuries and a half, out of gear. When the hostilities closed, the lands were still there; and in those sections which had escaped serious invasion like the Southside, the plantation buildings were yet standing.

It should be remembered that, when the new regime came in after Appomattox, the only property which the people as a whole still possessed was their farms and plantations. Here the older citizens had continued to reside while the conflict was in progress; and hither most of the soldiers of the disbanded army were compelled to return at once, as the only spots where they could be sure of an immediate subsistence. The impression that the former plantation system of Virginia went to ruin contemporaneously with the surrender of General Lee is remote from the truth. It maintained itself in a measure, in spite of the change in the system of labor, until the generation of youths who were living at the close of the war had grown to manhood. These found the life in the altered country too devoid of social and pecuniary advantages to tempt them to remain under the old ancestral roofs, where their parents were to linger until the end. It is true that many estates had passed from their original proprietors through forced sales for debt; but as all farm products were, during a decade at least, sold at a high price, there was less transfer of ownership at first than has been usually presumed.

There were many counties in the state,—more particularly in the remote sections of Southside Virginia, then the principal seat still of the black population,—where the freedmen, almost as a body, remained. Very many of the younger blacks wandered restlessly away in pursuit of novelty; but most of the elderly members of the race, accustomed, during a life-time, to their cabin-homes, were disposed to linger in their familiar localities. In consequence, there was not as great a wrench in passing to the wage system as might have been expected. In retaining so many individuals of this older generation, the counties so fortunate as to possess them were left in a situation to preserve substantially, for a considerable time, the economic status which they had occupied under the previous system. It followed that there were numerous farms and plantations in many parts even of the old slave-holding divisions which were cultivated as carefully and successfully, after the close of the war, as they had been before it began.

During many years, the change in these favored sections was a social one rather than an industrial one. If the surface of the country had an aspect of neglect to a large degree; if the proportion of wood and abandoned fields was greater than the proportion of cultivated ground; still there was no real difference between the appearance then and what it had been under the old system of labor. The radical alteration in the industrial status of the community really began with the emigration of the young white men between 1875 and 1885. This, to some extent, as we have stated, was hastened by the fall in agricultural prices, with the result of making hired negro labor less profitable.

One of the earliest and most significant indications of the impending radical revolution in the province of Virginian agriculture was the shrinking area of the individual farm and plantation. From the middle of the seventeenth century to the opening of the War of 1861-65, there had been a very perceptable tendency in the larger landed estates to increase in extent. This was due, before the introduction of artificial manures, to the need of virgin soil for the production of tobacco in perfection. Such soil could only be got at that date by widening the plantation boundaries, so as to take in hitherto untilled ground. Another motive was the advantage of possessing as much acreage in wood as possible in order to afford room for cattle to wander more freely in search of food. A third motive had its origin in the special social consideration enjoyed by the landowner whose estate spread out in thousands of acres about his mansion.

The abolition of slavery set forces in action which soon checked this tendency of landed estates to grow in size. In a few years, the former movement was reversed. In the first place, free labor was not as reliable for the heavy work of clearing new soil of timber as slave labor had been. The planter was now satisfied if he could retain the free labor which remained with him to cultivate the fields already open for tillage. Moreover, the profits of agriculture, after the first interval of high prices had passed, did not encourage the purchase of more land. In addition, the change in the conditions of the new social life radically modified the old pride in land-holding. The young men decided to leave the farms and plantations, instead of adopting, like their fathers, the pursuit of agriculture as a calling in life.

The next movement was natural enough. The large estates began to disintegrate by subdivision. This was hastened by the payment of private debts. Many of these had been brought over from the period that preceded the war, but the majority had been created or at least increased in the stress of the times which followed that event. It was further hastened by the augmented unreliability of negro labor as the older freedmen began to die off. It was still further hastened by the deaths of the elder landowners, which gave their sons who had emigrated the opportunity to divide and sell the land which they had inherited. How far the subdivision had gone by 1900 was revealed in the fact that negro free-holders had acquired title to 990,790 acres in a total area of 19,907,883 acres in the state. In other words, they had become the owners of every twentieth acre. Of the land which they had secured, 368,840 acres were situated in the thirty Tidewater counties; 570,278, in the forty-two counties of the middle division; and only 51,672 in the twenty-eight counties of the Great Valley. The average value of this land by the acre was only four dollars and twenty cents. The cheapness of that form of property during the years pre-ceeding 1900 explains the negroes' ability to secure so large an area.

The farms purchased by small white landowners, who had increased their holdings very materially when the large estates came into the market, had made a further curtailment in the original groups of large landed properties.

Virginia, by 1900, was ripe for the introduction of a more generally intensive system of culture than had prevailed at the beginning of the new era. By that time, there had arisen a stronger disposition than had existed under the old regime for the state to participate directly in the advancement of agri-culture. Before we come to describe the various agencies that were used for this purpose, it will be necessary to mention the crops which were produced during this first stage in the modern development of that great interest.

Virginia, owing to the diversity of its configuration, soil, and climate, offered, at this time, as it still does, five important physical divisions: the Tidewater, the Midland, the Piedmont, the Valley, and the Appalachia. In Tidewater, the soil was composed of marl, clay and sand; in Middle Virginia, of a chocolate clay, red clay, and sandy loam; and in the Valley and Appalachia, of limestone. The climate varied sharply at long intervals in some parts of this area from great heat to great cold; but the average temperature for summer ranged from 83° to 90,° and for winter, from 20° to 44.6.° The mean annual temperature was 60.8° to 48.5.° Violent disturbances of the air were of rare occurrence.

The staple crops consisted of tobacco, maize, wheat, cotton and hay. Tobacco had, at one time, been produced in all the counties of the Tidewater and the Southside; and also in a considerable belt north of the James. It was now restricted chiefly to the counties of the Southside. Here too the cotton plant was cultivated. Maize and hay were produced in varying quantities in every division. The principal scene of wheat culture was in Piedmont and the Great Valley, although this crop too was found here and there in every part of the State. This was the case also with the grasses and legumes; but the grasses grew in the lushest abundance in the Valley and the Southwest. These two divisions, together with the Piedmont, were the ones in which the commercial fruit tree flourished with the most congeniality. Vegetables were produced in extraordinary profusion and variety in the light soils of the counties situated in the vicinity of Norfolk or on the Eastern Shore. The peanut was found in equal profusion in the counties lying between the James River and the Nottoway. The attention paid to the raising of livestock was most conspicuous in the counties of the Piedmont, the Valley, and the Southwest. The animals bred were sheep, hogs, horses, and cattle for the dairy and the abattoir.

PHILIP W. McKINNEY
Governor 1890-1894

It will throw additional light on this phase of our subject
if we select a typical county in each division of the state and
name its chief productions during the years that immediately
preceded 1900. The following is a representative list: Accomac, wheat, corn, oats, fruits and vegetables: Norfolk
County, corn, berries, potatoes, cotton and fruits; Dinwiddie,
tobacco, wheat, corn, oats, peanuts and hay; Charlotte, tobacco,
corn, oats, wheat, vegetables and fruits; Lunenburg, tobacco,
wheat, corn, fruits and cotton; Pittsylvania, tobacco, corn,
wheat, oats and grass; Pulaski, corn, grass and fruits; Augusta,
corn, wheat, oats and fruits; Clark, wheat, corn and fruits;
Loudoun, corn, wheat, grass and fruits; Essex, corn, wheat,
grass, and vegetables; Northumberland, corn, oats, wheat, grass,
fruits and potatoes; Powhatan, tobacco, wheat, corn, oats and
potatoes; Fluvanna, tobacco, wheat, corn, oats and grass; James
City, corn, oats, peanuts and apples; Middlesex, corn, wheat,
oats, fruits, and grass; and Hanover, corn, wheat, oats, and
fruits.

These counties, as a rule, were situated widely apart.   In
a general way, it may be said that the principal crops of Virginia
at this time were hay, corn, wheat, oats, tobacco, Irish potatoes,
sweet potatoes, peanuts, apples, peaches, pears, and grapes.
About fifteen million acres were under actual cultivation in
1899.   There were then about forty-eight thousand tenants,
white and black,—in addition to the owners of land and their
hired laborers,—employed in cultivating the soil.

There were three offshoots of this soil which showed after
1870 an extraordinary increase in volume.   The first of these
were fruits; the second, vegetables and berries known as trucks;
and the third, peanuts.   In the course of 1889, forty-six of the
hundred counties of the state were largely engaged in the production of fruits for sale in the markets of the United States
and Great Britain.   So superior was the quality of the several
varieties during the following year, that five prizes were
awarded Virginia for specimens displayed at the Paris Exhibi-

tion. Apples were now dispatched from the orchards of Albemarle and Frederick counties directly to Liverpool, Glasgow, and London. The success attending apple culture encouraged the extension of orchards to lands which previously had been reserved for the production of cereals, or allowed to lie untilled. The area in fruit had so much expanded by 1900 that we find in one orchard alone, situated in Southwest Virginia, forty-four thousand trees. This culture had, by this time, spread on a great scale to Patrick and other counties in that region. In 1902, there were growing in Virginia not less than eight million apple trees, two million peach, about two hundred and sixty thousand cherry, three hundred thousand pear, about one hundred and eighty thousand plum, and not less than eight hundred and thirty thousand grape vines. The largest orchards in the State, a few years later, were those belonging to the Diamond Orchard Company in Roanoke County, and to the Scott Company in Floyd.

It was estimated that, in a successful year, the return in income amounted to as much as five hundred dollars per acre in some of the orchards. In 1905, Frederick County disposed of two hundred thousand dollars worth of apples alone. A barrel of this fruit brought from one to two dollars under the tree. All the way from Rappahannock County to Nelson, and from Nelson to Bedford and Patrick, the same story of abundant proceeds from similar sales was told in the course of the same year.

The peach crop, though much smaller in volume, was proportionately as profitable. The experience of Mr. Ballard, of Crozet, was not a rare exception to the rule. He obtained twelve hundred dollars from the harvest of one acre and a half.

Larger in volume, more stable in price, and, perhaps, more profitable also, was the production of trucks in the circuit of counties that spread out around Norfolk, as far to the east as Accomac and Northampton, to the north as Isle of Wight, and to the west as Nansemond. These trucks consisted of the straw-

berry, the potato,—both Irish and sweet,—kale, cabbage,
spinach, asparagus, tomatoes, radish, onions, and peas. The
two counties on the Eastern Shore were the scene of the most
abundant out-put of potatoes that was to be noted in the United
States at that time. The expansion in the area given up to the
production of all these varieties of vegetables in Virginia did
not really begin until 1870. The pioneers of the industry are
said to have been three market gardeners from New Jersey.
Before the close of the last decade of the century, the income derived from the sales of trucks had swelled to six million dollars.
As the close of another quarter of a century, the value of the
potato crop of Accomac and Northampton counties alone
amounted to thirteen millions of dollars. By the year 1909,
Virginia had become the most productive trucking region in the
whole country. The volume of its sales had now reached fifteen million dollars in value annually.

While this development of the trucking interests was in
progress, the area planted in peanuts, which embraced lands
in Dinwiddie, Surry, Isle of Wight, and the tier of counties
situated immediately westward, was steadily broadening every
year. This too was a comparatively new crop. The cultivation
of cotton also received a new impulse in the counties lying next
to the Carolina border. In variety of products, this part of
Virginia could justly claim priority. Passing through that
region, one saw in contiguous fields a respective growth of corn,
wheat, oats, tobacco, cotton, grass, vegetables, and fruits. The
soil was equally well adapted to each.

Another interest that began to expand more rapidly in importance by the eighth decade was livestock. The herds of cattle
had been very much reduced in number by the devastation of
the war. A few years afterwards, close attention was given to
the breeding of beef cattle and sheep in Southwest Virginia,
and also in the Valley, both of which sections enjoyed the
advantage of limestone pasturage. Milk, cheese, and butter
proved to be profitable articles for shipment to the cities. At

this time, an enormous amount of butter and cheese was imported into Virginia for consumption. The raising of cattle became in time such a large source of revenue in those parts of the state that were blessed with an abundance of grass that a successful effort was made to improve the numerous breeds. Those preferred were Jersey, Holstein, Durham, Alderney, and Ayrshire. Less attention was paid to the production of hogs, as their ownership was more precarious. Still the best porcine blood was represented in the herds that were in existence, such as Berkshire, Poland-China, Essex, and Chester. This was also the case with the sheep, which, as a rule, belonged to the Southdown, Shropshire, Cotswold and Merino varieties.

The three most important agencies employed by the state to advance the welfare of its agriculture, before the end of the Nineteenth Century, were the Board of Agriculture, the Commissioner of Agriculture, and the Agricultural and Mechanical College. The most successful of these was the Commissioner of Agriculture, who acted under the direct supervision of the General Board. One of the earliest incumbents of this office,—who was appointed at a time when the functions of the department were passing through their first stage of exercise,—was George W. Koiner, who continues to fill the position with a ripeness of information, a soundness of practical judgment, and a vigilant zeal, that reflect the highest distinction on his administration. His first employment was that of a farmer in one of the most fertile and productive counties of the state. This gave him his earliest insight into the needs of Virginian agriculture, which has been further deepened by the opportunities for observation which he has enjoyed during his long occupancy of his office.

In the year 1896,—and the same condition continues, as a rule,—the duties of the Commissionership were as follows: (1) the publication of a handbook of the agricultural advantages which the state had to offer; (2) the analysis of all the brands of fertilizer sold to its farmers and planters; (3) the preparation of voluminous tobacco statistics; (4) the special investigation of the best means of treating soils, improving the staple crops, increasing the prosperity of fruit-growing and trucking, and repressing the depredations of insects and other pests; (5) the holding of county institutes for the benefit of the farmers and planters of the surrounding region; (6) the distribution of healthy seed; and (7) the publication of bulletins relating to every phase of the agricultural interests.

Furthermore, the incumbent of the Commissionership was called upon to post widely weekly weather reports that gave warning of approaching droughts or storms. He also sought to augment the native population by means of immigration. At a later date, other functions were exercised by him. These were created by additional enactments of the General Assembly. Among the laws was the one that regulated the action of the commission merchants through whom the crops were sold; another required the distribution of anti-hog cholera serum; while another protected the wholesomeness of foods. This latter was accomplished by the inspection of samples in the laboratory of the Department. Seed too were subjected to the same analysis in the botany division.

The most constant side of the Commissioner's work related to fertilizers. As Virginia was an agricultural state, the volume of artificial manures which it called for, especially for such crops as tobacco and trucks, was huge in its proportions. Had the fertilizer companies been permitted to dump their output on the farms and plantations without check, the effect, through poor or fraudulent stuff, would have been disastrous. The cultivators of the land were protected by the rigid inspection of every ton of fertilizer that was offered for sale. It was estimated in 1900 that the farmers and planters of the state expended as much as four million dollars annually in the purchase of artificial manures. In 1910, it was six million. No appropriation was made by the General Assembly for the enforcement of the fertilizer law. The charge for analysis and inspection was borne by the sellers of the article. During this year, so large a sum as twenty-eight thousand dollars was collected from this source by the imposition of a tax of only fifteen cents on every ton sold.

MUNICIPAL MARKET, NORFOLK

In 1911-12, the General Assembly authorized the erection of a grinding plant to supply the farmers and planters with raw lime, to be paid for at a rate of only ten cents a ton in excess of the actual cost.

In 1902, a test farm was laid off in Charlotte County. The object of this farm was to use the most modern means of finding out the proper way of increasing the volume of production of the cereals, and also of grasses, tobacco, vegetables, and fruits. Among the fruits raised there, after its establishment, were numerous berries, and also several varieties of grapes.

One of the grains was sorghum; and among the vegetables were rare kinds introduced from foreign countries.

There were also several experiment stations organized during the same period. The most important of these was located at Norfolk, in order to promote the interests of the truckers residing in that part of Virginia. This was the only one at that time to be found in the United States. Its work was carried on in cooperation with the Federal Government, the Virginia Polytechnic Institute, and the Southern Produce Exchange. There were subsequently a second station in operation at Blacksburg; a third at Alta Vista; and a fourth, for a time, in Augusta County.

A great service was rendered to every branch of agricultural production in Virginia by the series of bulletins issued by the Department. These publications were sent to every farmer whose address could be obtained. The variety of their contents is revealed in the list for the year 1912. The subjects discussed in that list were Alfalfa, Value of Hog Cholera Serum, Hog Raising in Virginia, the Apple Orchard, Preparation of the Soil, Home Mixture of Fertilizers, Stock Raising in Virginia, Potato Growing in Virginia, and Poultry Raising in Virginia. In 1911 alone, a million copies of these bulletins were distributed without charge among the farmers and planters of the State. They were supplemented by institutes, which were held in different parts of the country. In 1892, there was one in session in the first, second, third, and ninth districts, respectively; and two in the sixth, seventh, and eighth, severally. The number varied from year to year, largely owing to the fact that their chief support was derived from local subscriptions. Their usefulness admitted of so little doubt that, in spite of this handicap, they steadily increased in importance. Equally informative were the agricultural fairs which were now held very generally in the State.

During the interval covered by this chapter, the size of the farms had been falling off. While this was going on, the average number of acres in the landed estates had declined from two hundred and forty-five in 1870 to one hundred and six in 1911. The number of farms had, by 1910, been increased by sixteen thousand, while their value had risen to six hundred and thirty million dollars. In 1900, this value was only one hundred and twenty-nine millions. In the interval between 1900 and 1908, the proceeds from the corn crop alone advanced from sixteen million and a quarter to thirty-five millions. At this time, the wages of negro laborers by the month with board was ten dollars and fifty cents; without board, they were fifteen dollars and a half.

CHAPTER V

PRODUCTS OF THE FOREST

Among the profuse and virgin natural resources of Virginia, when that region was explored by the voyagers of 1607, the noble forests then in existence adjacent to all the great rivers emptying into Chesapeake Bay, were the most remarkable feature of the aboriginal landscape. The chroniclers of the events that took place after the arrival of Captain Newport and his followers in those hitherto unploughed waters, record, with an enthusiasm shared by them all, the impression left on their minds by the vast array of towering trees that met their astonished eyes on either side of the swelling flood of the Powhatan; and Captain Smith, in his subsequent discoveries as far as the mouth of the Susquehannock, was equally struck with the thickness of the woods which overshadowed the shores of the Bay.

As the English settlements gradually reached out from Jamestown to the valleys of the Appomattox, Pamunkey, Pianketank, Rappahannock, Potomac, and Nansemond, the same magnificent growth of trees was found in all those interior areas; and when the wave of population passed the line of the falls in the rivers, and spread over the back region that extended all the way to the Blue Ridge, the forests were seen to be of the same imposing aspect. Perhaps, the custom of the Indians in destroying the underbrush and leaving considerable space between the trees, fostered the growth of the individual tree by giving it the benefit of that much more room for sunlight and air, and that much more freedom also for the expansion of its limbs. It was said of these forests that a man on horse-back could traverse their aisles at a gallop, without risk of running against a bole.

232

Apparently, the only openings in the woods along the banks
of the streams had been created by the Indians when clearing the
ground for their cornfields or for a convenient site for the wig-
wams of a new village.   Here and there, in the wide area of the
forests, extensive savannahs, overgrown with grasses, weeds,

Courtesy of Norfolk-Portsmouth Advisory Board

A TYPICAL STAND OF PINE TREES NEAR NORFOLK

and flowers, were discovered; and this was the case especially
in the uplands west of the falls.   The early trappers and hunters
saw in these natural meadows herds of buffalo and elk quietly
browsing on the succulent herbage.   The only broad area that
lay spread out unbroken by forests was the Valley of the Shenandoah.   The aspect of that beautiful garden was, at the date
of Spotswood's first sight of it from the crest of the Blue Ridge,
apparently as free from trees, except along the water courses,

as it is in our own time. The Valley was a magnificent preserve for the aboriginal animals which had been feeding on its pasturage during uncounted centuries. Originally cleared by the fire-brand of the Indians, it had been kept clear, like the prairies of the Far West, by the same destructive torch.

What were the principal species of tree that covered the region of Tidewater when the feet of the first explorers intruded into those immemorial shades? The most conspicuous along the more or less sandy coast, was the pine, which still grows there so prosperously, and which still scents the winds blowing out to sea. This tree spread, during a later age, over all the abandoned plantation fields.

In the aboriginal forests of this region, the walnut is said to have formed one-fourth of their remarkable growth. There were three varieties of it observed in the beginning. The oak formed a still larger part of these original woods. The trunks of many specimens were so enormous in girth and height that planks twenty yards in length were sometimes cut from them. A companion tree was the cypress, which sprang up like tall columns from the muck of every inland swamp. The ash was almost equally as common; and the mulberry, in many places, grew so thickly as to form a beautiful grove. The cedar was seen in stately groups here and there in the woods, in dark contrast in summer with the leaves of the oak, ash, and walnut. The sassafras in autumn created ruby patches in the deserted fields. The elm, the locust, the maple, the chestnut, the chinkapin, the cherry, the crabapple, the persimmon and the plum tree were all indigenous to the aboriginal soil. These numerous species are still to be seen almost everywhere in Virginia.

The forests observed by the first explorers were soon heavily depleted by the axes of the cultivators of the ground. In opening up the surface of the country to the hoe and plough, vast areas in woods were changed to tillable fields. What remained of the original forests was used without any real regard to their permanent preservation. But the destruction of trees was a form of waste that nature was quick to remedy, at least in a measure. The genial soil and the copious rains conspired in less than a generation to fill up every gap in the cut-over wood.

It is, perhaps, true that no forest that has succeeded an aboriginal forest was ever quite equal to the primeval growth; but there were, at the close of the War of 1861-65, a wide area in trees which differed little,—in aspect at least,—from the woods that had covered the whole land in the beginning. The peculiar system of agriculture which encouraged the creation of large plantations had been the means of preserving a few of the forests that had come down from the seventeenth century. The thinness of the population had cooperated in this preservation to such an extent that any one traversing the country was disposed to conclude that forests, and not open fields, predominated everywhere, except in the Valley of the Shenandoah, parts of Piedmont, and along the banks of the rivers threading the coastal plain.

It was not long after the close of the War of 1861-65 that the impoverishment of so many of the landowners led to the sale of the finer species of trees springing from their soil. There were soon in many sections of the state, especially in Tidewater, wide areas that had been denuded of the matured forest growth, leaving behind only the tangled debris of severed limbs and masses of luxuriant undergrowth. The demand for tillable ground was not sufficiently great to induce the conversion of these forlorn and unsightly stretches of skeleton woodland into cultivated fields of tobacco, corn, wheat, or cotton. They were simply abandoned to the subtle restorative processes of nature.

The investigations for the computation of the census for 1910 disclosed the fact that nearly sixty per cent. of Virginia's surface at that time was composed of woodland. This did not include the area given over to marsh or brush. Approximately, fourteen millions of acres were covered with trees that were of a size to be cut and used, or were in the way to a serviceable condition through the stages of natural growth. An additional

million acres could be easily converted into superior woodland by
transplantation, or by simply abandoning the soil to the forestation of time.

The course of this natural forestation was generally the same
in all the counties lying well east of Piedmont, both north and
south of the line of James River. A field that had been sufficiently long under tillage to be exhausted was allowed to lie
idle, with its last corn or tobacco rows still unobliterated. A
growth of broom-straw, by the end of the first or second year,
extended solidly, or in thick patches, over the face of the ground.
It was not long before delicate little pines began to peep here
and there through the heads of this tawny waving sedge. Several years more, and the pines had spread all over the ground in
a green mass, which threw so thick a shade that the last stalk of
broom-straw under their bows was stifled and ultimately disappeared. The pines grew taller, until they formed a stately
array of straight columns that raised the bushy compact foliage
of their tops to the open heavens. Through these tops, the
wind sighed in the noblest cadences of Nature's music.

Gradually, the pines began to die, leaving small gaps to allow
the penetration of the thin and struggling sunlight. Quickly a
hardwood sapling appeared here and there in these gaps; and in
time, this intruding growth spread itself from end to end of the
former abandoned field and, later on, pine forest. The last pine
tree, like the last stalk of broom-straw, vanished, and there remained a new grove of oak, poplar, and other indigenous hardwood trees. These would maintain themselves for a long period
before their acorns or scions would be called upon to fill any
gap that had been made by natural decay or by the strokes of
lightning. No foreign growth, however, would steal in to
smother these hardwoods. Only the axe or forest fire could
destroy their ranks permanently.

In spite of axe and plough, there are still wide areas of
woodland in Virginia, much of which has passed through the
several stages of reforestation just described. The most im-

portant areas are found, (1) along the slopes and in the close foothills of the Alleghany mountains facing the Great Valley; (2) on the middle plateau of the Piedmont division, in which we include the western counties of the Southside; and (3) all over the coastal plain, from the falls in the rivers to the margin of the Chesapeake Bay. Practically denuded of timber is the region lying in the eastern angle between the Blue Ridge and the Potomac River, and along the sides, both eastern and western, of the same chain of mountains as it approaches the Carolina border. Only those sections of wood which are situated in remote and obstructed spots have escaped the axe in a body.

The area of untouched aboriginal woodland is not thought to exceed five per cent of the entire extent of the Virginian forests. The remainder has either been deprived, to a measurable degree, of its finest species of trees, or been cut over thoroughly more than once, after renewal by natural growth.

Let us descend more to particulars. It was estimated previous to the World war that, in the region known distinctively as the Coastal Plain, not less than two-thirds of the surface was covered with timber of unequal size and value, owing to the fact that the original growth had, through the axe, given place to a secondary, if not to a tertiary, growth. The species of trees in this region ranged all the way from the loblolly pine and the several kinds of oak, to the gum, poplar, and hickory. In the marshy spots, the cypress and maple sprang up in abundance.

The middle plateau of Piedmont, like the Coastal Plain, is for two-thirds of its area covered with timber of varying importance. This timber has, in many places, sprung up on lands which had been stripped of the merchantable trees by the axe at least once, or had been exposed, at one time, to the devastation of forest fires. Only a small extent of ground remains in wood which has never been rifled. The species of tree most commonly seen in the forests still surviving in this section are the pine, the oak, the hickory, the poplar, the chestnut, the maple, and the gum.

Along the western and eastern slopes of the Blue Ridge, which, from their steepness, are inaccessible to the lumbermen in many places, a considerable amount of virgin timber is still to be found. Most of the surface, except on the crest of the chain, is covered with forest growth, although here and there it is stunted in size, owing to the occasional infertility of the soil. Extensive sections have been cut over or practically destroyed by forest fires. The species of trees that grow on these slopes are the chestnut,—which, however, in recent years, has been decimated by disease,—the oak, poplar, hickory, beech, maple, pine, and hemlock.

The Shenandoah Valley offers the greatest area of cleared ground to be seen in any of the divisions of the state. This is because the soil there is remarkable for its productiveness. Moreover, unlike the Piedmont, the Coastal Plain, and much of the Southwest, it was not overgrown with forest when it was first occupied by white settlers. In aboriginal times, it formed the open hunting-ground of the Indians; and such was its character when Spotswood gazed down from the top of the Blue Ridge on its beautiful landscapes. Doubtless then, as now, there were groves rising here and there, and patches of isolated timber in inaccessible spots; but these only served to accentuate the extent of the unshaded expanse of land.

The region of the Alleghanies still contains the largest quantity of virgin timber to be found in the State, as so much of its area is so rough and so precipitous that the removal of its forest growth to the degree observed elsewhere is impracticable. Here the principal species are oak, chestnut, poplar, maple, hickory, and beech. Pine and hemlock are to be observed only in small quantities.

In 1909, the Federal Forest Service valued the merchantable standing timber of Virginia at one hundred million dollars. It was estimated that, at this time, the quantity of this timber reached the enormous dimensions of thirty billion feet board measure of usable material. By the end of another decade, the value of the standing timber had risen to a figure as high as three hundred and ten million dollars. Of this vast store, about forty-three per cent. consisted of pine and other soft-woods, and the remainder, of oak, and other hardwoods. Pine and oak together made up about seventy per cent of the whole.

It was shown by the census of 1910 that, during the previous year, Virginia was in possession of a larger number of saw-mills than any other state in the Union. The average annual cut during the three intervals, 1915, 1916, and 1917, amounted to over three billion and a half feet board measure, valued at thirty-five million, three hundred and twenty-five thousand dollars. The different articles embraced in the list of what was made from this material consisted of lumber, laths, shingles, cordwood, veneer, slack staves, headings, cooperage, cross-ties, pulp wood, mining props, poles, and the like.

In 1919, it was estimated that the annual cut of standing timber out-ran the restoration of denuded lands, through natural growth, to the extent of sixty-two per cent. This disproportion was increased by the destruction caused by forest fires, and by the gross indifference, in the cutting, to the future of the trees too small for the axe. The depleted wood was left in no condition to heal its wounds in a normal manner, under the kindly influence of heat and rain.

About the middle of the second decade, the rank disregard, by landowner and lumberman together, of the community's interest in the preservation and proper use of the forests led to the first important legislative step for their protection. This was the creation of the office of state forester, and the appointment to it of Mr. Chapin Jones, who had acquired a ripe experience in that province of public service in a neighboring state. Mr. Jones, at the same time, was elected to the professorship of forestry at the University of Virginia.

An apparent lack of keen interest on the General Assembly's part in the duties of the new state forester was revealed by its failure at first to make an appropriation for the prosecution of his labors. The University assumed the cost of this undertaking, in the beginning, to the extent of five thousand dollars. But both in 1916 and 1918, the State set aside the sum of ten thousand dollars in order to defray the expenses of the new office. This amount was steadily increased, until, in 1926, it reached a figure slightly in excess of twenty thousand dollars. In the meanwhile, the University had assigned to the forester ground for the creation of a State Forest Nursery. He had also been employed at that seat of learning in the instruction of a class that was studying the various features of his specialty.

Under the influence chiefly of Mr. Jones, a more intelligent and conservative policy in handling the forests had, by the middle of the third decade, come into play. A forestry staff of five trained and experienced men had been appointed, and forest wardens had also been selected for all the counties in which a service for fire-control had been organized.

The special duties imposed by law on the State Forester were clearly defined in the Code of 1919. They consisted (1) of making a study of the most effective methods for the preservation of the forests; (2) of spreading, by reports, bulletins, lectures, and addresses, the latest information thus obtained; (3) of directing the measures that had been adopted for the prevention or control of forest-fires; (4) of assisting the owners of land in the utilization of their woods to the highest advantage; (5) of managing a State Forestry Nursery, and distributing the young trees for the purpose of reforestation; and (6) of investigating the effect of denudation of the forests upon the flow of water in the streams.

At different times, the state has considered it wise to purchase forests, or to accept the gift of them from private citizens interested in the conservation of wooded areas. It is the duty of the State Forester to oversee these reservations and protect them from devastation.

It will be perceived from this extended enumeration of his different functions, that the position occupied by the State

Forester is one requiring constant watchfulness, unremitting activity, and profound information. It will be pertinent now to mention some of the obstructions which have hampered him in carrying out the duties incident to his office. The foremost of these duties, especially in the beginning, has been the acquisition, by personal investigation, of a thorough knowledge of the actual condition of the forests in every part of the commonwealth. So far, this investigation has been limited to a small number of the counties. The reason for this fact has lain entirely in the meager appropriations granted by the General Assembly for the prosecution of the work, which can never serve its purpose, in the most effective manner, until it has extended over the whole surface of the state. A study was made in 1924 and 1925 of the forests of Surry and Brunswick counties by Alfred Akerman, the district forester for Southeastern Virginia. The reports which followed these detailed investigations begun by an expert indicate the advantages which would accrue, should the same careful observation be brought to bear on every forest area in the state. Additional studies had been made, by 1925-26, in the counties of Bland, Wise, Russell, Buchanan, Tazewell, Dickinson, Lee, Washington, Southampton, Nottoway, Chesterfield, Alexandria, and the Valley Coal Fields. The results of these investigations were described in special bulletins.

It was through such publications as these that the Forestry Department disseminated the information which had been collected about the different provinces of its work. These publications were supplemented by the administration reports of the State Forester. Among the various subjects covered by the contents of the bulletins and reports were (1) the Forest-Fire Laws of Virginia; (2) the Forest Warden's Manual; (3) Farm Forestry in Virginia; (4) the Forest Resources of Virginia; (5) Common Forest Trees of Virginia; (6) Trees for Reforestation in Virginia; (7) the White Cedar of the Dismal Swamp. The list is too long for more extended quotation.

But the communication of information was not limited to the diffusion of printed articles. Many owners of land applied in person, or by letter, for the special instruction which they wanted for the preservation or the restoration of particular areas of wood in their possession. These inquiries had no connection with valuations of standing timber or estimates of losses by fire. They were rather in the nature of consultations, in which expert advice was asked and given, under the influence of the general principle that, in helping the individual landowner to take proper care of his own forest, the state or district forester was conferring a benefit upon the community as a whole. Even the trouble of a personal inspection was cheerfully borne, and no compensation was required beyond the payment of the expenses incurred in making the visit. The calls of this kind have now become so numerous that the demand for additional district foresters has grown very urgent. In those cases in which the standing timber can be culled to advantage, and this surplus disposed of, information is imparted as to the right manner of selecting the trees to be cut down, and the most profitable market in which they can be sold.

Of the sixteen million acres to be found in the State which are covered with some form of forest growth, about five hundred thousand are embraced in the forest reservations of the Federal Government. For this area, the amplest protection against fire is created by the vigilance of its custodians. Any agency for warding off entirely this kind of destruction from the enormous extent of woods not enjoying the Federal guardianship could not now but be limited, owing to the heavy expense which would be entailed upon the State and the individual owners in providing successfully against it. It was estimated by the state forester, in his administrative report for the calendar years 1924 and 1925, that, during that period, not less than a million dollars' worth of timber was consumed in the conflagrations which had swept through the woods. To this was to be added the damage caused to the soil by the heat; the diminution in the number of wild animals and birds; and the retarding effect on the power of reproduction in the remaining plant life. It has been said that, if the prevention of forest fires could be made universal in the state, the productiveness of the woodland area would be doubled in a few years.

The nearest approach which has been made to a substantial curtailment of the loss by fire has been effected through the appropriation by different counties of an annual sum to be used, in conjunction with funds granted by the state and Federal Governments, for the remuneration of forest wardens. Not all the counties have taken advantage of this offer to cooperate, owing to the fact that the charges to be incurred would add appreciably to the existing burden of their local taxation. The force required embraces a chief forest warden, wardens for separate districts, and wardens also for separate smaller localities. Both the district and the locality wardens are under the control and the direction of the chief warden; and it is he who prosecutes all offenders against the laws for fire precautions. The principal guardians, however, are the district wardens, who are supposed to patrol, with vigilant eyes, the respective areas assigned to their care. They inspect the heating arrangements of the school-houses; they supervise the process of clearing for new grounds on a great scale by the partial use of fire, and they keep under strict observation the employment of fire about the precincts of saw-mills. The duties of the local forest wardens, on the other hand, cease as soon as a conflagration has been extinguished and its origin ascertained.

The volunteer system of fire prevention or suppression has proved to be successful only in those parts of the state where the land-holdings are contracted, and the population, in consequence, more or less concentrated. It was estimated that, during the years 1924 and 1925, about one-half of the surface in forest had been brought under the protection of wardens.

The work of fire prevention undertaken by the counties with the cooperation of the Federal and State Government has been effectively supplemented by the action of landowners and land-owning companies, whose interests were vitally involved in the success of these public agencies. Fire protective associations have been incorporated for large areas in wood. Towers have been built there on high points for the clearer observation of the surrounding forests; and watchmen have been stationed in these structures to send out an immediate warning, by the telephone, whenever the smoke from a fire is seen in the distance. Fire crews have been organized to give assistance so soon as a con-flagration is reported. During 1924 and 1925, about twenty-two hundred fires are calculated to have occurred. The following are recorded as the principal causes: lightning, railroad engines, lumbering, brushburning, camp-fires, smokers, and incendiaries. From twenty-six to twenty-nine per cent of the number could not be traced to their origin. The tangible dam-age ranged from two hundred and eighty-two thousand dollars to six hundred and twenty-four thousand. The indirect damage greatly added to these figures.

The present State Forester has not only energetically as-sisted in preventing the destruction of the existing forests, but, through the distribution of seedings to landowners at low prices, and to state institutions free of charge, he has already, to an important degree, contributed to the reforestation of areas which had been denuded of their original forest growth. These seedings have been obtained from the Forest Nursery situated near the State University.

The next great work of the department will be to supply the trees that will be needed for the ornamentation of the borders of the public highways. Already, many of these highways run through woods, but long stretches are still unshaded and una-dorned. The highways of France and other European countries reveal the beauty that can be created by such an addition.

CHAPTER VI

PRODUCTS OF THE MINE

In our description of the first settlement of Virginia, allusion was made to the fact that the hope of finding gold and silver in the virgin land over-sea, had, at the beginning, been the most powerful influence of all that had excited interest in the impending expedition for its exploration. When the voyagers, after landing on Jamestown Island, had completed the erection of a village and fort for shelter and protection, their minds were quickly turned to the possibility of discovering in the surrounding country the outcroppings of the precious metals. Nor were they disappointed so far as surface indications went. Wherever the earth was dug up with the spade, mineral substances were detected. So early was the prospecting of the soil for traces of metal undertaken, and so energetically was it pushed, that, when Newport set sail for England, he was able to take back with him a genuine, though, doubtless, a very small, nugget of gold, which had been picked up, probably, in the debris at the foot of the great falls in the Powhatan, where it had found lodgment, after being washed down from one of the veins brought to light in the next century in the region of the modern Buckingham County.

In addition to this nugget, Newport took into the hold of his vessel a mass of earth, which was intermixed with sparkling particles that bore every appearance of being gold ore, but which proved, on analysis, to be worthless dirt. The Company were not discouraged by this fact, but directed him, on going back to Virginia, to continue his search. There was, on his arrival at Jamestown a second time, a repetition of the original investiga-

245

tion. One chronicler of that day testified that "there was then
no talke, no hope, no work, but dig gold, wash gold, refine gold,
load gold." The quantity of promising dirt which Newport
again carried back to England exceeded the quantity which he
had transported thither on his first return voyage. The upshot
was the same. The spangles turned out to be entirely spurious.

At a later date, Lord Delaware, accompanied by experts,
explored the wild region situated west of the Falls, with a view
of gauging its resources in gold and silver. Nor was he altogether unsuccessful in his purpose. The remembrance of this
fact lingered long enough to induce Governor Harvey, many
years afterwards, to send out an expedition along the same
path; but the arrival of winter cut its progress short. After
this region had been taken up by emigrants from the counties of
Tidewater, the deposits of gold here and there led to its systematic mining, although the veins were not extraordinarily fine in
quality or abundant in output.

One of the first articles noticed by the English on the persons
of the Indians was the copper plate. This metal, however, was
not obtained from local mines, but by trade with the tribes inhabiting the shores of the Great Lakes in the Northwest, in
which modern exploration have brought to light the presence of
the richest copper beds in the world.

The working of the iron deposits near the banks of the Powhatan began within a few years of the first settlement. These
deposits consisted apparently of bog-ore alone. A furnace was,
as we have stated in our first volume, actually erected at Falling
Creek in the modern Chesterfield County, but it was destroyed
during the Indian Massacre of 1622. It was not until 1714 that
a second furnace was built. This was situated at Germanna, in
Spotsylvania, and was the property of Governor Spotswood. In
1727, a second furnace was erected in the same county in the
vicinity of Fredericksburg; and about the same time, a third, at
Accokeek in Stafford. All these furnaces were supplied with
ores from mines in their respective neighborhoods.

Another metallic substance which was known by the first voyagers to exist in Virginia was antimony. A mine for the extraction of this article by the Indians was discovered near the banks of the Potomac. It was used by them for personal adornment. One of the first savages seen after the landing at Cape Henry had been sprinkled with the powder of this material. Its appearance led the voyagers to think that the stuff was really pulverized silver, and they took it as an indication of the existence of precious metals in the new Country. An alum spring was afterwards found in the course of the exploration of the Potomac River.

By the time that the War of 1861-65 began, the mineral wealth of Virginia had been partially gauged; but it was not until our own times that its real extent has become fully known, and an effort has been made to use it for utilitarian and commercial purposes. We propose now to give a sketch of the principal mineral substances which have, in our own era, been extracted from the soil of the State to increase the wealth of its people.

The systematic mining of gold in Virginia began in Orange County in 1832, and from this date until 1850, the value of the annual output amounted to a figure that averaged between thirty thousand and fifty thousand dollars. Afterwards, the quantity declined. The mining was resumed subsequently to the War of 1861-65, but the milling and reduction plants proved, as a rule, to be unprofitable, owing partly to the refractoriness of the ores, and partly to the inexpert handling of them. The principal deposits have been found in a belt that starts in Maryland and runs across the counties of Stafford, Fauquier, Culpeper, Orange, Spotsylvania, Louisa, Fluvanna, Goochland and Buckingham. This belt, in its narrowest part, does not exceed fifteen miles; and in its widest, twenty-five. In length, it extends to about two hundred miles. Traces of gold have been discovered in scattered counties lying outside of this belt, such as Appomattox, Prince Edward, Charlotte, Halifax, and Franklin. The deposits in these five counties, except Halifax, have been too meager and tough to justify any attempt at their reduction. In Montgomery, Floyd, and Grayson Counties, which lie on the western slope of the Blue Ridge and well isolated from the belt, recourse has been had to sluicing and panning to separate the particles of gold from the dirt. Some of the mines in the main belt are still worked to some advantage to their owners.

The history of the output of the Franklin mine in Fauquier, one of a group of five, is fairly representative. From ten samples of the ore from this mine, the assay has revealed a value of twenty-four dollars and twenty-five cents a ton. The ore in some of the remaining groups is of a higher quality. The assay has shown a value in at least one of these running up to about ninety dollars a ton. In Stafford, five mines were worked at one time. One of these, the Rappahannock, was two hundred feet in depth. From another, the Rattlesnake, a large number of pure nuggets were formerly extracted. The ores from the mines in Culpeper, Spotsylvania, Orange, and Louisa Counties ranged from four dollars to forty in average value by the ton. The return from some of the concentrated ores ran as high as two hundred dollars. In one mine situated in Spotsylvania County, there was found, at a depth of twenty-eight feet, a pocket which yielded one hundred and sixty thousand dollars from a space only three feet square. The Tellurium Mine, which lay partly in Goochland and partly in Fluvanna, is said to have benefited its owners to the extent of one million dollars. From the Fisher Mine in the same locality, as much as three hundred dollars per ton has been obtained; and from the Hughes, in Fluvanna, as much as seven hundred and eleven dollars; but the average return has not exceeded thirteen dollars. The ores mined in Buckingham have shown the same average value as those produced in the counties previously mentioned. The principal mines here number as many as thirteen.

It is estimated that the value of the output of gold and silver from the beds in Virginia amounted, in the interval between

CHARLES T. O'FERRALL
Governor 1894-1898

1799 and 1879, to the sum of three million dollars; between 1879 and 1892, to about sixty-seven thousand; and between 1892 and 1905, to about eighty-two thousand.

A number of minerals distinguished for beauty and durability, or for beauty and rarity, have been extracted from the Virginian soil. The county which has been most productive in such substances has been Amelia, because peculiarly rich in mica deposits, the principal bed of these precious mineral forms. The largest diamond that had been found in the United States before the year 1884 was discovered in Chesterfield by a laborer engaged in turning up the earth. This diamond was valued at four thousand dollars, although slightly injured by the presence of a flaw, which diminished its power of refraction. In color, it was of a faint greenish whiteness. Garnets, similar in luster and tint to the famous hyacinth gem of Ceylon, have been taken from the Amelia mica beds. These beds have also been productive of pure white beryls. A deposit of amethyst has been discovered in Amherst County. This occupies the space of only a few acres. Chlorophane has been found in Amelia, a substance that possesses the remarkable property of emitting a phosphorescent light when heated by the warmth of the hand. Other precious mineral substances of the same general nature lying in Virginian soil are cyanite, feldspar, staurolite and allanite.

Copper was mined methodically in Virginia as early as the year 1730, when it is reported that as much as an hundred weight of ore was, on a single occasion, sent to a Northern furnace, to be smelted. Subsequently, beds fairly rich in this mineral were opened in Mecklenburg County, but only to be abandoned after a partial working. The principal existing deposits are situated in the Virgilina district in Halifax County; near Keysville in Charlotte County; near Front Royal, in the Valley; southward, in the neighboring counties on both sides of the Blue Ridge; and along the plateau in Southwest Virginia formed by the counties of Floyd, Carroll, and Grayson.

The prospecting in the Virgilina field has been extended over many thousand feet, and the shafts have been sunk to the depth of several hundred. The veins run to a width of four feet or more. One of the mines, the High Hill, had produced up to March, 1904, about two hundred and thirteen thousand pounds of refined copper. In addition, about twenty-five hundred pounds of refined silver had been obtained from the same ores. The deposits of copper in Charlotte, Buckingham, and Albemarle Counties, have not turned out to be so profitable as to justify their persistent development. A more energetic attempt has been made to utilize the deposits in the counties adjacent to Front Royal by means of shafts, drifts, and small openings. The native ores in these localities have been discovered in combination with numerous other mineral substances.

A more productive region has been the Gossan lead that lies on the Floyd, Carroll, and Grayson plateau to a length of eighteen miles. Before the War of 1861-65, this region supplied the market with a large quantity of copper. The metal ran as high as one-fourth of each ton of ore. The depth of the vein underground rarely sank as low as sixty feet, while its width sometimes extended to one hundred. Several other counties, more especially Loudoun, Culpeper, and Orange, contain traces of copper in the red sandstones and shales, which enter so largely into their geological formation. The grade has proved to be so inferior that it has not permitted exploitation to any advantage.

The earliest lead mines in Virginia to be worked were those situated on the New River, in the Southwest. These were opened before the Revolution. The presence of zinc in the neighborhood was not immediately discovered. During the War of 1861-65, its existence in the same locality was first noted, but it was not systematically developed until the exploitation of the Bertha Mine began. The quality of the zinc was found to be of such purity that there arose a keen general demand for it. This caused the erection of a smelting plant at Pulaski. Lead and zinc have been detected also in Albemarle County at Faber. It

JAMES HOGE TYLER
Governor 1898-1902

was from the mines in this county, and in the counties of Southwest Virginia, that the material for the manufacture of the bullets used by the Confederate soldiers was obtained.

As we have seen, the mining of iron ore was the first undertaking of that character to occur in colonial Virginia. More or less fitfully, this industry was pursued throughout the eighteenth century, and also through the first half of the nineteenth. The principal centre of the interest lay in the region watered by the mountain tributaries of the James River, where a large number of isolated furnaces were in operation. At first, the products of these furnaces were exported by means of that stream; but the difficulty and expense of that manner of conveyance were influential in curtailing the production of pig-iron, and in consequence, the extraction of the raw ore. After railroads had penetrated that part of the State, not only were the number of local furnaces very much increased, but the quantity of ore shipped away was enormously augmented. This addition came largely from the mines of Cripple Creek and Craig County, which had now a free connection with the world at large through branches of the Norfolk and Western and the Chesapeake and Ohio Railways. These roads have been duplicated in other directions, with the result of opening up a still wider area of country productive in iron ore.

The principal ores mined have been the red hematite, the brown hematite, the magnitite, and the carbonite. The presence of these ores is not confined to the Alleghany Mountains. They extend also to the Great Valley, the Blue Ridge, and the Northwestern division of the Piedmont Plateau. This Piedmont area consists of a narrow strip, about one hundred and fifty miles in length, running down to the North Carolina boundary, and lying from fifteen to thirty miles away from the parallel line of the Blue Ridge. The Blue Ridge area is also a narrow strip, with a length of about one hundred and fifty miles. The third area extends along the Floyd—Carroll—Grayson plateau for a distance of sixty miles. It too is contracted in its width. The largest amount of ore is taken out of the Oriskany measures. Next in importance, come the deposits situated in the region of New River and Cripple Creek. At one time, the deposits in the environment of the Great North Mountain were also a source of profit.

About 1910, there were seventy-nine mines and twenty-seven furnaces in operation in Virginia. The means adopted for working them included the steam shovel, pick and shovel, milling, sluicing, and hydraulicing. The output in 1918 was valued at a sum exceeding ten million dollars; and about nine million was at this time, invested in the industry.

The first prospecting for tin beneath the soil of the State occurred previous to 1860. The scene of the earliest exploitation of that mineral lay in Rockbridge County. The existence of deposits in that county had been long known, but nothing was done until 1883 to make commercial use of them. The first shaft was sunk in the month of November during that year. The Irish Creek area, which spread over a space of twelve square miles, was found to be the richest in this ore. The proportion of tin to the ton, however, was not high, for it amounted, when assayed, to a figure that only reached five per cent of the whole. In some cases, the average sank to three and a quarter per cent. The geological and mineralogical conditions of the Rockbridge area were similar to those of the county of Cornwall in England. The Virginian deposits, in their situation, length, thickness, and purity, bear a favorable comparison with the celebrated mines in that part of the British Islands.

The presence of nickel beneath the surface of the Floyd—Carroll—Grayson plateau, and also in Amherst County in the vicinity of Lynchburg, was early detected, but little advantage has been taken of its existence there. Cobalt has been found intermixed with it in small proportions. Traces of nickel have also been discovered beneath the soil of Fauquier County. The highest average of pure metal have, as shown by the assays, been from three to four per cent, with a fraction of one per cent in copper, and a still smaller proportion in cobalt. The principal use to which this nickel has been put in manufacture has been in the production of nickel steel for heavy forgings, marine engines, wire cables, and electrical apparatus.

One of the most widely distributed metallic substances in Virginia is the Pyrite; but it is not often sufficiently concentrated in quantity to be worked with a profit. It is only in Carroll, Louisa and Prince William Counties that the deposits have proved to be commercially valuable. The mines in these localities supply about fifty per cent of the output from the whole of the United States. They are the largest in extent to be found in the entire country.

Prospecting for baryte began in Prince William County as early as 1845. Later this mineral was mined in Campbell, Pittsylvania and Smyth; and at a subsequent date still, in Tazewell and Russell. Baryte, like pyrite, is to be found in other parts of the State, but it is generally in association with limestone, in which it is deposited in pockets or in loose lumps and nodules. In mining this ore, the shaft is sometimes sunk to the depth of one hundred and sixty feet. Again, the ore is often reached a few feet below the surface indications of its presence. Occasionally, blasting has to be employed to break down the limestone in contact with it. Baryte is now used as a pigment in itself, and not, as formerly, as an adulterant of white lead. It is also used to increase the weight of certain varieties of cloth and paper.

The phosphates mined in Virginia in many places appear in three forms: (1) phosphatic marls, so commonly employed as a fertilizer and in the manufacture of cement and quick lime; (2) phosphatic rock; and (3) pebble phosphate. Nitrates are found only in the caves of the Shenandoah Valley, but in sufficient quantity there, though mingled with dirt from the accumulations of ages, to serve numerous purposes. The nitre in these deposits has fallen from the roofs of the caverns in which it is imbedded. Quartz is discovered in considerable masses,—in association with mica and feldspar,—in Amelia County, and also in the counties of Fairfax, Roanoke, and Franklin. It is used in the manufacture of cheap jewelry, and also of lenses. Diamonaceous earth, another form of silica existing in Virginia, has been turned to account by converting it into polishing powders and scouring

Courtesy of The Norfolk-Portsmouth Advertising Board

VIRGINIA PORTLAND CEMENT COMPANY

soaps. Corundum, emery, ocher, ilmenite, rutile, and other kinds of exides have been mined, to serve, like quartz, which is of the same family, for the special purposes to which they are adapted.

The oxides of manganese are the most important of all. The first mining of this ore occurred, in 1857, in the Shenandoah Valley in the vicinity of Waynesboro. It was subsequently extracted from the deposits discovered in Amherst County. Since that date, more manganese ore has been obtained in Virginia than in any other State of the Union. Virginia, in fact, contains the largest number of manganese mines that have been systematically worked in this country. The deposits have been found in every one of the three divisions: Tidewater, Piedmont, and Valley. From the Valley, the greater part of the total output has been taken. The ore is detected there in pockets, or in the form of nodules, and ranges in thickness from a few feet to an hundred or more. The work of the miners in securing the ore has been in open pits or cuts, or in shafts and tunnels. In manufacture, the manganese, in association with compounds, is used in the case of certain alloys, oxidizers, and coloring materials. It is also employed as flux in the smelting of silver ores, in chemical production, and in the manufacture of glass; but especially in the manufacture of iron and steel. It is particularly effective in the manufacture of chilled cast-iron car wheels.

Virginia has been endowed by nature with a great variety of valuable clays. It has been said that, in 1904, the value of the clays used in the United States was greater than that of the entire output of the gold, silver, copper, and petroleum, obtained from beneath the soil; and that it was only surpassed by the value of the output of coal and iron. The clays of Virginia have been designated the residual and the sedimentary. The residual have come from the decay of the rocks; and the sedimentary, from the deposits from large bodies of water. The residual is generally used in the manufacture of brick and tile for drains. One variety, however, has been found in parts of Piedmont so free from all trace of iron that it has proved to be specially adapted to the manufacture of white-ware of different kinds. This variety is the well-known kaolin. Sedimentary clays exist in the Tidewater region, and also in the Great Valley, which is supposed to have been at one time the site of a wide lake. The clays of this nature are converted into brick. The most profitable beds lie in the vicinity of Alexandria, the product of which, after passing through the kiln find a constant market in Washington City. Beds have also been discovered in the neighborhood of Fredericksburg, and also near the towns of Wilmont, Layton, and Milford, which are situated in the same section of country. The sedimentary clays discovered near Richmond are second only to those which lie exposed on the surface in the outskirts of Alexandria, but they too are only suitable for the manufacture of common brick. Other beds are found near Petersburg, Bermuda Hundred, Norfolk, and Suffolk.

Virginia has, from an early period, been known to be unusually rich in beds of granite adapted to the construction of every kind of building. The deposits of this stone extend throughout the region bounded on the west by the Blue Ridge, and on the east, by the Coastal Plain. The counties in which the largest quantity of granite has been observed are Dinwiddie, Chesterfield, Henrico and Spotsylvania. The quarries in the vicinity of Richmond, Petersburg, and Fredericksburg are among the most valuable that have been worked in the United States. The beds near Richmond cover the widest area so occupied in Virginia. From their output, the magnificent building of the State, War, and Navy Department in Washington has been constructed.

Slate has been discovered in large quantities in numerous localities in Virginia. The most important deposits are situated in the counties of Buckingham, Albemarle, Amherst, and Fauquier. The Arvonia belt in Buckingham is the most valuable of them all. Professor William B. Rogers pronounced the slate obtainable from this belt to be, "in texture, density, and capacity of resisting atmospheric agents, unexcelled by any similar material in any part of the world." The same belt crops out also on the northside of James River, in Fluvanna County. In that section, its width does not exceed one mile and a fifth. South of the river, the width contracts to one mile. Some of the quarries are remarkable for the extent of their area. The average quarry spreads out five hundred feet along the cleavage, three hundred feet from edge to edge; and it is also three hundred and fifty feet in depth. The product of all is slightly graphitic and magnetic in quality. A slate of dark green and red colors has been obtained from a quarry at Esmont, in Albemarle County. Another kind, of a dark gray tint, has been

Courtesy of Virginia State Chamber of Commerce

CHALK MINES NEAR COLD SPRINGS

found in the Fauquier belt. This is also the color of the slate quarried in Prince William and Stafford Counties.

Sandstone has been found in each of the principal divisions of the State. From the quarries on Acquia Creek, there were extracted the blocks that were used in the construction of the first Federal buildings erected in Washington City. Among these buildings were the White House, the central part of the old Capitol, and the older parts of the Treasury and Patent

Offices. From the quarries of Albemarle, material was obtained for the making of the locks and culverts of the James River and Kanawha Canal. Much of this material is now used in a crushed state as a ballast for railway beds. What are known as Newark sandstones are found in seven or eight widely separated areas. But not many of the deposits of this stone have been opened. The Potsdam sandstones are for the most part confined to the western slope of the Blue Ridge. They are especially suitable for the composition of cement. The Oriskany sandstones in Bath and Highland Counties, are as a rule, too friable for use in building.

Soapstone has been discovered in the Piedmont region, and it has been quarried there in large quantities. The principal sites of the beds lie in the Counties of Fluvanna, Buckingham, Albemarle, Nelson, Campbell, and Franklin, on the one side, and Louisa, Fairfax, and Orange on the other. It is also found in the Southwest. But the most important deposits are situated near Green Mountain in Albemarle and Nelson. The chief use to which this material, so soft and greasy to the touch, is put is in the manufacture of wash or laundry tubs, electric switch boards, and insulators and laboratory sinks. It was formerly used for other purposes,—in the manufacture of slate pencils, for instance, and also of fire brick. The refuse is sometimes employed as a lubricant.

Limestone has been discovered in the three principal divisions of the State. Its most extensive beds, however, lie in the Valley. The limestone of the Coastal Plain is impure in quality, while that of the Piedmont is thought to be too crystalline. The variety found in Tidewater is designated as marl, which is very much used for the improvement of agricultural lands. In association with limestone deposits are discovered several kinds of marble, which are known by their color. This color is either dun, mottled, blue, gray, white, red, or black. They are nicely adapted to purposes of ornament as well as to solid building.

The first coal beds to be opened in the United States were those situated near Richmond. This occurred in 1750. In 1822, over fifty thousand short tons of this material were obtained from these deposits. It was not until 1882 that the production began to be pushed on a very large scale. By that time, the Pocahontas district had been made accessible by the construction of the Norfolk and Western Railway. The building of the Clinch Valley branch enlarged the area for the use of the pick. This latter field was situated in Wise County.

The coal areas of Virginia are found in the Piedmont and Mountain regions. The Piedmont province embraces the Richmond Coal basin, which extends to Amelia County on the west. The Mountain embraces the areas of Frederick, Augusta, Botetourt, Pulaski, and Wythe Counties; and also Tazewell, Russell, Scott, Buchanan, Wise and Lee further down. Wise and Tazewell are the largest producers. Along with the development of more coal-fields has gone the production of coke in enormous quantities. It is estimated that the coal beds of Virginia contained originally twenty-two billion short tons. Up to the close of the year 1908, sixty-one and one-half million short tons had been taken out of the mines of the State. In 1919, the output amounted to nine million, one hundred and eleven thousand short tons. The value of the product was estimated at eleven and a half million dollars.

CHAPTER VII

PRODUCTS OF THE SEA

One of the most striking features of aboriginal Virginia in the eyes of its earliest English explorers was the presence of so many streams wherever they penetrated. They compared the number to the veins in the human body. Between every two hills, there flowed a brook; and at every turn in the estuaries, there entered a creek as large at its mouth as a small bay, but tapering back into the country until it assumed the proportions of a mere rivulet. At not much distance apart, along the western shore of the Chesapeake, there debouched the waters of four mighty rivers. Indeed, it would be difficult to find elsewhere on the face of the globe, within the same area, such noble floods as the Powhatan, the York, the Rappahannock, and the Potomac; and their tributaries, like the Nansemond, the Appomattox, the Chickahominy, the Mattapony, the Pamunkey, and the Shenandoah, were all rivers of an imposing size where they entered the main streams.

Here was ample room for the movements of vast swarms of fish, either seeking food or searching for spots where they could deposit their eggs. So dense were the schools of them that it was said by the first voyagers that the Indians were in the habit of killing thousands, during the breeding season, in the brooks and creeks, with the strokes of a stout stick; and at a later period, it was also asserted that, in the spring, a horse fording a stream, could not avoid treading on the fish, so thickly did they mingle with the water. In the upper reaches of the Chesapeake, Smith and his companions supplied themselves with a meal by scooping up with a frying-pan as many fish as they needed from the schools, which, everywhere, were breaking the surface of the water into sparkling silver.

There was a countless number, respectively, of shad, sturgeon, herring, and rock. In addition, were found grampus, porpoise, sole, butt, mullet, salmon, seal, roach, plaice, eel, lamprey, cat, perch, tailor, sun, bass chub, flounder, whiting, flat-back,

BOATS FOR FISHING AT OCEAN VIEW

One of Norfolk's Ocean Resorts

jack, carp, breme, and stingray. In places, the navigation of the rivers was obstructed by banks of oyster shells, which had been accumulating in the course of ages. The other shell-fish vied with the oysters in abundance.

When it is recalled that the natural store of fish had, during thousands of years, been exposed only to the Indian spear, the sea-hawk's talons, and the teeth of their own fiercer varieties, it will be perceived that there was no real strangeness in the existence of such great swarms of them at that time. It was not until the country had been fully occupied by the English that these swarms began perceptibly to diminish. In the latter part of the seventeenth century, the General Assembly actually felt compelled to pass a law for the protection of these inhabitants of the river and sea depths; and that law has, in one form or another, been constantly reenacted down to our own times. Without it, there was danger,—and still is,—that some valuable species of fish would be almost entirely destroyed; just, as, long ago, the elk and buffalo disappeared from the verdant meadows of the Rappahannock and Roanoke, and the passenger pigeon, from the forests of Piedmont and the Coastal Plain.

It was not until the War of 1861-65 had closed, bringing in a juster conception of the necessity of husbanding the natural resources of the State, that a really systematic attempt was made to find out and enforce the best means for halting their gradual decay or open destruction. The first practical step taken relative to the fishery interest of Virginia was the appointment, in 1874-75, of a commission to protect and enlarge that interest in accord with thoroughly modern methods. At one time, fish of the most valuable varieties, like shad, rock, and sturgeon, had run freely up to the headwaters of the main streams in order to deposit their spawn. They were caught in season all along the James, the Appomattox, the Rappahannock, and the Potomac, beyond the great falls in those streams, by the riparian owners; and formed an enormous addition to the food resources of the adjacent plantations. The building of the canal parallel to the banks of the James made large dams necessary to supply the water for the new highway. Dams were also erected in the other rivers for mills or to improve their navigation. Gradually, the larger fish found it impossible to pass these obstructions, and the old abundance of them in the upper tributaries ceased.

Effective, but in a less degree, in producing a decline in the inland supply, were the pound-nets planted in the waters near the mouths of the great rivers, for these prevented the proper proportion of the fish from moving on to their spawning beds above.

One of the earliest acts of the commissioners was to urge the passage of a law that would compel the erection of fish-stairs at every important dam in the State; and an equally earnest effort was made by them to reduce the closeness of the meshes of the nets in the pounds.

Another measure for the preservation of fish, by their larger propagation in the future, was the erection of hatcheries to supply the eggs needed for restocking the streams. These had been authorized by the General Assembly. One of the first, if not the first, of these hatcheries was established at Lexington, under the supervision of Marshall McDonald, a name of great distinction in the history of the Virginian fisheries. A second hatchery was established at Berkeley. From these centers, the young fish were taken and distributed in the principal rivers. In 1875-76, all such rivers in eastern Virginia were stocked with black bass, and some also with brook trout. During the same year, over three hundred thousand embryo salmon from California were obtained for similar dispersal, after first passing through the hatchery at Lexington.

By 1878, these measures, looking to propagation, had begun to show a more or less successful result. An increase in the number of brook trout, shad, black bass, and salmon had become clearly perceptible, although dams in the Potomac, and in the Roanoke at Weldon, still blocked the upward penetration of those great streams, and their vast network of tributaries. Again, the commissioners earnestly demanded the removal of all such obstructions everywhere, as the only hope of restoring the inland fisheries to the condition which had prevailed one hundred years before. The failure to remove these obstructions would render the continued planting of young fish a practically useless act in the long run, as they would find their way to the sea and be unable to return.

Marshall McDonald, in 1878, was appointed the State Commissioner, and the work of propagation and protection was continued with increased skill and energy. In the course of the fol-

lowing year, seventy-two thousand young bass were released in
the streams of Augusta, Rockingham, Prince Edward, and
Louisa Counties. The Rappahannock was soon stocked with
shad; and so was the Potomac. About one hundred and sixty
thousand fish of this variety were caught in Virginian waters
during the same year. A second instalment of salmon eggs,
procured from California, were also hatched at Lexington, and
about two hundred and seventy-six thousand salmon minnows
distributed in the James, Shennandoah, and Rappahannock. A
permanent hatchery was, in 1879, established in the latter
streams. In a few years, the young salmon from these breeding places disappeared; but the black bass became acclimatized
and remained.

Menhaden, at this time, were caught in purse-nets. The
season's harvest numbered as many as three million, which produced at least eight thousand gallons of oil and three hundred
tons of guano. Later, the number of tons produced rose as
high as ten thousand tons of guano, and over two hundred and
thirty-five thousand gallons of oil. About five hundred men and
eighty vessels were employed in the industry, while about one
hundred and eighteen million of fish were consumed in the different forms of manufacture.

Year after year, the streams continued to be supplied from
the hatcheries. In 1895, for instance, over six million and a
half Spanish mackerel were liberated in these waters. But complaint was now heard that, in spite of these measures to stimulate propagation, the supply of fish in the rivers had begun to
show a distinct tendency to shrink. The damage through the
pound was one of the causes of this depletion. It is said that,
in 1875, there was but one pound at the mouth of each of
the principal streams. In 1891, on the other hand, there were
nine hundred and sixteen in all. The pregnant fish found it
difficult to pass the meshes, and the spawning grounds up
stream, in consequence, were closed to a large proportion of the
migrants.

During the last years of the nineteenth century, the oyster had remained the most popular form of sea-food. It was estimated, in 1877, that four hundred square miles of tidal bottom suitable for the culture of this shell fish lay near the shores of the estuaries of the James, Rappahannock, Pianketank, and

Courtesy of Virginia State Chamber of Commerce

THE LARGEST OYSTER SHELL PILE IN THE WORLD

York, and also of Mobjack Bay. These beds were known as oyster rock. It was claimed that the Chesapeake Bay, which included the area just mentioned, had an advantage over the other parts of the United States in the breeding of the oyster, not only because of the character of its bottom, but also because, in that Bay, the saltiness of the sea-water was modified by the addition of fresh-water from the numerous debouching rivers to precisely the right degree of temperature for the prosperity of this shell-fish.

The annual value of the oyster catch rose from two million dollars in 1893 to three million and a quarter in 1900. In 1907, the value made a higher leap. In that year, the sales amounted to five million and a quarter dollars. To this income from oysters, there was to be added the proceeds from the sale of Spanish mackerel, blue-fish, sheepshead, porgie, spots, bonito, hog-fish, and mullet. At this time, about fifteen hundred vessels of several kinds were engaged in garnering the harvest of the Virginian fisheries.

A Board of Fisheries was created by the General Assembly in 1898; and ten years afterwards, a Commission of Fisheries was appointed, with the special view of arresting the depletion of the natural rock, then in such conspicuous progress. A system of protection through police-boats and local guards was now put in force. There were three steam vessels and one schooner embraced in this little fleet. The tonguers numbered about six thousand, and the dredgers about five hundred. The oyster area covered about fifty thousand acres. At this time, the State rented an acre for twelve and one-half cents annually during the first four years; twenty-five cents, the next five; and fifty cents during the succeeding ten years. It was calculated that, in 1903, the income from the sale of Virginian oysters amounted to three and one-half millions of dollars, and from ordinary fish, four and one-half millions. The revenue to the State, without deduction for expenditures, reached about fifty-eight thousand dollars.

A close inspection had been instituted to prevent the repeated invasions of the oyster rock. Seed had previously been openly taken from the beds and carried off to Maryland; undersized oysters had been gathered up and sold; stakes, marking the lines between natural rock and leased bottom, had been pulled up and destroyed.

ANDREW JACKSON MONTAGUE
Governor 1902-1906

By this time, 1891, a very complete map had been made of all the State's oyster grounds by Lieutenant James B. Baylor, of the United States Coast Survey, acting under the authority of the General Assembly. A division had been drawn between the natural rock, which was open to the use of tonguers and dredgers in general, and the remainder of the bottom, which was reserved for leases. The area of the former, according to the survey, embraced two hundred and twenty-six thousand acres; the area of the latter four hundred thousand. The popular impression had been growing that the Commonwealth had not been deriving the revenue from its oyster grounds which it had a right to expect; and this survey was one of the first and most effective steps that was taken to ascertain precisely the area which should be remunerative to the State's Treasury. In 1906, the net profit did not exceed forty-nine thousand dollars, although a large steamer and several other vessels were now in commission to prevent abuse of the oyster rock. The quantity of seed-oysters had declined, and destructive scrapers had taken the place of the dredges. These were often found illegally at work in the closed season. In 1907, however, the net revenue to the State rose to sixty-seven thousand dollars; but fell to forty-three thousand in the course of the following year,—a fluctuation caused by the difference in the seasons and also in the prices.

About two hundred and seventy million menhaden were now annually captured. From these, oil to the value of eight hundred and fifty thousand dollars, and guano to the value of six hundred and forty thousand, were manufactured. There were ten fertilizer factories in operation.

In 1907, W. McDonald Lee had become the chairman of the Commission, and his thorough knowledge of the Chesapeake fisheries, and his energetic and zealous performance of the duties of the office, left a permanent impression on the further development of this great interest of the Commonwealth. The industry was now obstructed by the play of certain hostile influences. A report, encouraged by the producers of oysters in the North and far South, spread that the Virginian rivers were polluted; and that their oysters, in consequence, were dangerous to the stomach. The demand for them fell off, the price decreased, and many tonguers were forced into other employments, in order to earn a livelihood. This scare continued during several years.

At this time, the Commission's duties consisted chiefly of protecting the young oysters on their native grounds; increasing the output of the marketable oysters; and guarding the interests of the men employed in the several branches of the industry. To strengthen the Commission in the performance of these duties, the General Assembly, in 1910, adopted a new oyster law.

It had been noticed that, whenever the supply of oysters on the natural rock increased, the disposition of those persons who were in possession of leased bottoms was to give up their assignments and join the great body of tonguers in using the free areas. During the years in which the impression of pollution was general, the expiring leases were not so often renewed; nor did those who failed to hold on show any disposition to take advantage of the natural rock. As the number of lessees and ordinary tonguers alike fell off,—and this number was said, as early as 1908, to embrace one-half of those previously employed,—the production decreased in the same proportion, although it was observed that the oyster beds were hardly ever before covered with such an abundance of these shell-fish.

Possibly, the interval of more or less suspended exploitation was a benefit to both the leased bottoms and the natural rock, by allowing the oysters to increase at a more rapid rate than they would have done had the annual harvest maintained its former volume. It was said, in 1911, that the imputation from outside of the State of unwholesomeness in the Virginian oyster, as the result of supposititious pollution, had already cost the Commonwealth and the producers the sum of four million dollars. The shuckers and canneries also lost heavily from the same cause. To augment the evil springing from the spread of this report, the exact location of the lines of the Baylor Survey

CLAUDE R. SWANSON
Governor 1906-1910

in some of the waters had become confused. This was particularly so at this time in the James River. Sharp disputes arose
there from the encroachments of the lessees on the natural rock,
and of the tonguers on the leased bottoms. Both claimed that
they were not guilty of any intrusion. It became necessary to
restore the original lines near the mouth of this river, and subsequently in the other estuaries, by a second survey.

The existence of this uncertainty about so many of the lines
while it lasted, further discouraged the lessees of the planting
grounds. In the course of four years, the area under culture
declined from seventy thousand acres to forty thousand. This
diminution began in the year following the most prosperous year
in the history of the industry; namely 1907. Nevertheless, the
output of the fisheries in 1911, four years later, was still large.
The income derived in the aggregate during that year amounted
to three and a half million dollars for oysters; a million and a
half for ordinary fish; one million and a quarter for menhaden;
and a million for crabs and other shell-fish. The State's share
in these proceeds was near forty thousand dollars. This represented a decrease of nearly ten thousand, in comparison with
the revenues from this source in 1905, before the alarm about
pollution had set in.

By 1913, the private bottoms were leased at the rate of one
dollar an acre. Only one-fourth of the area suitable for exploitation was now in actual use. This signified that one hundred and seventy-five thousand acres were lying idle. On the
other hand, the many thousand acres open to the public as natural rock were now worked by a host of men, ranging from ten
thousand to twelve thousand tonguers and dredgers. Notwithstanding this fact, the revenue of the State from the double
area had now declined to thirty-two thousand dollars. This
stimulated the Commission of Fisheries to still greater activity
in restraining the various forms of depredations to which the
oyster beds were still exposed. The little navy was really unable
to protect adequately so vast a space; but so far as was possible

it was kept incessantly on the watch. It was partly due to this fact, no doubt that, in 1914, the revenue of the Commonwealth from the fisheries was substantially increased,—from the planting grounds alone, the income during that year, amounted to fifty-four thousand dollars.

The laws which the State was now most resolute in enforcing were those relating to the protection of the fish from too destructive methods in securing them; the return to the water of all, including oysters, which were under size; and the prevention of the removal of seed from certain localities. The Commission were authorized to employ special policemen to carry out all the regulations. These special policemen furnished their own boats, but, apparently, were not called upon to give their entire time to the duties of guardianship, which included the periodic examination of the dredgers to find out whether they were observing the culling law, and also whether they were operating under valid licenses. The regular fleet of the Commission consisted at this date of two steamers, one schooner, and six launches.

How important the oyster industry was, as compared with the other branches of the fisheries, was indicated by the fact that, of the ninety-three thousand dollars derived by the State, in 1914, from those sources in the aggregate, seventy-two thousand was the portion collected from the oystermen as a body. At least forty thousand persons at this time obtained their livelihood, either directly or indirectly, as heads or members of families, from this industry. The bulk of the revenue came from the working of the natural rock. Indeed, the demand in the markets was so nearly filled by the catch on this natural rock that the ability to lease the rest of the bottoms was seriously affected for a period. The lessee was subject to special expenses. For instance, he had to plant his young oysters; he had to watch constantly to prevent the intrusion of depredators; and, finally, he had to pay a rent of considerable amount.

At one time, seed-oysters were not permitted to be taken out of Virginia, even under the supervision of the Commission. This

Governor 1910-1914

law was ultimately repealed, but seems to have been subsequently reenacted. The law which prohibited the investment of foreign capital in the use of oyster rock was also repealed, on condition that the outside companies making such investments should be first chartered by Virginia.

The protection of the fisheries was now enforced with increased vigilance. There were nine vessels of one kind or another employed in the performance of this duty, while eleven special policemen were similarly engaged. The revenue obtained by the State just before the World war began, from the two principal branches of the industry; namely, the oyster and the ordinary fish, amounted, respectively, to seventy thousand dollars and fifteen thousand dollars. During the war, the income from the fisheries increased; but the rise in prices was counterbalanced by the advance in wages, which followed from the scarcity of labor then prevailing. In the course of the same period, the effort to augment the supply of fresh-water fish by means of hatcheries was successfully renewed. The Commission acted in close cooperation with the United States Bureau of Fisheries in carrying out this work of propagation.

In the space of sixty-five miles lying between Old Point and the mouth of the Potomac, there were, at this time, about two thousand pound-nets, which were more or less obstructive of the passage of fish seeking their inland river spawning grounds. It was difficult to remove the barrier thus created; but regulations were adopted which diminished the evil substantially.

The controversy over the disregard of the lines of the Baylor Survey, both by the private planters and by the exploiters of the public rock, had never ceased. The planters still asserted that the free tonguers and dredgers were encroaching on their boundary stakes; the latter declaimed, still more vigorously, against the intrusions of the planters on the open rock. In consequence, it again became necessary for the State to run many of the original lines anew, and to mark them again for their lasting preservation. In the course of carrying out this

work, it was found that both sets of complainants were correct,
—the planters had, in some places, taken illegal possession of
public rock; and the free tonguers and dredgers, in their turn,
had, in other places, thrust themselves into the leased areas
without authority. The planters had been specially indifferent
to the rights of the free tonguers and dredgers in the natural
rock situated in the Rappahannnock River. This course of
ruthlessness was vigorously reprehended by the Commission, as
on the free use of the natural rock depended the prosperity of
the oyster industry. This prosperity had, in the waters of some
of the tidal rivers, been already curtailed by the discharges of
oil on the surface by numerous vessels coming in from the sea
or passing out. This unwholesome coating was equally destructive of the growth of the ordinary fish.

The State was not content to confine its attention to the
preservation and propagation of sea-fish. A department was
created about 1919-20 to protect the different varieties of inland
fish, and also of game birds. It was an important act of this
department that it had purchased a farm for the purpose especially of breeding the partridge. This farm, which was situated on the Chickahominy, embraced an area of twelve hundred
acres. It was very successful in raising quail for dispersion in
the various counties in which that bird had grown scarce through
persistent over-hunting or through unpropitious seasons. As
a means of putting a stop to local depredations, wardens were
appointed for each of the ten congressional districts. Under
them, additional wardens served in the guardianship of special
localities. It was under the supervision of the local and district
wardens that the birds sent out from the State farm were distributed. In 1821, over twelve hundred quail were hatched
from the eggs of eighty-four hens. A thousand of these were
liberated in the various areas reserved as sanctuaries.

But the department was not restricted to the propagation
and protection of birds alone. It was also incumbent on it, as
we have mentioned, to preserve the existing supply of inland

fish. The vast increase in the number of carp in the inland streams had already diminished the number of those fine species of fish, like bass, perch and shad, with which they had been stocked at so much expense. How were these carps to be destroyed? That was a problem. Many of the streams were now thoroughly polluted by the refuse from the tanneries and sawmills which was allowed to fall into their current. It was said that, at this time, the Shenandoah, through this cause alone, had been deserted by its former finny denizens, which were of a peculiarly excellent quality.

The task preserving and protecting the inland fisheries did not require the same persistent alertness as the task of preserving and protecting the salt-water fisheries. The open depredations and encroachments to which the latter were subject never ceased. This was due to the greater value of these fisheries, and the greater number of persons who looked to them for a livelihood. At least fifteen thousand people in 1922-23 depended on them as their only means of subsistence. Not less than seventy thousand persons were, for the whole or a part of their time, engaged in the various branches of this great industry. It was calculated, in the course of this year, that the output from the public rock was worth two million and a half dollars, and from the private planting grounds, one million. The value of the product of the crabberies was estimated at seven millions. The State, in 1622, derived about seventy-nine thousand dollars from its fisheries. The income increased to one hundred and one thousand in 1923.

Four years afterwards, keen alarm was felt that, unless the existing methods of using the oyster fishery were altered by putting a stop to improvidence, the industry would practically disappear by the end of a brief space of time. In order to preserve the natural supply, it has been recommended that all reseeding should take place under the supervision of the State; that scrupulous culling should be strictly enforced and that the season for taking oysters should be reduced to the five months coming between October first and March first. It was said as late as 1927 that the natural rock has been depleted to the extent of seventy per cent. In the meanwhile, the problem of pollution has not been finally solved, but its settlement has recently been taken over by the National Government, which is in a better position to remove or reduce the evil than the State has proved itself to be.

CHAPTER VIII

PRODUCTS OF HAND AND MACHINE

Previous to the War of 1861-65, as we stated in our first volume, there existed in Virginia a very considerable variety of manufactures, carried on, in many instances, on the scale of plantation crafts, in which black and white mechanics alike were engaged. Even in the production of cotton-goods, now turned out in enormous quantities, the bulk of the output of each mill was not then imposing from the modern point of view. This fact is clearly illustrated in the figures for 1840, 1850, and 1860, on the one hand, and 1890, 1900, and 1910 on the other. The last date is within the limit to which the present chapter is confined.

In 1840, there were twenty-two cotton factories in operation in Virginia; in 1850, there were twenty-seven; and in 1860, sixteen. After the close of the war, there were, in 1890, nine; in 1900, seven; and in 1910, ten. In other words, during the first period of twenty years, there was an annual average of twenty-two mills in operation; but during the second, there were only seven. And yet the capital invested in the average seven for the interval of 1890-1910 was as high as $21,440,095; and of the average twenty-two for the interval of 1840-1860, as low as $4,575,463.

During the last interval, the number of wage-earners ranged from 1,816 to 2,963; and during the former, from 2,000 to 5,103. The value of the product of the cotton mills in operation between 1840 and 1860 amounted to but $3,422,418, although there were as many as twenty-two mills in existence then. On

First Telephone Station in Richmond

the other hand, the value of the product of the cotton mills between 1890 and 1910 amounted to $11,877,650, notwithstanding the fact that there were only seven mills. In 1900, when there were only seven mills, the number of spindles rose to 126,827.

These figures confirm the correctness of the statement that the volume of production in cotton manufactures in Virginia, before the War of 1861-65, was not in proportion to the number of mills, as tested by the present standards of output.

During 1892, there were seventy-two different forms of manufacture pursued in the state. We have already referred to the production of cotton goods. A few other of the more important varieties may be mentioned.

The production of plank in the saw and planing mills was, at this time, an industry of magnitude, owing tu the vast area in forest and the depression in agriculture. There were at least twenty-five mills of the largest dimensions at work and capable of turning out an enormous quantity of dressed lumber. These did not include the mills that were moved from place to place in the forests. There were also paper-mills, woolen and knitting mills, and mills for the manufacture of stoves and furniture. There were establishments too for the manufacture of flour, cornmeal, woodwork of the finer sorts, shoes, clothes, fertilizers, iron, and other articles too numerous to be specifically named. There was also a large number of important canneries and tanneries. The tobacco factories were especially numerous in Richmond, Petersburg, Lynchburg, Farmville, and Danville; but many others were in operation in the smaller towns.

Already, in 1892, the various chambers of commerce were advertizing the advantages which the presence of mineral wealth, in an extraordinary quantity, in the soil of the state, and the existence of perennial water-power, were offering to outside capital for the development of manufactures on the largest scale. Vigorous local associations, like the Shenandoah Valley, the

Rappahannock Valley, and the Hampton Roads Port Commissions, had been incorporated for industrial as well as for commercial purposes of impressive magnitude.

By 1899, the progress of manufacturing development had reached an extent that was reflected in the rising prosperity of every important town in the state. A more detailed reference to the nature of these manufactures will throw a significant light on this progress. Let us consider the accomplishment of the larger centers of population in this department of industry.

In Bedford City, in 1899, there were in operation two roller and two woolen mills. In addition, there was a mill for the production of sassafras oil. Less extensive manufactures also existed there. In Bristol, there had been erected an iron furnace, a foundry, machine works, a tannery, and several lumber and planing mills. The annual output of these and other establishments in that town was valued at a million and a half dollars. Buena Vista possessed a mill that produced twenty-five thousand pounds of pulp daily, and twelve thousand pounds of high grade paper. It also counted a woolen mill, an iron furnace, and a tannery. In addition, it manufactured saddles and harness, and converted into different forms a large quantity of hardwoods.

Danville could count among its buildings at this time eleven warehouses for the storage of leaf tobacco. It had already become the largest loose leaf tobacco market in the world. It also manufactured a great quantity of cotton goods in the Riverside Cotton Mills, which were among the most imposing in the United States. It possessed, among other important establishments, several factories for the production of wagons.

Lynchburg was then, as it had been during several generatins, a seat of tobacco manufacture. It was also engaged in the manufacture of cotton-goods in a large way. Its industries included, too, many small manufactures of a varied character. Newport News was already well-known for an extensive shipbuilding yard. Over five thousand men were employed in its different departments. Norfolk, at this time, possessed fourteen lumber factories, six cotton and woolen mills, ten fertilizers mills, seven peanut cleaning establishments, three ice factories, two flouring mills, a brewery, a creosote plant, several cotton compresses, foundries, machine shops, and other shops of equal

Courtesy of Virginia State Chamber of Commerce

LYNCHBURG COTTON MILLS

importance. Petersburg was chiefly noted for the manufacture of tobacco and cotton goods; but it also produced a large quantity of other kinds of manufacture, such as iron, fertilizers, and woodwork. In Portsmouth were situated three big lumber mills, two ship-yards, two carriage factories, chemical works, oyster packing establishments, and cigar factories.

Richmond, even in 1899, was remarkable for the magnitude and variety of its manufactures. Its iron establishments, like the Tredegar and the American Locomotive Works, its flour mills, its tobacco factories, and its paper mills, were among the most important in the United States. In addition, it manufactured a vast quantity of fertilizers. It also contained box, meat-juice, and baking powder factories, and other establishments of the same general nature.

Roanoke had already begun to expand in its manufacturing interests. It possessed a plant for bridge construction, three large iron furnaces, three large planing mills, two tobacco factories, and two important printing establishments. Staunton, at this time, had gone almost equally as far in laying the path for its future advance in the same industrial province. This was also true of Radford in the Southwest.

The following embraces a complete list of the different branches of manufacture carried on in Virginia in 1899; namely, agricultural implements, artificial ice, bakers' products, spirits, brooms, brick, tile, boots, shoes, baking powder, candy, canned-goods, cigars, cigarettes, cheroots, clothing, cotton-goods, butter, cheese, carriages, wagons, cornice and sheet metal, medical drugs, chemicals, flour, corn-meal, groceries, foundry iron, knitted-goods, lime, cement, planing mill products, printing, engraving, paints, oil, glass, lumber, saddles, harness, leather, soap-stone, granite, stoves, tobacco, tents, awnings, trunks, woolen-goods, wooden-ware, paper, paper boxes, tin boxes, staves, and cooperage.

It was calculated that the capital invested in these various manufacturing industries during 1899 amounted to seven million and a half dollars; and that the value of their output exceeded ten and one-half millions. There were not less than three thousand men and women employed in cotton manufactures alone. This represented an increase of twelve hundred persons over the number engaged in that branch of work during the previous year. Of the entire number employed, about twelve hundred were female operatives. Two hundred and sixty-eight of these were under the age of sixteen.

The amount of daily wages received at this time by men and women respectively in the cotton factories was not the same. In the weaving-room, a woman was paid seventy-six cents and two-fifths of a cent; and a man one dollar and sixteen cents. In the clothing-room, the wages were, for the members of the two sexes, respectively, seventy cents and ninety-three cents; in the spinning-room, forty-nine and one-half cents, and sixty-two and two-fifths cents; and, lastly, in the carding-room, respectively, sixty-six and one-fifth cents, and eighty-seven and two-fifths cents. In each situation mentioned, it will be perceived that the female operative fared the worst.

In 1900, the total value of the product of the thirteen woolen mills then running approximated the sum of four hundred thousand dollars. There were now employed in these mills about five hundred operatives, of whom two hundred were males whose years ranged above sixteen, and seventy-three whose years ranged under that age. The ages of only thirty-four of the female operatives were less than sixteen.

During the same year, eight knitting mills made a report to the state government of the volume of their output and the amount of their income during the previous twelve months. These mills had a fund of one hundred and ninety thousand dollars invested in their business. The amount of goods which they had turned out during the interval mentioned was valued at seven hundred and fifty-six thousand dollars. In the operation of these eight mills, two hundred and eighty-six men over sixteen years of age and seventeen under, were employed. The corresponding figures for the women were three hundred and fifty-six and one hundred and forty-two. In this branch of industry, it will be preceived that the female operatives outnumbered the male.

The amount of wages received by persons of the two sexes respectively, varied substantially. In the knitting-room, for instance, the men were paid ninety cents, and the women, seventy, while in the finishing-room, the men were paid ninety cents and the women, fifty-nine.

In the province of contracting work, there does not seem to have been any sex division among the operatives. Apparently, they were all men. In 1901, the daily wages received by the different kinds of craftsmen needed in this department of work were as follows: the cooper was paid two dollars and twenty-six cents; the carpenter, one dollar and eighty-three cents; the bricklayer, three dollars and thirty-nine cents; the plumber, two dollars and seventy-five cents; the tinner, two dollars and thirty-eight cents; the plasterer, two dollars and seventy-nine cents; the lather, two dollars and sixteen cents; the stone-cutter, three dollars and forty-six cents; the mason, three dollars and twenty-seven cents; and the painter, two dollars and twenty-four cents.

It may be noted here that, at this time, the colored plasterer received only one dollar and ninety-four cents, and the colored lather only one dollar and seventy-six cents. This was, in the one case, eighty-five cents and in the other, forty cents less than the white plasterer and the white lather were paid.

One of the most profitable forms of manufacture at this time was that of cigarettes, cigars, and cheroots, long a characteristic industry of Virginia. In 1900, twenty-eight establishments of this kind reported sales, during the previous twelve months, that aggregated four and a half million dollars. About four hundred and fifty thousand dollars were invested in that business. In printing and engraving establishments, about five hundred and sixty-five thousand dollars was the value of the annual products. The value of the output of the breweries was about one hundred thousand; of the output of paper, wood, and tin boxes, about seven hundred and thirty-two thousand; of the output of fish-oil, about two hundred and sixty-seven thousand; of the product of the tanneries about four million and six hundred thousand dollars; of the product of the canneries about one hundred and thirty thousand. On the other hand, the value of the output of the manufacture of agricultural implements and stoves respectively was the same; namely, three hundred and three thousand dollars. Over four hundred thousand dollars was invested in the manufacture of carriages, wagons, and buggies; and the value of the product amounted to nearly seven hundred and one thousand dollars.

In 1901, the value of the product of the flour mills was in the neighborhood of three and a half million dollars. This indicated an increase in value, in the course of a single year, that amounted to twelve hundred thousand dollars. About ninety-seven thousand dollars were paid to the operatives in this branch of industry. The capital invested was nearly one million, two hundred thousand dollars. On the other hand, the capital invested in the iron industry was seven million and a half dollars; the value of the annual product was over five million and a half; and the wages were four million. The capital invested in the manufacture of tobacco was still larger. It amounted to six million dollars for thirty-one establishments alone. The wages paid out were over seven million and fifty thousand dollars, while the capital exceeded two million and a half. The daily remuneration in this industry for men ranged from one dollar and ninety-two cents to one dollar and forty-five; and for women, from eighty-nine cents to forty.

Soon after the year 1902, the wages paid out in the manufacturing plants steadily advanced in the case of the majority of the operatives, but in the case of the minority, they showed a decline. In the instance of the brick kiln, the white employee received ten cents less by the day in 1904 than he had done in 1902. The colored brickmaker, on the other hand, received twenty-six cents in addition. The white helper in the same business was paid nine cents more in 1904 than he was paid in the year 1902. The black common laborer was also paid twenty-seven cents more. In the sawmills there was an increase in the rate of wages for the white operative as well as for the black, though the advance was indicated by only a few cents.

In the manufacture of ice, the common laborer was paid three cents more than in 1902.

In the breweries in 1903, the principal working-men received two dollars and fifty-six cents by the day. In 1904, they received ten cents more. The drivers of the brewery wagons lost fourteen cents in 1904 as compared with the amount received by them in 1903. In the canneries, there was a decline in the wages of some of the employees, whilst there was a small advance in the wages of others, with the balance in favor of the majority. In the manufacture of carriages, wagons, and buggies, the same condition was to be noticed, without there being any apparent reason for its existence. In some cases, the advance and the decline were equally insignificant. Thus the common laborer received higher wages in 1903 than he did in 1904, but the difference was two cents only. The general trend was in the direction of a falling off. In the case of the painters, this amounted to fifty-eight cents; in the case of the trimmers, to thirty-four cents; and in the case of the wood-workers, to sixty-four cents. The rate of wages in the sawmills also fluctuated, but not to the same degree. In nine of the principal departments of these mills, the working-men, in 1903, were paid an average wage, by the day, of one dollar and thirty-four cents; and, in 1904, of one dollar and thirty-one cents. Here there was a shortage of only four cents; which represented a loss of less than a dollar in the course of the whole month.

Numerous women, at this time, were employed in the knitting mills. It will be to the point to compare the rate of remuneration allowed them with that adopted for the men. In 1904, the male and female operatives in these mills received the same wages in the binding department, namely, forty cents. In the cutting department, the women received ninety cents in 1903, and eighty cents in 1904. On the other hand, the male cutters received one dollar and seventy cents in 1903, and one dollar and fifty-two in 1904. The wage of the female knitters in the former year was eighty cents, while the wage of the male was one dollar and three. In 1904, the wage was respectively sixty-eight and one dollar and one cent. The female loopers received in 1903 seventy-three cents; the men ninety. In 1904, only women were employed, and they were paid eighty cents.

Many women, in 1904, were engaged in the manufacture of round and square boxes. In this work, their wage did not exceed seventy cents. Men, on the other hand, were paid one dollar and sixty cents, which was as much again as the female operatives received.

In the manufacture of paper and pulp, about sixty-nine women were employed in 1903. Precisely double that number of men were also engaged in the same industry. During the same year, women received only eighty cents as compositors, while the wages of the male compositors ranged from two dollars to two dollars and forty-five cents. In the tanneries, the only competitors of the white men were negroes. Miscellaneous laborers of both colors in these plants were paid the same amount at this time; namely, one dollar and twenty-five cents. In tobacco manufacture, there were, in 1904, many women employed. In several branches of this business, they were remunerated with a somewhat larger wage than the men. Thus for the manipulation of certain machines, they received one dollar and four cents as compared with ninety-five cents received by the male operatives. As general helpers too they were paid three cents more; but as pickers, they received twenty-seven cents less. Their wage in the boot and shoe factories was also smaller than the wage of men. This was also the case in the silk mills, in which many female operatives were employed.

By 1907, the wages of the working men and women in the different manufactures had increased very materially. The following list will show the advance in the remuneration in the case of the more important operatives: bakers, 30 per cent; blacksmiths, six; boilermakers, ten; brewers, also ten; bricklayers, twelve; carpenters, ten; cigarmakers, eight; machinists, ten; milling-men, ten; painters, twenty-five; plumbers, also twenty-five; sheet metal workers, twenty; engravers, ten; tailors, also ten; and typographers, twelve.

The year 1908 was marked by industrial depression, but there was an increase in the wage scale of the following manufactures: woodenware, cotton-goods, leather, paper, pulp, woolen-goods, canning, boxes, ice, spirits, printing, binding, and engraving. On the other hand, there was a decrease in the wage scale in the manufacture of iron and machinery, cigars, cigarettes, cheroots, lumber, trunks, bags, overalls, shirts, wagons, carriages, stoves, agricultural implements, silk, boots, shoes, knitted-goods, and furniture.

The following were the number of hours adopted in the most important factories, which we will designate by their products: agricultural implements, nine to ten and a half; blast furnaces, twelve; boots and shoes, ten; canneries, nine to ten; carriage and wagons, nine to ten also; cigars and cigarettes, eight to nine and a half; fertilizers, ten; furniture, nine to ten; glass, eight to nine; gloves, eight and a half to ten; knitting mills, nine and a half to eleven; overalls and shirts, eight to ten and a half; paper and pulp mills, ten to twelve; paper boxes, seven and a half to ten and a half; printing and engraving, eight to ten; sashes, doors, and blinds, ten; silk mills, ten; and stove works, eight to ten; tanneries, eight to ten; trunks, seven and a half to ten and a half; wooden ware, eight to twelve; and woolen mills, ten to ten and a half. The hours for children and women were less extended—for children, in all cases; and for women, in many.

By 1907 an improvement was to be observed in the condition of all the factories. A more spacious type of building was now erected than had been erected before. The rooms were more open to the fresh air; the sanitary arrangements were more modern in their character; and the provisions for ensuring the operatives' comfort, while working, were more adequate and more considerate also. Virginia was now becoming in all its towns and cities an important manufacturing community; and one of the conspicuous evidences of this fact was the adoption of every mechanical improvement that had been suggested by the experience of the North. Each successive year now witnessed a perceptible advance. In 1910, for instance, the gain in the value of the manufactured product amounted to sixteen million of dollars. Thirty-five industries alone showed an increase in this respect that equaled nine hundred thousand dollars. In 1912, the advance in the value of the product of forty-three industries over the value of the product of 1911 came to nineteen million dollars. Fifty-one different forms of manufacture were listed in 1915. The total value of their product was put at two hundred and twelve and a half millions of dollars. This indicated a net increase of twenty-six and a half millions over the returns for 1914.

How far were wages raised by the growing prosperity of Virginian manufacturers? The following are the figures for some of the more important white craftsmen in the various industries. The brickmaker received by the day the sum of one dollar and fifty-two cents; the mason, five dollars and eight cents; carpenters, two dollars and eighty-seven cents; plasterers, two dollars and forty-one cents; stone-cutters, three dollars and four cents; blacksmiths, two dollars and seven cents; coopers, one dollar and fifty-two cents; common laborers, one dollar and forty-nine cents; machinists, three dollars; painters, one dollar and fifty-four cents; brewers, three dollars and twenty-eight cents; upholsterers, two dollars and sixty-four cents; bakers, two dollars and twenty-two cents; wheelwrights, one dollar and sixty-eight cents; sawyers, one dollar and seventy-one cents; cabinetmakers, one dollar and fifty-eight cents; and ship carpenters, two dollars and ninety-four cents. This list of wages might be indefinitely extended.

Perhaps, the most remarkable feature in these rates was the fluctuation from year to year; but, in the long run, the trend was towards an increase.

The remuneration for women still fell short of that allowed male operatives in the same industry. A few illustrations of this fact may be given. In the knitting mills in 1914, for instance, the female cutters received fifty-four cents less for a working day; the female finishers, thirty-four cents less; and the female knitters, forty-three cents less. In the cotton mills, the female carders received seven cents less; the female dressers, forty-five cents less; the female warpers, thirty-seven cents less. In the silk mills, female helpers received eighty cents less; the female finishers, twenty-three cents less; the female weavers, seventy-three cents less.

The same degree of difference was to be noticed at this time, as a rule, in all the industries in which women participated as operatives. It was only in a few that they obtained, in one or more departments, either equal or superior wages. The female packers in the manufacture of cigars and cigarettes, for instance, received sixteen cents more than the male. In the knitting mills, the female spinners received twenty-five cents more.

How far did the negro take part in the tasks of the factories of Virginia previous to the World war? We have seen that, in the times of slavery, members of that race performed most of the mechanical tasks required on the larger plantations. There were also many free blacks occupying stands in the villages and small towns. During a considerable interval after the War of 1861-65, the ordinary crafts in the rural districts were filled by the older negroes, who had learned their trades under the former industrial system. It was estimated, in the census report of 1900, that there were, at that time, in Richmond, eighteen hundred blacks employed in the mechanical trades and industries. These figures included the negro operatives in the iron and steel works, and also the negro operatives in the tobacco factories and saw-mills. They disclosed a falling off as compared with the number who were similarly engaged in 1890. This shrinkage in the ranks of negroes earning a livelihood in trades in the capital was observed throughout the state. By

1910, the number of white operatives employed in manufacturing or mechanical establishments in Richmond had swelled to about seven thousand, while the number of colored operatives had shrunk to nine hundred and forty. Ten years later, the number of white operatives in the same city had increased to over ten thousand, while the number of colored had only increased to thirteen hundred, an addition of four hundred only in the interval.

The wages of the black operatives were, at this time, not often equal to the wages of the white. As a rule, the wages of the former were distinctly lower even for the same character of work. This was seen in the history of the building trades about 1906. These trades were fairly representative in this particular. A white bricklayer, in the course of that year, received five dollars and thirty-one cents daily; a negro only one dollar and eighty; the ordinary white laborer, one dollar and ninety-five cents; the common negro laborer, one dollar and eighty cents; a white carpenter, two dollars and fifty-seven cents; a black, one dollar and seventy cents; a white plasterer, three dollars and eighty-three cents; and a black, two dollars and thirty-two cents.

A more particular reference may be made to special crafts, like, for instance, those of the painter and the paper-hanger. The wages of a white painter was ninety-three cents more than the wages of a black; of a white plasterer, who coated the walls, twenty-five cents more; and of a white paper-hanger, one dollar and twenty-eight cents more. A long list running along the same lines might be added.

As we shall perceive when we come to describe the condition of manufactures in Virginia after the World war, the remuneration of the negro operatives, like that of the white, was substantially increased, under the influence of the inflation which prevailed then so generally.

VIII

THE WORLD WAR AND ITS SEQUENCE

CHAPTER I

THE VIRGINIA COUNCIL OF DEFENSE

The Council of National Defense was appointed in 1916, about two years after war had been first declared in Europe, and nearly eight months before the United States joined the ranks of the belligerents. Its general purpose was to organize all the resources of the country as a whole for prompt and efficient use in case the nation should be drawn into the hostilities that were then devastating the European continent and disrupting the safe navigation of all the seas of the world. It was not until April, 1917, that the United States was compelled by the ruthless policy of Germany to join in these hostilities. Instructions were then received by the State Government of Virginia, along with all the others of the Union, to appoint a State Council of Defense, whose functions, within the bounds of the commonwealth, were to be a duplication of the functions of the National Council within the bounds of the United States at large. In compliance, Governor Stuart selected, first, an Agricultural Council of Safety; secondly, an Industrial Council; and thirdly, a General Council of Defense. In the course of the following year, all these bodies were consolidated into the Second Virginia Council of Defense.

There was a general impression in the state, in the beginning, that the only really important part which its people would be called on to play in the conflict would be to aid in supplying the materials rather than the men who would be needed to prosecute it. This feeling had originated in the fact that, for nearly three years, the United States had been engaged in sending food

297

HENRY C. STUART
Governor 1914-1918

and munitions oversea for the benefit of the Allies, without sending men; simply, however, because there had, during that period, been no open and formal breach with the Central Powers. But this impression was soon lost after energetic steps had been taken to organize the military power of the community. It was then perceived by all that the state's participation in the war was to be direct and without reservation. It was the duty of the State Council of Defense to overlook the enforcement of every local measure adopted for the success of the Allied cause. This applied to the action of all private agencies as well as of all public. Both the Agricultural and the Industrial Councils were subordinate to the Council of Defense.

The first meeting of the State Council of Defense was held in May, 1917, about one month after the declaration of war by Congress. The resolutions passed on this occasion indicated that the members present recognized that Virginia's share in the hostilities would involve as much the production of food as the enrollment of men. The military plan recommended apparently to Congress included both specifically, as practically of equal importance. Certain industries, besides agriculture, were also to be actively promoted, and trained labor was to be kept ready for mobilization whenever the need of it grew insistent. The provisions for drafting included in the military plan suggested was far-reaching in its scope. Thus not only were the young men who had passed the physical examination to be all enlisted, but also every man of the right age, and in good health, who, for one reason or another, was permanently or temporarily unfitted for military service. In addition, every man whose advance in years exempted him from enrollment for active duty at the front should have his name recorded, and also every boy below the age assigned for enlistment. One object of this provision was to obviate a shortage of labor, should it at any time appear to be impending; but a more important object still was to obtain a complete knowledge of the extent of the man-power of the state. This was for the special use of the

Council of Defense. To the Industrial Council was assigned three indispensable duties: (1) the conservation of labor; (2) the recruiting of labor; and (3) the financing of the farmer. To the Agricultural Council, on the other hand, were assigned the duties of increasing the production of all the food crops and the prevention of waste. The Secretary of the State Council of Defense was required to take charge of the dissemination of information about the various activities to be inaugurated, while a press agent was employed to arouse and sustain the patriotic spirit of the people of the state.

One of the early recommendations of the State Council of Defense, addressed to Congress, was as to the advisability of adopting prohibition as the policy of the nation during the progress of the war. This advice was placed on the ground that the efficiency of the soldiers would be thereby increased, and their supply of food conserved. Of more practical significance, however, was the activity of the council in encouraging the sale of Liberty Bonds by every means in its power. One of the ways suggested was that the banks should lend money to persons for investment in these securities, which were to be held back until the amount borrowed had been returned. The State Council of Defense also urged that the only excuse for exemption within the age limit, in carrying out the selective service law, should be, that the person coming up for the draft should be engaged in the production of food under abnormal circumstances; or in the pursuit of an employment, like munition making, for instance, which was directly connected with the efficient prosecution of the war.

Only a few months after Virginia was drawn into the conflict, the question was taken up by the State Council of Defense as to the propriety of organizing a Home Guard, who were to assume the duties of the existing National Guard, as the latter were now likely at any time to be drafted under the call of the President. Governor Stuart, to whom the advisability of this step was submitted, had it already under consideration as a

means of preserving the safety of each city and county in the
Commonwealth; and his plan was to obtain Congress' authority
to give these troops the status of Federal soldiery—to the extent
of their equipment at least.

The people of the state had first to consent to the organization of these bodies among them. By the governor's advice,
the State Council of Defense issued a public address to influence
popular opinion in favor of the creation of a Home Guard so
soon as the National Guard should be transferred to military
camps, which was now imminent. The need of such a guard
for the protection of every community would then become at
once urgent, since the existence of war might encourage an outbreak of local lawlessness at any hour. The result of the appeal
was the organization of two military bodies for local defense;
namely, the Virginia Volunteers and the Home Guard. The
former were subject to the call of the state's military authorities;
the latter, to the call of the local authorities alone. The State
Council of Defense recommended that the railroads of the state
should subordinate all passenger service to freight, so as to
hasten the transportation of food designed for the troops; and
manufacturers and merchants were urged to make use of the
rivers as far as possible as the primary means of conveyance.
An appeal to the people to burn wood instead of coal was also
issued at this time, although in one place at least, Norfolk, fuel
of the former kind had, within ten days, advanced from $10
to $16 a cord. The object of this recommendation was to reserve
all coal for communities in which it was difficult to obtain wood.
Another reason was that coal would be shipped in a larger
quantity to the railway car. This would create a proportionately
smaller demand for transportation, and thus leave more cars
for the movement of food to the front.

This seems to have been the last business considered by the
First Council of Defense. Governor Davis succeeded Governor
Stuart in February, 1918, and one of his earliest acts was to

WESTMORELAND DAVIS
Governor 1918-1922

accept the resignations of the members of the original board and and appoint in their place incumbents of his own selection.

Before proceeding further, however, it will be necessary to consider the valuable work that was performed by subsidiary organizations during the existence of the first State Council. One of the most important of these subsidiary organizations was the subordinate Woman's Committee of the Council of National Defense, which had been appointed for Virginia under the chairmanship of Mrs. Beverly B. Munford. Mrs. Munford had won a high reputation for unselfish patriotism and uncommon executive ability as the head of the Cooperative Education Association of the state. The following were declared to be the purposes which the General Woman's Committee of the National Council had in view: (1) The registration; (2) the production, consumption, temporary storage, and final distribution of food; (3) the protection of women engaged in industry; (4) the training of women for special services; and (5) the maintenance of the material and spiritual inner defenses of the national life. Upon Mrs. Munford, as chairman for Virginia, was imposed the duty of creating a subordinate committee for that state for the coordination of all the work done there by women's organizations. These organizations were consolidated by her into a single permanent body, which also constituted an auxiliary committee of the State Council of Defense. There were sixty-four such organizations in the different cities and counties, and their usefulness was increased by this combination under a single guiding chairman, who, in turn, acted under the direction and supervision of the State Council of Defense.

The negro women of Virginia had also been previously drawn into separate organizations of their own for war work, but they were now made subject to the same regulations as the white women. It was calculated that as many as fourteen thousand women, white and black, were now similarly employed. The committee which represented them all kept before them the purposes recommended by the Woman's National Committee;

namely, the conservation of food; the elimination of preventable
diseases; the supervision of women in industry; the promotion
of the Liberty Loan; the safeguarding of moral and spiritual
forces and the like. The Central Committee appointed, in July
(1918), twenty-three local chairmen, who were required to report, to the state headquarters in Richmond, the extent to which
these purposes had been carried out in the several cities and
counties.

A second subsidiary body that acted under the direction of
the State Council of Defense was the Commission of Religious
Forces, which had been appointed by the executive of the commonwealth. Its members were drawn from all the denominations. The design in creating this commission was, through it,
to inflame the patriotic sentiment of the people by appeals from
the pulpits. In these appeals the causes of the war were to be
described, and the necessity of combatting the ruthless spirit
which had been exhibited so flagrantly on both land and sea by
the Central Powers was to be enforced. More than one great
public rally was held by this commission at which ministers of
the Gospel delivered earnest and powerful addresses. The same
commission also sent out a circular letter to every clergyman in
the state asking for the cooperation of all the congregations in
observing the regulations adopted for the successful prosecution
of the war. The strongest emphasis was laid on the conservation of the food supplies and the protection of the young soldiers
in camp from every demoralizing influence. The negro commission, modeled on the same earnest and effective lines, were
equally zealous in arousing the energies of their own preachers
towards advancing the same moral and practical work.

A third subsidiary organization of importance was known
as the Speakers' Bureau. The head of this bureau was Mr.
Lewis Machen. He was instructed by the State Council of
Defense to summon, through the local commonwealth's attorneys, a public meeting in every county, at which the people were
to be urged to uphold with patriotic zeal the military policy of

the National Government, and to carry out cheerfully all the requirements of the draft law.

The national organization known as the Four-Minute Men had created a division in Virginia under the chairmanship of Mr. Machen. Its purpose was similar to that of the Speakers' Bureau. It furnished men of distinction to deliver special addresses on the occasion of concerts and theatrical perform-, ances, or wherever there were large assemblages of people. These addresses were directed chiefly to the counteraction of the hostile propaganda that had been subtly spread throughout the country.

A medical section had been created by the National Council of Defense at the beginning of the American participation in hostilities. This organization was represented in Virginia by a committee of physicians, who were accepted by the State Council of Defense as closely affiliated with itself. Local subordinate committees were appointed in all the more populous counties and towns. These committees cooperated with the examining boards, and also secured medical officers for the army. It favored the exclusion of all medical students and internes from enrollment in the draft, and urged their assignment instead to the enlisted Medical Reserve Corps. It also arranged for speeches to be delivered at public meetings by representatives of the surgeon-general's office.

As early as April, 1917, the Virginia Agricultural Council of Safety had been organized in subordination to the State Council of Defense. The main purpose which this body had in view was to increase the supply of food for the troops at the front, by encouraging the adoption of more intensive methods of farming, and also by widening the area under actual cultivation. Each member at its second meeting was asked to submit a plan looking to the fullest utilization of all the varied agricultural resources of the state, and also to suggest to what extent other organizations—like the Cooperative Educational Association, for instance—could give assistance in the special work of the Agricultural Council. One of the first to offer aid was the principal war society of the negroes. A central office was opened in Richmond, and steps were promptly taken to form local councils of safety. District committees too were named to stimulate the farmers to increase the volume of their food products. They were also to promote a spirit of economy in the different homes. Under their supervision were the distribution of food, the control of farm labor and farm loans, and the direction of publicity. Or to enter further into particulars, they encouraged the production of wheat, rye, meat, milk, potatoes, beans, and fruit; increased the attention paid to canning and preserving; prevented the slaughter of breeding cows, sows, and ewes; drew operatives from industrial plants to assist on the farms and plantations at crowded seasons; and helped in the organization of the Federal Farm Loan Associations.

About eighty-seven counties were successful in founding local councils of safety. Even those among them which had previously been given up almost exclusively to the cultivation of tobacco showed their zeal for the cause by reserving the largest area in their history for use in planting corn or sowing wheat. In Pittsylvania, for instance, the acreage in wheat was increased 40 per cent, and in corn, 33 per cent. Prince William County was especially active in swelling the quantity of dried fruits, vegetables, preserves, pickles, and jellies which it had been producing. In the aggregate, an enormous amount of the articles were accumulated.

In ninety-five counties demonstrations were given of the best methods of canning, and also of saving food supplies in general. Nearly three thousand meetings were held for this purpose, which were attended by approximately two hundred thousand people. Additional interest was aroused in food conservation through the influence of the numerous school and civic leagues, acting under the ardent leadership of Mrs. Munford, as president of the Cooperative Education Association. The Department of the State Dairy and Food Commission also

assisted through the work of its numerous inspectors, who were
sent into the county districts in every direction. They organized local councils, and also gathered up useful information
about manufacturing plants, and also about cooperative buying
and selling associations and the like.

The Virginia Industrial Council of Safety was appointed
by Governor Stuart for the purpose of increasing the volume

SHAM BATTLE AT NAVAL BASE, NORFOLK

of manufactures for the war; and also for the conservation and
distribution of the labor employed in this branch of industry.
The latter object was substantially accomplished by curtailing
the activities of unscrupulous labor agents from other states
who were seeking, most frequently secretly, to draw away the
supply of workingmen then engaged in the manufacturing plants
of Virginia. Every outside solicitor was soon required to pay a
license tax of $1,000, and to give bond in the sum of $10,000.
The aim of this ordinance was principally to protect the negro
laborer from the imposition of promises which were never intended to be really carried out.

Another commendable act of the Industrial Council was the adoption of a rule designed to break up the loafing of young men, both black and white, on the street corners. The chief of police of each city and town was instructed to take a census of these idlers and to enter a record of their addresses, so that they might be summoned at any day into some form of active service for the prosecution of the war.

In February, 1918, the first State Council of Defense came to an end, with the close of Governor Stuart's able and energetic administration, and the second State Council of Defense took its place by the appointment of the new governor, Westmoreland Davis. Instead of choosing its membership from among the citizens at large, he confined his selection, with a few exceptions, to the incumbents of various state offices already in existence. The chief advantage of this act apparently was that, as these men were already in the service of the commonwealth as auditors, directors, or commissioners, the pecuniary cost of recruiting them for the second State Council would be more or less negligible. An additional reason was based on the supposition that a council composed of state officials was more likely to be homogeneous and unified in spirit than a council drawn from the body of the citizens at large.

One drawback to this step, however, would seem to have been the onerousness of the duties which these officials were already called upon by the commonwealth to perform, independently of war demands on their time. Another was, that the first State Council of Defense represented more distinctly and directly all the local divisions of Virginia, and were, therefore, more in touch than the second council with the sentiments of the inhabitants of these separate regions, and through that fact possessed a higher degree of influence with the people as a whole.

The following auxiliary committees of the general council were promptly filled, namely: The Agricultural, the Industrial, the Medical, the Woman's the Ministerial, the Property Protection, the Police and Military, the Public Instruction, the

Transportation and Highways, and the Speakers' Bureau. Subsequently, three other committees were appointed, namely, the Fire Protection, the Religious Forces, and the Labor. The executive secretary of the State Council of Defense was selected to serve as the official mouthpiece of all these bodies. It was ultimately found that, instead of these committees performing their war functions in a really independent spirit, calculated to stimulate their activity and sense of industrial responsibility, they became more or less mere advisory adjuncts of the State Council, with even this duty considerably hampered by the pressure upon them of the regular business of the commonwealth, which they had sworn to attend to as state officials. This fact seems to have exalted the importance of the second State Council of Defense, without its efficiency being increased in a practical way beyond what good advice could add.

The executive secretary became the principal figure in the war work. This was Mr. Machen, the head of the auxiliary Speakers' Bureau. He was a thoroughly well informed and capable officer. By him a bill was drafted for the General Assembly's approval which provided that the acts of the first and second State Council of Defense so far should be legal *in toto;* and that a course should be laid down by the Legislature for the second council, now in existence, which it could pursue without apprehension that it was exceeding its powers as limited by the law of the state. The principal object of this bill, which was passed, was to bring about a precise accord between the operations of the state government in the prevailing crisis and the purposes which the National Government was endeavoring to carry through. Hardly had steps been taken to accomplish this object, when the second State Council of Defense had to decide the question: what should be the method of pushing its work in every community? It was admitted that this had to be done primarily through local councils, but in what manner? This question had not seriously perplexed the first State Council of Defense, but to the second council the problem seemed to be difficult to solve in a satisfactory way.

It was finally proposed that a plan of organization should be first presented to the State Council of Defense, and, afterwards, a plan of work suitable to the conditions which had to be met

BATTLESHIPS AT ANCHOR OFF
OLD POINT COMFORT,
FORTRESS MONROE

in order to win success. As a part of the plan of work, it was suggested that special addresses should be delivered by members of the council itself before the numerous church conventions which were now coming together in the state. The influence of these bodies in promoting interest in the war and its vigorous prosecution was dwelt on with emphasis; and so was the assist-ance of the various school conferences which were also meeting at this time. It was also suggested that the eleven hundred organized community committees of the Cooperative Education Association should be requested to serve as sections of the county and city local Councils of Defense.

The plan finally adopted called for local councils. Under this plan, the executive committee of each local council was composed of the executive chairman and the chairmen of the several separate committees. The purpose of the local executive committee was to assign definite tasks to each subordinate local committee, and to enforce a prompt performance. It was considered to be peculiarly incumbent on each of these local executive committees to promote the success of the stamp drives, and also to assist the Red Cross, the Young Men's Christian Association, the Knights of Columbus, and the Jewish Welfare Board, in advancing the different enterprises for the prosecution of the war which they should undertake. These executive committees also kept in close affiliation with the National Government, so as to receive immediate information of any expansion in its general policy or alteration in its plans; and this information they were required to convey to the State Council of Defense in order to prevent any conflict in action. All the purely patriotic bodies working for the success of the war were also supervised to prevent any inconsistency or inharmony in the performance of their respective functions.

In addition to the local executive committee, which, as pointed out, had charge of the enforcement of these special duties covering a wide field, there were a publicity committee and a neighborhood committee. The publicity committee had under its control all public demonstrations, patriotic rallies, and emergency instruction. The neighborhood committee's duty was to approach individual citizens within limited areas, and to communicate with them directly, when that course, it was thought, would be the most effective. There were sixteen other committees of local councils whose object may be mentioned as showing the minute division of the functions of these local bodies scattered about the state. These committees had jurisdiction over finance, food production, home economics, food distribution and control, motor truck express, farm labor, labor in general, health welfare, law, thrift, economy, housing, home relief, loyalty, conservation, and negroes.

These various committees of the local councils were able to reach every side of the life of each community, and every section

BATTLESHIPS AT SEA OFF NORFOLK

of its inhabitants, from the richest to the poorest. On the other hand, as already pointed out, they also touched the vital machinery of the National Government in carrying on the war. This they did not do directly, but the contact was as effective as if it had been made through Washington, and not through Richmond. The Council of National Defense sent an order or suggestion to the State Council of Defense, which, in turn, remitted it to the subsidiary auxiliary bodies; and they, in their turn, remitted it to these local councils. The process might be the reverse. The bucket might start at the bottom of the well and rise to the top. The theory was perfect in itself; and that it did not always function fully and harmoniously was due to the slipping of a cog, which could not be anticipated or prevented at the time.

There were about twenty thousand persons employed in keeping this state system in order by performing faithfully the duties which had been assigned to them individually or as members of well defined bodies. All these persons, with few exceptions, had volunteered their services without expectation of any remuneration. How purely gratuitous was their attention to the war business was revealed in the case of Mr. Keely, who represented the National Government in Virginia as the Federal field secretary. His salary consisted of 100 cents a year. It was necessary, however, that some money should be at the disposal of the State Council of Defense. The General Assembly had appropriated the sum of $5,000 to cover all the expenses that could not be avoided; but this sum proved to be insufficient; and the governor, in order to make good the deficiency, appointed a committee of bankers to solicit contributions. These men represented every important district in the state. When the end of the war arrived, and all activities had ceased, there was left in the state treasury to the credit of the State Council of Defense $168.

It will not be possible to enter in detail into the manner in which the various committees of the local councils performed their several duties, for these duties covered a very wide ground, involving the success of the whole war scheme. In connection with transportation by car and truck, the state, represented by George W. Coleman, the road commissioner, agreed to expend one-half of the road fund in assisting in the construction of Federal military highways. The local councils too endeavored by every means in their power to aid the Federal Bureau of Housing in meeting the acute need for more room in the crowded towns. They strove to improve the situation of the women engaged in the war service of the National Government in Virginia. When the demand for food became more pressing in

Europe, the local councils encouraged the farmers to increase the acreage in corn and wheat, and enlarge the number of live stock which had been previously raised. They adopted additional means of fire prevention as suggested by the Council of National Defense; and they also heartily supported all the regulations that were proposed by that council to advance thrift and economy among the people. They were equally responsive to a second suggestion of that body; namely, to issue war pictures and to encourage the singing of community songs.

CHAPTER II

MILITARY AND POLITICAL SERVICE

The policies that related to mobilization belonged exclusively to the military jurisdiction of the National Government. All the steps taken to effect it began with that Government, and were directly under its general control. The State Council of Defense had no right of independent initiative in connection with these measures, and its power touching them ended either with advice, or with simply carrying out instructions as received. This occurred in the case of most of the War Department's activities. It was as an agent merely that the Virginia Council of Defense, for instance, informed the people of the exact nature of the draft regulations. These had been adopted by the War Department in the course of the Stuart administration.

At an early date the Council of National Defense directed that advisory boards should be appointed in every county and city by the state. These boards were to carry out the instructions which were to govern the expected draft. Instead of the State Council of Defense appointing the members of these boards, that body transferred this power to the president and executive committee of the State Bar Association; but the State Council kept a close oversight over the duties of these local councils through the adjutant-general of the state, one of its own members. The regulations relating to the draft were strictly enforced by the local councils and the State Council; and the response of the young men, except in very rare instances, was prompt in action and patriotic in spirit.

315

The 12th of September, 1918, had been fixed by the President of the United States as the day for the registration of all men in the whole country between eighteen and forty-five years of age, unless they, for one reason or another, were exempt from military service. A previous Act of Congress, dated May 18, 1917, had prescribed the age limit as twenty-one in one direction and thirty in the other, both to be inclusive. It will thus be perceived that the interval was substantially extended at either end of the period for enlistment. A severe penalty was to be inflicted, should any one, between these ages, fail to appear at the time chosen for the ceremony of registration. The mayor of each city and town of the state was instructed by the governor to issue a proclamation to inflame popular feeling in support of this measure; and the city and county councils were also directed to cooperate with the draft boards in securing a complete registration of the available military forces of their respective communities. Every possible medium of publicity was also employed to call the people's attention to the approaching ceremonial of draft day. In order to arouse martial enthusiasm, Secretaries Daniel and Baker, both of whom had been at one time vigorously opposed to participation in the European war, patriotically placed the finest military bands of the army and the navy at the disposal of various large cities in the state.

The impression made on General Crowder, the provost-marshal of the army, by the prompt response to the Government's directions, was so favorable and so satisfactory that he publicly commended the state and county councils of Virginia for their zealous and successful performance of their duties.

Apart from the men specially exempted, on account of their physical disabilities, or their incumbency of certain official positions, no favor was shown to any class as a class, with the exception, to some extent, of the farmers, whose services in the fields had become peculiarly valuable, owing to the shrinkage in labor. The latter was so short, indeed, that a large number of soldiers had to be furloughed in the summer of 1918 to give assistance in harvesting the crops. At a later date, when an epidemic of influenza had broken out to a degree beyond the control of the country districts, already deprived of so many of their local physicians, a large contingent of doctors was obtained from the military arm to combat the evil.

An important aid to the military service after the main registration in Virginia had been finished was the publication

BIG GUNS IN ACTION AT FORT STORY

of a booklet of legal rules for the guidance of the soldiers and sailors so recently enrolled. Its object was to inform the draft men of the character and scope of their civil and political rights, and to impress them with the legal consequences of evading the full performance of their duties in camp and field. It does not appear to have been distributed as freely among the soldiers and sailors themselves as among the members of the legal advisory boards, who were expected to use the information which it contained in personal consultation. It was also distributed very generally amongst the county clerks and the chairmen of the local councils.

The State Council of Defense was zealous in investigating the war risk insurance in which many fraudulent allotments and allowances had come to light at an early date; and it was also instrumental in preventing the lapse of many policies which had been improperly discredited. The State Council also endeavored to promote some form of industrial training among the young soldiers who were awaiting classification. In this course it had the ardent support of the public school authorities. It also assisted the military arm in intercepting deserters; and impressed upon the local councils the urgent need of their cooperation.

In the registration for June, 1917, which was the first undertaken, 181,000 men had been enlisted for active service. Over one-third of these Virginians made, on this occasion, no claim to exemption under any head. The registration included 95 per cent of the proportion within the age limit estimated by the Census Bureau to belong to the population of the state. This was 2 per cent in excess of the proportion allowed by that bureau for the rest of the country. The gross quota of the nation at large numbered about 1,150,000 men.

In May, 1918, an amendment to the Selective Service Act was adopted by Congress, which provided for the registration of all who had passed their twenty-first year during the interval since the original registration in June, 1917. Under the authority of this amendment, the enlistment was made, with the result that 14,600 men were added to the previous enrollment. About 10,000 of these were white, and about 4,000 were colored. In September, 1918, the total registration numbered 259,429 men. This, added to the registration in June, 1917, and June and August, 1918, brought the total for the period of the war to 465,619. Besides these, about 15,500 white men, and about 8,500 colored, were certified for military service on December 1st, 1918. The total number of Virginian soldiers actually inducted into military service were 78,524. About 9,000 of these were attached to the navy, and about 500 to the marine corps.

Owing to the withdrawal of so many troops from Virginia—
first in 1916, to serve as a cordon on the Mexican border, and
afterwards, in 1917, to fight on the battle-fields of France—it
became necessary for the state government to provide a domestic
military force for the preservation of order in the different communities, both urban and rural. There were now many inflam-
matory local influences at malignant play, which might, at any
time, come to the surface and cause serious popular disturbance.
A large number of persons had been brought to Virginia to work
in the munition plants and at the several army and naval bases.
Many of these, if not actively lawless, were indisposed to observe
strict rules of discipline outside of the limits of their employment. The atmosphere in which the entire population lived
was one that vibrated with the excitement and restlessness of
the hour; and there was always a danger that hostile circumstances would arise which could only be met with the strong
arm of military power.

It was the possibility of some outbreak like this taking place
at any moment that led Governor Stuart in July, 1917, just a
few weeks after the country had formally entered into the World
war, to authorize the organization of home defense companies,
which were to be known as "Virginia Volunteers." These companies were each to consist of at least sixty-four men, but not
more than 100, with a captain and two lieutenants, one sergeant
and one corporal attached. The response to the governor's
appeal was immediate. The wisdom of the call was universally
recognized, and an ample supply of men for the protection of
person, health, and property was quickly assured.

Among the companies organized, a few may be mentioned
as typical, in character, of the entire number. Among the first
to be enrolled was the Hanover Grays, which had begun to drill
even before the executive summons had been issued. In August,
1917, the Albemarle Rifles was formed, to be followed by the
Buckingham Guards, the Colonial Rifles, the Hopewell Rifles,
the Bath Rifles, and seventeen other companies, of equal zeal

and gallantry, all of which, like those already referred to, bore, as their distinctive titles, the names of the localities to which they belonged. In some cases, these were cities; in others, country districts. Among them was the famous organization, the Richmond Light Infantry Blues, which was mustered in as a battalion. Equally famous was the Richmond Grays, which

CAMP LEE

was mustered in as two companies. The largest company enlisted was the Valley Riflemen of Staunton, which embraced 200 men.

The Virginia State Volunteers were simply a trained militia, which was governed by the adjutant-general and its own officers only. It was the duty of these Volunteers to answer any call which the civil authorities should make for their military service, and, unlike the Home Guard companies, which were designed for local purposes alone, were liable to be ordered to any part of the state where disorder impended. The age for active duty ranged from eighteen years to forty-five. All these companies wore the khaki uniform—only slightly different in detail from that of the regular army. In some instances, they were compelled, owing to shortage in arms, to purchase the rifles which they used in drill and actual service. Adjutant-General Stern is said to have held in storage a complete equipment of overcoats, blankets, and pouches for any one company that should be called out to suppress any commotion that might occur. It was observed that even the slight experience of military discipline obtained in the career of a volunteer, spurred some of the men, in their eagerness for a taste of real war, to join, as soon as they were able, the regular forces of the army and navy. Many soon became subject to the normal draft and were drawn automatically into this larger field.

But one incident occurred in 1918 that required the intervention of the Volunteers. This took place at Hopewell, the site of the great Dupont Munition Works. The cause of the disturbance there arose from the friction between white and colored employees of that corporation. The critical situation was modified by the prompt arrival of several companies on the scene; and before night had closed in, peace had been restored, without the need of bloodshed. The retention of the troops on the ground for a few days had the effect of making this return to quiet conditions permanent.

As early as July, 1917, an attempt was begun to organize Home Guards in every city, town, and county of the commonwealth. The Virginia Volunteers, as we have mentioned, were really a militia liable to be ordered to any part of the state where disturbance had actually broken out or was seriously threatened. The Home Guard, on the other hand, was simply a higher branch of the local police, whose duty, like that of every form of special police, was directly subject to the instructions which were given by the sheriffs, constables, and mayor. Unlike the Volunteers, they had no connection with the office of the adjutant-general beyond receiving the state's formal authority to organize; nor had they any connection with the state troops. Apparently, a Home Guard was established only by those communities which had failed to set on foot a Volunteer company. The entire number of Home Guard companies, indeed, did not exceed twenty-nine, of which twelve were stationed in cities, and seventeen in counties. This deficiency arose from the fact that not many communities were able to furnish sufficient men— apart from those subject to the draft—to make up both a Home Guard and a Volunteer company. In the country districts, the men who remained undrafted were generally farmers; and these were often too much engaged with their crops to have the time to walk or ride a considerable distance to attend the drills. They had, indeed, in many cases, been exempted from service only because the demand for their labor in the fields was so urgent. There was no similar demand in the cities, beyond the production of munitions, and, in consequence, the large towns, where the need of organized protection was greatest, enrolled in some instances as many as six companies of Home Guards, whom they equipped and supported. Richmond possessed as many as twelve, a large proportion of whose members supplied their own arms and equipment. In both Danville and Richmond, Home Defense Leagues were formed; and this was also done in Portsmouth. There was, in fact, no town of any importance in the state which did not organize at least one Home Guard. And this was also done by the most populous counties. Albemarle County, for instance, formed at least two. The existence of these companies was influential in preserving order even though they were rarely called upon to intervene. Above all, by the excellent opportunities which they offered for acquiring knowledge of military drill and the rules of military discipline, they fitted many raw citizens for active participation in the war, even though they should never leave their native state.

The ground covered in the operations of the Virginia units on the continent of Europe is too broad to be treated in a work of this kind with any approximation to completeness even in outlines. The events of those sanguinary campaigns in which the Virginian troops took part in but small proportion to the millions actually engaged, belong, not to the history of their commonwealth, but to the history of the whole world. These troops were so inextricably mixed with the soldiery from other parts of the United States, taking the country at large, that it would be difficult to give a description of their share in the conflict, except as separate contingents. There were thirty-two Virginia units in all. Of this number, eleven never participated in the struggle abroad, as they were never taken oversea. Of the twenty-one that landed in France, six were never marched to the front. These had their only experience of service behind the lines. They embraced (1) the two colored engineer battalions, whose duties limited them to rough construction work; (2) the two fully equipped Base Hospitals, numbered 41 and 45, furnished by the University of Virginia and the Medical College of Virginia, respectively; and in addition, (3) the two units consisting of the One Hundred and Eleventh Field Artillery, and the One Hundred and Fourth Ammunition Train.

There were seven units occupied in doing valuable work of different kinds near the first line, but were never drawn directly into the fighting. These seven units were attached to sanitary trains, ambulance corps, military police, and similar branches of the service.

At least eight units of the Virginia troops, however, entered the very thick of the conflict at the front. The names of these may be mentioned: The One Hundred and Sixteenth Infantry, formed by the First, Second and Fourth Virginia Infantry Regiments; Company B of the One Hundred and Twelfth Machine Gun Battalion; the Three Hundred and Seventeenth and Three Hundred and Eighteenth Infantry, and the Three Hundred and Fourteenth Machine Gun Battalion, organized from among the Virginian members of the Eightieth Division; and finally, Battery B, Sixtieth Regiment, drafted in Roanoke, and Battery F, Sixtieth Regiment, drafted in Richmond. The Richmond Light Infantry Blues had converted their organization from an infantry into a horse battalion, in order to hasten their participation in the events of the battle fields.

The first embarkation of Virginian troops for Europe came off in August, 1917. Two other sailings followed before the end of the year. The first, in 1918, occurred in January; and there had been four more before the middle of June arrived. The last took place in July.

The One Hundred and Sixteenth Infantry, in July and August, 1918, participated in the operations on the front line in the section of Haute Marne, and, subsequently, were engaged in the bloody offensive in the Meuse-Argonne. Companies B and D of the One Hundred and Twelfth Machine Gun Battalion shared in these conflicts. From September 26th to November 6th, the Three Hundred and Seventeenth and Three Hundred and Eighteenth Infantry and the Three Hundred and Fourteenth Machine Gun Battalion, of the Eightieth Division, were deeply involved in the movement of the Argonne offensive. Batteries B and F of the Sixtieth Regiment, which were principally trained for active service in France, also took part in the same memorable advance. The One Hundred and Seventeenth Trains Headquarters and Military Police were stationed at first in Lorraine and Champagne, but were afterwards transferred, in succession, to Chateau-Thierry and St. Mihiel, where Pershing's attack proved so successful. Subsequently, they were posted in the Meuse-Argonne.

The One Hundred and Fifteenth Hospital and One Hundred and Fifteenth Ambulance Company were associated with the Twenty-ninth Division during its operations on the east bank of the Meuse River, while the Three Hundred and Nineteenth Ambulance Company took part in the sanguinary scenes of the Meuse-Argonne offensive. Ambulance Section 517 served in the Ypres, Champagne, and Argonne sectors. Section 518 had a still more varied history. It served first in the Vosges, and, afterwards, in the sectors of Amiens and Chemin des Dames. It was later on closely engaged in the struggle that took place along the line of the Oise-Sambre Canal. The One Hundred and Eleventh Field Artillery landed in France in July, 1918, and having completed its training, was about to leave for the front when the armistice was proclaimed. The Horse Battalion, also too late, arrived on French shores in the course of the same month.

Base Hospital No. 45, equipped by the Medical College of Virginia, established itself at Toul, while Base Hospital No. 41, equipped by the University of Virginia, took possession of the old school at St. Denis. Among the noblest memorials of America's share in the World war are the records which describe the service that was performed by these two hospital units. Although Hospital No. 41 was designed for 1,000 beds only, it was called upon, before the close of the conflict, to find room for 3,000. Fifty-two marquise tents were erected for the accommodation of more patients, and numerous Beaseneau tents were added for the same purpose. Halls and kitchens were also converted into wards, and the cooking was done under shelter out of doors. When the armistice was declared, this hospital alone was administering to the needs of 2,900 patients. At the height of Foch's offensive, the convoy would, on some days, bring in as many as 400 wounded soldiers. Although, between August 16 and January 17, 1918-19, 4,800 cases were treated, there were only sixty-eight deaths, of which twenty-seven resulted from pneumonia following influenza. Base Hospital No. 41 received one-fourth of all the wounded who were brought to Paris from the front, although there were ten other establishments of the same nature situated in the city.

The following figures reveal the extent to which individual officers and soldiers attached to the Virginian contingents achieved special personal prominence. Ten won the Distinguished Service Medal of the Army; seven the Distinguished Service Clasp; and ten the Navy Cross. Five were cited by the Commander-in-Chief. Five won the American Expeditionary Force Citation, and six the Meritorious Service Citation Certificate. One hundred and nine were cited by the First Division Commanders; twenty-six by the Second Division Commanders; and ten by Brigade Commanders. Twenty-two won the Silver Star Citation; seven, the Miscellaneous Citations; four, Commendations; and fourteen, recommendations for the distinguished service medal and cross. Eighteen won the Croix de Guerre; five, the Legion of Honor; and three, the Medal of Honor. Five received the Belgian and Italian Medals; two, Polish; three, Portuguese; one, Rumanian; one, Servian; three, Russian; one, Grecian; one, Montenegron; and one, Czecho-Slovakian.

Virginia, as we have seen, performed with alacrity the part which she was called upon by the National Government to play. She promptly provided her proportion of the troops needed for the prosecution of the war oversea; and her authorities, both local and state, without exception, were most energetic in stimulating the production of food crops for the support of the Allied Armies. These were the chief military duties imposed upon Virginia by the conflict. She was equally assiduous, when war actually started, in the performance of all her civic duties. The President of the United States, throughout the hostilities, and during the period of reconstruction which followed, was a native of Staunton; the Secretary of the Treasury, for a time, was a native of Lynchburg; the Chairman of the Foreign Affairs Committee in the House was a native of Appomattox; and the Comptroller of the Currency was a native of Richmond. These men exercised, in one case a supreme, and, in the other cases, a most important, influence on the course of military and political events.

Mr. Wilson did not escape private and public criticism previous to the entry of the United States into the war in the spring of 1917. It was thought, first, that his policy "of watchful waiting" in Mexico, before the conflagration in Europe began, had produced on the German mind the erroneous impression that the President could not be provoked to join in a European war, even by the most aggravated encroachment on American rights. This contemptuous feeling removed that apprehension of American interference which a bolder attitude on his part might perhaps have engendered among the Germans when the depredations on American shipping began. The pressure of the Administration on the European conflict during the first two years of the fighting amounted unfortunately to as little as that of a second rate power. In other words, it was practically negligible for the time being. A bolder Executive, it was asserted after Belgium had been invaded, would have offered an open protest against the reduction of solemn treaties to the status of worthless scraps of paper. The expediency of such action, however, would have been questionable where the treaties involved only European interests.

The Presidential call upon the people of the United States to obliterate all partisanship from their minds, even to the extent of suppressing all thought of the war, was going perhaps beyond the demands of a normal neutrality, and placed the country in the position of possessing no opinion of its own at a time when the whole world was outraged by the Germans' conduct in Belgium and their ruthless indifference to the rights of neutrals on the sea. This spirit reached the extreme of caution when the Secretary of the Navy forbade in his department the public or private singing of any of the Allied war songs.

The Administration, during a long period, could find no more pertinent expression of its convictions than argumentative Presidential notes to the Central Powers, which the latter hardly took the time to answer. In the meanwhile, their delegations in the United States were plotting in the shadow of the White House itself to cripple the aid which this country was giving to the Allies in the form of munitions and food supplies. Frequent carping against Great Britain's firm sea policy at an hour when she was struggling for her very existence, and announcements in public addresses that "peace without victory," alone was to be desired, although the future welfare of the whole world was known to be really dependent upon the crushing of the enemy—such acts and such words placed the real sentiment of America in an unhappy light, which was aggravated by the later utterance, "too proud to fight," which fell from Presidential lips after the destruction of the *Lusitania*, the foulest crime in history since the Massacre of St. Bartholomew.

OLD AND NEW LIGHTHOUSES AT CAMP HENRY

The only substantial justification for the Administration's failure to call at once for war was that, in its judgment, the public opinion of the country was not yet ready to take the plunge. This impression on its part was not universally accepted as correct. The people were, quite probably, as ready to follow the President then as they were in April, 1917, when a state of war was formally declared by Congress on his recommendation. There was no other course to pursue if the dignity and self-respect of the American people were worthy of preservation at all.

The course of the President in prosecuting the war after the United States entered it, was not open to pertinent criticism. His action in fact was prompt and vigorous. The popular weight behind him carried the whole national force into the conflict. The American brilliant record in providing food and munition from this side, and in assisting in the battles on the other, reflected honor on the country's spirit; and this spirit, so powerful in its display, had an important, if not a decisive, effect on the final upshot of the contest.

Virginia was more closely identified with the patriotic labors of Mr. Glass and Mr. Flood than with those of Mr. Wilson, for these two men had represented her, during many years, in Congress. Mr. Glass had won extraordinary distinction as the principal author of the Reserve Board Act. This reputation for great financial ability was increased by his career in the National Treasury, where his profound knowledge of the duties of the position, coupled with a conservative spirit and a rare sagacity, made him one of the most competent secretaries who has ever filled that powerful office.

Mr. Flood, as head of the House Committee of Foreign affairs —perhaps the most important at that time in the Lower Chamber—performed his part in the mighty drama, then in progress, with marked ability, thoroughness, and devotion. Mr. Williams, as Comptroller of the Treasury, was distinguished for his unbending integrity and uncompromising firmness in performing his delicate functions. If, by his rigid sense of duty, he sometimes created enemies, this hostility was of the kind that made most men honor and respect him all the more.

Two Virginians filled ambassadorial positions abroad during the war, namely, Thomas Nelson Page, and Joseph E. Willard. The one was accredited to the Court of Italy; the other to the Court of Spain; and both remained acceptably in office throughout the progress of hostilities.

CHAPTER III

VIRGINIA CITIES—THEIR HISTORICAL ASPECT

It is a fact of significance that, with three exceptions, the important cities of Virginia are the expanded towns of the eighteenth century. Roanoke, Newport News, and Hopewell alone, have sprung up on sites, which, fifty years ago, were simply unoccupied fields, or, at best, the ground on which a private residence and its curtilage had been standing. This was notably the case with the site of Hopewell, which, within the memory of persons living, had been, for the most part, the site of a famous colonial home, the home of the Eppes family, while the site of Roanoke had, at one time, been a part of the ancestral estate of the Watts family.

As the colonial settlement of Virginia developed in the orderly form of a gradual spreading out of population from Tidewater to the Blue Ridge, so the growth of the modern cities of the state has been a steady expansion from roots which had been in existence, in most instances, for at least a century and a half, if not two centuries. Norfolk, Hampton, Williamsburg, Richmond, Petersburg, Fredericksburg, Alexandria, Winchester, Staunton, Charlottesville, Lynchburg, Harrisonburg, Lexington, and Wythesville, had been incorporated either before the Revolution, or before the termination of many years afterwards. One impressive result of this fact has been that each of these towns, now so modern in their character, possesses a history that is intertwined with the history of the commonwealth at large, both when it was a colony, and, subsequently, when it had become a state. This has given the

330

distinction of a historical individuality to each of these cities, which has been increased in charm, and not diminished, by the glow of their recent advance in wealth and population.

This definite romance which comes from age is but one of the several peculiarities which identify these cities with the ancient centers of urban population in England, from which so many of them derived their names. Norfolk, Hampton, Richmond, York, Winchester, Suffolk, Bristol and Warrenton, hark back, in this respect, to old English towns, the chronicles of which reach to the era of the Normans. Of an equally distinct, but less prominent, English historical suggestiveness are the names of Alexandria, Staunton, Lexington, Orange, Fredericksburg, Culpeper, and Charlottesville. Other towns, such as Lynchburg, Wytheville, Pulaski, and Franklin, have an identification with a history that goes back to the Revolutionary age.

In entering the most prosperous of the Virginia cities, like Richmond and Norfolk, for instance, the well-informed visitor becomes conscious at once of the presence of a back-ground that reflects a past, which, from the point of view of our more or less youthful country, is really an extended one, and as varied as it is extended. Norfolk rises in memory's eye as a colonial port on a broad estuary of the great Bay, with the British flag flying at the peaks of its vessels. It was hardly to be distinguished from a port of the same size situated on the English coast. Its trade was of the same general character, and its sailors were of the same race. The English seashore towns imported heavily from the West Indies; so did Norfolk; and, in many cases, in the same bottoms. The men and scenes, and the hogsheads and casks, along the docks, were plainly reminiscent of English wharves. There the negro alone would be missing.

The vision summoned before the inner eye by Richmond was in a still longer vista. Almost down to the end of the seventeenth century, the site of the future town was known as the World's End. Until the Huguenots built a village at Monocan

west of the Falls in the James, the spread of the tidewater
population had not passed the barrier of the forests that reached
to the base of the Blue Ridge. The residence and trading shops
of the first William Byrd were, during a long series of years, the
last outpost of Virginian civilization in that quarter of the colony. The place did not then contain even a frontier fort. It
was simply the home and trading stand of a single proprietor.
Here the characeristic scenes of such a spot at that time were
to be observed—the Indian, with his rifle and pack of pelts,
ready for barter with the store-keeper; the store-keeper spreading out his goods to tempt the savage's taste; the numerous
factors lounging about with their guns and horses and awaiting
the command to return to the wilderness for another harvest of
furs; the master, in the midst of it all, silent, and, perhaps, not
devoid of some distrust of his taciturn copper-colored guests.

This was a scene of the frontier. Afterwards, the slowly
growing village passed before the mind's eye through a long
period, not without disorder, as Bacon's rebellion disclosed.
Then followed the events of the Revolution, and we behold
great figures of that mighty era whose voices were heard in the
conventions which assembled in the halls of the town. And
finally, there unrolls the panorama of the War of 1861-65, when
every street echoed to the tramp of soldiers, and the roll of
drums, and the blare of trumpets, and the strains of martial
music.

It is no reflection on the historical background of the other
Virginian cites to say that, in the midst of their prosperity, they
were unable to call up such a wonderful background as this—
one so rich in stirring or picturesque scenes, and one so animated with the presence of political and military heroes. Not
even Williamsburg, that sits today under her urban trees justly
conscious of her classic fame. There the ghosts of the most
aristocratic society that ever flourished on our continent still
flit about, carrying with them the bright colors of the old
colonial costumes, the elegance of powdered hair and silver shoe-

buckles, and the charm of polished manners not unworthy of St. James itself. To pass down the long street is to be lost in dreams of a past that vies in interest with the one suggested by the streets of some old English town, which counts its age by the centuries. Only here, there is also to be felt, on either hand, the breath of the wind that accompanies modern progress.

The oldest college building in Virginia, if not on the continent, stands in the very shadow of the imposing new structures which the press of an ever-increasing number of students has required to be erected. Here we have mingled those two traits which the conservative yet enterprising instincts of the English stock of people have always cherished: namely, a just regard for the sentimental claims of the past, and, at the same time, a clear recognition of the superior claims of the present.

Williamsburg would possess a romantic interest even if it had no other power of appeal beyond its association with Jamestown, which lies only a few miles away. Practically, the new capital was simply the old transferred through the forest to the higher and more wholesome site of Middle Plantation. The noble view of the broad waters of the Powhatan seen from Jamestown is shut out of sight from Williamsburg by the thick screen of trees that rises between it and the spacious stream; but the presence of the river, and the inspiration of the events which occurred along its banks in colonial times, seem still to pervade the atmosphere of the whole region. We have only to leave the highway running from the modern Williamsburg to Richmond to find ourselves in a road which leads down to some one of the baronial estates that have given the Lower James so conspicuous a place in the social history of Virginia. Perhaps, it is the home of William Byrd, the second, the most accomplished gentleman associated with the colonial period, the black swan of his age, and the perfect embodiment of every brilliant characteristic that has been claimed for the Old Virginian plantation life in the reign of the king. The imposing mansion stands there still, irrefutable evidence of the solidity as well as

of the beauty of that past civilization. Perhaps, it is Shirley,
not far off, which is equally remindful of the same age and
equally suggestive, in its wide halls, spacious apartments, old
world furniture, and noble portraits, of some ancestral English
home of our own day. Perhaps, it is Berkeley, where one of
the Presidents first saw the light, or Sherwood Forest where
another one resided. Or perhaps it is Brandon, so closely
identified with the social life of the last century.

On the other side of Williamsburg, there spreads away, like
some spacious lake, the silver waters of the York. A little creek,
rising on the eastern slope of the town, finds its way through
the short intervening distance to the bosom of this broad stream.
But that stream differed from the James in possessing no great
estates—at least along its southern banks. It was really an
estuary of the bay. The lands situated on its southern margin
had never, like those along the James, been subject to overflow
that left behind it a rich alluvial deposit suitable to the production of great crops of wheat, maize and tobacco. It was an
opulent soil that made the wealthy colonial family and the fine
old colonial mansion, with its thronging interests and traditions.
There was no room for that affluent social life on the southern
side of the York because the ground there was comparatively
poor.

On the northern side, on the other hand, the existence of
Carter Hall and Rosewell, homes of the Burwells and Pages
respectively, shows that the York could, in part at least, repeat
the generous style of living for which the valley of the James
was so celebrated. On its banks at Yorktown, we find in our
own era a town that is invested with some of the most inspiring
memories of American history. The long street of quaint structures and the old custom-house point drowsily to the time when
the town was an important port of entry for ships bringing into
the colonies the diversified merchandise of Europe. The tall
statue, so imposing in its artistic beauty, reminds the spectator
that the spot had other associations besides those which were

purely commercial. Did not Cornwallis surrender on this spot, caught between the upper American military millstone and the French nether? As the first tocsin of the Revolution was rung by Henry only a few miles away, under the roof of the House of Burgesses, so its last bell sounded when O'Hara, in the name of his humiliated master, delivered up his sword to Washington's designated lieutenant. "All is well, and Cornwallis has surrendered" soon echoed from town to town, up and down the Atlantic Coast, and far off over the plains behind, and deep into the valleys of the Alleghanies.

Independence was not the only result of the great scene which has made the ground of Yorktown forever sacred to liberty. A never-to-be-forgotten lesson in unselfish patriotism was taught there, for the inspiration of future ages, when General Nelson, with Roman firmness, directed his cannoneers to fire their heaviest shells at his splendid home rising from behind the enemy's lines.

Let us return to the banks of the James. Just at the point where the modern Newport News stands, the river merges in the broad waters of Hampton Roads. In the early Colonial times, when the site belonged to Daniel Gookin, it was notable in the minds of all mariners plying that way for a spring that gushed from the earth in a phenomenal volume. It was from this spring that water was taken aboard for the ocean voyage. Later on, a substitute was found by many seagoing vessels in the water of Lake Drummond, so deeply tinctured with the taste of the juniper tree, presumed by sailors to be so preservative of freshness. Perhaps, near the very spot where the spring at Newport News—known in those times as Newport's News —poured out of a bank, the modern docks and ship yards which have made the place so famous, now spread out in extraordinary vastness.

Young in years as Newport News is, the name of the city is one of the oldest in Virginia. Here was illustrated a conceit in nomenclature that was often employed in that age. How did

this double-barreled name arise? The most plausible explanation points to the combination of the names of Captain Newport
and Captain Newce, both skilful ship-masters and brave colonial
officers. It is thought by some that the spot was so designated
because here Captain Newport received discouraging news of

Courtesy of Virginia State Chamber of Commerce

NEWPORT NEWS

the settlers at Jamestown, when he was bringing over the First
or Second Supply, in order to preserve them from starvation.

But which ever version is correct—and the first explanation
is almost unquestionably the true one—the modern city of Newport News had a recorded history several centuries before it was
actually founded. That narrow section of river coast was so
called when stout Daniel Gookin's pioneer cabins were the only
habitations, except those of the Indians, situated in all that
region. It bore this name when little fleets of aboriginal canoes
plied up and down the great shining stream, reaching inland as

far as the eye could see. It bore that name when the Dutch men-of-war, in Governor Berkeley's time, pursued the English merchantmen to the mouth of the James and burnt them to the water's edge. It bore that name when, in the War of 1812-15, the British cruisers sailed by to carry havoc into the land. It bore that name still, when the *Merrimac* rammed the Federal wooden frigates near shore

The thriving city was not thought of then, but when it did arise, what a stirring history it inherited at once, a history older than that of Plymouth, or New York, or Richmond, or Charleston, or Cincinnati, or Chicago!

And a similar priority could be claimed by Hampton, lying not far away on the beautiful curving coast that ran down to the bay. This town is today one of the principal shell-fish marts of Virginia. It still maintains the reputation which that region acquired in the time of John Smith, for did he not record the fact that he spent Christmas here with the Keconghtan Indians, and that, on this occasion, he was feasted with oysters and game to a degree of repletion hardly to be surpassed in the most opulent contemporary home in England? The most extensive cornfields seen by the voyagers of 1607 were situated in this quarter; and after all the time that has elapsed since then, one can almost deceive himself into thinking that he still hears the gentle rustling of the vast array of corn-blades, as the breeze stirs the emerald stalks. Here was a scene of abundance which the starving creatures behind the palisades at Jamestown, not many months afterwards, must have recalled with a feeling of longing that deepened their sense of despair.

It is quite possible that the first African slaves to be landed on North American soil were first disembarked here. They were subsequently found, hoe in hand, on Governor Yeardley's plantation higher up the great river. Hampton felt the British stroke in the Second War for American Independence; and from her shore the epochal combat between the two marine monsters, the *Merrimac* and the *Monitor*, could be plainly discerned.

Further towards the bay rises the ramparts of a great Federal fort, the successor of a large earthwork that stood on the spot as far back as the earliest days of the colony. In the wide waters off shore, Newport, in the spring of 1607, searched long, and, at first, in vain for a passageway deep enough to accommodate the hulls of the *Sarah Constant* and *Goodspeed;* and it was not until he skirted the point on the north side that he found the channel of the river, with ample room for his keels. A garrison within a few weeks was placed there. Its chief duty was to watch the glimmering capes for strange incoming vessels. The nightmare of the hour was the strong probability that a fleet of Spanish cruisers would, at any moment, hove in sight. This might mean the impending destruction of the little settlement at Jamestown. On at least one occasion, a single vessel did enter the Roads and drop anchor off the primitive fort; but she repressed her hostile purpose, and was satisfied with simply placing on shore a couple of disguised spies, one of whom, Governor Dale, with characteristic sternness and decision, swung to the yard's arm of his vessel.

Here at the point, all the newcomers were required to stop on their way up the James; and here they obtained their first view of Virginia from the side of the land.

In the course of the next century, the sad eyes of the fugitives from Acadia looked across these waters, eager, perhaps, to find another home here, but destined instead to pass on until they had reached the marshy bayous of Louisiana. And when another long period had gone by, the files of a great army in blue were seen disembarking from a fleet of transports and establishing their encampments in the vicinity of the modern fort. A few years more, and the late Chief Magistrate of the Confederacy was to be found here, shut up within narrow walls, but awaiting his fate with imperturbable dignity.

Cross the James to Smithfield, where the famous ham of that name has long rivaled the most succulent product of Westphalia in the Old World. Its excellence is due to the flavor of the local breed of hogs, which run wild in the woods, and about the dug-over peanut fields, and feed greedily on the acorns and the dwarfed peanuts left in the hill. Without taking on a proportionate fatness, the Smithfield pig, nevertheless, acquired an uncommon sweetness and delicacy in its flesh. What chance has the noble old English church near the town—where generations of the people of Isle of Wight County have worshipped—of attracting the attention of the average visitor, when, for him, the atmosphere of the community seems to be as reminiscent of hams as Champagne and Bordeaux are of grapes; or the English Kent, of hops; or Italian Piedmont, of olives; or the Bermudas, of lilies; or Carolina, of rice; or the Virginian Southside, of yellow tobacco.

But the old church is a beautiful shrine, nevertheless, as suggestive of the ancestral English stock as any of the numerous venerable churches that rise along the banks of the Thames near Oxford, or the Mole near Guilford, or about Boston in the Fens, or among the chalk hills of Tunbridge Wells. This edifice resembles a tablet erected in some stirring prosperous community to remind the people, as they hurry by, of the remote colonial civilization, so peaceful and so removed in spirit, and yet so full of charm and color and culture.

We pass on by Portsmouth, so long associated with warships and memories of the *Merrimac;* by that noble naval hospital, which looks down the wide Roads, until the seascape blends with the horizon; on by the Dismal Swamp, with its skeleton trees, rising above the wine-colored waters, and its fire-fly lamps at night, pointing the way for the canoe of the mystical maiden and her lover. Further on still, by Suffolk; solid in the prosperity which she has won, so largely by the handling of that most prosaic of all fruits, if fruit, not vegetable, it can be called—the peanut. Does not that city justly boast

of a bank, the shares of which command the highest price of
any like shares on the exchange—excepting only the stock of
a single bank in New York City?

From here westward to Franklin and Courtland the highway winds through fields of fluffy white cotton or tall Indian
corn; or spreading peanut vines; or the still greener vines of
the potato—a region apparently capable of producing any crop
under the sun.

Turning northward, we reach, within a few hours, Petersburg, renowned in history for its success, during so many
months, in resisting the vast army of Grant. The fortifications
still belt the town. We enter the main street through an environment that once trembled to the roar of heavy siege guns, and
over ground once saturated with blood. The crowds along
the thoroughfares have not forgotten the past, as numerous
monuments testify. Here are great tobacco and cotton factories,
which reach out their aromatic hands as far as Sidney and Hong
Kong; but, perhaps, the visitor at first is content to recall that
it was the incomparable William Byrd, the second, who founded
the town; that not far off, John Randolph, strange meteor from
another world, was born; and that here died that British commander who was pronounced even by his foes to be the "proudest
soldier of the proudest nation on earth."

In Hopewell, Petersburg's nearest neighbor, we have an
enterprising community that reminds one more of the growth
of Western cities than of the growth of Virginia, for not even
the gourd that sheltered Jonah had a much more rapid expansion
after the first seed was sown. It had its birth in the hothouse
of war-times; the cessation of war activities threatened it with
extinction; but, as in the case of the runner who has caught
his second breath, the future promises for it a rate of progress
not previously surpassed. Here the new spirit abroad in Virginia springs from a ground peculiarly hallowed by the story
of the past. Across the water rise the roofs of Shirley and
Westover, monuments of that leisurely day which has cast a

spell over the whole valley of the Lower James. This spell is
not really broken, but, on the contrary, merely deepened, by
the throbbing energy of the new center of modern manufacture
on the West Shore, which blows its smoke over so many scenes
associated with a more romantic history.

Fredericksburg, many miles to the north, sits, like Richmond,
on the ledge of rock that marks abruptly the western border
line of the coastal plain. The Rappahannock comes tumbling
down from a higher level to form itself into a placid, slow-
moving stream that seeks far off the embrace of the sea. John
Smith saw these falls in the course of his voyage up the bay,
just as he had seen the falls at Richmond, a few weeks earlier,
in Captain Newport's company. A more interesting fact still
is told of the first years of the ancient town's settlement, for
it has been seriously asserted that there formerly rested on its
soil a tombstone which casually recorded that, underneath, there
reposed the remains of an Englishman who was one of those
who had borne the pall at Shakespeare's funeral. The correctness of this statement, if every really made, has very properly
been disputed; but claim to belief has been romantically supported by one of the most beautiful sonnets in the language.

Fredericksburg has other and more substantial reasons to
arouse historical interest. Did not some of the Knights of the
Golden Horseshoe pass through the town on their way to the
rendezvous at Germanna? Spotswood, erect in his saddle, led
the way. Some of the explorers, no doubt dreaming of the Shenandoah so lately seen, returned by the same road to their distant
homes in Tidewater.

But a more commanding figure yet dominated the ancient
borough at a later time. It was not so much Washington, as
Washington's mother, tall and imposing in bearing, who rises
before us as we wander about the ancient streets. No matron
looks down from the vista of Roman history with a sterner gaze
than this venerable parent of the immortal Father of his Country. There came a day when the earliest of American sea-com-

JOHN PAUL JONES
From the Statue by C. H. Niehaus
at Washington, D. C.

manders, then a young and obscure exile from his oversea country, was to be seen lounging with his friends at the street corners. No one then suspected that, in John Paul Jones, the qualities of a marine hero had been planted by nature.

Down further in the stages of time, a great battle was fought here. That plain spreading to the hills on the south side of the river was the scene of the gallant Pelham's feat of stopping with two cannon, for a time, the advance of a great hostile army, while his commanders, Lee and Jackson, looked down from the heights behind in wondering admiration of the courage of their youthful, lionhearted lieutenant.

Alexandria, sitting at the feet of the national capital, could boast a longer history than the town across the river. She had been a flourishing post when Washington was an open field in part, and in part a straggling wood. The most vivid association belonging to the place goes back to that morning when the brave but obstinate martinet, Gen. Edward Braddock, set out, at the heal of several regiments of complacent red-coats, on his fatal march to the Monongahela. There was a youthful but stalwart aide at his side, who understood the subtlety of the Indian warrior, and the deceitfulness of his method of warfare; but the self-sufficient British officer failed to listen to the warnings uttered by his thoughtful Virginian lieutenant.

The pews are still pointed out at Alexandria where George Washington and Robert E. Lee worshipped in Christ Church. Many a famous American and European passed through these streets in the far past on their way to visit the two noble mansions at Mount Vernon and Arlington.

A flight across the Blue Ridge and we land at Winchester; perhaps, already embosomed in the blossoms of its glorious apple orchards. Nature has scattered on all sides the most beautiful gifts that spring can offer from her bountiful bosom —the poetic charm of misty mountain ranges, which reflect the cerulean tints of Virginian skies as Como and Maggiore reflect those of Italian; the sweeping landscape dotted with groves and farms, and blooming orchards; and nearer at hand, the town, shaded by its masses of trees, and bustling with trade. The sight of it calls up three eminent figures: Washington, preparing his troops for a second attack on Fort Duquesne; Old Lord Fairfax, uttering the despairing wish to be put to bed for good when informed of the closing success of the American cause; and Stonewall Jackson, driving out the Federal armies with the irresistible force of a whirlwind.

We pass on up the valley—the terrain of the most brilliant military campaign that has occurred since the young Bonaparte fought on the plains of Lombardy. Harrisonburg, Staunton, and Lexington are reached in succession, after we have traversed one of the most beautiful sections of the United States. In sight are ramparts of lofty mountains towering at a distance on the eastern and western horizons, while close at hand spreads away the combined panorama of fields, clothed in wheat and maize, meadows, waving with clover, orchards, groaning under the weight of apples and peaches, and white farmhouses, standing amid their verdant groves. At Lexington, the past and the present again come together inextricably, for here are the tombs of Lee and Jackson, and also the imposing buildings of two famous modern colleges. And here too an immortal lesson in patriotism is taught by the monument to the youthful heroes who perished at the Battle of New Market. This is, perhaps, the most pathetic, and, at the same time, the most inspiring memorial to be seen standing on the soil of Virginia.

Charlottesville, which we reach after crossing the pass at Afton, where one of the noblest landscapes in the world is to be descried, has a more classic charm than any other spot in the state, for here rise, on a neighboring mountain, the beautiful proportions of the Monticello mansion; and down in the plain below stand the Palladian pavilions and lofty Rotunda, which we owe to the taste and persistence of Jefferson. Scattered around the town are artistic statues to the great figures of the Revolution and the War for Southern Independence. A village has existed at Charlottesville from the early settlement of the County of Albemarle.

Lynchburg cannot as yet claim the accumulated historical glow of age, although its annals go back for a long period in the past. The only important historical incident in the history of Danville was its conversion into the Confederate capital after the fall of Richmond. These two centers, like Roanoke, Bristol, and Hopewell, are less remarkable for historical interest than for commercial and manufacturing greatness. They have been built up on the basis of that new spirit which has, in recent years, been transforming the character of the whole state. This change takes in the old towns, which have been associated with the history of the general community almost from the beginning, as well as the new towns which are of very modern growth.

JOHN M. MILLER, JR.
President First and Merchants
National Bank of Richmond
Photo by Dementi

GOVERNOR HARRY F. BYRD

HON. HARRIS HART
State Superintendent of Public
Education
Courtesy of Department of Public Education

JOHN W. CRADDOCK

HON. GEORGE W. KOINER
Head of Virginia State Department

S. L. SLOVER

CHAPTER IV

MANUFACTURES AND FINANCIAL FACILITIES

The development of manufactures in Virginia has now reached such an extent that the state may almost claim that this new department of its interests is just as important as its agricultural. But whether this assertion would be strictly correct or not at the present time, there can be but small doubt that the outlook for the commonwealth's manufactures is more promising of a voluminous expansion than the outlook for agriculture. It is true that the latter still has wide room for enlargement in spite of the fact that, during several centuries, it has been the main local pursuit. Local manufactures, on the other hand, are on the threshold of their growth. Their future seems unlimited, in the light of the recent increase of the American population, which, apparently, has hardly passed its first stage.

It was natural enough that the Virginians should, during their antebellum history, have directed their principal attention to agriculture. The soil of their state was adapted to an extraordinary variety of crops. Wheat, maize, cotton, tobacco, and vegetables, could be produced in it with abundance. This encouraged the growth of the plantation system, which was already dear to a people who had come originally from a country where rural life had always exercised a strong fascination over the popular mind. It is true that England had, for many generations, shown her ability to maintain a great system of manufactures at the very time that she offered a paradise of agriculture.

It was not until the abolition of slavery destroyed the old plantation organization in Virginia, that conditions arose which

347

would really foster a new spirit among its people that would make the development of manufactures on a large volume practicable. It did this by shifting the population, within a few decades, to a great extent, to the towns. The country was no longer the profitable place for employment which it had once been; nor did it any longer offer the social advantages which it had formerly done.

Another factor also promoted the growth of manufactures. During the first years which followed the end of the War of Secession, the number of railways in Virginia knitting up the state with the United States at large was comparatively few. There was no line to Washington without the intervention of a steamboat. The Chesapeake and Ohio stopped at Richmond, at the one end, and at the New River at the other. The Seaboard Railroad had no straight connection with the capital. The Atlantic and Danville and the Virginian were not yet built; nor had the two railways in the Shenandoah Valley been laid.

One of the foremost elements in the expansion of Virginia's manufactures within recent years is the fact that every large town in the state has direct access by more than one railway to the markets of this country. Some, like Charlottesville, are penetrated by two great trunk lines running to the four great points of the compass. Some, like Richmond and Norfolk, have a half dozen lines reaching out north, south, east, and west. The reaction of this fact has been mutual. The presence of the railways has encouraged the growth of manufactures; the growth of manufactures has encouraged the construction of new railways and doubletracked the old. The railways have brought in the raw materials in abundance for manufactures; and the railways have also carried away the finished products.

In a previous chapter, a description was given of the progress made by Virginian manufactures during the first years that followed 1876. We have come now to the condition of this great interest as we find it today.

The principal manufacturing city in the state is Richmond, the capital. It possesses not only numerous lines of transportation by rail, but also several lines by water, which are valuable in protecting freight rates, upon which the prosperity of manufactures is so directly dependent. An additional advantage lies in the water-power created by a fall of eighty feet or more in the local current of the James, which has now been turned to use by means of hydro-electric plants. A second advantage is the accessibility to the coal-fields of the Alleghanies, which are tapped by the Chesapeake and Ohio railway. A third advantage is the immense volume of pure water furnished by the storage reservoirs. A still greater advantage is the presence of adequate labor long known for its conservative disposition, and untainted by the anarchistic tendencies displayed in so many of the manufacturing centers of the North and West. Conspicuous in the ranks of local labor are women of both races. The negro has taken a useful position in many branches of work, and in some, like the manufacture of plug tobacco, he enjoys a monopoly.

In a general way, it may be stated that the principal industries of Richmond embrace the manufacture of tobacco in all its varied forms, iron, and steel, fertilizers, paper and paper products, wooden-ware, flour, meal, and their products, and the products of the printing press and the packing house. The number and nature of the smaller articles entering into a complete list of the output of the Richmond factories is too extended to be fully specified. The great iron, flour, and fertilizer establishments of the city would alone give it a position of business distinction. It claims to possess the largest wood-works in the world; the largest blotting paper plants; the largest bottled flavoring extract factory; the largest cigar factory; and the largest mica mill. It leads the South in lithography; in engraving; in the manufacture of blotting paper; in the manufacture of paper-bags; and in the sales of automobile supplies.

It is estimated that the annual sales of Richmond's products amount to $250,000,000. On the other hand, the annual sales in the jobbing and wholesale business alone exceed another $200,000,000.

In 1865, the financial resources of the city were too small to be enumerated. Sixty years later, the combined resources of its banks had expanded to $266,000,000; its combined capital and surplus, to over $20,000,000; and its bank deposits, to $134,000,000. It is now the seat of the Fifth Regional Reserve Bank. Local financial institutions are housed in their own buildings, which are valued at $25,000,000. There is a total number of thirty-two financial organizations in Richmond, all of which are under either national or state supervision.

Petersburg, as a manufacturing city, enjoys today all the advantages that accrue from the possession of several trunk railways—these are the Atlantic Coast Line, the Seaboard Air Line, and the Norfolk and Western Railroad. The Atlantic Coast Line joins her, on the one hand, to the towns in the Eastern Carolinas, and also in Georgia and Florida; and, on the other, to Richmand, Washington, and New York. The Seaboard Air Line throws open to her the trade of the thriving centers in the Middle Carolinas; and the Norfolk and Western Railroad, the trade of Southside Virginia and the Southwest.

Petersburg, by the presence of a water-way at its front door, also possesses a straight path to the sea. This advantage has enabled it to obtain competitive freight rates in the shipment of merchandize both to and from the North. The double opportunities of transportation to and from the Carolinas, by the existence of two great railway systems, have been especially promotive of the town's expansion in trade towards the South, in spite of the rivalry of Richmond in the same field. She enjoys the same freight rates to Philadelphia and New York as Richmond; and also rates lower than those which Lynchburg has to meet in her business intercourse with the same Northern cities. She is in the possession of the same advantages as Richmond, too, in obtaining her supply of coal from the Alleghany mines; and in the falls of the Appomattox, she is able to secure hydro-electric power for the propulsion of her various plants whenever desired.

The country accessible to Petersburg, as far as the Carolina border, is richly productive of crops that enter into manufactures. A vast quantity of tobacco, for instance, is grown in the soil of this region which is equally well-adapted to cotton and peanuts, while the growth of timber there is remarkable for its abundance, its variety of species, and its fineness of quality. The supply of native labor has, so far, proved adequate for the numerous purposes for which it is needed.

The ground on which the two cities of Petersburg and Hopewell now stand forms at present two separate industrial districts, but they can be correctly described as the Petersburg-Hopewell industrial area, and treated, in a general way, as one. Petersburg proper embraces the central town and the outlying villages of Ettrick, Matoaca, and Swift Creek. The primary industries carried on within these boundaries consist of the manufacture of tobacco, cotton, and lumber, in the numerous forms to which they are reduced for sale. Additional articles included in the list of important manufactures are trunks and valises, machinery, fertilizers, fireworks, clothing, finished and retanned leather, straw-hats, books, and other printed matter, and products of the grist mill. Peanuts too are prepared here for the market in extraordinary quantities. Other manufactures, like agricultural implements, boxes, carriages and wagons, mattresses, saddlery, harness, silk-goods, and tools.

The wholesale and distributing business of Petersburg, in the territory accessible to its merchants, amounts in value to many million dollars.

In 1912, the du Pont Company purchased in the vicinity of City Point an area embracing about eighteen hundred acres for use as the site for gun-cotton, nitric, and sulphuric acid works. When the great European war broke out in 1914, the establishment was converted into a gun-cotton plant to supply the demand for artillery ammunition. Before the end of two years, 14,000 persons were employed in the various departments; and, soon afterwards, the number increased to 18,000. The close of the World war seriously affected the prosperity of Hopewell by abruptly cutting short the manufacture of munitions. The prospect of an early addition to its manufacturing plants has recently restored the full promise of its first incorporation. It is estimated that $15,000,000 are already invested in its factories.

The population of the Petersburg-Hopewell area, according to the estimate of the Federal Bureau Survey in 1926, was about thirty-eight thousand.

The City of Newport News, like Hopewell at the beginning of the World war, is especially remarkable for one great industry. This industry is ship-building on an immense scale. Practically by the will of one man, Collis P. Huntington, there was established here a ship-yard which constitutes one of the greatest plants of its kind in the world. This plant, unlike others of a different character, has not suffered from the deflation which followed the peace. The volume of its business has, in recent years, reached proportions larger than were ever known by it before.

The population of Newport News has been estimated at 48,000, a rate of growth which has brought it close to the size of Roanoke, its only present rival in Virginia in rapid expansion. The aggregate value of its property is assessed at $36,500,000. In the course of the year ending with June 30, 1927, the post-office receipts increased $5,000,000. Its bank resources at the latter date were recorded at nearly $15,000,000; its deposits at $12,000,000.

Newport News enjoys the advantage of a direct connection by water, not only with the cities of the North, but also with those of Europe. It has convenient intercourse by the same means also with all the towns situated along the coast line of the Chesapeake Bay. The double tracks of the Chesapeake and Ohio Railway, reaching to the coal mines of the Alleghanies, have made the city one of the largest export coaling ports in the United States. Its coal piers are among the most spacious to be found in the entire country. Equally notable for their

Courtesy of Virginia State Chamber of Commerce

NORFOLK MUNICIPAL GRAIN ELEVATOR

extent are the warehouses reserved for cotton, tobacco, and other bulky commodities.

Hampton's industry is chiefly devoted to the preparation of marine and truck products for the market. Fish, oysters, and crabs are here handled in unusual quantities for shipment. Portsmouth, like Hampton, is not primarily a manufacturing town, but in the Federal Navy Yard, shipbuilding and repairs are carried on on an extraordinary scale. The prosperity of the

23—Vol. 2

city is further sustained, like that of Suffolk and Norfolk, by the various industries springing from the presence in the vicinity of a wide area reserved for the production of vegetables for the Northern markets at various seasons of the year. Among these industries is the manufacture of barrels, boxes, and crates for the transportation of the products of the trucking fields. There are numerous articles of other kinds which, in the making, add to the wealth of the city.

The prosperity of Suffolk, like that of Portsmouth, is largely derivable from the handling of the products of the trucking fields. The principal source in this province, perhaps, is the peanut, which forms so important a crop in the region situated in the southeastern part of the state.

No city in Virginia has been impeded in fulfilling the destiny assigned it by nature to the same degree as Norfolk. Had the General Assembly, ninety years ago, recognized that every interest of the state called for the construction of a railway, and not of a waterway, from Hampton Roads to the Ohio River through Richmond, and chartered a company to build it, Norfolk, and not New York, would, perhaps, have been the principal port in the United States for the exportation of the products of the Middle West. Possibly the War of Secession—in which Virginia had no real interest from a material point of view—would have been staved off, at least to the extent of not involving her, had Norfolk, by 1861, reached the proportion of a great center of population by the enormous trade which would have been poured into her lap by a rail counterpart of the Erie Canal. The influence of such a vast emporium would hardly have been favorable to the state's withdrawal from the Union, in spite of the existence of the institution of slavery within her borders. Quite probably the presence of such a city would, before 1860, have gradually created among her people an irresistible disposition to abolish that institution. The disappearance of slavery, combined with a direct rail connection with the Middle West, would, perhaps, have made the sentiment of the state turn irresistibly to the side of the Union. But the funds of the Commonwealth continued to be sunk in a canal until it was too late to recover the advantages which had been snatched away by her great seaboard rival in the North.

Notwithstanding its sole dependence upon the general resources of a more or less contracted area in the South, the city continued to grow. When she at last found herself in pos-

SHIP AT ONE OF NORFOLK'S PIERS

session of more than one great rail highway to the West, her ability to use these means of transportation was seriously diminished by the legitimate rivalry of the New York Central and Pennsylvania railroads, which, with the Baltimore and Ohio, occupied a position that gave them control of the main traffic from the plains and towns of the West to the seaboard. Coal mined within the borders of the two Virginias alone escaped the suction of these Northern railways. For the same reason, the transportation of cotton from the Carolinas, and tobacco, corn, and peanuts from Southside Virginia, could not be shunted off by land, at least to the North.

In the meanwhile, the use of the great harbor had not expanded to the degree justified by its natural advantages. What other harbor in the United States could offer so safe an approach from the sea; such a broad and deep channel when the capes had been penetrated; and such general freedom from ice

Courtesy of Norfolk-Portsmouth Chamber of Commerce.

S. S. George Washington

One of world's largest steamers entering
Norfolk harbor without aid of tugs

and fog and hurricane? Here was room for all the navies of the world combined. Why was not this room taken up to a larger extent? No doubt the existence of a high tariff has had something to do with this condition, for the profits of a voyage are as much dependent on imports as on exports; and when the cargo is practically confined to the voyage in one direction, this result is a restriction, to that degree, upon the development of the port.

But in spite of this drawback of the tariff, the volume of exports has been enormous. The commerce between the United

States and Great Britain, in 1926, amounted to many million tons in exports and also many million in imports. Of these exported millions, a very large proportion were shipped from the wharves of Hampton Roads. During the same year, fifty-four per cent of the unmanufactured tobacco exported from the United States passed out to sea from the Roads. The amount of coal exported reached 20,000,000 tons. Approximately 500,-000 bales of cotton were received at the Port; and of these, 125,000 were shipped to the British Islands. Many thousand barrels of apples and millions of pounds of corn-starch left the same wharves. In 1926, 20,000 vessels, engaged in the river, coastwise, and foreign trade, dropped their anchors in the Roads.

The principal energies of the people of Norfolk have quite naturally been directed to the development of their Port; but, in recent years, close attention has been paid to increasing the number of the local factories. The expansion in this branch of their local interests is as yet on the threshold but the proximity to raw materials, on the one hand, and to the sea for shipment of finished goods, on the other, is a combination of advantages that will quite certainly advance rapidly the fortunes of this branch of industry.

Norfolk is connected with Danville by the Atlantic Danville Railway, a part of the Southern system. Danville is said to be the largest loose tobacco market in the world; and it enjoys the additional distinction of possessing the second largest cotton-mill. There are ten enormous loose leaf sale warehouses situated within the confines of the municipality, under the roofs of which about fifty million pounds of tobacco in this unmanufactured form are sold. The quantity consigned to private parties comes to as much more. The Riverside and Dan River Cotton Mills add a vast sum to the wealth of the city. The value of the two plants is computed at $30,000,000. Approximately six thousand persons are employed in their various departments, and 76,000 bales are consumed in their manufacturing processes. It produces daily 257 miles of cloth. The sales exceed $18,000,000 a year. The Danville Knitting Mill creates employment for 500 persons. The number of machines in use under its roof is a thousand or more. Among the other forms of manufacture pursued in the city are tobacco, clothing, furniture, flour, paints, wooden-ware, wagons, trucks, rugs,

Courtesy of Virginia State Chamber of Commerce

WATER POWER DEVELOPMENT, ROANOKE

tents, candy, bread and ice. The resources of its banks exceed $15,000,000.

In 1882, Roanoke, which deserves the name of "Magic City" that has been given to it, counted a population of 400. In 1927, the number of its inhabitants was estimated at 67,000. Its total population, as a combined community, embraced, at that time, 80,000 persons at least. Of these, only 18.35 per cent were colored, and only 1.73 were foreign born. The city has 192 miles of streets. Its real estate is assessed at $48,000,000, upon a basis of fifty per cent of its actual value. Since 1923, its postoffice receipts have risen from approximately $347,000 to $428,000. The combined resources of its banks amount to $40,000,000. It has two trunk lines of railway, which connect the city with the North, the West, and the Southeast. The freight service to Hampton Roads does not consume more than twelve hours, while the journey to Washington, Philadelphia, and New York, is limited to a little more than a single night's travel.

The number of industries in Roanoke range as high as one hundred; employ over eighteen thousand workers; and show an annual product valued at $68,500,000. The largest artificial silk-mill in the world is situated in this city; and it also contains the largest railway shops in the South, and also the largest structural steel plant and the largest tin-can factory. The prosperity of the Magic City is, perhaps, partly, though indirectly, due to its possession of fifty-one churches for white people and fifteen for colored.

By the census of 1920, the population of Lynchburg numbered 30,000; but within its community limits over forty thousand persons now reside. According to the assessment of 1924, the value of its real estate exceeded $28,000,000, while the value of its tangible personal property was $22,000,000 more. It is supplied with water from an artificial mountain lake that has a capacity of 500,000 gallons. In the Norfolk and Western, Chesapeake and Ohio, and Southern railways, Lynchburg possesses three of the greatest trunk lines in the Eastern states, which afford her people a daily passenger service of sixty trains. It is calculated that there is spent annually here about $1,000,-000 in building operations within the corporate bounds alone, a sum duplicated by a similar expenditure in the suburbs.

About eighty-five articles of a widely varied character are manufactured in Lynchburg. These have a value that exceeds $75,000,000 annually. These products include cotton-goods, cast-iron pipe and pipe fillings, plows, farm wagons, candy,

and bark extracts. All of them are manufactured on an imposing scale. The largest bark extract plant in the United States
is situated here. The output of candy runs above ten million
pounds annually. The sale of tobacco in forms for export has
swollen to an enormous volume.

But it is in shoe manufacture, called into being, in the beginning, chiefly by the genius of three men, John W. Craddock,
A. P. Craddock, and T. M. Terry, that Lynchburg has taken
its most conspicuous place in the great business life of the
South. The Craddock-Terry Company was founded in 1888, and
incorporated in 1898. So rapidly did its output expand from
the start, that its operations were, in 1914 and 1921 respectively,
extended to St. Louis and Milwaukee in the West. It is estimated
that not less than 400,000 cases of shoes are annually shipped
from Lynchburg, the greater part of which is produced by the
six modern shoe-factories situated in the city.

There have been established here eight financial institutions
of the first rank, including commercial, trust, saving, industrial,
and loan banks. The total resources amount to over $30,000,000.
In the course of ten years, the deposits have increased to the
extent of $7,000,000, while the total financial resources have
doubled.

Winchester, Fredericksburg, Charlottesville, Alexandria, and
Staunton, are towns of growing manufacturing importance.
Winchester possesses woolen and knitting mills, and also establishments for the manufacture of gloves, boxboards, brick, flour,
and fruit products. The total resources of its four banks amount
to $10,000,000. Charlottesville also is the site of a variety of
profitable manufactures. The largest woolen mills in the South
are situated here. In addition, in close proximity, are plants
for making electrical safety appliances, sheet-metal works,
creameries, food products, and undergarments.

If we pass from the history of Virginia's manufacturing
growth, as illustrated in the different cities mentioned in the
previous paragraphs, to that history as illustrated by the State

as a whole, the conception of the expansion which has been going on in this province of industry will be very much widened. In 1912, the value of the total output was $158,420,968.32. By 1917, these figures had grown to $303,371,820.17. In 1918, the capital invested was $306,831,315; and the value of the products, $905,003,885. The male employees numbered 133,489; the female, 21,532. By 1920, the capital invested had risen to $362,328,506; and before the end of 1923, this sum had been increased by nearly $3,000,000. The value of the output now was $463,825,890. The number of white male wage earners approximated 58,000; the number of the colored male, 23,000. The corresponding figures for white women were 15,500, and for colored, about 9,000. At this time, fifty-two different branches of manufacture were pursued in the state.

At the session of the General Assembly for 1922-23, a new Child Labor Law was enacted, which applied to all gainful occupations, except to those connected with farms, gardens, and orchards. No child below sixteen years of age was permitted to be employed; and those offering their services were required to submit a certificate of physical fitness.

In 1925, the capital invested in manufactures amounted to $379,559,950, and the value of the output to $561,146,931. One hundred thousand male operatives were at work in the factories, of whom 75,000 were white, and 27,000 colored. The number of female operatives was about 29,000—of whom 19,000 were white and 9,000 colored. The wages of members of the two races varied appreciably in favor of the white. In the same way, the wages of white men and white women revealed a marked difference to the disadvantage of the women. The present tendency is towards a nearer approach to equality. The condition of the factories, from every point of view, has shown a substantial improvement.

In our description of the manufacturers of the different cities, we referred incidentally to the financial facilities enjoyed by all of them for the support of their various branches of industry. One of the most impressive differences between the new order of business affairs in Virginia as compared with the old is the presence of a bank, not only in every large and small town, but also in nearly every village. Each year has seen an increase in their number. The capital of these banks has shown a steady enlargement. In 1926, for instance, thirty-three state banks added to their capital stock an aggregate sum that ran into several millions. In 1895, the total assets of the Virginia state banks amounted to $25,040,000. By 1915, this sum had swelled to $91,550,000, and, by 1926, it had grown to $277,487,-000. The number of banks had expanded from eighty-five in 1895 to 271 in 1915, and to 339 in 1926. These figures do not include either the number or the assets of private banks.

In 1926, the resources of the national banks in operation in Virginia amounted to $400,206,000. This, together with the resources of the state banks, gave the sum of $677,693,000 for banking facilities. The total resources of the Building and Loan associations were estimated, during the same year, at a figure exceeding $48,000,000.

Of the numerous banking institutions in operation in Virginia in 1926, nine were the property of the negro race, and under the management of trained officers of their own color.

CHAPTER V

PROCEEDS OF AGRICULTURE

In the year 1919, Virginia, in the volume of all its crops, occupied the position of the twenty-sixth state among the forty-eight that composed the sisterhood of commonwealths. By 1926, it had advanced to the position of the twenty-fourth. At this time, the main products of its fields, apart from most of the trucks, were corn, wheat, oats, barley, rye, buckwheat, Irish potatoes, sweet potatoes, tobacco, hay, cotton, peanuts, sorghum, beans, and broom corn.

The value of the corn crop was, in 1924, about the same as it was in 1926. It was in each of these years approximately $39,000,000. The value of the tobacco crop, which exceeded $29,000,000 in the year 1924, fell to $25,000,000 in 1926. The value of the hay crop, which was about $25,000,000 in 1924, had, by 1926, declined to $19,000,000. White potatoes brought $3,000,000 more in the latter year—when the value of the product was $18,000,000—than they did in the former. The value of the wheat crop was, in 1924 and 1926, $12,500,000 and $15,000,000, respectively. The apple crop was sold for $12,000,000 in 1924, and for about $9,000,000 in 1926. The cotton crop varied from $4,500,000 in value, in 1924, to $3,000,000 in 1926. The peanut crop was more profitable in the former year than in the latter. In the interval, it advanced from $4,000,000 to $5,250,000. The figures for sweet potatoes were virtually the same.

Calculating the value of all crops, including those not mentioned, and it is found that, in 1924, the total approximated

363

$178,000,000, and in 1926, $172,000,000, a falling off to the extent of $6,000,000.

Between 1918 and 1926, inclusive, the number of acres planted in tobacco shrank from 226,000 to 188,000. In 1918, the number of acres planted in corn exceeded 1,500,000, and in wheat, 1,050,000. In 1926, the figures for the first was 1,700,000; and for the second, 687,000. The number of acres planted in white potatoes was, in 1918, 135,000; but, in 1926, 1,000 less. The acreage in cotton advanced, in the same interval, from 44,000 to 101,000. The area in peanuts shrank from 138,000 to 131,000.

Taking the acreage as a whole, and considering also the value of the entire round of crops, it is found that the former, in the interval between 1918 and 1926, fell off from 4,600,000 to 4,570,000. The decline in value was still greater— $294,500,000 in 1918, it sank to $172,100,000 in 1926.

Tobacco has been the principal money crop of Virginia since the day that John Rolfe proved that it could be made to vie successfully with the Spanish leaf in the markets of London. It is still the largest source of farm revenue, although the growing population of the state, and the greater attention paid to intensive tillage, has diminished its relative importance. The leading types of the plant now cultivated and sold in Virginia are the Burley, the flue-cured, the fire-cured, and the sun-cured. The production of each of these types in 1920 was, in number of pounds, respectively, 2,000,000, 114,932,000, 45,600,000, and 9,048,000. The corresponding figures for 1926 were 3,700,000, 82,350,000, 43,800,000, and 7,150,000.

The price of Burley by the pound, between 1920 and 1926, fluctuated to a remarkable degree. In 1920, it was about 14 cents; in 1922, it was about 16; and in 1926, about 15. The price of flue-cured rose from 22 cents in 1920 to about 23 in 1926. In 1920, the price of fire-cured tobacco by the pound was about 9 cents. In 1922, it rose to 19 cents; but, in 1926, fell to 7.8 cents. The value of sun-cured by the pound rose in 1921

THE FIRST FACTORY TO MANUFACTURE
CIGARETS BY MACHINERY

to 18 cents from 9 in the course of the previous year; but fell from this figure to about 9½ cents in 1926.

Neither the volume nor the prices of these different commercial forms of tobacco kept step with each other. Thus we find the greatest production of fire-cured in one year, and of sun-cured in another. The production of flue-cured was equally independent. In the same way, there was little consistency in the production of the same variety from year to year. The Burley variety has only in recent years been cultivated over large areas. Its production is mainly confined to Southwest Virginia, a division of the state that resembles in soil and climate the area of Kentucky where Burley makes up the principal crop.

The fluctuation in price of the different kinds of tobacco has been due to the increased or diminished demand for the leaf in foreign countries. In 1926, for instance, the exports dropped to 18,000,000 pounds, after having risen to 48,000,000 in 1923. The several varieties of Virginia tobacco has been compelled, in recent years, to compete with imports from both Tennessee and Carolina. The principal market for the sun-cured has been Richmond, while Danville purchases the largest quantity of flue-cured tobacco. South Boston is its most active competitor. Lynchburg is the chief market for the sale of the fire-cured tobacco, but both Farmville and Blackstone have pushed that city closely as purchasers of this type of leaf.

Virginia ranks third or fourth in the volume and value of its truck crops, as compared with other states that devote a part of their acreage to this form of production. During bad seasons, it falls to the place of fourth or fifth. No crop is so sensitive to weather as these more or less delicate off-shoots of the soil. A late season is especially injurious to the profitableness of the output. One night of heavy frost will extinguish the chief part of this profitableness, or even destroy it altogether. Some species of truck enjoy the advantage of two seasons. This is so in the case of cabbage, string beans, and spinach, which are shipped in the spring and autumn alike.

The greatest trucking district is situated in the vicinity of
Norfolk, Portsmouth, and Suffolk, and on the eastern shore.
Not less than fifty-two varieties of vegetables and fruits are
exported to the northern markets from this region. The principal salable varieties are beans, cabbage, cucumbers, lettuce,
onions, green peas, early potatoes, spinach, strawberries, tomatoes, and watermelons. In 1926, over 141,000 acres were
planted in these varieties. The value of the production in 1925
amounted to $23,000,000. There was, in the ensuing year, a
decline to $19,000,000. The strawberry offered the largest
quantity of fruit. There were over 19,000,000 quarts of this
berry harvested. The potato crop of this year filled over
9,000,000 baskets.

What has been the extent of the profitableness of the various
farm products of Virginia in recent years? A comparison
pertinent to this question may be made between the statistics
of 1919—the year that followed the close of the World war—
and those of 1926. These together cover the interval of eight
years since that event. We will take the income derived from
tobacco, potatoes, wheat, fruit, and trucks separately, and from
all the other crops in the aggregate. In 1919, about $48,000,000
was received from the sale of the tobacco crop. In 1926, the
proceeds were only about $25,500,000. This shrinkage was the
result of the deflation which, by this time, had reached its
lowest level in nearly every province of agriculture. The return
from the potato crop in 1919 was about $27,000,000. By 1926,
the return had sunk to about $18,000,000.

In 1919, the crop of wheat sold for $27,000,000, but, in 1926,
it sold for approximately only $15,000,000. The crop of fruit, in
1919, brought in about $18,000,000; but, in 1926, only about
$12,000,000. Trucks sold for $15,500,000 in 1919; but for only
about $7,000,000 in 1926. All other crops were, in 1919, dis-
posed of for $41,500,000. In 1926, they returned an income of
$35,500,000, a loss of $6,000,000.

If we take the total sales during these two years, respectively, we find that, in 1919, the crops in the aggregate brought in an income of $176,772,000; but in 1926, an income of only $112,703,000—a loss of $64,000,000.

No perfectly accurate statistics are obtainable for the returns from the forests during these two years. Such statistics would probably add a large sum to the amount of the farm incomes; but the same shrinkage would be equally noticeable in this item for 1926—as compared with the like item for 1919—that was so conspicuous in the case of all the other crops specifically enumerated by us in the previous paragraphs.

Did the farmer not find some compensation for the heavy decline in price for his crops by a corresponding falling off in the price of the articles which he was required to purchase, such, for instance, as farm implements and domestic food and clothing? No one in Virginia in our times has observed more carefully the difficulties confronting those engaged in the pursuit of agriculture than Hon. George W. Koiner, the long and thoroughly experienced commissioner of that state department. Writing in his report for 1921, he said: "How can the farmer be expected to return to prewar prices and prewar production if everything he has to buy to produce his crops remain at postwar prices? In July, 1914, pig-iron sold for $10.25 per ton; in July, 1919, for $27.75 per ton; in November, 1920, for $38 per ton—an increase, since 1914, of 270 per cent. For comparison: Corn in July, 1914, sold in the Chicago market for 72 cents per bushel; in July, 1919, for $2.19 per bushel; but in November, 1920, dropped back to 83 cents per bushel. This was true of other commodities as well. In 1920, tobacco sold at 50 per cent below cost of production, yet manufactured product is selling approximately at war prices. Hides are selling below prewar prices, yet harness and shoes are selling for double prewar prices. Wool sells for about 20 per cent less than prewar prices, yet clothing costs as much. These inequalities extend to everything the farmer makes, to be manufactured later."

Before we take up the subject of live stock, let us consider how the farmer has fared in the value of his land. In 1916, an acre of good soil for the plough was appraised at $46. By 1927, the appraisement had risen to $59. This represented an increase of $13. During the interval, however, the value of an acre of this nature fluctuated to a conspicuous degree. Thus, by 1918, it had risen to $61, and by 1920, to $73. From this high figure, it fell to $58 in 1925; but, in the course of the following year, it rose again—at least to the extent of $1. During the interval between 1916 and 1927, poor plough land never exceeded $34 in value; and by 1927, it had sunk to $29, as compared with $22 in 1916.

An important step in gauging the profits of land is the ascertainment of the rate of wages paid the laborers employed in cultivating it. In 1913, the amount with board was $16.10 by the month, and 86 cents by the day. Fourteen years later, the rate with board was $30 by the month, and $1.60 by the day. In 1913, $23 without board was paid by the month, and $1.11 by the day. In 1927, the corresponding figures were $42, and $2.10. There was an advance for a time in the rate of wages, whether payment was made with or without board. It was not until 1921 that a recession was observed; but the general tendency to a lower scale was resumed in 1924.

In the production of crops in Virginia, during many years, a large quantity of fertilizers has been used. This is especially so in the case of trucks and tobacco. In former times, as we have pointed out, the chief means of obtaining a suitable soil for the young tobacco plant was through opening up new ground by cutting away the woods. This process was, to a certain extent, supplemented on well-managed farms by the application of coarse manures produced by dropping leaves or cornstalks in the muck of cowpens or stable yards. Afterwards, a habit arose of using the guano gathered up and imported into the United States from the west coast of South America. Ultimately, the manufacture of purely artificial fertilizers began; and the volume of this product has increased to an extraordinary degree. It has now become so general in its use that strict inspection laws have been adopted to ensure purity of substance. The demand, however, has varied. This is indicated by the amount of the tonnage disposed of from year to year. In the course of 1910, 356,183 tons were sold in Virginia; and in 1920, 465,227; but the amount declined to 435,223 tons in 1926, owing to the depression then prevailing in the price of tobacco. The year in which the largest quantity of fertilizer was bought in Virginia was in 1917, when the tonnage amounted to 495,091.

As was to be expected, the areas in which the greatest proportion of this stimulant was expended were, first, the region of trucks lying around the cities of Norfolk and Suffolk and the towns of Smithfield, Emporia and Franklin; second, the region embracing the Eastern Shore, the Northern Neck, and the Pamunkey Valley; and, thirdly, the region extending from Charlotte County to Pittsylvania. The consumption of fertilizers in the first of these regions amounted to 114,600 tons; in the second, to 102,800; and in the third, to 61,700.

In a previous chapter on the subject of agriculture, we gave some description of the development of Virginia's interest in commercial apple and peach orchards. Attention to the production of these varieties of fruits has been continuously shown throughout the plantation period. No mansion of any pretension in the state was then lacking in an orchard; and the number of trees embraced in many of these areas ran into the thousand scale. Originally, few of the orchards were designed for the sale of their annual product. The fruit was raised, as a rule, for the use of the planter's family and slaves, or for the fattening of his herds of hogs. Probably, a market would have been found for the surplus apples, peaches, and plums, had the proper facilities existed for their temporary preservation and ultimate transportation. They were, however, too perishable without scientific protection and shipment, and, in those times, the proper methods of handling them were not generally known,

even when there were railways near at hand to convey the fruit
to market. Nevertheless, the most classic incident associated
with the Virginian apple records the fact that numerous barrels
were once sent to the American minister in London, Mr. Steven-
son, of Albemarle County, to serve as a gift for the Queen.

The earliest large commercial apple orchards in the state
were two that were established in Albemarle prior to 1890;
and one, about the same time, in the vicinity of Winchester.
The crop from this third orchard amounted to as much as 5,000
barrels. The first large commercial peach orchard was planted,
in 1867, in Botetourt County, by J. C. Moomaw. It contained
about 4,000 trees. The fruit from them was retained for consumption in the owner's cannery. By 1890, the County of
Botetourt, and the neighboring counties, Bedford, Roanoke,
Scott, Washington, and Pittsylvania, possessed 370,000 trees;
and Essex, Westmoreland, and Fairfax counties, an additional
121,000. In the meanwhile, the orchard spray for the control
of insect pests and destructive infectious diseases had been
brought into successful use. The next step was the adoption of
refrigeration and cold storage. This made possible an important
extension of the season for marketing; and it also enabled
shippers to forward their product to more distant points. This
was, in reality, the beginning of the foreign trade in a large way.

The steady increase in the volume of sales down to a recent
year is revealed by the reports for certain counties which may
be selected. The shipments for Bedford, for instance, rose
from 54 cars, in 1903, to 230, in 1924. The proportion for
Botetourt was 120 cars in 1903, and 478 in 1924. The corresponding increase for Roanoke was from 148 in the former
year to 592 in the latter. Nelson County, in the same interval,
advanced from 80 cars to 1,574; and Albemarle County, from
180 to 1,622. Augusta County offered a still higher proportion.
In 1903, it shipped only 255 car loads, but, in 1924, it shipped
2,000.

The increase in the region of the Upper Valley was more conspicuous still. The shipment during this interval advanced in Clarke from 42 to 550; in Warren, from 110 to 550; in Rockingham, from 75 to 910; and in Shenandoah, from 58 to 1,009. The increase in Frederick County was the most remarkable of all. The number of car loads expanded from 475 to approximately 4,000.

Virginia is now the third in the list of apple-producing states. The volume of its output is exceeded only by that of Washington and New York. About 3,200 commercial growers are now actively interested in this industry in Virginia; and their average annual profits, during the interval between 1923 and 1925, were estimated at $6,000,000. Approximately 62 per cent of the farms under cultivation in Virginia are reserved chiefly for the production of apples. The total number of trees growing exceed 10,500,000. Of these, 4,300,000 are used for commercial purposes. Much of the rest is disposed of casually in local markets.

The "commercial" apple crop is described as "that portion which is available for consumption as fresh fruit," which is admitted to be an unsatisfactory definition, owing to its vagueness. In the interval between 1916 and 1919, the total production of apples amounted to 95,500,000 bushels. Of this number, about 50,000,000 baskets represented the volume of the commercial crop. This crop has, in that interval, varied from 42.1 per cent of the whole production in 1921, to 58.5 in 1923. During the interval between 1819 and 1919, the commercial output increased from 6.5 per cent of the total amount to more than 43 per cent. Virginia and California were the only two states of reputation for the excellence of their fruits which disclosed, in the interval between 1920 and 1925, an increase in the number of their apple trees already capable of bearing. Virginia is the largest producer of apples exported in barrels. Between 1924 and 1925, at least 789,217 barrels were transported to the foreign market. This formed 53 per cent of the barreled apple exports of the entire country.

Hampton Roads has now become an important point of shipment abroad.

The principal foreign market is found in Great Britain. The consignments are distributed throughout the kingdom from the ports of Liverpool, London, Hull, Manchester, Southampton, and Glasgow. Some of the English firms receiving the fruit have their representatives in Virginia, and, by assisting the grower on the ground with the means for handling and shipping his crop, obtain a lien on its sale. Exports of Virginian apples are also made to the continent of Europe, and also to South America.

Ample accommodations exist in Virginia for the cold storage of apples, in anticipation of an advance in price. Nearly 2,000,000 barrels can thus be safely preserved for this purpose. At least sixteen very fine species of apples are to be found in the orchards of Virginia. This number is increased by those which are designated simply as "miscellaneous."

It is estimated that the commercial peach crop of Virginia amounts annually to at least 500,000 bushels. In 1925, the number of commercial peach orchards in the state exceeded 700. They contained approximately 570,000 trees. These make up about one-fourth of the peach trees standing in the state. The remaining proportions are grown on the farms for the use of the fruit in the home, or its sale in some small town near by. There were, by the report of the last census, about 62,000 farms in Virginia which disposed of the product of their orchards in this manner.

What is the explanation of the fact that, with the exception of mules, there is a smaller number of live stock in Virginia today than there was in 1910? In 1910, the number of horses was 312,000. On the other hand, in 1927, there were 224,000. In 1910, there were 356,000 milch cows; in 1927, there were 340,000. In 1910, there were 461,000 sheep; in 1927, there were

380,000. In 1910, there were 709,000 hogs; in 1927, there were 558,000. Other kinds of live stock were 433,000 in number in 1910, and only 367,000 in 1927.

Horses fell off in value from $107 a head, in 1910, to $66 in 1927. Milch cows, on the other hand, rose during this interval from $30 a head to $45; sheep, from $3.90 to $10.30; swine, from $6.50 to $13. The increase in price made good the decline in number in the case of sheep, milch cows, and hogs alone. Thus, 709,000 head of swine were valued at $4,609,000 in 1910, while 558,000 head in 1927 were valued at $7,254,000; 356,000 milch cows were valued at $10,573,000 in 1910, while 340,000 head were valued, in 1927, at $15,300,000; 461,000 sheep were valued at $1,798,000 in 1910, while 340,000 were valued at $15,500,000 in 1927.

In 1910, there were 60,000 head of mules in Virginia; in 1927, there were 103,000 head. The latter were valued at only $955,000 more than the former, although there was a difference of 43,000 in number. The explanation lay in the decline in price which took place in the interval. This decline was represented by the difference between $130 and $85. In the case of each branch of live stock which has been mentioned, there was a considerable degree of fluctuation in value, with a general tendency either upward or downward.

Dairying did not become in Virginia an organized industry on a substantial scale until 1907, when the State Dairymen's Association was formed at the Jamestown Exposition. At first, there were only thirteen members; and even today not more than 5,000 dairymen and dairy-farmers can be counted in the body of the farmers at large, who now number about 194,000 in all. The men who derive their principal income from dairying specialize in the industry. One set ship their product to the towns and cities in the form of whole milk; another dispose of their product to the creameries in the form of sweet and sour cream for churning; the third convert their milk into butter, and market it in that form.

The influences which have encouraged the growth of dairying have been: (1) The improvement in the means of reaching
the market with rapidity; (2) the increase in the number of
towns, which supply a steady and reliable custom; and (3)
subdivision of the land, which has raised up a new class of

A FINE HERD ON ONE OF VIRGINIA'S DAIRY FARMS

intensive farmers eager to augment the opportunities for swelling the profitableness of their properties. Moreover, Virginia
is remarkably exempt from long spells of either very hot or very
cold weather. The western blizzard is unknown here. The
terrible cyclones, so common on the Great Plains, are shut out
by the Alleghanies and the Blue Ridge. Snow rarely continues
to lie more than a few days on the ground. The rainfall is
abundant, and the springs and streams are perennial. In the
Piedmont, the Valley, and the Southwest alike, the soil is adapted

to the growth of nourishing grasses. It is especially suitable for the production of leguminous plants.

With the constantly broadening market, the disposition to improve the quality of the herds, as the source of the milk supply, has rapidly increased. This improvement is effected,

A TYPICAL VIRGINIA DAIRY FARM

not only by importation, but also by the breeding of the finest varieties of stock for the dairy. More intelligent attention too is paid to the character of the food consumed. The use of corn silage has now extended throughout the regions devoted chiefly to dairying.

In 1926, the average production of milk to the cow was reported to the state authorities by 900 dairymen. The figure noted for this average production in the counties at large was

5,500 pounds. The highest average was discovered in Henrico, which possessed many dairies, because of the proximity of the City of Richmond. Warwick County, owing to the presence of Newport News, made also a very favorable showing. For the same reason, namely, the nearness of large cities, the average production was high in the counties of Fairfax, Chesterfield, Pittsylvania, and Prince Anne.

The character of the output, whether whole milk, or sweet and sour milk for churning, depended chiefly on the situation of the dairies. Those accessible to Washington, Richmond, Norfolk, Roanoke, Newport News, Danville, and Petersburg, exhibited a preference for whole milk. Wherever a great distance made the transportation of fresh milk both precarious and expensive, a disposition was shown for the shipment of sweet cream alone. The counties lying still farther away limited their production for export to cream for churning.

In the course of the ten years between 1914 and 1924, the production of butter in Virginia was increased to the extent of nearly 300 per cent. This advance was to be attributed, not only to the improvement in facilities for marketing, but also to the more scientific care exercised in breeding and feeding the cows. In 1912, there were in operation in Virginia only twenty-seven creameries. At the present time, there are forty-three, together with thirty-three regular receiving stations, which ship to creameries situated within or without the state.

In 1925, the total annual production of eggs by the average Virginian hen was estimated at 117. During the following year, this rate advanced to 120. All poultry products were valued at $28,137,000 in 1926. This represented an increase of nearly $4,000,000, in comparison with the return in 1919.

Computing the gross income of the farmers of Virginia in 1926, it is found that they received $188,417,000, as compared with $182,427,000 in 1925. In 1919, the amount was $283,741,000.

CHAPTER VI

RAIL AND MOTOR TRANSPORTATION

The first railway charter issued in Virginia was issued in 1827. In the course of that year, the Winchester & Harper's Ferry Railroad was incorporated. Thirty-three years after this event, 1,350 miles of trackage had been constructed within the boundaries of the state and were in actual operation. These public improvements had been made practicable by means of large public and private subscriptions.

As we have seen, the sentiment of the people of the commonwealth who resided east of the Alleghany Mountains had been opposed to appropriations by the National Government for a purpose apparently so local in its scope as the building of state railways; and yet they clearly recognized that the public interest demanded the adoption of such means of transportation as essential to Virginia's advance in prosperity. It was this feeling, and a certain local pride also, which stimulated its citizens to raise a larger fund by public and private assistance alike than, perhaps, they would otherwise have been led to do. It was admitted too that justice and expediency required that something should be done to diminish the isolation of Western Virginia. Had not the War of 1861-65 intervened, there is no reason to doubt that the Central Railway, which was slowly pushing its way westward, would, in a comparatively short time, have reached the region now embraced in West Virginia, and been extended to the Ohio River. As it was, by 1860, the Valley only had been crossed.

The policy followed in laying down the other roadbeds was to link up with lines that already joined the Virginian border on more than one side. The Petersburg & Weldon, for instance, tapped a railroad that ran southward as far as Georgia. The Richmond & Danville was expected to unite the Town of Danville with a link that was to be continued to Greensboro. The Virginia & Tennessee was to join at Bristol with a line that was to run down the valley of the Tennessee River to Knoxville.

We have already referred to the deterioration in the condition of the railroads of the state which resulted from the enormous traffic during the War of Secession, and the lack of the proper facilities for duplicating the rails. So serious became this decay that it was found necessary to reduce the speed of passenger trains to ten miles by the hour, and of freight trains to eight.

It was not until the close of the Reconstruction Period in 1870 that a revival in the existing railways, then suffering from extreme dilapidation, began to show itself distinctly. The first stimulus was given by Commodore Maury's memorable pamphlet, *Physical Survey of Virginia,* which was written with the view of arousing interest in the development of the material resources of the state. This, in that scientist's opinion, was to be done chiefly by the erection of certain convenient lines of railway, and by the use of Hampton Roads as a great national seaport.

During the interval between 1870 and 1885, approximately 1,000 miles of new railways were built in Virginia. The extent of the ones in existence at that time was computed to be 2,500 miles. The most conspicuous railway achievement of this period was the consolidation of the railroads that joined Norfolk and Bristol into a single line, known in our day as the Norfolk & Western, and the consolidation of the lines that extended from Washington to Danville into the Virginia Midland Railway. The three railroads that ran from Harper's Ferry to Lexington up the Great Valley became a part of the Baltimore & Ohio

JOSEPH R. ANDERSON

system. The Shenandoah Valley Railway was completed by 1882. This road, which extended from Hagerstown to Lexington, was subsequently purchased by the Norfolk & Western. By 1884, a line of railway had been laid the entire length of the Accomac Peninsula; and by this means, the agricultural products of the Eastern Shore found quick access to the great markets of the eastern cities. A few years earlier, the old Central Railroad had changed its name to the Chesapeake & Ohio. It had now passed the Alleghany Mountains on one side and reached the sea on the other.

Formerly, the Richmond, Fredericksburg & Potomac Railroad had ended at Acquia Creek, from which place passengers and freight were transported to Washington by steamboat. Ultimately, this railroad was extended to that city and became a part of the great Atlantic Coast Line. At a later period, the Richmond & Allegheny Railway Company bought the properties and franchises of the James River & Kanawha Canal Company, and built a track along the site of the former towpath. This road was finally merged with the Chesapeake & Ohio Railway.

During many years, the gauge of the railroads in Virginia was different from the gauge of the railroads in the North. This fact signified that a transfer of both freight and passengers in crossing the Potomac was always necessary. With the increasing prosperity of the state, the inconvenience and expense resulting from this condition became intolerable, and it was decided that a change should be made that would permanently remove them. The alteration, which extended over nearly 1,000 miles of railway, occurred between the hours of 3:30 A. M. and 4 P. M., on the 1st day of June, 1886. At this time, a provision of the Reconstruction Constitution forbade an appropriation of public money for the assistance of new or old railroads. Before the War of Secession, as we have seen, the state subscribed to three-fifths of the stock of all projected lines. For the construction of the Virginian Railway, the last independent line built in the state, the capital was furnished by its incorporator, one of the principal beneficiaries of the great Standard Oil Company. This road extends from Norfolk to Roanoke, and from the latter city runs into the coal regions of West Virginia. The grade from the mountains to the sea is so sharp that the impulse given by gravity alone is almost strong enough to carry one of the road's enormous coal trains to the piers on Hampton Roads. These piers are among the most modern in their appliances to be found anywhere in the world. This is also true of the piers of the Norfolk & Western in the same city.

An important addition has been made to the Seaboard Air Line by the extension of that system to Richmond. This line, by the use of the Richmond, Fredericksburg & Washington Railroad, has become one of the principal passenger railways between the northern cities and the great winter resorts of Florida.

The extent of the industrial advance which has been made by the state in the course of the last four decades is reflected with singular clearness in the improvement of the roadbeds and the general equipment of the local and through lines of railway. Many persons not yet very far gone in years can recall the rough tracks in the '70s and '80s, when the rails were frequently so worn down or flattened out as to appear unsafe for use, and were proved to be really so by the number of accidents to rolling stock which they caused. The cars were only too often counterparts of the overtaxed rails. They were sometimes kept going until not even a coat of new paint could hide their thorough dilapidation. The interiors, in the way of seats and toilets, were equally suggestive of the prevailing impoverishment. The general aspect of the trains also reflected the provincial character of the local communities, just as if they too had only an indolent connection with the world at large. The number in use each day was small, since the degree of travel on all the lines was limited. One day train and one night train each way on each railway embraced the entire means of conveyance. So early was their hour of starting on their daily runs that it was said at the time that the Virginian people were slandered, whenever they were charged with laziness, for, on the occasion of the most ordinary journey, did they not always have to rise before dawn to catch their train?

The transformation which has taken place during the extended interval that has since passed has been extraordinary. The Atlantic Coast Line, the Seaboard Air Line, and the Southern Railway, starting their luxurious trains from the City of New York, rush them through to Florida and the Gulf without change of cars, one following another in comparatively close succession. And so with the Chesapeake & Ohio Railway in its communication with the West, whether from Washington or Richmond. Many persons still clearly recall the day when the number of passenger trains passing westward or southward through the Town of Charlottesville over the old Central and Midland railways did not exceed four each way, during every twenty-four hours. Now some twenty-five fast trains pass both ways in that length of time, many of them running without a break as far as New Orleans or Cincinnati in one direction, and New York in the other. Most of the lines have been double-tracked to accommodate the heavy traffic. The greyhound has taken the place of the snail, and the hare of the tortoise.

The improvement in rail transportation, enormous as it has been, has not been as notable as the improvement in vehicular transportation on the highways. The extraordinary change in the latter particular is attributable primarily to the introduction of the motor car.

The word "bottomless" was often applied in old times even to the best roads in Virginia, so deep was the mud here and there, which impeded the passage of wheels at certain seasons of the year, or in spells of bad weather at all seasons. The preservation of the principal highways was left to the care of the local authorities, who turned it over to the responsibility of an elected local official. One of the common sights on the public roads of the colonial and post-Revolutionary period was the four-horse family coach. Now this was not really an indication of family pride and ostentation. Its use was a habit that had its origin in the necessity of combining all the equine strength available to pull the lumbering vehicle over the heavy roadbed. Not infrequently, an additional couple of horses were required to be attached to the traces if the assurance of reaching the destination in view was to be put beyond all peradventure.

It was only in the mountain districts and the Great Valley that gravel or plank surfaced roads were to be found often enough to excite comment, although the turnpike road was not entirely unknown in other regions. But for the invention of the motor car, it is quite possible that an hundred years would have elapsed without Virginia having built a system of great highways for traversal by vehicles from one point in the state to another, or beyond its borders on all sides. The commonwealth had, for several centuries, been given up chiefly to agriculture. The country everywhere was a series of farms and plantations more or less isolated even from each other. If any one had to leave home on an important trip, was there not the nearest railroad ready to convey him? What more was wanted?

How could a people of moderate wealth find the means to establish a great ramification of highways? There were for a long time no powerful interests to draw the Virginians into the world at large, and they were, therefore, content to jog quietly along the roads which they already possessed. No phenomenon appeared on the face of the Heavens when the first modern motor car rolled down a Virginian street or public road; but that car really portended far greater changes than any comet ever foreran. Gradually it was to produce a complete alteration in the Virginian's love of a family coach and even of the buggy, which had proved the best vehicle for surmounting the drawbacks of the country roads. The fascination of the new means of locomotion was quickly felt by all who tried it, and the number who did so increased with extraordinary rapidity. The popularity of the car soon extended to the remotest country districts, where there were no trained mechanics at first to repair damages, and where the roads were altogether unfit for rubber tires. Every additional purchaser of a new car was an additional enthusiast; and these enthusiasts became so numerous that entire communities were converted.

The earliest symptom of this craze for swift movement was the popularity of the bicycle. Every one for a time was to be seen on wheels; but the joys of this vehicle palled as the motor car came upon the highway, with its superior speed, its greater ease in manipulation, and its more imposing appearance.

The country's demand for good roads began about 1895; but the Highway Commission, which was to utilize this demand, was not formally established by Act of Assembly until the spring of March, 1906. The motor car was responsible for its creation, and to the motor car should be attributed its triumphs, for the motor car made possible the popular sentiment which called for the commission.

What was the task before that body? A report as far back as 1892 gives the number of improved roads in the state at that time; and in the interval between this date and 1906, there had been no important increase in the extent of the hard-surfaced beds. The total roadways that had been macadamized by 1892 aggregated about 625 miles. This improvement was confined to twenty counties, which represented a proportion of one-fifth of all the counties of the state. The counties that could boast of the largest number of macadamized roads were Clarke, Wythe, Frederick, Loudoun, Rappahannock, and Shenandoah. In none did the extent of the hard surface already laid down run over fifty miles.

It was not until the spring of 1906 that a Highway Commission was established by Act of the General Assembly, under the chairmanship of P. St. John Wilson. His assistant was George P. Coleman.

Courtesy of Virginia State Chamber of Commerce

NEW CONCRETE HIGHWAY BETWEEN WASHING-
TON, D. C., AND RICHMOND, VIRGINIA

A difficult problem to solve was: How should the counties raise the funds that would be needed by them to defray their share of the expense of road building? The machinery and equipment which they were able to furnish was, unfortunately, very inadequate. On the other hand, the only assistance that the commission could give at first was in the form of convict labor. A formal application had to be made to that body for this aid by the county wanting it. Every such county had to supply the materials and tools that would be required for the construction to take place within its borders, and also to agree to conform to all the plans that the commission should prescribe and to submit to the supervision of one of its engineers. The next step was for the commission to requisition the superintendent of the penitentiary to assign to the use of the particular county such a number of convicts as would be desired.

In December, 1906, five bands, composed of fifty such men each, were placed upon the roads. In the course of the following year, there were applications from fifteen counties for the building of thirty-two highways, extending over 203 miles. Ninety-two miles were actually surveyed and platted in nine counties during that period. The railways showed a fine spirit of cooperation by transporting without charge the convict contingents, with their camp equipment, and road machines.

In 1908, a substantial addition was made by the state to its appropriation for the maintenance of the commission. One year later, the annual sum reserved for its use in aiding permanent road improvement was fixed at $250,000. An important provision adopted at the same time required that every county seeking assistance should contribute as large an amount for road building within its bounds as the state was ready to supply.

The interest in road construction was now growing more earnest and intelligent. Already seven counties had authorized their boards of supervisors to issue bonds for the purpose of securing the funds which they needed for road improvement. The demand for convict labor soon became so great that the commission was unable to meet it completely. It was clearly perceived by this body that such a form of labor for the highways offered several serious drawbacks. The most important of these was, that it had to be performed by convicts in groups under guard. The men could not be strung out for fear that many of them would take to the bushes and escape. Their highest usefulness was exhibited in the quarries, where the surface material was prepared.

As there was no stone to be found in Tidewater Virginia, a mixture of clay and sand was applied there after the bed had been properly graded and drained. The state made no provision for dirt roads.

In 1909, the General Assembly contributed about $90,000 to the construction of macadam highways, $11,500 to the construction of gravel, and approximately $25,000 for the construction of sand and clay. In all these instances, convict labor was furnished to the counties in which these roads were situated. Bond issues continued to be negotiated by the counties to supplement the appropriations by the state. In 1909, every county in Virginia, except ten, applied for the assistance of convict labor. Roads were now under construction in forty counties; and eight besides were awaiting state aid before beginning work. There were, during this year, fourteen convict camps engaged in this branch of public service. The steadily increasing interest of the public in good roads was revealed at this time in the formation of the Virginia Good Roads Association, and also in the number of donations for the promotion of highway improvement made by citizens in their private capacity. In 1910, 270 miles of surface were laid in macadam, gravel, or clay and sand, after they had been scientifically shaped and graded. This was double the extent of the similar construction done in the course of 1909. Sixty counties had shared in this work. Not less than thirteen were now bonded for local road improvements. The smallest obligation assumed in this form was $30,000, and the largest, $200,000.

The state, in 1910, distributed the sum of a quarter of a million dollars among the different counties to assist them in the construction of scientific roads, and this appropriation was again increased by the generosity of individual citizens. In the course of the following year, ninety-three of the one hundred counties were in the enjoyment of the state's subsidy, whether in the form of convict labor or of money. Some of the counties began now to bond themselves for the same purpose to the extent of $600,000, and even $700,000.

At this date, the cost of convict labor by the day was estimated at approximately 50 to 67 cents. This was a lower outlay than for the same length of time in the course of the previous year. It was then 66 to 71 cents. In 1909, it was 72 cents. The cost of free labor on the roads, as compared with convict, revealed a large difference in favor of the greater cheapness of the latter. This difference amounted to at least $1,500 a mile. The work on the roads included not only the construction of beds, but the erection of new bridges or the repair of old. In 1911, sixty-seven counties obtained the assistance of the state for the improvement of their road surface; and fifty-three, a similar assistance for the construction of bridges. In 1912, alone, ninety-three bridges were either built through this co-operation, or formally contracted for. Only five counties had failed to apply for the state's aid.

In the course of this year, about 147 miles of surface were macadamized, 63 graveled, and 179 covered with soil or sand-clay. Twenty-eight counties had, by this date, authorized bond issues for these purposes. The showing for 1913 was equally favorable for each type of construction. Thirteen counties this year alone issued bonds for road improvements. This included new bridges.

The Highway Commission had been becoming more and more solicitous that a law should be passed which would compel the counties to keep roads, once constructed in a scientific manner, in good condition. Neglect these roads, it was said, and nothing in time would be left to prove that they once existed, except the still unpaid bonds, which had been issued to provide the means for their construction.

In 1914, during the commissionership of George P. Coleman, there were 403 roads under construction in ninety-six counties. This building also included the erection or repair of ninety bridges. A large part of this work was done by convicts obtained from the penitentiary in Richmond, assisted by jailbirds furnished by the counties. The state convicts numbered 1,100, and the local jailbirds about 500 in all. They were scattered about in separate camps in thirty different counties. The length of their hours of labor each day did not run beyond ten; and the average cost did not, for that period, exceed 52.9 cents. The extent of the new surfaces finished during this year came to 152 miles of macadam bed, 103 of gravel, 534 of soil or sand, and 3½ of shell. Bonds to the value of $400,000 for new road construction were issued in the course of these twelve months.

Commissioner Coleman recommended, at this time, that the convicts assigned to labor on the highways should be divided into four separate classes. First, there should be set apart in one group the dangerous men who had been sentenced to long terms. These should be stationed in quarries under guard for the preparation of the needed stone material. The second group should be composed of men who had been sentenced for short terms. These were to be dressed in blue or brown uniforms and distributed among the counties in the different camps engaged in grading and laying down the roadbeds. The third group should consist of small gangs, dressed in khaki, who were to be employed as yardmen, engineers, or superintendents in the different camps. The fourth group should be dressed in ordinary clothes, and should serve as patrolmen in the maintenance of the roads.

The General Assembly, during the session of 1915-16, passed an act that provided that the income from the automobile and garage licenses should be reserved as a special fund for the

Highway Department's use in assisting the counties to keep up the roads already constructed, on condition that they, in turn, would supply an equal amount for the same purpose. This fund did not become available until 1917; and, at first, it was not sufficient, even when supplemented by the counties' contributions, to furnish the sum needed.

A state system of roads now became necessary if Federal cooperation was to be secured. Such cooperation would signify a Federal appropriation beginning with $100,000 in 1916-17, and ending with $500,000 in 1920-21.

In the course of 1916, 700 miles of roadway were constructed at a cost of $1,600,000. Now, for the first time, every county in the state applied, either for money, or for the assistance of convict labor. In thirty-three counties alone, 1,800 convicts and county jailbirds were employed in road building at a cost of 57.50 cents for each day of labor, which still embraced a period of ten hours. In the area of improvement, there was now to be observed for the first time, in the list of computed lengths, an item of concrete. This extended only for a distance of ten miles. The gravel roads had increased to 637 miles; the soil, to nearly 2,000; the shell, to 18. Twelve counties, during this year, issued road bonds; and the sum of these obligations of all the counties had now reached the magnitude of $8,500,000. The aggregate addition to the roadbeds in 1917 was 14½ miles of concrete, 104 of macadam, 32½ of gravel, and 264 of soil. Bonds were issued during this one year to the extent of over $412,000.

By an Act of Assembly, passed in 1918, a state highway system—pertinent, however, only to certain sections of the roads—was created. Under this act, over 1,500 miles of improved roadbed were transferred to the commission. This area had cost about $700,000 to build, including the expense of the convict labor furnished. The commission decided to resurface and widen these old roadways. The county highway system seems to have embraced 2,300 miles, maintained by the joint funds of the state and the counties.

All the counties, except four, in 1919, applied to the state for aid. Thirty-three separate camps were placed about Virginia in order to afford shelter for the 1,200 convicts and county jailbirds employed in the construction of the roads. The average cost by the day of convict labor at this time was $1.12⅓. This increase had followed the rise in all prices since the beginning of the World war. Between 1918 and 1923, the expense of building had varied with the types of construction. The total charge for the laying down of 1,049 miles of all types was computed at nearly $2,000,000. Between October, 1921, and September, 1922, there were 2,260 miles under maintenance. A few months later, the commission assumed the care of 4,200 miles of roadway as a part of the state highway system. The new chairman of the body was H. G. Shirley, who had enjoyed an exceptional experience in the province of road building.

The great thoroughfares of the state, most of which have been fully or partially completed, are in 1927 the Lee Highway, from Washington to Bristol; the Jefferson Davis Highway, from the same city, through Richmond, to the Carolina border; the Valley Pike; and the Pocahontas, Tidewater, and Spotswood Trails. The Pocahontas Trail runs from the capital city to Newport News. There is a second highway to Norfolk by way of Petersburg. Several other important highways are in course of rapid construction.

The state system is maintained and lengthened by means of a gasoline tax. The people of Virginia wisely refused to issue an enormous amount of bonds for the extension of their hard-surfaced roads. Not only have the existing highways facilitated the passage of private cars, but they have also led to the establishment of motor-bus lines, which now connect all the centers of population, both great and small. It has already given a strong impulse to tourist travel through all parts of the state.

CHAPTER VII

STATE BOARD OF HEALTH

One of the most remarkable characteristics of the Middle Ages was the ignorance of all the natural sanitary laws, which are so clearly understood in our own era, and, as far as possible, so strictly enforced. If that impression of foul living which we get by the study of those times—even of a period as late as the seventeenth century—is absolutely correct, then it is impossible not to wonder how men, at least in the towns, escaped extinction in a body. With every street an open sewer to carry off the domestic refuse; with practically very little ventilation to purify the air in the rooms of houses; with no means to halt an epidemic when it had once started, except to allow it to burn itself out to the last victim, like a conflagration that has nothing more to consume—the only cause for surprise would seem to be that any city could, in the course of a long period, retain any inhabitants at all.

It is easy to conceive what the condition of London must have been when the plague, following the Restoration, had wreaked its havoc upon hundreds of thousands of unfortunate people exposed to its malignant breath. Strange must have been the public attitude of mind, afterwards, which could find consolation in the destruction caused by the terrible fire which succeeded. It was a demoniacal cleansing of the filth of centuries; and the gain was greater than the loss, in spite of the incineration of so vast a metropolis. The fatalistic spirit was stronger in those days than in ours. "Are not these fearful

393

diseases," the populace argued, even in the hour of suffering and death, "the visitations of Almighty God?" In silent misery, they submitted, as if to the inevitable; and when the besom had passed, the survivors resumed their callings without having learned a single lesson that would prevent, even in part, a recurrence in the future of the same calamity.

Naturally, the purely rural districts in those times were more wholesome localities than the towns; but even there, the conditions must have been inimical to true health among the inhabitants at large. Hygiene is essentially a modern science. In a quiet way, it has done more to make this world a comfortable place to live in than all the great mechanical inventions put together. Preventative sanitation is the consummation of modern philanthropy, which has brought about more well-being, moral as well as physical, than any other device of human genius; and its marks more distinctly and beneficially the boundary line between the old and the new than the telegraph or the locomotive. In fact, it is civilization's last and greatest triumph.

When men began to realize that the observance of sanitary laws would diminish, if not prevent, the worst of the ancient diseases, the first experiment was made in the towns by establishing a vast net-work of sewers; by prescribing the plumbing for private residences; by cleaning up the streets; by purifying the water; by improving the ventilation of houses; by inspecting the food; by prohibiting the use of pernicious drugs; by isolating contagious sickness; by stamping out chronic diseases.

It was not long before it was perceived that the rural districts were just as much in need of sanitation as the urban; and that they were equally capable of being freed from the maladies, which had, in the past, brought so much sorrow into human life through the naked force of ignorance and its offspring, neglectfulness. It was quickly recognized that here was a service to the public which could only be performed properly by performing it through the agency of the state; at least, to the extent of general direction and supervision. Cooperation between commonwealth and locality was essential, it is true. But without the resources, knowledge, and appliances of the state, the most successful results could not be reached, when it came to the point of either preventing or curing insanitary conditions. If the aid of the state was required to sustain properly a system of universal education, that aid was still more indispensable for the maintenance of an equally universal system of hygiene. The two had much in common. The one was instruction for the benefit of the mind; the other was instruction for the benefit of the body. Both had an element of philanthropy in their character. There rises up in both the propulsive spirit of a true crusade; the stimulus of an unselfish devotion to mankind's welfare, which carries its own reward.

We know of no finer examples in Virginia's modern history of this inspired attitude than can be found in the reports of Dr. William H. Ruffner, who inaugurated the public school system of the state, and the reports of Dr. Ennion G. Williams, who, with able assistance, practically created the Virginia State Board of Health, as we know it today. This is public service in its highest manifestation, for its ulterior aim is to improve directly and radically the condition of a vast multitude of men.

As early as 1872, only seven years after the close of the War of Secession, the General Assembly of Virginia authorized the establishment of a State Board of Health, to be composed of seven distinguished physicians, selected from different parts of the Commonwealth. The appointments were made. This board was impowered to investigate unhealthy conditions wherever they existed to an alarming degree; but its principal function seems to have been to act in an advisory capacity touching any matter of hygiene or medicine brought directly to its attention as affecting the safety or usefulness of prisons, asylums, and hospitals. By act of Assembly at the session of 1899-1900, the Medical Society of Virginia was granted the right to select the members of the Board; subject, however, to the approval of the governor. By the same Act, the Medical Society was authorized to submit to the judge of each county or corporation court, the names of those physicians of that county or city, who, with the clerk of the court, and the chairman of the Board of Supervisors, if a county, or the mayor of the town, if a corporation, were to serve as a local Board of Health.

It was not until 1903 that an appropriation was made by the General Assembly for the support of the State Board. The next step on its part was to increase the number of members to twelve. Each congressional district was to be represented by one member, and the City of Richmond by two, all to serve a term of four years. An epochal feature of this reorganization by the Legislature was the appointment of a health commissioner, who was to occupy the position of the board's executive officer; without, however, possessing a seat as one of its members. The new officer was required to be a man deeply versed in bacteriology and sanitary science. His appointment was a proof of the board's intention to widen the public usefulness of their organization.

The new Commissioner was Dr. Ennion G. Williams, of Richmond, who was destined, by his zeal, energy, enthusiasm, and efficiency, in performing the duties of his office, to win distinction in the contemporary history of the state. His assistant was Dr. Roy K. Flannagan, who proved to be a most competent coadjutor. An expert bacteriologist was also employed. A new era had really begun for the State Board of Health.

One of the most momentous facts of the hour was the light which had been thrown by the science of bacteriology on the causes of diseases; the manner in which they were transmitted; and the proper means of preventing their incubation and spread. Vital as this information was in its significance, only partial use had previously been made of it by local, state, and national authorities. The possibilities of such use, however, had been demonstrated on a magnificent scale in the suppression of yellow fever on the Isthmus of Panama. The reorganized Virginia Board of Health, under the leadership of Doctor Williams, which

ENNION G. WILLIAMS.

began in 1908, was one of the first of the state boards to apply modern scientific knowledge to the improvement of public hygiene by a system of prevention as well as of cure, extending to every rural and urban district in the Commonwealth.

In 1916, the number of the Board's members was increased to fourteen, so as to include in its circle a representative of the dental profession, the importance of which calling, in the control of disease, was now very generally perceived. A second additional member, chosen without regard to professional attainments, represented the state at large. Eight years afterwards, the membership of the board was cut down to seven. The five great geographical divisions of the state were represented by one member respectively, and the state at large by two. At least three were always to be selected from the membership of the Medical Society of Virginia, and one from the Dental.

The name of the board was changed in 1927 to the State Department of Health. There was no alteration in its powers, or in those of the health commissioner, who continued to be Doctor Williams. He had now served for a period of about nineteen years, with a steadily increasing reputation. Among the men in political life who had taken a deep interest in the work of the board was Capt. W. W. Baker, the delegate in the General Assembly from Chesterfield County, and Governor Swanson. Both, in their separate spheres, rendered services of extraordinary value.

Having described the general character of the Board of Health, it will now be pertinent to enter with some particularity into the nature of its functions. As these varied to some degree from year to year, it will be necessary to follow their development as outlined in the successive annual reports.

Let us begin with 1909. One of the first duties of the Board in its initial year was to issue a monthly series of bulletins containing a vast amount of practical information promotive of the public health. The list for that year is indicative of the nature of all these bulletins. They related to School Hygiene,

Small-Pox and Vaccination, Sanitary Rules, Oyster Pollution, Care of Infants, Carriers of Disease, Good Water in Town and Country, Hookworm, Health Conditions in Virginia, Measles and Whooping Cough, and War on Consumption. The number of these bulletins distributed in 1909 ran into batches of thousands. This printed health propaganda was supplemented by a continuous stream of notices of health subjects published in the columns of the daily press. These were at first followed by a series of "Health Talks," published in the summer editions of the daily journals. In addition, there were the public lectures delivered by the commissioner and his assistants at the invitation of different associations scattered about the state at large. These were made more impressive by lantern studies. There were also public exhibits illustratory of tuberculosis and other diseases.

As a further means of checking consumption, steps were taken in 1909, under the general supervision of the Department of Health, to erect a sanatorium at Catawba. The first patient was received in July of this year, since which date that beneficent institution has been taxed to its utmost capacity. A second disease which, at the same time, received the most solicitous attention was typhoid, the principal scourge of small towns and rural districts. As soon as an outbreak was reported to the commissioner's office in Richmond, his assistant was dispatched to the spot to investigate the cause of the epidemic; and if necessary, a bacteriological laboratory was established there for the closest tests. The same special examinations were made, in 1909, in the case of small-pox, diphtheria, and pellagra.

Equal attention also was, during this year, paid by the commissioner to the condition of the various water supplies of the state, for to them was generally traceable the contemporary outbreaks of the filth diseases. Another subject intimately connected with such diseases, and as carefully considered, was the disposal of sewerage. On this source of so many epidemics, the most watchful and experienced eye was constantly kept. In the same spirit, the causes of oyster pollution were fully studied. Schools and factories were also inspected. On the recommendation of the department, acting through the commissioner, new sanitary arrangements and purer water supplies in different places were introduced. Another step on the part of the department at this time was the establishment of a Bureau of Vital Statistics; and also a Bureau for the Registration of Communicable Diseases. Deaths too were recorded under the same auspices.

Such was the nature of the department's functions during the year of its first practical organization, namely, 1908-09.

Two years subsequently it was divided into additional bureaus for the more convenient supervision of special branches of work. The Catawba sanatorium was enlarged; an intensive campaign against the hookworm was started; the local boards of health, erected during the previous year, were successfully reorganized; the use of the laboratory was extended; the inspection of railway stations and public buildings was made more thorough; and a large quantity of diphtheria antitoxin distributed through the state.

A bureau of sanitary engineers was now created, which served a useful purpose in several ways. It was incumbent upon this bureau to begin the investigation of a water supply when the department's aid was sought by any locality in need of it. It also made an examination of sewerage disposal in the towns and cities. In both cases, the representatives of the bureau instructed the local authorities as to the proper methods to be followed. They were also authorized to assist with their counsel private individuals who wished to install the best sanitary appliances in their homes. A general recommendation was publicly issued in favor of the use, in every rural habitation, of a dry closet for the deposit of excrement; and it was sought to impress upon the people at large in all the rural districts the vital importance of erecting these sanitary structures. The most modern methods of sanitation in this particular were urged

DR. WALTER REED

by the department when the inspection of school-houses was made by it, in association with the Department of Public Instruction.

The work of the Department of Health, in the course of the ensuing years, was on even broader lines. The cooperation between that department and the local authorities grew closer; the machinery for the study and prevention of disease was substantially improved; the sanatorium at Catawba was enlarged; the laboratory tests were made more expansive; the distribution of antitoxins was carried out more liberally; vital and mortuary statistics were recorded more fully; and the labors of the Bureaus of Inspection and Sanitary Engineers were extended over a wider field.

It was natural that this great activity by the Health Department should, from this time, arouse a deeper interest in the minds of the people at large upon questions involving the public health; especially in its domestic ramifications. In no previous year, indeed, had so many schoolhouses been inspected with such care by the local authorities as well as by the agents of the Health Department; nor had so many sanitary outbuildings been erected; nor so many sanitary wells been constructed; nor had so many towns installed perfected water supplies, or laid down modern sewerage systems. A keener vigilance was shown by persons in the sanitary condition of their homes, and a greater eagerness to utilize every means recommended in the public bulletin for the protection of the individual and the family health.

At this time, the principal problems of public hygiene presented themselves for solution in the rural districts, where, naturally, it was more difficult to solve them successfully owing to the absence of the right organizations. It was in this field that the most beneficial work of the Department of Health was now accomplished. During an indefinite period in the history of these rural communities, only the crudest attention at best had been given to those great sanitary laws which it was essential to obey, if the public or individual health was to be preserved. The indifference of the country people in the past arose from ignorance rather than from intentional neglect. They continued to live as their fathers had lived before them. It was only the fresh air of the open spaces which kept them from falling victims more readily to the defective sanitary conditions that prevailed so generally in their homes.

The population of the country far exceeded that of the towns and cities, and it was subject, with equal certainty, to the same diseases as the urban population; and in some cases, in a more malignant form. The most frequent of these were typhoid and hookworm. Both were conveyed through the mouth by means of some form of excreta. If these could be removed entirely from all contact with individuals, the danger of such diseases occurring would be extinguished, for they were purely filth diseases. Was it practicable to eliminate the filth? It was here that science stepped in to show what could be accomplished in this particular. If the causes of these diseases could not be entirely wiped out, at least they might be held in check. How was this to be effected on a secluded farm, where there was no protected water supply, no sanitary closets, and no sewerage? The most promising means was the dry closet, and, in 1912, as we have seen, the Department of Health was especially energetic in enforcing the necessity of introducing it.

How thoroughly justified that department was in carrying out this campaign of education at this period, is revealed in the multitude of cases of typhoid which are recorded for the years 1909, 1910, 1911 and 1912. The estimated number for each of these years, in succession, was 14,398, 11,843, 11,803 and 8,740. The actual number of cases was respectively 7,472, 6,771, 5,959, and 4,608. It is indicative of the success of the department's labors that, from 1909 to 1912 inclusive, as the preceding statistics prove, there was a steady decline in the prevalence of this disease. Indeed, during this interval of four years, the number of positively known cases fell off nearly one-half—a result attributable directly to the popular recognition of the wisdom of following the recommendations that the department had been so long pouring into the public ear. There was a drop in two years from 11,803 cases to 8,740, a difference of 3,063.

What a preservation of human life! What a diminution of human suffering! What a saving in expense! Well might a community rejoice, even from a naked economic point of view, in such a beneficent showing as this!

The upshot of the campaign against the loathsome hookworm was still more successful. This disease was spread by the discharge of hookworm eggs from the bowels of the victims. These eggs were taken into the mouth of a second victim, to be hatched in his intestines, and in this new form, to continue indefinitely the evil which they had already inflicted. In the war made by the department on this malignant pest, that organization had the assistance of the Rockefeller Sanitary Commission.

In 1914, thirty-seven counties of the state were selected as a field for inspection. Fifty-five thousand persons residing in this area were carefully examined; and of this number, 17,000 were found to be afflicted with this disease. In thirty additional counties, the children were subjected to a similar examination, and it was discovered that at least 7,500 of these had fallen victims. In twelve counties, less than ten per cent of the population suffered from the hookworm; in ten, from 20 to 30 per cent suffered; in nine, 30 to 40 per cent; in seven, 40 to 50; in two, 50 to 60. In several counties, the number of children infected amounted to two-thirds of the entire number. In 1812 the commissioner calculated that 20 per cent of all the school children in the state were victims of this disease.

In addition to these campaigns against typhoid and hookworm, the department was, at this time, actively employed in an effort to destroy the germ of malaria. This was, in some parts of the state, almost ubiquitous. The methods adopted were those inculcated by the successful contest with this evil which had been carried on in the tropical countries under the guidance of modern science.

The department, as we have already mentioned incidentally, was always ready to inspect on the ground the water supplies of the different cities in response to the request of their respective authorities; and also to test the purity of these supplies by laboratory methods applied in Richmond. In 1914 the towns of Alexandria, Alta Vista, and Appalachia, and sixty smaller centers, took advantage of this means to find out the quality of the water stored in their respective reservoirs. The importance of this test was fully recognized by the commissioner. "The final conquest of typhoid in rural Virginia," he wrote more than once, "will depend particularly on the installation of a safe supply of pure water." He considered this as essential as the construction and regular use of the sanitary dry closet in the home, or the use of the typhoid vaccine matter in infected families.

The department was especially solicitous to assist with its counsel, or in any other way lying in its power, every effort of the negro population, on their customary cleaning-up day to make a thorough job of that domestic proceeding. It was clearly perceived that the health of the whites was directly involved in the hygienic condition of the blacks, as the large proportion of their servants, and most of their laundry-women, were drawn from this section of the community. Many cases of smallpox and other contagious diseases that appeared from time to time among the white people arose in this way. The negroes were crowded at night into unwholesome parts of the towns; but their work as laborers carried them everywhere during the day, and made them active propagators of disease, should their bodies have become infected. At this time, the ratio of deaths among the whites was 11.4 per cent in 100,000. The ratio among the blacks, on the other hand, amounted to as much as 19.1 per cent for the same number of individuals.

The department took a special interest in the small towns, because they often suffered in an aggravated form from the evils which were experienced by the cities and country districts. These towns were frequently victims of epidemics of disease for no other reason except that they lacked the modern system of sewerage, and were equally wanting in the means to procure an abundant quantity of pure water. The sewerage consisted too often of the natural surface drainage, while the water was obtained from pumps. On finding out that conditions like these prevailed in some particular small town, the department distributed among its citizens numerous bulletins or pamphlets that related directly to the best way of removing the evil; and afterwards dispatched an inspector to go over the ground thoroughly, and in doing so, to advise with the householders. Not satisfied with their promise to institute a change, he usually returned, after an interval, to see whether the instructions which he had given had been carried out.

In some instances, after a water supply had been installed under this influence, no effort of importance was made by a town to prevent any contamination of its water-shed. Subsequent inspection by the department invariably led to more effective protection.

The department's activity was always increased by a mild winter, for it was anticipated that such a season would bring out a greater swarm of pestilential insects, which were known to be propagators of disease. This was anticipated particularly in the case of the flea. Warnings were dispatched far and wide before the spring arrived, urging a warfare upon all disease-bearers of this kind. If an epidemic from this or any other cause broke out in any part of the state, the department's epidemiologist was promptly dispatched thither. He was always accompanied by a sanitary engineer and the director of the state inspectors. If their report revealed that there was an imminent prospect of the outburst of an aggravated type of disease, the department's emergency hypochlorate plant was at once installed, in order, at the start, to sterilize the drinking-water.

As the years passed, the work of the department continued along the same general lines, with an increased efficiency and a keener enthusiasm. It was said in 1916 that its labor in spreading the latest knowledge of contagious diseases, and in educating the people in the laws of hygiene, was only limited in scope by the means at its disposal. The quantity of pertinent bulletins distributed was now larger than ever before. The responsiveness of the General Assembly was shown by their appropriation of $5,000 towards the success of the campaign for the extinction of tuberculosis, in which the department was acutely interested. Under its influence, a sanatorium for negro consumptives had been established in 1915-16.

Another phase of work which also enlisted the department's interest to a remarkable degree was the health of mother and child. Fifty thousand bulletins bearing on this subject were sent out in the course of this one year alone. In consequence of an intensive sanitary campaign carried on in 1915-16 in fourteen counties, 3,000 sanitary privies were erected. An active warfare was now begun for the suppression of rabies, and an enormous amount of antitoxins were distributed for the cure of diphtheria and tetanus, and also vaccine matter for the prevention of typhoid. An epidemic of infant paralysis was checked in 1917 by energetic intervention on the part of the department.

Notable events that occurred during this year was the appropriation by the counties of a fund of $17,000 for the prosecution of sanitary work, and the appointment of twelve additional public health nurses for service in the cities and rural districts of the state. In 1918, when the United States was engaged in the World war, the department, although crippled by the withdrawal of some of its officers for foreign duty, was as strenuous as ever in the performance of its local sanitary labors. It inspected, at this time, ninety-four towns in the state having a population less than ten thousand in number. It was disclosed that thirteen had no public system of sewerage; and in sixty-one, there was not a single sanitary privy.

During 1918-19, a great epidemic of influenza broke out. The department promptly issued over one hundred thousand bulletins containing special directions for combating this destructive disease. Under its supervision, Dr. Paul Barringer visited the mining and railway centers of Southwest Virginia, and delivered there a series of addresses pointing out the best methods for preventing or curing the prevailing malady. Elsewhere, equally able and successful spokesmen represented the department at this critical hour. Schools were closed and new hospitals were opened. The department was now in close affiliation with the county boards of health, and, by counsel and direct coperation, increased the value of their services. It was also in touch with the Federal Board of Health.

The period that has followed 1920 has been marked by still greater activity on the part of the department; and its usefulness has, with the progress of the years, continued to broaden along the lines, which, as we have seen, it had been pursuing during the earlier period of its existence. The extraordinarily diverse and extensive functions of the department, during this recent period, have been summed up by the indefatigable commissioner of the board substantially as follows: it investigates every serious outbreak of disease, especially if that disease is a communicable one; it publishes bulletins relating to the cause, prevention, and cure of every malady of this character; it maintains a laboratory for the examination of specimens obtained from persons suspected of such infection, and also for the analysis of drinking water sent by towns or districts; it administers free treatment in all cases of supposed rabies; it directs the collection of birth and mortuary statistics; it dispenses, at wholesale prices, antitoxins for diphtheria and tetanus, and vaccine matter for smallpox, whooping cough, and typhoid; it operates sanatoriums for white and colored patients; it passes upon all the plans for establishing public water supplies and sewerage systems, and offers the assistance of its sanitary engineers in the construction of these public works; it carries on an intensive campaign in rural districts and small towns for the eradication of typhoid, malaria, and hookworm; it recommends the best methods of reducing infant mortality; it cooperates with the authorities of town and country in making general sanitary surveys; and it aids in the organization of local boards of health.

But this is not the entire extent of its beneficent work at the present time. It appoints the members of the health organizations in towns which do not enjoy the right to do this alone; it assists the local school authorities to carry out the sanitary regulations touching the school houses, and periodically inspects the physical condition of the school children; it cooperates with the Virginia Anti-Tuberculosis Association in combatting that disease; it employs a state supervisor of nursing; it inspects all the hotels at intervals, and also the water served on trains; it exercises on occasion the powers of quarantine; it operates at Coeburn, in Wise County, in association with the Federal Government, a hospital for the diagnosis and surgical and medical treatment of trachoma. And finally, it supplies lecturers to the medical colleges to discuss the different phases of public health, in order to encourage the study of these phases by the young men present, since so many of them are destined to become the health officers of the state.

CHAPTER VIII

PROHIBITION

Virginia, during the whole of its history before the War of 1861-65, and for many years afterwards, was widely renowned for its genial and delightful hospitality. Most of the social habits of her people had been simply a continuation, under another sky, of the habits which had distinguished their English ancestors, and which still distinguished their contemporary kinsmen oversea. When the first settlers sat down along the banks of the Powhatan, they did not give up any of their inherited tastes. On the contrary, they remained as tenacious of these tastes as ever, and the passage of the years made no difference in this respect in their descendants. By the time that several generations had gone by, there had been built, in all parts of the Colony then taken up, a succession of homes, in which the people lived in extraordinary abundance, rendered possible by the fertility of the land. No suggestion of frugality or parsimony ever came up, because there was no need to cultivate such qualities. The hand had only to be put forth to pluck the fruits of a mild climate and a rich soil. There was not only enough for all, but more than enough. A spirit of apparent wastefulness was really a mere phase of a generous and overflowing plenty. Why store and hoard for the morrow when the morrow was certain to be simply a counterpart of the bursting present?

But there were other influences besides fields of grain and tobacco, teeming gardens and orchards, and pastures filled with cattle, to promote this spirit of domestic enjoyment. That old

410

plantation system, which began in Virginia before the Pilgrim Fathers were ever heard of, tended, it is true, to isolate the landowners physically, but this fact only brought out more clearly their social instincts by leading them to cultivate more ardently the pleasures of hospitality. The exercise of that virtue prompted them to live always liberally. There were to be found in the American Colonies no other tables garnished with as much that was good to eat and drink as the tables that groaned under their heavy loads in the Virginian mansions. The taste for good liquor especially was undisguised. As far back as 1686, William Fauntleroy kept in his cellar as many as ninety gallons of rum, twenty-five gallons of lime juice, and twenty dozen bottles of wine, reserved for the use of his private board alone. This abundance of spirits in a plantation home was not at all rare throughout the whole of the seventeenth century. Wherever a body of gentlemen, large or small, gathered together, whether it was to dine in a friend's residence; or to appraise the value of an estate; or to pass upon a public bridge; or to hold the county court, a liberal quantity of liquor of all kinds was invariably placed near at hand to assuage their thirst.

The taverns of those times kept ready for sale, not only such fierce stimulants as whiskey and brandy, but also the finest wines of France and Madeira. These taverns were frequented by persons of all classes, in their hours of leisure, for the comfortable potations and the pleasant social intercourse which they offered. In the seventeenth century also, the private banquetting hall was not unknown. An association of genial neighbors would get together to subscribe for the erection of such a structure; and after it was built, each in turn would meet all the costs of a feast, in which the sparkling glass went cheerfully around the board.

The love of mellow liquor was also general in the eighteenth century. Even as staid and restrained a character as Washington took his wine with relish; nor did he consider it derogatory to his dignity to distil at Mt. Vernon a brand of whiskey of superior quality, which helped materially to drive the malaria of the adjacent Potomac marshes out of the blood of his white and black dependents. Was there ever a more sober gentleman than Thomas Jefferson? And yet he is said to have invented a table so easily turned within its stationary outer rim that his guests were never known to complain of any slowness in the passing of the liquor. The "morning draught" was a popular expression in those early times. Every man who was not an extreme Puritan,—and there were few persons of that type in any neighborhood of Virginia in that day,—took this draught regularly, and was grateful that the malignant diseases could be kept at a distance by such pleasant means. There was no alteration in the kindly attitude towards the mint-julip and toddy during the years that followed the Revolution, down to the War of Secession. The julip and toddy cups were cherished as souvenirs of colonial ancestors, and were regarded as all the more precious because they recalled the most glorious social era in the history of the community.

While nearly every citizen drank to some extent in the ante-bellum period, there is no evidence of such excess in the general life of the people as to become a scandal. The Virginians of that period were a liberal, generous, genial and happy race of men who respected their wives, their homes, and their religion, and were responsive to every honorable and chivalrous sentiment. Was such a type as this disposed to violate the decencies of society by frequent and ill-timed indulgence of a thirst for spirits? Drunkards there were, but they were marked individuals in their respective communities. Over-indulgence was not unknown even among sober men, but there were bounds to their use of liquor, a line which they never crossed.

Even after the close of the War of Secession, when the people had so many sorrows to urge them to seek self-forgetfulness, there was no change for the worse in their habits of drinking. They continued, as a rule, to make the same moderate use as before of all the pleasures of this kind in their reach. Indeed, liquor circulated no more than during the previous years. The community had not turned about in this respect. If anything, it was more restrained in its enjoyments than it had been formerly.

What then was it which, in time, altered the Virginians as a body so far as to induce them to adopt prohibition as the per-

HISTORIC RALEIGH TAVERN OF WILLIAMSBURG

manent policy of their social and political life? What had so changed this conservative race of men to such a degree as to cause them to take exactly the opposite tack from the one which they had been pursuing ever since their ancestors at Jamestown and Williamsburg had set them the example of a rational appreciation of exhilarating spirits? The question is a puzzling one. Quite probably a mixture of influences produced this social phenomenon.

One of the fundamental, if not the most powerful of these influences, was the practical extinction of that old rural gentry, of high family position, which had ruled the social and political life of every community in Virginia throughout the Colonial and post-Revolutionary periods. These men set the tone in every Virginia county. They constituted as much of a social aristocracy as was possible under a Republican form of government. Prohibition has never been an acceptable doctrine with any set of men who possess all the opportunities for social enjoyment which wealth can offer. Such men do not look at life from a Puritan point of view. Nor did these old Virginians; and the opinions which they expressed, and the example which they set, carried far among those of their neighbors and friends who were not so fortunately placed as themselves in a worldly way. Their influence in the social arena was even more powerful than it was in the political. Prohibition is a social policy primarily, and as long as this ancient gentry survived after the War of Secession, this policy made no real progress.

When prohibition was adopted in Virginia, the political and social ascendancy had fallen into the hands of a section of the community which had occupied a less influential position so long as the powerful rural gentry ruled, but now that this gentry had, as a class, disappeared through impoverishment, the former subordinate division of the old society assumed their place of priority. It cannot be asserted that this section taken as a body was animated by a rigidly puritanical spirit; but it can be affirmed that it was governed by a strong and active religious spirit. The most conspicuous members of this new controlling element of citizenship were closely associated with several great religious denominations which had been always noted for their sectarian zeal and uncompromising loyalty to their own standards of morality.

The old drinking inclinations of the people had undoubtedly a side open to censure. How natural then that these religious denominations should unite in directing all their energies to the adoption of a public policy which they felt sure would put an end to what they sincerely conceived to be an evil, by tearing it up root and branch.

The history of Prohibition in Virginia reveals that the movement advanced in more or less slow gradations. First, an endeavor was made to throw restrictive regulations around the flow of the liquor traffic in different districts of the State. This was the well-known policy of local option. This policy was necessarily crippled in its operation by the ease with which the citizens of one county, cleansed by local option, could obtain all the liquor they needed from an adjacent county that still patronized the open saloon. There might be some inconvenience in visiting distant bar-rooms and country-stores outside their own dry county's jurisdiction, but when the thirst was keen, no obstacles were allowed to stand in the way.

The zeal of those who, at first, favored local option was so much whetted by this disregard of the spirit of this law that they began to work for the extension of prohibition to the area of the entire State; and in the end, this policy was adopted, after local option had spread to the greater proportion of the counties. The evolution of Prohibition was completed by its adoption throughout the Union, under the authority of the Eighteenth Amendment to the Federal Constitution. This final measure had been preceded by Congress' passage, during the War, of a Protective Act. This, however, had continued virtually null, owing to the fact that no provision for carrying it out had accompanied it.

The two most important Acts relating to the enforcement of Prohibition in Virginia, after the adoption of the original Act establishing it, were the Mapp and Layman Acts known by the names of their patrons. These Acts are too voluminous in detail to be presented here, except in bare outline. They defined at length what was to be considered ardent spirits, and forbade the manufacture, use, sale, and transportation of such. They also specified the steps to be taken in a search; prohibited all advertisement of liquor; laid down the rules to govern trials in cases in which the Acts had been violated; created the office of commissioner, and stated its functions; defined the character of punishable intoxication; prescribed what should be held to be soft drinks, and how they should be sold; and, finally, authorized an appropriation by the General Assembly to compel the observance of the law.

There were other features of the two Acts which are not necessary to be mentioned here. Many of the provisions for the enforcement of Prohibition had been adopted in previous measures of the Assembly. The law was especially strict in regulating the dispensation of liquor by druggists, as this was practically the only way in which it could be sold without violation of the law. One of the striking characteristics of the first statute was its excessive voluminousness and its extreme minuteness. Few Acts recorded in the General Code of Virginia have been strung out in such astonishing detail. It seemed to be foreseen by the Assembly that the smallest loophole would be taken advantage of by the lynx-eyed opponents of the law; and that every possibility in this particular was to be met by the exhaustive wording of the text.

Such a law was essentially different from the average one putting a restraint upon or punishing individual conduct. Most laws of this nature relate to some act which is acknowledged to be wrong by those who are guilty of it, even at the moment of its commission. The use of liquor was, in its very nature, no crime. Men who commit murder are aware that they do commit a crime, and men who steal do not disguise from themselves the fact that, in stealing, they too have been guilty of a serious offense. As far back in history as the records go, the use of spirits has been universal in every country. It was not even condemned in the most sacred of all books in the eyes of Christians,—the Holy Bible. The Prohibition Law was one of the first enactments that endeavored to make a crime of conduct which had been previously considered legitimate for thousands of years.

Naturally, the passage of such a law was not accepted universally as perfectly right in itself. The originators of the Act in Virginia probably had this fact in mind when they drafted a statute so drastic, so voluminous, and so iron-bound in its provisions. They expected that this would prevent its violation. Actual Prohibition necessarily raised a bitter controversal spirit. This is the fate of every law that seeks to interfere with the ordinary social habits and domestic rights of men, especially if they have been possessed and enjoyed by the race throughout the progress of the ages. Public policy will not be considered by all citizens as a justification of such an Act; nor was it in the eyes of a great many persons in Virginia, even though that State, taking the majority of its people together, was one of the firmest of all the Commonwealths in the support of the new regulation.

It will be pertinent now to make some examination of the degree to which the law has been enforced in the Virginian communities.

The first report that was drafted by the new Department of Prohibition was submitted for the year ending October 31, 1917. The Commissioner in this report complained with truth that his power was practically restricted to these rights: (1) to name his assistants; (2) to distribute the State's appropriations in harmony with his own judgment; and (3) to perform the duty of a sheriff so far as it called for a simple arrest. Apparently, his general functions were merely those common to every peace officer in the Commonwealth. One of the drawbacks of his position was that it was of such recent origin that no precedents had as yet been established to guide him in the performance of what was expected of him. He had to create his own precedents; and how far he could go was a question which caused much hesitation in his own mind. And in his case, this doubt was deepened by the fact that every act on his part which amounted to the creation of a precedent was watched with scornful or hypercritical eyes, or received with open public denunciation by the host of citizens who regarded the Prohibition law as an outrageous infringement on their personal liberty of conduct.

Knowledge of this hostile attitude comes to the surface in many of the reports of the successive commissioners. There is often an acrimonious resentment reflected in these reports, when discussing the obstacles to the successful administration of the Prohibition Law raised by its opponents. This sharp personal tone is rarely, if ever, perceptible in the records of the other departments of the State Government. As a matter of fact, the only good ground for surprise is that the obstructions to the enforcement of the Act were not far greater in the beginning than they really proved to be. The law had no forerunner in the history of Virginia. That fact alone would have made its administration difficult, even if it had raised no widespread feeling of antagonism in itself.

The Prohibition Department was, in reality, only required to supervise the working of the statute. It was the ordinary police's duty to enforce it. But the Commissioner's impression seemed to be, certainly at first, that his department was wrongly expected to compel the observance of the law as well as to supervise its operation, while the regular constabulary were to be permitted to look on placidly. Many peace officers, according to the Commissioner, were in collusion to neglect and even to defeat the statute. This attitude on their part at this early stage was attributable, not so much to indifference to duty, as to the difficulty of realizing that the act of drinking, which they had never considered to be criminal, had suddenly become an offense in the eyes of the law simply because the majority of voters in the different communities of the State had determined to make it such. There was nothing wrong in itself in the moderate use of liquor. These recalcitrant peace-officers were perfectly aware of this fact; and, in consequence, they were often apathetic, if not actually inimical, to carrying out the law.

When the original Prohibition Act was adopted by the General Assembly, that body appropriated the sum of fifty thousand dollars for a period of two years to facilitate its enforcement. Those citizens who had opposed the passage of the original Act were not made less antagonistic by their knowledge of the destruction of revenue which would follow. The liquor licenses had brought in a large income to city and country districts alike. This was now practically wiped out. In its place, each town and each county found it necessary to impose a new burden on the taxpayers in order to enforce the Prohibition Law, and to remunerate its agents.

The department, in the teeth of the existing opposition,—which had its origin in more reasons than one,—was compelled to assume a resolutely aggressive front as the only means of carrying on the work of prevention and repression with which it was charged. A large number of detectives were employed; and this number was steadily increased from year to year. Many lawyers were enlisted in the duty of prosecuting offenders in the courts, while many correspondents were engaged in reporting the various infractions which fell under their eyes in their several communities. In addition to these agents, the department engaged the volunteer services of many private persons who were interested in the successful enforcement of the law. Furthermore, the Women's Christian Temperance Union and the State Anti-Saloon League stood like a rock behind the department, and aided it by the various powerful means which lay at their disposal. In the meanwhile, the department publicly claimed that it was organized on an efficiency, and not on a political, basis. It was observed that it rarely employed the negro as a detective.

One of the most difficult problems which the department had to solve arose in connection with the drug stores. By law, these stores enjoyed the privilege of selling liquors for medicinal purposes, subject to certain definite but rigid restrictions. But it was found to be impossible to exercise close supervision over their prescriptions. A strict enforcement of the law was equally difficult in the case of hotels, the proprietors of which were permitted to use spirits to some extent in their preparation of certain dishes. A license was required to make this legal. And this was so too in the case of hospitals, chemical laboratories, and factories which produced flavoring extracts. A few distilleries were licensed to sell pure grain alcohol within the borders of the State.

Before the adoption of the Eighteenth Amendment, which made prohibition the universal policy in the United States, a large quantity of liquor flowed in surreptitiously from Kentucky, Maryland, and New York City. The liquor from Kentucky found an entrance through the lonely mountain passes on the border; that from Maryland came through by way of Alexandria, the Potomac River, and the Chesapeake Bay; that from New York, was transported by sea. The profits were so extraordinary that bootleggers took, without hesitation, the most extraordinary risks in conveying it from these several quarters into Virginia.

The railways entering the State from Washington were apathetic in searching their trains, as they asserted that it was no duty of theirs to interfere with the liberties of their passengers,—especially of those who had come from a State like Maryland, which had refused to adopt the Prohibition Law in the first stage of the public agitation for that policy. Without such assistance, the Prohibition agents naturally hesitated to board trains and make arrests. In the same spirit, they were reluctant, at this time, to halt bootleggers speeding along the public highways. In both cases, it was necessary for them to be fortified with warrants, unless they had positive evidence of the guilt of these bold violators of the Prohibition Law. In 1917, as many as one hundred distilleries were broken up in Virginia.

The question soon arose whether the existing Act did not violate one of the clauses of the State Constitution; but when the point was brought to judicial test in the Court of Appeals, the exception taken was not allowed. This was not the first time that the Prohibition Law had been submitted for formal interpretation. One court decided that the word "home" did not include the surrounding buildings, and, therefore, the privileges of exemption which it enjoyed could not be validly extended to these adjacent structures when used in the manufacture of domestic spirits even of the permissible strength. Other interpretations equally radical were given of various phases of the statute. But the majority of the cases at this time involved the guilt or innocence of accused persons. In this year, over two thousand instances of trials for violation of the law occurred in the Circuit Courts.

In June, 1918, an amended Prohibition Act went into operation. It differed from the old Act only in its provisions for the correction of defects which had seriously obstructed the enforcement of the original statute. For that reason, it enlarged the powers of the Department and augmented its duties. There still lingered the popular impression that this Department was established, not so much to prevent the use of ardent spirits, as to prevent their sale. Here again the difficulty of putting an absolute curb on the dispensations of the drug-stores beyond the limit defined was a constant plague to the Prohibition agents. The great majority of these stores endeavored to conform to the statute with conscientious strictness; but there were some that were callous to indirect violations of the law in their prescriptions.

Another leakage into private receptacles took place through express offices. Not less than two thousand of these offices were located in the State, and while it was perfectly well-known that innumerable illegal packages were passing through them, it was practically beyond the power of the Prohibition agents to stop this illicit transit. It was equally a matter of public notoriety, at this time, that a large number of the valises carried by travellers on the railways contained considerable quantities of liquor for private use. It was not often that the presence of this forbidden stuff was brought to light for confiscation and for the punishment of the owner. The motor-cars plying between the country and the towns were also a means of carrying on a traffic still more serious, for the liquor which they conveyed was designed for sale. It was only when these cars broke down that their contents were usually detected.

In the arrest of persons in trains and motor-cars, there was always a danger of the use of weapons by culprit and agent alike, and there were instances in which this happened, with the result of lives being lost on either side in the altercation. One inspector, who had shown a remarkable degree of bravery and determination in the performance of his duty, was murdered near Alexandria. It will be recalled that, at this time, the Eighteenth Amendment had not come into effect. This made the enforcement of the State law more difficult to press successfully. This condition confronted the inspectors on water as well as on land. "Enormous quantities of liquor," the Commissioner stated in 1918, "are brought into Hampton Roads by the members of crews. Sometimes, whiskey in a great ship is found in about every compartment of the vessel,—in the cabin state-rooms, life-belts, the smoke-stack, the ventilators, the forecastle, the anchor chains and the engine and boiler room; indeed, even in the dining room, saloons, and parlors, and in the coal bunks. Frequently, more than three thousand bottles are detected. Barges, sailing-vessels, ocean-going tugs, and fleets of motor-boats, bring in whiskey."

The Commissioner added, with evident depression, that the traffic showed no sign of abatement.

Large quantities of liquor were distilled, at this time, by moonshiners, in the remote fastnesses of the mountains, for sale in Piedmont and the Eastern lowlands, country and town alike. This product from the Alleghanies and Blue Ridge was supplemented by the same illicit manufacture in the neighboring counties of Nelson, Mecklenburg, Halifax, Pittsylvania, and Carroll. Even more copious was the surreptitious outpour in communities much nearer the hills, like Franklin, Floyd, and Pulaski. Some of these stills had been in operation long before the adoption of either the State or the national policy of Prohibition. They resembled old established institutions, although their existence was only known in a general way, or if known particularly, the fact was kept very quiet. As a rule, they used only small crude stills which could be moved off in a few minutes, whenever there was reason to suspect a raid by the revenue agents. Even this early in the history of Prohibition in Virginia, stills were frequently discovered in the heart of some of the cities of the State.

But wherever the liquor may have been manufactured, there was no dam to stop its wide-spread diffusion. "There are one hundred counties in Virginia, twenty-two cities, and one hundred and eighty-four towns," said the Commissioner, "and into all of these localities, these streams pour." He earnestly recommended that five or six inspectors should be stationed in each county, two in each town, and fifteen in each city. About five hundred and ten jail sentences for violation of the Prohibition Law were entered in the country courts in 1918, and over fifteen hundred in the courts of the cities. There were nearly twenty-five hundred prosecutions.

By the time the United States entered the World War, the demand for surreptitious liquor had increased, owing to the exhaustion of the supplies stored away some years before the original State law had passed. The bootleggers, in consequence, became extremely active, and through them a flood of liquor found its way into the State by way of the Capes, the Chesapeake, and the railways running down from the North. The rise in prices beyond the Potomac halted this traffic very perceptibly, and a large demand at once sprang up for illicit corn-whiskey manufactured in Virginia. Liquor that formerly sold for one dollar, or one dollar and a half, by the gallon, now brought from twenty to twenty-five dollars by the gallon. The antagonism between the inspectors and bootleggers which followed became bitter in the extreme. The inspectors were accused of assault, of murder, of highway robbery, even of drunkenness. "They are charged," said the Commissioner indignantly, "with every thing that has a tendency to intimidate them in the performance of their duty."

The accusation of ruthlessness on both sides was unfortunately only too just. Apparently the sole result accomplished was to divert the traffic from the boats and railroads to the illicit distilleries in the country, where it was far more difficult for the State to suppress it. In 1921, fines to the amount of $205,-435 were imposed, and three thousand violations of the law were prosecuted. In the course of the following year, the general enforcement of the Prohibition Act was placed under the jurisdiction of the Attorney-General of the State. During the two years ending with the first of September, 1923, fourteen thousand persons were arrested for contempt of the Act; and over six hundred and ninety-two thousand dollars were collected in the form of fines; and about eighteen hundred stills were captured and destroyed.

The suppression of the illegal manufacture and sale of liquor had not so far been successful to the degree expected and desired by the Department of Prohibition. The further progress of time has not made any material alteration for the better in this condition, in spite of the zealous activity of the Department. This has been due to the inherent difficulties of the situation which had to be surmounted.

CHAPTER IX

EDUCATION

In a previous chapter, we gave a description of the growth of the public school system previous to the outbreak of the World War. It will be pertinent to supplement this description with an account of the development of the same system since the war actually began, down to a recent date. What have been the lines along which its expansion has extended? How far has this expansion yet reached? These are significant questions touching one of the most vital provinces of the State Government. The Department of Public Instruction had, by this time, passed under the administration of Hon. Harris Hart; and largely through his sagacity, experience, and devotion, it has become one of the most useful and inspiring in the contemporary history of Southern Education.

What was the condition of the public schools during the initial year of this later period, namely, 1917-18? The shortcomings, at this time, were declared by the Superintendent to be inadequate buildings, restricted equipment, short terms, and underpaid teachers. So far as buildings were concerned, a vigorous and resolute attempt was now in progress to enforce the transformation of all school-houses of one, two, three and four rooms to a single definite type. During its previous session, the General Assembly had made a large appropriation for the benefit of the schools, on condition that the terms thereafter should be spread over seven months. It was clearly recognized that the school which was most in need of competent teachers

425

ROTUNDA OF THE UNIVERSITY OF VIRGINIA

was the rural school; and it would be all the more imperative that such teachers should be found, if the terms were to be lengthened at an increased expense to the tax-payers.

In 1917-18, there were many thousand instructors employed in performing the work of the public schools. At least one-half of their number were engaged in giving instruction in the one or two-room rural school-houses. This half received, in the way of salary, in the neighborhood of fifteen hundred thousand dollars gross, which was only twenty-eight per cent of the whole amount paid to the teachers as an entire corps. It was clearly perceived by the Superintendent that it was a very short-sighted policy to direct the preponderant attention to the town schools, which were so much better able to find additional funds for their own use through local taxation. So small in proportion to the number of children of school age was the number in regular attendance in the rural districts that it was urged by many persons interested in the success of the public schools that the tuition should be made compulsory in order for its benefits to reach every child in the community. What was expected to serve as a partial substitute for a compulsory system when this was decided to be impracticable? The only substitute that was then considered to be feasible was to establish vocational schools in certain counties, where there was need of a special kind of instruction. The terms of these were to last only ten weeks, but long enough to be distinctly useful.

The conditions upon which the rural high school was now organized were (1) that its length of term should be prolonged for a period of at least nine months; and that seven months should be the shortest length of the term in the elementary grade taught in conjunction with the higher; (2) that a permanent record should be made of the work accomplished by every pupil; (3) that at least eighty minutes' supervision daily should be given by the principal to the teachers' performance of their duties; (4) that not less than thirty-five pupils should be embraced in the high school section; and also at least three teachers, including the principal; and each of them must have won a certificate of proficiency; (5) that not less than three teachers should be employed in giving instruction in the elementary courses; (6) that the program of studies should embrace the subjects of English, Mathematics, History, Science, and Electricity; (7) that each pupil should devote at least two years to the acquisition of the foreign language; (8) that satisfactory facilities for laboratory work should always be provided and carefully maintained; and finally, (9) that a library should be attached to each high school.

These requirements indicate the progress which had been made in the development of the high schools in the rural districts. Many persons still living can recall the difference between these new rural high schools and the old field schools supported by the voluntary contributions of the surrounding planters of antebellum and reconstruction times. The typical old field school stood in some upland broomsedge pasture, or pine belted opening in the forest, within a convenient radius of the adjacent homes. The school-house itself was often an old deserted overseer's house, or even a pioneer's cabin, abandoned, many years before, to slaves. From the modern pedagogic point of view, the building was rude, and even repulsive in aspect, with barely room enough to accommodate the persons of a dozen boys; and yet here under this old shingle roof, and by this great wood-fire, the pupils were often taught by a scholar of ripe attainments. Perhaps, he was the clergyman of the nearest parish aiming to eke out his salary. Perhaps he was a man of fine literary tastes who had proved to be a failure in practical life. A pure love of classical learning often sprang up like a flower under his tuition, and there many an eloquent gospeller, able lawyer, and patriotic statesman, was trained.

These very simple, almost repulsive, temples of learning in the woods are now replaced by the high schools, the requirements of which we have just described. The traveller comes upon them, often unexpectedly, near some church or store on the public roads. The buildings are generally excellent; the surroundings neat and orderly; while the interiors contain every appliance for the preservation of health and the stimulation of culture in teacher and pupil. Where there were, perhaps, ten pupils in the lonely old field school, there are now, even in the remote rural public high school, an hundred or more. The teachers are, for the most part, women; and what some may lack in knowledge and pedagogic efficiency is made up by the refinement of action and thought which they unconsciously diffuse around them by their mere presence.

In the examinations for public positions held in 1918, about nineteen hundred white candidates participated, and about eight hundred colored. The preparation which they had received had been acquired as follows: approximately, two hundred and thirty-eight whites had graduated in high schools, and about one hundred and sixty-four blacks also. Three hundred and fifty-four whites had spent three years in completing their high school work; two hundred and sixty-five whites, two years; and one hundred and ninety-five, one year. The corresponding figures for the negroes had been one hundred and thirty, eighty, and forty-one. About eight hundred and forty-two whites, altogether had received a high school training with or without graduation, and about four hundred and fifteen blacks.

During the session of 1917-18, Virginia possessed five hundred and twenty-two high schools of all grades. Approximately, twenty-seven thousand pupils were instructed in them, under the guidance of nearly eighteen hundred teachers. The average salary of these teachers by the month in the towns amounted to seventy-seven dollars and a half; and in the county, to eighty-six dollars and sixty-six cents in the highest grade, and seventy in the lowest.

At the time of the passage of the Smith-Hughes Act, there was in existence in Virginia a system of Congressional District agricultural high schools. They resembled, not so much vocational schools as those rural schools which possessed a special department of agriculture and economics and also a farm to illustrate the different phases of those sciences. These farms were maintained by State appropriations. The number of such schools in operation was eleven in all; that is to say, one for each Congressional District. After the Smith-Hughes Act had become law, these district schools were merged in those high schools which gave a course of instruction in agricultural subjects designed to prepare the recipients for the pursuit of farming as a calling in life. Altogether, there were, after this change, not less than nineteen such high schools in Virginia; and for each of these a special supervisor had been appointed.

By the end of another four years (1920-21), the high schools in which a course in practical agriculture was taught had increased to sixty-two in number. Eight of these were reserved for the negroes. Members of both races showed a keen interest in the purpose which this agricultural tuition had in view, and earnestly desired the enlargement of that branch of study. It was, indeed, a subject which came home to nearly every boy entered in this particular type of rural school, for they were, in the large majority of cases, the sons of farmers and intended to follow that calling themselves in their mature lives. It was essentially a vocational course, by which the community's welfare was bound to be ultimately promoted to a notable degree.

The popularity of these high schools was further increased by the practical aid which their supervisors gave the surrounding farmers in cooperative marketing,—more especially as relating to the sale of peanuts, tobacco, and cattle. Furthermore, classes were held in the hours of evening for the benefit of adult farmers. The teachers in these high school agricultural departments were men who had been well-prepared to perform that part,—the whites at the Virginia Polytechnic Institute; the colored at the Institute situated at Petersburg.

As late as 1920-21, complaint was heard from the school authorities that the education of the negroes in the public schools was seriously handicapped by the deficiencies of their teachers, and by the irregular attendance of the children. There were about eighty-five thousand colored children who could be relied upon to make the most of public school instruction. The position of teacher in these schools was filled by men and women who had received a fair degree of training for their work, but who, in most cases, were capable of acquiring a higher degree of pedagogic knowledge. There were, at this time, as many as twenty-three training schools for members of their race in the State. A course of two years of high school lessons was offered in all these schools, under the guidance of twenty-five male and ninety-one female teachers. In two of these schools, the term extended for a period of seven months; in sixteen, for eight; and in five, for nine.

At this time, the Cooperative Education Association was performing an energetic part in advancing the eminently practical purpose which it had always kept in view in carrying out its noble mission. Its work extended to every one of the hundred counties embraced in the area of the State; and also to each one of the twelve important cities. About fifteen hundred local leagues had been organized by it. Of this number, four hundred and fifty-five were engaged in promoting an improvement in health conditions. There were twenty-four employed in social and recreational labors; three hundred and thirty-eight in stimulating interest in the alteration for the better of the public highways and two hundred and eighty-seven in the advancement of farming. There were numerous other branches of the public welfare which enjoyed the benefit of their attention. The membership of the Association embraced as many as thirty-eight thousand persons; and they were able to raise a fund annually which came to as much as one hundred and eighty thousand dollars for expenditure upon their patriotic mission.

What was the general condition of the public schools during the period covered by the years 1925 and 1926? At that time, the school population of the State approximated seven hundred and two thousand children of the required age. Of these, about five hundred and fifty-one thousand were enrolled; but only four hundred and twenty-five thousand were in daily attendance on the average. Only a small proportion of the school population was now enrolled in private and parochial schools.

A limited compulsory law was at this time in existence, which fact sensibly reduced the margin between enrollment and the average daily attendance. One of the questions now raised by the public school related to the best means of cutting down this margin to the vanishing point. Proper facilities were certainly one of them, and this was dependent upon public taxation, which, in turn, was dependent upon the financial resources of the people. As much as seventeen millions of dollars were now annually spent on the schools' operation, maintenance, and instruction. This was derived from general taxation, local taxation, and, to some extent, from individual gifts. Under some unavoidable circumstances, the School Boards were compelled to borrow.

The larger proportion of the school children are now as before enrolled in the elementary schools. Naturally, this branch of the general system has demanded the first and most constant attention, and, consequently, it has shown the most perceptible signs of improvement. Necessarily, there has been more room for it there. This improvement has been reflected especially plainly in physical aspects. During 1925-26, seven hundred and eighty-four one, two, and three room schools met all the requirements of the State Board of Education. During the previous year, the corresponding number had been only five hundred and sixty-six. This indicated a very decided step forward for so short a period as twelve months. It is estimated that it afforded an additional thirty-six per cent of children opportunities for education which they had not enjoyed so favorably before.

Another indication of amplified facilities was the increase in the number of busses used for the transportation of pupils to and from school in the rural districts. In 1925-26, the entire number in service was one thousand eighty-one, an addition of nearly three hundred to the number in use during the previous years. The number of children hauled expanded from twenty-five thousand to twenty-nine and a half thousand. There were now 390,465 enrolled in the counties as compared with 101,866 enrolled in the cities. Besides the regular schools, there were many others that were open only during the months of vacation. These were organized to give opportunities of tuition to children who were prevented by good reasons from attending during the ordinary session.

The prosperity of the accredited high school was very perceptibly stimulated by the policy adopted by the State Board of Education in 1925-26, in order to increase the thoroughness of the instruction. This was made the more imperative by the marked augmentation of the number of students embraced in the enrollment for that year. There were now nearly fifty-nine thousand entered in the total list.

The improvement in the character of the instruction in the public schools followed very naturally from the more thorough training which the teachers were receiving in preparation for their calling. In 1917-18, the college professional certificate, the highest awarded, was won by only twenty-one of the white instructors, and five of the colored. On the other hand, in 1925-26, three hundred and ninety-three of the whites were in this catagory, and twenty-one of the blacks. The collegiate certificate, which is bestowed on the graduates of standard colleges and institutions for the training of teachers, was won in 1917-18 by one hundred and sixty-one white instructors and five colored. By 1925-26, the corresponding totals were five hundred and ninety-five and thirty-one. There could not be a more remarkable proof of the improvement in the quality of the school instruction.

By this year, it was not possible to say truthfully that Virginia was lacking in the proper institutions for the training of teachers. There was an ample number at this time; and this number was restricted to colleges supported by the State. The private colleges were also contributing to the circle of competent public school instructors. This was equally so in the case of the colored teachers. It was a fact of interest that the various seats of learning sustained by public or private gifts had prepared for their vocation a large number of the public school teachers employed in the surrounding States.

As early as 1919, several standard plans for the new school buildings had been adopted by the State Department of Education with a view to improving the architectural aspects of the school-houses. The plan varied to suit the kind of structure which was called for, namely, the high school in town, the high school in the country, the elementary school, and so on. Blue prints and specifications were sent to every school board which had a building of any one of these types under contemplation; and these documents were, later on, delivered to the contractor submitting the lowest bid. In 1926, sixty-five buildings were constructed from the plans, and under the supervision, furnished by the State Department of Education. Their cost amounted to one million and a quarter dollars. During the same year, there was the following number of public school-houses of different types in existence and use in Virginia: one room, 3,460; two room, 1,529; and in excess of two rooms, 1,317. The property in this form owned by the public school organization was valued at, approximately, forty-six million dollars.

At the present time, special attention is paid to physical and sanitary education in the public schools. For this purpose, an elementary course has been arranged for the guidance of the teachers in the schools of lower grades. One part of this course relates to the exercises which take place on the play-ground, such grounds being now regarded as indispensable to every school of even subordinate importance. In some of the public schools in the towns, the teachers have been trained to give physical examinations, which enable them to carry out the health program more safely and more beneficially. In 1926, ninety per cent of the enrollment of eighty-eight counties and twelve cities were reported as having passed the annual physical inspection. The percentage of inspection for the total enrollment of the State amounted to nearly seventy-four.

The number of full-time departments of vocational agriculture in Virginia's high schools had, by the session of 1925-26, grown to one hundred and six. Instruction along this very practical line is imparted at one hundred and sixty-two places in the State, under the auspices of the public schools. The negroes are included in its benefits. It has been estimated that fifty per cent of the boys of both races who had enjoyed this instruction returned to the farm as their home in life. In addition to these former pupils in the agricultural departments of the public schools, there were, in 1926, about twenty thousand youths under twenty who had retired to the country after their school term had expired, but without having enjoyed any tuition in agriculture while pupils. A number of these were persuaded to come back to school in the months of January and February, when the tasks of the farms were at a stand-still, and take a course of agricultural study specially adapted to the character of their farms. All the boys in the regular agricultural departments are required to carry out certain enterprises on their home-lands as a means of further enforcing upon their minds the practical nature of their instruction at school.

Perhaps equally important were the vocational domestic economics taught in a designated number of the public schools. The branches in which instruction was received were dietetics, millinery, home-nursing, dressmaking, child-care, cooking, plain sewing, and interior decoration. During the year 1926, there were also one hundred and seventeen trade and industrial classes in operation in the State. These counted nearly three thousand students. Forty-four different trades and vocations were represented. These were distributed among twelve different industries of the first importance in the life of the community.

In all this remarkable progress of the public school, the negro population has actively shared; and their improvement, in the light of the handicaps to which they have been subject for various reasons, has reflected honor upon their eagerness to make the most of the opportunities for education which are now furnished by the State.

One of the most conspicuous results of the growth of the public school system has been the increased desire for the completion of the education thus obtained by attendance upon the instruction given in some advanced seat of learning. The higher the standards are raised in the public school, the more definite has become this aspiration. Every young man of promise, every girl of talent, who is successful in the studies of the foremost of the public schools very naturally wishes to secure a collegiate or university education in addition. This disposition has been developed to such a degree already that the principal scholastic institutions of Virginia are hardly able to accommodate the pupils who are seeking admission to their lecture-halls. An ever augmenting number of the matriculates each year are graduates of the public high schools.

This is especially the case at the University of Virginia, where the students who are natives of the State are not required to pay any tuition fee. The most interesting feature of advanced education in the Commonwealth is that which comes out in the relation of this great institution to the public school system, and in the influences which they are mutually exerting on each other. Great as Mr. Jefferson was in so many departments of human thought and action, he was, perhaps, most constructive in the department of education. The most perfect system ever devised in modern times for popular instruction was proposed by him long before serious steps had been taken, or even been considered, for the public education of every youth or child in each community. What was the nature of that system? It was a system of gradations: first, the elementary school; second, the college; third, the university. The elementary school was

EDWIN A. ALDERMAN
President University of Virginia

to teach the rudiments; the college, the classics; the university, the sciences and other subjects, with the right reserved to the student to elect his own courses. The most promising graduates of the college were to pass automatically into the university, which, by this means, was to become the reservoir for the reception of the best scholars which the State, at that time, could furnish. Under this regulation, the university would be the *alma mater* of picked students alone, the very finest exemplars of intellectual training which the different colleges could supply.

The projected circle of colleges was never erected as Jefferson had planned. The university alone was built; and it had, in consequence of that fact, to give up the character intended by its founder of being exclusively a university. It was compelled to sink in part to the level of a college, and, to that extent, to offer no higher instruction to the undergraduate at least than any one of the circle of colleges designed by him could have conferred. Fortunately, as time went on, the standards of independent colleges, like Hampden-Sidney, Washington, and others, and private academies like Franklin Minor's, and the Coleman's, advanced until they were able to supply the university with matriculates well-grounded in every line of scholarship.

As yet the high schools of Virginia are unable to contribute to the university a large body of students thoroughly prepared to pursue at once all the highest branches of learning; but the number is increasing, and there is a good prospect that, in time, Mr. Jefferson's circle of contributory colleges will, through the best of the high schools, come into substantial existence, and fully carry out the comprehensive plan which he had so near at heart during the last days of his illustrious life.

The solid improvement in the public school system of Virginia; its uninterrupted forward movement in all its departments; the increased competence of its corps of teachers; the rising appropriations granted to it by the State Government; the more intelligent and solicitous interest taken in its welfare

J. A. C. CHANDLER
President College of William and Mary

by the people—all point to a still more useful and energetic development of its activities.

Each step in its advance will have the encouragement of every seat of higher learning in the Commonwealth. The prosperity of all these seats is more or less dependent for stability on the work of the public schools. From them, they are getting an ever increasing number of pupils in a better state of preparation. They are also finding, with the growth of the public school system, a more enlightened appreciation among the people at large of the benefits that accrue to the individual and State alike from the spread of education. The atmosphere in which these colleges and universities move has already become more inspiring and stimulating. With the popular support now behind them, they feel as if there was no limit to their possible scholastic achievements. Already in all the State and independent institutions of higher learning in Virginia, we find this spirit abroad in such force that it is altogether likely that their advance during the next decade will exceed by many degrees that which marked the whole of the previous quarter of a century, if not of a half century itself.

We now observe a phenomenon which had no existence a few years ago. At one time, the belief prevailed among a large majority of business men that it was no advantage to a young clerk to have received an education beyond that which could be picked up in some school of moderate grade. Indeed, a fine education, they thought, would realy diminish his usefulness. No such notion as this is now generally held. A college education is considered essential in the case of important subordinates. The young man's chance of obtaining a position is impaired, not increased, by his failure to show a diploma.

It would be impossible to overstate the personal advantage which accrues from college affiliations to the really promising students drawn from the more obscure social sections of the community. The youth from the farm, the youth from the urban mechanical shop, is thrown into a new social sphere; rubs elbows with a different type of companion; finds that there are sides to life which he had never before known; gazes into a world of new interests, wider and deeper than any which had ever met his vision previously; is moved to aspire to a career far higher than the one which his father had followed; feels that there is no bar strong enough to obstruct his progress if he has been blessed by nature with talent and energy. It is true that there are thousands of students of inferior social origin who never rise above the place where birth had originally established them; but there are thousands also for whom the combined tuition of public high school, college, and university, has created the opportunity to lift themselves to a higher personal and family plane; and this opportunity they have seized with decision and utilized with avidity.

Thomas Nelson Page

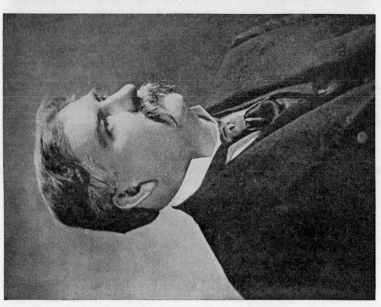

Armistead C. Gordon

CHAPTER X

LITERARY INFLUENCES

Why is it that Virginia has not been more voluminously productive in the field of literature? We have seen that, under the old order, the authors of distinction associated with her soil could be counted on the fingers of the two hands—Poe, Thompson, Philip Pendleton Cooke, John Esten Cooke, George W. Bagby, Mrs. Terhune, James Barron Hope, Daniel B. Lucas, Mrs. Margaret J. Preston, William Wirt, and Henry St. George, and Beverley Tucker—such was the almost complete list, unless it would be appropriate to add to it the political writers, Jefferson and Madison, and the political orator, John Randolph of Roanoke. If Poe is excepted, there is no purely literary figure in this group whose works enjoy a fame that has spread far beyond the boundaries of the State. Not one of that circle, indeed, besides the author of the *Raven,* is known today by name to every educated person, even to those who possess a fair knowledge of the American literary productions of that now remote period. In spite of their undoubted merits, they cannot be rated at the very highest in the history of the literary past. Virginia could not, on the strength of most of these authors, assert, with confidence, a claim to any special literary genius.

During the years that have followed the War of Secession, the State has taken a higher and more original position in literature. Amelie Rives, A. C. Gordon, Thomas Nelson Page, Ellen Glasgow, Mary Johnston, and James Branch Cabell, have, by their novels and short stories, won a place in contemporary fiction quite as conspicuous as the one occupied by the imaginative

443

writers belonging to the most literary States of the Union. Nevertheless, there is still reason to be dissatisfied with the numerically restricted, rather than the inherently impoverished, showing which Virginia has made since she started so brilliantly, in a literary way, with the incomparable journals of that colonial black swan, the second William Byrd.

What has been the cause of that limited literary fruitfulness which is so plainly seen to have existed if we look down the vista of her long history? Did the deficiency arise from lack of homogeniety in her citizens? Leave out the German population in the lower Shenandoah Valley, and there is left a stock of people as purely British as the inhabitants of England and Scotland, the two homes of a splendid literature. It is true that the Upper Valley was seated by immigrants known as the Scotch-Irish, but the Irish part of the hyphen is not derived from a certain blood, but from the original place of settlement of a mingled Scotch and North English colony. The Huguenot group, which made its home at Monacan, in 1700, was too small to modify the British strain. In time, it was absorbed in the mass of the Virginians, among whom they had taken their place as newcomers from over sea. And so too the few French and Dutch people, who, during the seventeenth century, had arrived in separate families, left no impression on the Virginian British stock.

If purity of race has been one reason for literary fertility among the people of England and Scotland in the past, why did not the same purity turn out to be as fecund in their descendants residing in the valleys of the James, the Rappahannock, and the Potomac? Were the English of the early and later generations of brighter minds and more lively spirits than the Virginians? In other words, had the Virginians degenerated in mental force, in power of invention, and in keenness of insight, because their ancestors had withdrawn from the hills and vales of the mother country to found new homes across the water? As a matter of fact, it was noted as far back as the seventeenth and eighteenth centuries by discerning travelers that the Virginia mind of the best quality was more vivacious than the English mind of equal caliber, which tended rather to heaviness and solidity than to nimbleness and alertness of wits. The general prevailing sunshine throughout the year in Virginia, and the rapid variations of temperature in the atmosphere there seem to have a stimulating influence on Virginian mentality, just as the lowering skies and more equal temperatures in England appeared to have a more or less dull and lethargic effect on English mentality, without, however, diminishing its vigor and weightiness.

By the eighteenth century, the Virginian people had erected a community as highly individualized in its way as any community of the same size then to be found in England. There was, it is true, an inequality between them in the point of wealth; but the difference in this particular was not sufficiently great to curtail their ability to secure the best instruction of their time. The sons of many of the leading plantation families had been educated in England. They had first attended the private schools there; had afterwards gone to the public schools; and subsequently had completed their courses at Oxford or Cambridge. Some had lingered for a training in law in the Inns of Court of London; or in medicine, in the schools of Edinburg. They returned to Virginia with their minds ripened by the learning which they had acquired under those noble scholastic roofs, and by the impressions which they had accumulated in the streets of the great English cities, or in the drawing-rooms of stately English homes.

Did their culture, after their arrival in Virginia, disclose itself in any form beyond a taste for reading and the polish of their personal bearing? Byrd alone showed, by the product of his pen, that his natural genius had been pricked into literary fruitfulness by the stimulating influences of the intellectual accomplishments acquired in the English academies.

The large collections of volumes which existed in Virginian mansions, during the seventeenth and eighteenth centuries alike, indicate that books were among the most popular recreations of

MARY JOHNSTON

ELLEN GLASGOW

the families of the best position. Old volumes were read and reread, and handed down to the next generation. New volumes were imported in the vessels arriving twice a year at the plantation wharves; and their titles revealed that the quality of these books was of a very high order.

Had an imaginative writer of Jamestown or Williamsburg thrown off the manuscript of a novel, he might have found some difficulty, even in the eighteenth century, in hunting down a publisher in the colony; but there was no reason why he could not have obtained one in the England of Johnson, Goldsmith, and Richardson. And had he issued a story of genuine merit through the English press, he would have gained readers, not only in Virginia, but also in England. But no book of this kind deserving the name of a romance was ever written in the colony, even in the eighteenth century, although Fielding and Smollett, at this very time, were composing and publishing works of fiction which are still considered to be among the greatest masterpieces in the language.

The colonial society that preceded the Revolution was polished in manners, fashionable in habits, and discriminating in literary and musical taste; but all this education ended only in making the lives of the planters pleasant to themselves. Their mental activity was satisfied with conversation or oratory in the House of Burgesses. That activity never sought to spend itself upon the composition of a great book; at least, of an imaginative cast. Just before the outbreak of the Revolution, and after it began, and during the years that followed its close, an extraordinary genius was exhibited by certain citizens in the production of political treatises. Questions of government called forth from statesmen like Richard Bland, Thomas Jefferson, James Madison, and others not quite so famous, papers of an ability which have never been surpassed in the history of political disquisition. But there was, nevertheless, no impressive revelation of the imaginative power; in short, no pure literature in the highest creative sense of the words. The State had felt recently the throes of nationality; had zealously cooperated with the American people at large; and, in the end, had united in sharing with them all the enthusiasm of a great victory; and yet, so far as the contemporary records show, not a line of poetry of extraordinary merit was brought forth by a Virginian intellect to reflect the capacity of that intellect for the expression of grand patriotic emotions in the form of verse. It is this form which the heart, stirred by noble thought and feeling, always employs.

In brief, the literary productions of the Revolutionary era, if literary they could be termed at all, fell into a perfectly practical groove, which, however fine in itself, was entirely devoid of an imaginative bent,—not even reaching out to the province of history, unless Marshall's *Life of Washington* and Tucker's *Life of Jefferson*, can be referred to as belonging to that category. And so during the period which stretches from the year 1800 to 1861. It is true that the essays of William Wirt were marked by merit to an unusual degree; so too was his *Life of Patrick Henry;* but in both, from the nature of these compositions, the imaginative element is lacking. They are didactic, descriptive, distinctly historical. There is to be found in his writings hardly a sentence which indicates that he had a rare creative talent in either poetry or prose, although he was an admirable writer.

It was one of his contemporaries, St. George Tucker, who, in a single brief poem, *Resignation*, revealed his possession of at least a fair measure of real genius, for, in expression and thought alike, those stanzas are high above the ordinary run of verse. George Tucker, the distinguished professor at the University of Virginia during its early sessions, produced, in his younger years, several works of fancy that have now passed into utter oblivion, but which were deserving of a happier fate. Nathaniel Beverley Tucker was also a man of genius; and in the *Partisan Leader* and *George Balcombe* exhibited a high degree of mastery of the difficult art of fiction. These two works fell far behind the novels of Cooper and Scott, but they were, notwithstanding that fact, examples of what might be done in so picturesque a field. A more striking example still was the novel of *Hansford* written by the pen of a younger Tucker, perhaps the most remarkable historical novel ever composed by a Virginian, although we have excellent specimens of that branch of literature in the works of Miss Johnston in our own times. John Esten Cooke was also an imaginative writer of merit in the same province, in spite of a certain high-flown sentiment which distinguished much of his fiction. Marion Harland also won reputation as a painter of Virginian manners previous to the War of 1861-65.

During this long period, with the period the war added, the lyrical voice was rarely raised in song. Among the few stanzas which have survived are the lines written on the walls of Old Brandford Church in Petersburg, by Mrs. Schermerhorn; Philip Pendleton Cooke's incomparable *Florence Vane;* John Lowe's *Mary's Dream;* Lucas's *In the Land Where We Were Dreaming;* McCabe's, *In the Trenches,* and a few spirited poems by Thompson and others contributed to the pages of the *Southern Literary Messenger,* or the columns of the daily press. The poverty of Virginia's poetical ability in these years would be only brought out more distinctly by a further enumeration of her writers in that department of letters.

We will now ask again the question which we put in discussing Virginia's lack of literary fertility during the eighteenth century: what was the reason for her comparative barrenness in the early nineteenth? Why should New England at that very time be producing an extraordinary number of writers of sufficient merit to draw to themselves the attention of the English reading world? It is true that these writers, with the exception of Hawthorne, and to a less extent, of Emerson also, were largely echoes of the English school of poets and essayists of that day; but even as echoes, they were of a very refined quality. Omitting Poe, who really belonged to no age and no clime, there was no group, either in Virginia or the entire South, which approached them in literary skill and polish. And yet there was not a neighborhood in any of the older counties of Virginia, which did not possess as many citizens of culture as were to be found in the communities of Massachusetts of equal population. There were not so many towns in Virginia as there were in the Bay State, and, therefore, there were not so many public libraries; but there were quite as many private. No important planter's mansion was lacking in a collection of all the modern American and British classics. As so many of these homes had been in existence for a century or more, there had been time for their successive owners to accumulate the works of exceptional merit which had been published from generation to generation.

The remoteness and isolation of a large number of these ancient residences gave an increased value to books in the eyes of the inmates. By the limitation of recreations and amusements in that old plantation life, an interesting volume, indeed, assumed a double importance. Certain authors became favorites because they were constant companions in hours of leisure in summer and winter. In many of those Virginian homes, the literary atmosphere was far more pervasive than under the roofs of city houses, since in the latter, the room for amusement in other directions was so wide and so continuous. So well were volumes, like the *Life of Dr. Johnson,* known from the first to the last paragraph, that their contents were drawn upon for a thousand illustrations in ordinary conversation. Scott has been read and reread until every heroic or romantic scene pictured in his pages was stamped on the memory of the old and young alike. Cooper, Simms, and Kennedy enjoyed extraordinary popularity also. Irving was familiar to all. So were the novels of Dickens and Thackeray and Bulwer.

The day of trashy fiction overflowing from the press in a noisome stream had not then arrived. There were fewer books, and such as were published were of greater merit. When a fresh contemporary volume was lacking, the plantation readers went back to the classics—to Shakespeare, Fielding, Sterne, Cervantes, Swift, Addison and Pope. Many of the men had been so well-grounded in the Greek and Latin tongues that they were able to relish the beauties of the ancient masterpieces without the assistance of dictionaries or formal translations.

All these literary influences produced in a large number of the Virginian rural gentry before 1860 a cultivated taste that might justly have been expected to bring forth more than one form of literary fruit. But the members of that gentry rarely employed themselves in that way. They were not a writing people, although they were a reading people. In fact, they were content to read what the masters had written without writing themselves. Can any one read the letters of John Randolph, of Roanoke, without recognizing the brilliant genius for that form of composition which breathes through every sentence? And the same genius or at least a high degree of talent, will be found pervading the letters of all the distinguished public men of that day, like John Hartwell Cocke, Henry St. George Tucker, Chapman Johnson, William Wirt, William C. Rives, and very many others whose names could be properly mentioned in the same connection.

While the country squires and their families were deepening their literary culture by their relish for the great books written in their own language, the rôle of men of letters in Virginia was limited to a small circle of persons residing in the capital city. The foremost of these were John R. Thompson and George W. Bagby, men of decided literary talent, if not of large powers, in the province of literature, but not equal to the men of letters who, during the same period, had given such distinction to the town of Boston. It was doubtful even whether Richmond enjoyed as much literary fame, through its writers, as Charleston enjoyed at that time.

When the War for Southern Independence closed, the history of Virginia had been further enriched by a new series of events tinged with all the varied colors of the brightest romance. What subjects for writers of genius the long past of the Old Dominion

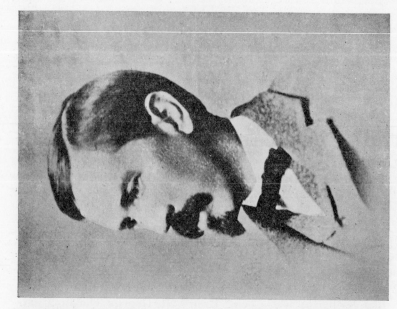

John Esten Cooke

George W. Bagby

now offered, whether these writers were poets, novelists, or historians! The first scenes in that past formed the noblest theme for an epic furnished by modern history, namely, the passage of the sea by the voyagers of 1606-07; the landing at Cape Henry; the foundation of Jamestown; the exploration of the Cheaspeake and its magnificent tributaries; the intercourse with old Fowhatan; the idyl Pocahontas; the massacre of 1622. Then followed, at a long interval, the deadly struggle between Bacon and Berkeley in the fastnesses of the primeval forests, and the burial of Bacon in the waters of Gloucester, under the cover of night. Another leap in time, and we see the figure of Spotswood standing on the top of the Blue Ridge against the sky, and looking down on the Paradise of the Shenandoah Valley; or it is the figure of William Byrd, gazing from the portico of Westover, or treading his way through the tangled woods of the Roanoke, or along the meadows of the Dan.

Still another leap, and we behold Washington, dressed in the buckskin of the frontier, returning through the winter snows from the outposts of the French beyond the Alleghanies. All this while, there had been a struggle with the Indians for possession of the outlying hills and valleys. But behind this constant warfare, there had peacefully expanded, in the plantation communities of Virginia, the most picturesque social life which has ever existed on the American continent. Williamsburg was the center of that life; and from this little town, there radiated to every important mansion in the country districts the charm and gayety of the capital.

The raid of Tarleton through Piedmont and the march of Cornwallis through Tidewater, a few decades later, brought upon the scene the red-coated campaigners of the Old World, and gave rise to events that will never cease to influence the fortunes of the Western Hemisphere. This wealth of episode was matched by the wealth of character illustrated in the personalities of the great Virginians of that day. And still behind it all, lay that old plantation society which had never lost its conservatism, its warmth, and its color. The War of 1812-15 precipitated on Virginian soil a number of incidents of a stirring and dramatic nature, but without altering the general spirit of the social life which had descended from the remote past. Then, like some mighty clap of thunder, sounded the explosion of the War of Secession, when the old State became a battleground from border to border, where one heroic and romantic adventure followed another.

What other country could furnish the novelist with a richer background than the one that arose in Virginia in that long interval between the landing at Cape Henry in 1607 and the surrender of Lee at Appomattox in 1865? Where could the poet find more inspiring themes? Where could the historian discover nobler subjects for the narrative power of his pen? Certainly not on the American continent.

What equal area in the western world at large has gone through so many political, social, and economic transformations as Virginia has done during the same extent of time? There was the period under the English crown, which lasted through the seventeenth century and the greater part of the eighteenth. The Revolutionary war which followed put an end to that status and converted a monarchial rule into a republican rule; destroyed the established church; and made the practical operation of the old social principles incongruous; without, however, eradicating them. Then followed, in turn, a twilight age, when the community was neither entirely English nor entirely American; and this continued until the institution of slavery, which had preserved so many of the old colonial social and economic ideas substantially unchanged, was overthrown and discarded. From that instant, there came into play a combination of new influences that tended to place Virginia in the same groove of development as had produced the prosperous North. The two previous stages; namely, the Colonial and the Post-Revolutionary, have been succeeded by the final stage, which may be correctly described as the stage of radically new economic and social principles, which have, at last, brought the community into close touch with what has come to be known as the typical American civilization.

During the first years that succeeded the War of Secession, those Virginians who were interested in intellectual and literary influences might well have speculated: what will be the effect of this enormous upheaval in Virginia upon the literary disposition of its people? Will it continue their previous limited productiveness or will it stimulate their minds to a new fertility? Sixty-two years have passed since the end of the War of Secession. What answer can be given to that question put so long ago?

The most conspicuous literary figures who have sprung up in Virginia in the interval since 1865 have been Thomas Nelson Page, Amelie Rives, Mary Johnston, Ellen Glasgow and James Branch Cabell. A writer of hardly less merit, but not so well-known, is Armistead C. Gordon, the author of the *Gift of the Morning Star*, and other works of imaginative distinction.

Page turned his eyes with most sympathy to those scenes of his own period which retained the delightful flavor of the then near antebellum past. As was natural in such an outlook, the shadow of pathos fell upon the life which he described so graphically. There was in his pictures too, what is equally natural in work so retrospective, a certain degree of romantic and sentimental over coloring. Time is likely to diminish the poignant vividness of this charming writer, as his presentation of his age will grow less and less intelligible in the course of years, because their passage will dull the force of that old Southern point of view.

Ellen Glasgow, in one of her novels at least, the *Barren Ground*, a powerful tale, has gone as far in bare and exaggerated realism as Mr. Page at times went in decorated and more or less expansive sentiment. The two writers, when considered together, illustrate, in more than one particular, the distance that lies between their respective periods, short as it really is. Page,

JAMES BRANCH CABELL

for instance, in his stories shows a keen interest in negroes, in consequence of their close social relations, in his day, with the lives of white people. Miss Glasgow, on the other hand, practically ignores the blacks and dwells with sympathetic care on the former so-called "po' white trash." She does this because the negro has really receded to the background of Virginian life, while the "po' white trash," now deserving of more dignified designation, have come prominently forward; at least, in the country districts.

Miss Johnston alone of these modern Virginian authors has perceived the wealth of Virginia's history for use in historical composition. She has caught with stirring fidelity the romantic reflection of colonial life and the thunder and the lightning of the great War of 1861-65, as illustrated in the adventurous careers of Ashby, Pelham, Stuart, and Jackson—men who closed their splendid lives on the battlefield. Cabell, on the other hand, has created a world of his own as foreign to Virginia as the scenes of Poe. His admirers are to be counted wherever there is to be found relish for delicate fantasy and whimsical humor. Local knowledge of Virginia does not heighten appreciation of his novels, for they are free of all local flavor.

When we pass from the region of imaginative invention to that of pure matter of fact—the province of description and narrative; the province of history and biography—it will be seen that the Virginians have not been entirely barren in that field. Among the numerous fine biographies which owe their authorship to sons of the soil, perhaps, the most notable are William Wirt Henry's *Life of Patrick Henry*, Miss Rowland's *Life of George Mason*, A. C. Gordon's *Lives of William Fitzhugh Gordon and W. Gordon McCabe*, and William C. Bruce's *Benjamin Franklin, Self-Revealed*. Eckenbode's studies of *Church and State* and the *Revolution in Virginia* are also works of great merit; and so is Wertenbaker's *Virginia of the Stuarts*. The description of different segments of Virginia's history given by Professors Lyon G. Tyler and Richard Lee Morton have thrown new light on the successive stages of her annals. The *Genesis of the United States* by Alexander Brown is a noble contribution to our knowledge of the events which led up to and followed the foundation of Jamestown. There have been other volumes written in exposition of Virginia's history deserving of the respect of scholars.

In the province of general literary productiveness, such as the works of professors, clergymen, scientists, physicians, and lawyers, the list has been a very respectable one in quality and not unvoluminous in quantity.

As yet no periodicals, except those of a historical cast published by Doctor Stanard, of the Virginia Historical Society, Doctor Tyler and Doctor Swem, have been able to survive during a considerable period. The *Reviewer* disappeared over the Carolina border after a brief but rather brilliant existence of a few years. The *Virginia Quarterly Review,* of recent origin, issued by the State University and edited by Dr. James S. Wilson, promises to enjoy a far more protracted lease on life. It has already taken a position comparable in interest and influence with the great periodicals of the North of the same imposing type. This periodical draws its contributions and patronage chiefly from the country at large, and not from the South.

The absence of numerous local magazines is a proof that the Virginians have not, in recent years, given serious attention to the production of poetry. Thomas Nelson Page, R. T. W. Duke, Jr., and James Lindsay Gordon, who were of distinguished talent in that art, are dead. Their most pleasing poems were issued in the old magazines; and to an almost equal degree, so were the poems of Armistead C. Gordon. There is but one slender sheet published in the State at this time, which is confined, in its contents to poetry. This is the *Lyric* of Norfolk, which has, in recent years, been adorned by contributions from the pens of M. Morland, Mrs. Leitch, Mrs. McCormick, Mrs. Kinsolving, and Mrs. Tunstall, all writers of growing distinction in their special province.

At this day, we rarely observe in the journals of the State, whether political or denominational, contributions of a purely literary cast. The Virginia *Press,* however, is creditable to the Commonwealth in its physical make up, fullness of news, thoughtful and practical editorial comment, and upright and honorable tone. The old type of editor, who possessed such wide influence in the community at large, has, however, passed. The veil of anonymity, which now hangs over the editorial sanctum, grows only more impenetrable as the years vanish in the rear.

What factors in the Virginia communities of our times are taking an active part in stimulating literary culture among the people? The foremost, perhaps, are the schools of English literature in the various local colleges and universities. We have already pointed out the wide influence which, after the close of the war in 1865, Professor Price exerted from his chair in Randolph-Macon College at Ashland. Numerous sympathetic disciples in other Southern seats of learning have continued his work. Indeed, the tradition of his instruction has never lost its power. There is not a seat of general learning in Virginia today, where accomplished professors are not grounding their students in the beauties of the English classics. Mere teaching, it is true, does not impart literary genius, but teaching does spread an atmosphere of relish for literature, which may flower into noble books in the course of time. More volumes are being written by Virginians each year. Already the novels from the pens of the most talented among them command the attention of the English-speaking world. The field of successful endeavor in other directions will grow larger. Each subordinate college and the University of Virginia will become a seat, not of receptive culture, but of productive culture, and the reproach of literary sterility in so many provinces so fertile in other countries shall no longer be correctly launched against the State.

A second factor that is certain to assist in giving a wider field to the prosecution of literary work in Virginia is the State Library, at present under the general oversight and direction of Dr. H. R. McIlwaine, a distinguished and useful scholar. As early as 1906, the General Assembly appropriated a large sum for the publication under his editorship of the Journals of the House of Burgesses and Colonial Council, and also for the creation of a department of archives, a department of bibliography, and a department of traveling libraries. These departments, during the successive stages of their development, have been in the immediate charge of capable men like H. J. Eckenrode, Morgan P. Robinson, Earl G. Swem, William Clayton Torrence, and F. B. Berkeley.

It is to the traveling libraries that we must look for the central library's most popular literary influence. As early as 1918, 164 collections were distributed in fifty-four counties. Nor were the stations to which these were sent restricted to the public schools. Four years afterwards, there were 330 stations receiving them. It is estimated that the schools then used two hundred and fifty sets, while one hundred and eighty were used by one hundred and forty-two study clubs. In 1926-27, two hundred and fifty-eight traveling libraries were dispatched to various parts of the State. These were assigned to special study clubs, high school libraries, community libraries, and graded school libraries. The reception of these books has greatly encouraged the organization of general public libraries and county libraries. Most of these associations have been small in proportions, but they have served a purpose which has already proved highly fruitful and stimulating.

The great collection of books in the State Library, now exceeding several hundred thousand volumes, has been already of incalculable value to students in various provinces of investigation. Especially is this true of research in the field of State history. The use of the photostat promises in time to make the store of material in the Archives Department far larger than had ever before been supposed to be possible. The greater the collection of information in this central depository, the more easy will it be to write the history of the State; and the wider and deeper will become the Virginians' knowledge of their own annals.

CHAPTER XI

BENEVOLENT AND RELIGIOUS INFLUENCES

Virginia is said to have been the first American community to found a hospital for the insane; and from that date to this, the Commonwealth has not failed to perform the duty which it owes to its unfortunate and helpless citizens thus afflicted. At the present time, the Commonwealth is in possession of at least five asylums for the amelioration of the condition of those disordered in mind. These refuges are situated in different parts of the State, so as to accommodate the more conveniently the unhappy patients of each separate region. The Western State Hospital is located at Staunton, and being thus placed, reaches out an assisting hand to the Valley from Winchester to Roanoke. The Southwestern State Hospital at Marion performs the same service for the afflicted in the country from Roanoke to Bristol. The Central State Hospital at Petersburg provides all that is needed for the care of demented negroes; especially among the black population south of the James. The Eastern State Hospital at Williamsburg is equally effective in its accommodations for the white insane belonging to the Peninsula. There is situated near Lynchburg a State establishment reserved for the care of epileptic and feeble-minded persons.

These different hospitals, through the generosity of the Commonwealth are endowed with every modern appliance for the cure of mental disease or the protection of patients whose condition is beyond hope of restoration to health. They are operated under the supervision of superintendents of distinction as alienists; and are in possession of spacious buildings and grounds. No means is left unutilized to place these establishments on the highest modern platform of humane utility.

In recent years, the State Board of Charities and Corrections has been converted into the State Board of Public Welfare, a title more in harmony with the now enlarged duties of that body. The general purpose for which it was appointed was, (1) to inspect and supervise all the county and city institutions of a reformatory and eleemosynary nature; (2) to organize and develop juvenile and domestic relations courts and county boards of public welfare; (3) to administer all legislation adopted for the benefit of children; (4) to carry out a programme for the proper disposition of the insane and feeble-minded after temporary or permanent withdrawal from the hospital; and finally, (5) to draft and put in force a plan for the education of persons belonging to the mentally deficient, dependent and delinquent classes.

The policy of the Board towards defective children was, perhaps, the most useful and successful in the entire round of its duties. It was estimated in 1926 that the various communities of the State annually committed to the care of this benevolent body not less than seven hundred children, for whose protection and reform nearly twenty-five thousand dollars was appropriated out of the public treasury. As far as possible, the Board has endeavored to carry out its duty of supervision over the child culprit by leaving him or her in his original home rather than by transferring him to a juvenile asylum.

During the session of 1919-20, the General Assembly empowered all the counties to consolidate their almshouses into district homes. In other words, each separate group of contiguous counties were permitted by this Act to establish one poor-house for the indigent and infirm to be found within the boundaries of that group. The object of this law was to diminish the expense of maintaining, say half a dozen alms-houses for half a dozen counties, by bestowing on those counties, taken together, the right to erect one alms-house which should serve

for them all. More healthy conditions could thus be created
and more comfortable arrangements be made for the unfortunate recipients of public charity. Through the influence of the
Board of Public Welfare, brought directly to bear, numerous
counties banding together have been led to erect, in the place
of their former primitive poor-houses, a model home held by
the group as the property of them all, for the support of their
decrepit and impoverished old people. Among these consolidated districts we may mention two of the most prominent:
first, Fairfax, Fauquier Prince William, Culpeper, and the City
of Alexandria; and, second, Alleghany Albemarle, Augusta,
Rockbridge, and Bath. This last district includes the cities of
Staunton and Charlottesville.

The Board now looks even further into the future than the
general adoption of this plan of district alms-houses. That body,
it is reported, ventures to think that the day will arrive when
the district alms-houses themselves will be consolidated into
a single State institution, like a modern Confederate home, but
on a greater scale, where all the really indigent and infirm old
persons of the Commonwealth could be spaciously housed and
completely protected from the pangs of further want. Such
an institution would quite certainly, like the Temple of Janus,
never be closed, for it would never be entirely empty, but its
establishment would undoubtedly reduce the cost of caring for
the helpless paupers to the lowest point that could be possible
reached. At the same time there is the drawback that, by concentrating the poor under one roof, an impression would be
created that the degree of extreme poverty prevailing in Virginia was greater proportionately to population than it really
was.

In 1926, a farm was purchased by the State as a place of
detention for youthful culprits of defective mentality. This
farm is closely connected with the State Farm. Another step
for the improvement of members of the criminal class was taken
in the State Penitentiary, where the prisoners are now not only

required to work,—in the course of which they learn a valuable trade,—but are also graded according to the character of their conduct, which enables the authorities to grant valuable privileges to those convicts who have proved worthy of trust. Another step in the same general direction has been the creation of a school of sociology at the University of Virginia, in which a program has been adopted that will assure research, during a period of five years, in the wide field of public welfare. The main purpose of this investigation will be to find out the best method for the care and treatment of the State's dependent, defective, and delinquent classes.

It will be pertinent to our subject to inquire as to the number of persons of these classes who have come within the cognizance of the Commonwealth through its different institutions, whether punitive, curative, or eleemosynary. The interval between 1910 and 1925, which embraces fifteen years, may be taken as indicative of the extent to which individual punishment, protection, or relief has been carried in the course of our own times.

During the year 1910, out-door relief was granted to about six thousand persons; but, by 1920, this number had shrunk to about four thousand; and at this figure also the beneficiaries stood five years later. A like decline was noted in the number of persons who obtained admission to the alms-houses. In 1910, this number approximated three thousand. By 1925, it had fallen off to about twenty-six hundred. During this interval, however, the expense to the public treasury of affording relief both in and out doors rose from three hundred and seven thousand dollars, in 1910, to nearly five hundred thousand in 1925. This increase resulted from the advance in prices in every department of living.

In 1910, the number of persons committed to prison was about eighteen thousand. The general reformatories received about three hundred adults and the juvenile about four hundred children. Fifteen years afterwards, the number of persons committed to jails and prisons in Virginia had expanded to twenty-eight thousand white. The inmates in the reformatories had only increased in number to a moderate degree. Considering the total number of persons confined in State institutions, it is found that there was hardly any difference in the enumeration for 1910 and 1925 respectively. The proportion for insane, feeble-minded, and epileptic patients varied little annually throughout that long interval. In 1910, there were about twelve hundred demented, and one hundred and twenty-four feeble-minded and epileptic. The respective figures for 1925 were fourteen hundred and thirty, and one hundred and thirty-five. During this protracted interval, however, the cost to the State of supporting these wards of the public swelled from half a million dollars to a million dollars and more.

There were about two thousand children detained in family homes in 1926. Many of them, after spending some time in these homes, were assigned to industrial schools for the purpose of their acquiring a trade.

The Virginian cities and counties numbered at least 115, and yet less than one-half of those communities had organized welfare boards. All of this latter group had appointed superintendents, whose time was devoted exclusively to the duties of the position. Fifteen of the larger towns in 1926 had established juvenile courts, with judges elected for the sole purpose of administering their business. In some cases, the Red Cross contributed to the support of these courts; but they were generally sustained by public funds. During the same year, there were ninety-five juvenile courts in operation in the rural districts. In other words, nearly every county in the State possessed at least one court of this nature, without counting the like court situated in any city located within its borders. The cases passed upon in the city juvenile courts in 1926 numbered about twenty-three hundred, while thirty-three hundred fell under the cognizance of the judges of the county juvenile courts.

The reformatories and refuges to which the delinquent children were assigned at this time embraced the Virginia Industrial School for white boys situated at Maidens, and the Industrial school for white girls situated at Bon Air. A similar school for colored girls had been established at Peaks, and for colored boys, at Hanover. A school for deaf and blind white children was in operation at Staunton, and one for colored at Newport News.

So far, we have been considering the means which the State offers for the relief of disease and poverty, the reform of youthful delinquency, and the punishment of crime. Let us now examine the part which the private organizations have played in promoting benevolence in the different communities of Virginia. There is not a city or town or county in the Commonwealth which has not formed an active association among its citizens to advance the cause of local charity. It will be pertinent to mention the names of the most conspicuous of them. Some have constituted chapters of the American Red Cross. This was the case in Arlington, Southampton, Bedford, and Montgomery counties and in the City of Portsmouth. Others were independent associations and leagues for community welfare. Such was the case with the organizations of this nature situated in Danville, Hopewell, Newport News, Norfolk, Petersburg, Richmond, Staunton, Roanoke, and Southampton. In Richmond, there was an association known as the Bureau of Catholic Charities, and another that was known as the Ladies Hebrew Benevolent Association. The Protestant Episcopal Church had formed the Missionary Society of the Diocese of Virginia.

Among the largest contributions to charity was the Salvation Army, which had established branches in several of the important cities of the State, such, for instance, as Alexandria, Charlottesville, Danville, Newport News, Norfolk, and Richmond. Equally active and successful was the organization which bore the name of the Travellers Aid Society. This association had offices open in the cities of Danville, Lynchburg,

Newport News, Norfolk, Petersburg, Portsmouth, Richmond, and Roanoke.

Among the largest contributions in 1926 by these private benevolent associations were $1,316.32 in Alexandria; $5,673.24 in Hopewell; $14,497 in Lynchburg; $24,686.39 in Norfolk; $11,149.17 in Petersburg; $3,237.83 in Portsmouth; $70,516.59 in Richmond; and $5,535 in Newport News. The Bureau of Catholic Charities in Richmond distributed, during the same period, the sum of $13,194.77; and the Ladies Hebrew Benevolent Association of the same city, the sum of $7,725.81.

It will be seen from these figures, pertinent to the largest communities only, that the total contributions by private charitable organizations ran up to a very large amount in the aggregate.

The chief expenditures by the State may be summarized as follows: hospitals, sanatoriums for tuberculosis, Confederate Homes, and pensions,—the sum of $3,186,722.67; corrective institutions, including the penitentiary, the convict farm and camps, jails, juvenile industrial schools and reformatories, and detention homes, the sum of $1,390,367,89; and finally, subsidies of various sorts,—the sum of $23,471. The State also contributed largely to institutions primarily supported by city and county. In its turn, private benevolence gave $2,613,526.30 to numerous beneficiaries, the most important of which were orphanages and children's agencies, homes for the aged, settlement clubs, neighborhood charities, family and visiting nurse associations, dispensaries, and hospitals. Numerous sums were also distributed by them among very many people who had made a personal appeal.

It is estimated that no less than $8,142,211.79 were expended, in the single year 1926, in different forms of charity by State county, city, and private benevolence. If we take the private and public resources of the Commonwealth, into consideration, this amount indicates that the people, as a whole, fully recog-

nized and carried out their obligation to assist the needy and
unfortunate to the extent of their pecuniary ability.

The most highly organized agencies for the advancement of
the purely moral welfare of the communities of Virginia during
the period now under discussion were the different religious
denominations. The most salient characteristic of these de-

OLD ST. PAUL'S CHURCH (EPISCOPAL)
Bombarded by British in 1776

nominations' relations with each other, and one of the most
powerful reasons for the good that they were able to accomplish, was the mutual amity which they maintained unfailingly,
in spite of the more or less identity of their respective fields of
labor. No conflict has arisen between them in the course of the
last century and a quarter; and this attitude of fraternal cooperation has only tended to grow as the spirit of democracy
has spread in the State in town and country alike. It would not
be imagined at this time that, during the last decades of the

eighteenth century, there was a grim struggle in progress between the Protestant Episcopal Church and the Baptists and Presbyterians, which ended almost in the practical destruction, —certainly for the time-being,—of the first of these denominations. The bitterness of the contest was natural enough, for the Dissenters, in the hour of the Established Church's ascendancy, had been treated with a shortsighted illiberality, which left a deep impression of un-Christian presumption and narrowness. But this did not justify the Dissenters in their participation, for the benefit of the State, in the stripping of the Episcopal organization of its property, with what appears, at this day, to have been a determined ruthlessness that was unworthy of their hour of triumph. To be tumbled down from a position of supremacy, such as the Colonial Established Church once occupied, was not a fate that leaves pleasant memories; but to be deposed in a spirit of hatred as the Episcopal Church was, was well-calculated to inflict a wound that could never be healed. But probably a generation had hardly elapsed before the past stabs of the Dissenters had been practically forgotten by the victims.

Why did this upshot occur? Because, as time progressed, the laymen and clergymen of the Protestant Episcopal Church in Virginia perceived more and more clearly that disestablishment was not only proper in itself, but also conducive to the greater prosperity of that church. Mr. Jefferson has told us that he was largely influenced in urging Disestablishment by the spectacle of the peace and good-will which were so observable in the relations of the different sects in New York and Pennsylvania, where all stood on a footing of equality, with the same privileges possessed and enjoyed by all. Apparently, there was no bickering and no friction between the denominations there. In Virginia, on the other hand, and at the same hour, the conflict between the Dissenters and the Established Church was irrepressible, and it was just as injurious to true Christianity as it was to the practical welfare of the community at large.

The sagacity of Jefferson's point of view was, in time, fully admitted by the religious denomination which suffered most from the change. Perhaps that denomination was never more ready to acknowledge the beneficence of his action than it is now when the Anglican order in England is internally torn by diversity of belief and practice, and the whole kingdom agitated by a feeling of religious bitterness, which would quite certainly have been duplicated in Virginia, had the community remained a part of the British Empire, and held on to the Old Established Church. As it is, there is no unbridgable schism in the Episcopal order here in the State. It maintains today on the whole the steady conservative evangelical spirit which it has always upheld under a noble line of Low Church Protestant Bishops. Its general attitude towards all the other denominations has always been in accord with the helpful democratic principles, which are still, and always will be, the essence of the religion of Christ. The dream of the great apostle of liberty, Jefferson, has been fully realized in his native State; all the ecclesiastical denominations are equally free; all are equally content; and all, with equal zeal, are working practically together to make the world about us a better and happier place in which to live.

Some years ago in Richmond, a venerated clergyman of the Presbyterian faith, who had guided the religious destinies of his congregation with unsurpassed fidelity and distinction, during a long and troublous period, was honored by the celebration of the anniversary of the beginning of his incumbency in his great office. In that remarkable gathering, every denomination in Virginia was represented, and the tributes paid to that man of God were as fervent when coming from the mouth of a Methodist, a Baptist, a Catholic, a Jew, and a Protestant Episcopalian as from the mouth of a Presbyterian. Such has been the characteristic conduct of the living descendants in Virginia of those fierce antagonists of the eighteenth century! The great lesson of tolerance has been learned; and what is still more to be admired, the great lesson of friendly and zealous cooperation.

And that spirit is quite sure to strike deeper down into the soil as the spirit of democracy grows and expands in the community at large.

To present an extended history of the beneficent activities of the different denominations in Virginia, in recent years, would require more space than we have at our disposal. We shall venture to give a brief description of the work of several as especially characteristic of the work of all. Let us begin with the Presbyterians, and consider first the steps which they have taken for religious education and practical benevolence. This denomination now possess the Union Theological Seminary for its theological students; Hampden-Sidney College, for its boys of collegiate age; Mary Baldwin College, for its college girls; the Danville Military Institute, for its academic pupils; and the Assembly's Training School for men and women who wish to secure a special preparation for vocational Christian service. It has also provided the Presbyterian Orphans' Home for the support and instruction of parentless children of its own membership, and the Sunnyside Home for aged and indigent women of the same faith. Annually, it furnishes an assembly ground at the Massanetta Springs for those persons, who, through the Bible Conference Encampment there, are seeking to find physical rest, combined with spiritual improvement.

The seed sown in these various soils has brought forth a beneficent fruit which has been shared by thousands.

The Presbyterian Home Mission Committee have afforded assistance to several hundred separate churches of their order. Numerous schools for the moral and mental training of the young mountaineers have been founded and supported by the same earnest agency. Sunday school work and also young people's work have been carried on by the church organizations with never relaxing zeal. In the course of 1926 alone, forty-three Presbyterian Leadership Training Schools threw open their doors, with a large attendance in each. In addition, Daily Vacation Bible Schools have been put in operation; annual Sunday School Institutes have been established; Mission Sunday Schools opened; and, also, in consequence of this activity, numerous church edifices have been erected in remote districts. The church also contributes to the support of the Davis and Elkins College, and also to the support of the Stonewall Jackson College.

These achievements of the Presbyterian denomination in the prosecution of its religious work are enhanced in importance by the record of usefulness which its affiliated institutions have made. This is particularly true of the Union Theological Seminary, Hampden-Sidney College, Mary Baldwin College, and the Danville Military Institute.

Virginia, during the long interval between the election of its first American Bishop, Madison, and the formation of the Diocese of Southern Virginia in 1892, constituted a single Diocese of the Protestant Episcopal Church. Previous to the Revolution, it had been included in the ecclesiastical jurisdiction of the Bishop of London. The Diocese of Southern Virginia was, in turn, divided in 1919, when the Diocese of Southwestern Virginia was set apart from its territory. We shall restrict our reference to the Diocese of Virginia, as the benevolent practical labors recorded of this Diocese have been duplicated in both of the others. In brief, the work that has been done in the original Diocese is substantially of the same character as the work that has been done in all.

The growth of the original Diocese is fully illustrated by a comparison between its condition in 1918-19 and its condition in 1923-24. The most significant difference, perhaps, lay in the manner of administration after 1919. The work of the various Boards and Societies previous to that day was carried on almost entirely by laymen who devoted to that purpose only their hours of leisure. By 1923-24, a Central Church House had been acquired in Richmond through the generosity of the Mayo family, and a vigorous business management for the whole Diocese had been organized. One result of striking value from this policy was the improvement in the resources of the Diocesan Missionary Society, and the consequent increase in its ability to make its functions more successful. Instead of thirty-eight clergy-men, two laymen and nine women workers receiving support from its fund, forty-nine clergymen and thirty-four women were pecuniarily maintained in 1923-24, while performing their duties in the local missionary field. The women workers in the moun-tain regions, especially, had no longer to rely on voluntary help. They were, at this time, paid a regular salary by the Diocesan Missionary Society. It was due largely to this Society that the number of clergymen was increased, since their full annual re-muneration was now assured by its contributions.

In 1919, there were only four Episcopal ministers employed exclusively in missionary work in the mountain districts. On the other hand, in 1922-23, there were, with Archdeacon Neve, seven so engaged. In addition, there were three rectors who gave up a part of their time to labor in the same isolated field. In 1919, a vacancy in the pulpit of a parish meant a temporary or lengthy termination of the services, and also a suspension of the Sunday School and other church activies. By 1922-23, a remedy for this had been found in the voluntary aid given in the pulpit by retired ministers, lay readers, and seminary students.

In 1919, there were six clergymen administering to the spiritual needs of negro congregations. There were still six in 1922-23; but the number of communicants had increased from 281 to 395. The number of Sunday Schools had grown from 14 to 18, and of parochial schools, from 5 to 9. Every colored mission congregation now possessed a branch of the Colored Women Auxiliary. During the interval between 1910 and 1923-24, four negro congregations were organized in Essex County alone, with a roll of eighty-one communicants; 136 scho-lars in their four Sunday Schools; and ninety-six pupils in their parish schools. This was the fruit of a single clergyman's devo-tion to his mission.

In 1919, the Diocese could show the possession of 147 Sunday Schools, with a list of 951 officers and teachers, and nearly ten thousand scholars. By the end of four years more, the number of schools had risen to 167, and the number of scholars to nearly eleven thousand. Since 1919, the number of communicants had augmented at the average annual rate of nearly six hundred.

Among the agencies which, at this time, were continuously employed in community work, was the Board of Christian Social Service. The Board of Religious Education was equally zealous and successful. There was also already a system of five church schools designed for both boys and girls. In 1923-24, the total enrollment of these schools embraced about five hundred and fifty.

Three years later, 1927, all those activities of the Diocese of Virginia, which we have mentioned were showing an increased energy and a still wider sweep of practical progress. The Diocesan Missionary Society was now conducting missions more effectively than ever among the mountaineers, the colored people, the inhabitants of the city slums, the backward people of the rural districts, and the prisoners in the jails. The Archdeaconry of the Blue Ridge alone possessed thirty-five chapels, forty Sunday schools, and ten day schools. It supported, too, a tuberculosis sanatorium. The church had erected an Industrial School in Greene County, which was now attended by a large number of pupils. It also assisted in the payment of the operating expenses of St. Paul's Memorial Church at the State University, which carried many students on its roll.

The work among the colored people has also steadily grown, until there are now nearly five hundred communicants, and over eight hundred children in the Sunday Schools.

The work of the Christian Social Service, under the direction of a city missionary, has taken the form of constant visits to hospitals, and also of aid to many unfortunate individuals. The usefulness of the Church schools has increased, while the purposes of the Board of Religious Education have broadened. This

latter has been accomplished by the establishment of a summer
school, and also of a summer institute; by securing college credit
for the study of the Bible in the State high schools; and lastly,
by the distribution of devotional and educational literature in
the homes of the Diocese.

The history of the other two great Protestant denominations,
the Baptist and the Methodist, reveals that, in their works of
benevolence for the improvement of conditions in Virginia, they
have shown an energy and practical ability unsurpassed, and in
some particulars, barely equalled, in the contemporary careers
of the sister Protestant churches which we have already named.
The vigorous spirit and resolute zeal breathed into their respective organizations by the hard treatment from which they suffered in colonial times, has never ceased to animate them down
to the present day. Among the most indefatigable agencies for
the promotion of good work in the different communities of the
State, will be found the organizations which these two denominations have created and are liberally supporting. Most notable
also are the educational institutions in which they are directly
interested, namely, the University of Richmond and the Randolph-Macon College, with their adjuncts. The first, founded by
the Baptists, and the second, by the Methodists, have made a
very large contribution to the educational welfare of the State.
Worthy of special commendation too are the many imposing
church edifices which these two religious denominations have
built in the various centers of Virginia's population.

We have already referred to the charitable work of the
Catholic and Jewish benevolent associations of Richmond. These
two great religious organizations, indeed, have performed a very
useful part in contributing to the general improvement of their
respective communities. They, too, have fostered the spirit of
good citizenship for the benefit of the public at large, as well as
the spirit of sympathy and helpfulness for the benefit of those
individuals who have needed assistance in want or sorrow. The
same noble work has been performed by the Christian and
Lutheran denominations to the full extent of their power.

CHAPTER XII

SOCIAL EVOLUTION

One of the greatest changes which the progress of time has brought in Virginia is to be discerned in the present characteristics of the State's social life as compared with the characteristics of that life in the past. Naturally, the peculiarities of her social framework have always been profoundly influenced by the peculiarities of her economic system. As the latter has passed through several stages of modification, so the former, in sympathy, has also undergone a marked degree of transformation. Nevertheless, some of the traits of the old social civilization of Virginia still survive. This fact is due principally to the homogeneity of its people, which remains almost as complete today as it was in the seventeenth and eighteenth centuries. This is a condition which Virginia has shared with most of the States of the Upper South.

The founders of all those Virginian communities which are situated east of the Blue Ridge were of the purest English stock, with the exception of the few inhabitants of Germanna and the neighboring settlements, and also of the Monacan village near the falls in James River. The people of the latter were sprung from the French Huguenots. It is true, as we have elsewhere pointed out, that some persons of Gallic blood had come into other Virginian communities from time to time during the seventeenth century, but these had intermarried with English men or women on the ground, and their grandchildren were not to be distinguished from the children of the same generation, who

477

could claim only English descent. And to a large degree this was true of the immediate posterity of the French settlers at Monacan. By the time the Revolution had arrived, which occurred after an interval of seventy-five years, that posterity had become so intermingled by marriage with the English stock of people that it had lost its principal Gallic peculiarities. For a time, the French village system was maintained, and the French language habitually employed by all.

After a considerable interval, the small French community slowly broke up, and following the example of the Virginians throughout the Colony, dispersed among separate plantations of their own. Wives were found among the native English stock, and thus the racial line became in time practically obliterated. Indeed, no trace of the French strain was left beyond the French family names, and the bright humor and lively wit of the French disposition.

As a matter of fact, at no time in the colonial history of Virginia did the region east of the Blue Ridge show any permanent indication of any differences in the white race inhabiting it. Virtually, the people there were as homogeneous as the people of the Eastern and Southern shires of England of that day, with whom they claimed a perfect identity of blood. Even the indentured white servants, who were imported down to the Revolution, were, as a body, of sturdy Anglo-Saxon descent, and were as conscious of that fact as their employers. The commerce of white men with slave negresses did not alter the racial status of the master stock, for the mulattoes who resulted took the same place in the social framework of the community as their negro mothers occupied. They too were slaves, and continued so until the end of their lives, like the very blackest of the bondsmen. The two streams flowed, without any recognized contact, side by side, from decade to decade, and from century to century. If any influence was exerted at all, the presence of the African slaves only intensified the racial loyalty of the whites, and made them only the prouder of their descent.

When the Scotch-Irish and the Germans overran the Lower and Upper Valley, a new element found lodgment in the Colony. The Scotch-Irish, after all, as we have already pointed out, were distinctly British. They hailed from the northern provinces of Ireland, but their forebears had originally been seated in Scotland and the North of England. Apparently, the intermarriages after their arrival in Ulster had been chiefly confined to themselves, although they too, in the mass, belonged to the Celtic stock, which could claim the greater part of the Irish population. But the racial kinship had not been close enough to make North Ireland, after the immigration from the land beyond the eastern strip of sea, share anything of importance with South Ireland. The difference in religion alone would have been enough to create an impossible gulf between the two peoples. The resemblance between the Scotch-Irish of the Upper Valley, and the pure English stock residing east of the Blue Ridge was so strong, in spirit at least, that, in a few generations, no real social difference was to be discerned in their respective habits and points of view. The line of demarcation, indeed, was gradually blotted out, although the Valley people of North Irish stock have never lost the stalwart piety, the manly vigor, the outspoken independence, of the original Ulsterman.

It cannot be said of the German element in the Valley that it has ever grown equally in sympathy with the older section of the Virginian population. That stock was too radically different from the Englishman and the Scotch-Irishman, when the German settlements were first made, to lose their identity by mergence in another race as time passed on. It is true that Spotswoods' pioneers were ultimately lost in the surrounding English population of North Piedmont. But on the west side of the Blue Ridge, in the Great Valley, the German communities were so thickly inhabited that they had no more difficulty in preserving their racial segregation than the people of Poland did under the iron hand of the Russian Czar. Intermarriage has had considerable influence in binding closer together the leading families of the Upper Valley and the leading families of Eastern Virginia; but this way of creating a tie between the latter and the German families of the Lower Valley was never brought into action to a degree that would be sufficient to affect the general character of those German communities.

Neither the Scotch-Irish nor the German immigrants took hold in Virginia long enough before the Revolution to exert any real influence upon the tone of the social life which had prevailed in its communities, in a well-developed form, from a period that went back as far, at the shortest, as the middle of the seventeenth century. It was from the social civilization founded in the early decades of that century that the Colony took its social tendency. It was this social bent, indeed, which gave Virginia, while still a dependency of the English Crown, the high repute which it enjoyed even in the most cultivated and polished circles of London. As a matter of fact, this was the social life in which the second William Byrd and the second Daniel Parke, who played so brilliant a part in the first drawing-rooms of England, were trained. Byrd enjoyed the warm friendship of some of the most celebrated men in England, men distinguished in arts, letters, and philosophy as well as in society. Parke was so much in the graces of Marlborough that he was selected to carry the dispatches of the great victory of Blenheim to Queen Anne in London, an exceptional honor to be paid a colonial subject. Doubtless among the Virginians who visited England, during the same period, there were others who were equal in social culture to Byrd and Parke, and who left as charming an impression as those two conspicuous gallants.

In an earlier chapter, we summarized the principal characteristics of the social life of Virginia during the first century of its existence as a community. As this social life was the basis of all that has followed, in spite of the great changes which have taken place during the long interval since, it will be pertinent to describe this spirit at least in a general way.

In the first place, it was natural enough that Virginia in that age should have been essentially English in every province of its community life. It was not simply that all its institutions had been drawn straight from England,—such as its framework of government, its system of law, its military administration, and its religious organization. It was not simply that the domestic habits of the people, their serious pursuits, and their modes of recreation, were mere continuations of what they had known in their ancestral home oversea. It is true that all these were exactly calculated to preserve the inherited spirit of their race when transferred to a new hemisphere, and to perfectly strange scenes. But, in reality, there was a more powerful influence than these to keep the English stamina unaltered among the people of the Colony. Down to the last quarter of the seventeenth century, all the leading men among them had been born and educated in England. When they arrived in Virginia, they were Englishmen in every fibre of their character, and in the entire bent of their minds. Their citizenship in the new land which they had entered, did not cause them to shed one single custom or to modify one single opinion which they had inherited in their homes in England before they had immigrated.

The Colonial founders of the Armistead family, the Banister, Bassett, Bland, Bolling, Beverley, Burwell, Byrd, Cary, Corbin, Carter, Claiborne, Custis, Fauntleroy, Fitzhugh, Harrison, Lee, Lightfoot, Ludwell, Mason, Page, Peyton, Randolph, Robinson, Scarborough, Spencer, Thoroughgood, Washington, and Wormeley,—all were natives of the English shires; all, in youth, had attended English schools; all had been trained in English sports on English play-grounds; all had worshipped in the churches of the ancient English cities and countrysides; all had drunk, at a very susceptible age, of the fundamental influences of English life; and all had been equally imbued with the spirit of English points of view.

Now, in no particular was the English characteristic of these men so deeply ingrained as in those ideas which governed their conception of the true constitution of society. "I was born a gentleman," exclaimed Cromwell, on one occasion, in addressing Parliament, "and in the old social arrangement of a nobleman, a gentleman, and a yeoman, I see a good interest of the nation and a great one." That was precisely the opinion which such men as John Page, Robert Beverley, William Claiborne, William Fitzhugh, William Byrd, the elder, Richard Lee, George Mason, William Randolph, Nicholas Spencer, Lawrence Washington, and Ralph Wormeley, held before they dropped from the shores of England, and which they continued to hold in Virginia until their last hour.

It was natural enough that men like these, together with the Cavalier immigrants as a body, should have unconsciously confirmed all the impressions as to what were the proper social lines of demarcation that had prevailed in the Colony before their arrival. Those lines only grew more perceptible with the accumulation of wealth, for that wealth took the form which has always been the principal buttress of the same condition in England. This form was land, which has always been the firmest support of the various aristocratic class systems which have flourished in the course of history, both ancient and modern.

The ever widening area of productive soil that fell into the hands of the most conspicuous families of the Colony, which was so purely agricultural in character, strengthened the social claims of these families by augmenting their financial importance. The larger proportion of the small estates belonging to the rank which Cromwell described as "yeoman" and this only accentuated the distinction of the families that were in possession of a broad domain of open fields and thick forests. The combination of inherited ideas respecting class differences, with the ownership of large properties that afforded the means to sustain social pretensions, created a social life in Virginia, which, in its essence, was the social life of England on a small scale.

There was no order of noblemen, such as the Great Protector attributed to his own country, but there was a clearly defined order of "gentlemen," and also an equally well defined order of "yeomen." Indeed, so distinctly was this admitted to be the case that citizens who belonged to one or the other of these two orders attached the terms "gentleman" and "yeoman" to the respective written names according to their social rank.

It did not follow that there was an unbridgable gulf between "gentleman" and "yeoman." The yeoman was as independent in his life and bearing as the gentleman, and they regarded each other with equal respect and bore themselves towards each other with equal courtesy. The yeoman recognized that there was a social difference between him and gentleman which placed himself on a lower social level, but that fact did not create any ill-feeling in his breast, so kindly were the social relations between the two, and so closely were their economic interests bound up together. On the other hand, the yeoman considered himself to be the social superior of the indentured servant, and the hired laborer, and acted in harmony with that impression.

No doubt too the presence of the African slave in every community tended to increase the force of class feeling among the whites. No matter how impoverished the thriftless white laborer might be, his position was regarded by gentleman and yeoman alike as superior to that of the black bondsman toiling in the tobacco fields or waiting at the dining table on the members of the planter's family.

As the eighteenth century advanced in time, the social peculiarities of the seventeenth,—which had been introduced into the different countrysides many decades before by native Englishmen,—became more deeply rooted and threw out wider and more vigorous branches. The full flower of Virginian social life,—the most aristocratic in spirit that has been observed on the North American Continent at any period of its history,—was reached in the course of the years that immediately preceded the Revolution. Owners of large estates in land and negroes could

WESTOVER

then be found in every one of the country-sides of Tidewater and Piedmont. These formed as distinct an upper class as any that was to be discovered in the England of that day. They possessed the same influence among their own neighbors as this class in England did, and they set the same example in their general style of living as that set in the same province by the contemporary English gentlemen of easy fortune. Westover, Berkeley, Brandon, Shirley, Wilton, and Malvern on the James; Sabine Hall and Mt. Airy on the Rappahannock; Rosewell and Carter Hall on the York; Mt. Vernon, Gunston, and Belvoir on the Potomac; Montpelier and Monticello in Piedmont,—these were merely the most famous homes, among the large number almost as imposing, that were situated in different parts of the Colony. Their proprietors stood out as conspicuously as though they belonged to a caste which was not the recent growth of a colony, but a transmission, without diminution of strength, from the immemorial communities of the mother country over sea.

The effect of the Revolution on the social life of Virginia was not as universally radical as might have been presumed. It is true that a Republican form of administration took the place of the former monarchical form, but the change was virtually a mere shift of the center of authority. The throne had never been very close to the social life of the Virginian people, except so far as it was represented by a Governor-General who surrounded himself with the ceremonials of royalty. But it was only the highest class of planters, who, by spending their winters in Williamsburg, were really conscious of the presence of this official in the Colony. To the mass of the inhabitants, following their callings in remote plantation communities, he was a figure known only by hearsay.

Undoubtedly, the Virginians as a body were loyal to the English Government and had no desire to separate from the kingdom, but when they did do so, there is no evidence that that fact made them a different people. They still had a governor in Williamsburg, who was only novel in having been elected by themselves. They still had their Council, now known as the Senate; their House of Burgesses, now known as the House of Delegates; their General Court, now known as the Court of Appeals; their bench of county magistrates, still known by its original name. Not even politically had the State been transformed in its fundamental spirit, in spite of the substitution of Williamsburg for London as the ultimate seat of authority.

In what particulars then had the communities of Virginia changed to an extent calculated to affect their social system perceptibly? These particulars were: the disestablishment of the Church, and the abolition of the law of primogeniture. Both of these regulations while they existed had exercised a decided influence in sustaining that social spirit, which, with its inclination towards marked class divisions, had been inherited originally from England. The Established Church sustained it by raising one religious denomination high above the rest, thus imparting to its membership an odor of social superiority. The law of primogeniture, and its accompaniment,—the law of entail, —sustained it by tending to concentrate the larger estates in the hands of a few, thus increasing the importance of families, and thereby fostering social pride and exclusiveness.

The reduction of the Established Church to the level of all the other denominations seriously and permanently damaged its social distinction. The members of that church had now, in the eyes of the law, not a single advantage of any kind over the members of the hitherto contemned sects. This was one step towards social equality throughout the community. By dividing the inherited lands up among all the children, instead of assigning them to the eldest son, their engrossment in this latter form ceased altogether. Estates now tended to curtailment by the operation of subdivision; and thus another cause of social prestige was practically destroyed.

The influence of the two changes mentioned undoubtedly altered to a considerable degree the social characteristics which were in existence at the beginning of the Revolution. But this alteration did not go down to the foundations of the entire social fabric which survived that event. And why? First, because the old plantation system remained; and second and above all, because the institution of slavery was as vigorous after as it had been during the Colonial era, although, from time to time, there were proposals in favor of emancipation. The plantation system was dependent upon the institution of slavery, but its social influence was independent of that institution. This influence was intensely conservative in the province of social life. It had shown itself to be such especially in the Colonial age, and it continued to do so after the alteration of the framework of government. And why? First, because the economic conditions remained the same as before; and second, because the isolation and seclusion of the plantation communities were as pronounced after the Revolution as before.

There was no new influence to change the old habits of the planters, and there were no new ideas stealing in to modify their old social points of view. The children of the men and women of the highest station who had passed through the commotions of the period of the Revolution were deeply imbued with the social ideas that their parents had held, and these ideas they passed on in turn to their own children. Perhaps, the most vigorous of these ideas was represented in their repugnance to the principle of social equality. This was shown, not only in their relations with the population at large, but particularly in marriage and purely domestic associations. Nor was this attitude inconsistent with a friendly and constant general intercourse with every rank of their neighbors.

But this conservative social spirit, descending from the past, did not continue because of the isolated plantation life alone. In a society which rested upon such a static institution as slavery,—as the Virginian social framework continued to do down to the close of the war in 1865,—the conservative spirit, not simply in social points of view, but also in all others, was the logical result of the situation. It could not have been otherwise without

jeopardizing the fundamental safety of the community. The
planters were forced by their environment to be conservative;
and they could not be conservative in regard to slavery without
unconsciously being conservative in regard to every other interest and sentiment of their lives.

The fact that the employment which occupied the time of
each section of the inhabitants; namely, agriculture, was substantially the only pursuit in every community of the State
tended further to preserve this conservative spirit. The planters had been producing tobacco and wheat chiefly during a period of two hundred years and more; these were their only
staple crops; and these they expected to go on cultivating for an
indefinite time. Their social life had followed the same unbroken pattern, and they did not anticipate that the future would
bring about any change.

The situation was not the same at the North. There was
there a combination of industrial and agricultural pursuits, with
the industrial predominating. But there was a more significant
difference even than this. Foreign immigrants had poured into
Northern cities and over the Western plains, taking with them
European conceptions of living and European modes of thought
utterly distasteful to the inmates of the plantation homes of
Virginia. Practically, no wave of this flood crossed the Potomac. In consequence, no alien notions, no alien manners, no
alien principles, crept in to confuse the inherited English social
ideas that had prevailed in the homes along the James, the York,
the Rappahannock, the Staunton, and the Ravanna, since the
settlements in these valleys had been founded in that past which
now seemed so remote. People of an almost exclusive English
stock they were in the seventeenth century; people of the same
stock they continued to be in the eighteenth; and people of this
practically unmixed stock they remained, keeping, throughout,
all the social conceptions and principles which they had imbibed
with the civilization that they had inherited, and which they had
never at any period of their history ceased to cherish.

The most radical blow which the social system of Virginia ever received was inflicted by the abolition of slavery. This institution was the keystone in the arch of that system; and after its removal by force, the whole structure, as it had existed from the seventeenth century, was at once weakened and ultimately ruined.

The old social system as we have seen had survived the severance from the British Monarchy. It is true, as we have pointed out, that it had been seriously impaired by the disestablishment of the Church, and by the revocation of the Law of primogeniture, but beyond this injury, it had revealed no tendency to complete transformation. Nor did it do so as long as it retained the firm support of the institution of slavery. The really destructive stroke in 1865 was not, however, immediately fatal. When the war ended in the course of that year, the only form of property which survived the catastrophe to any important extent was the landed estates. These estates, together with the slaves belonging to them, made up, even before the war, the principal financial resource of the Virginians. This resource, fortunately for the owners, outlasted the abolition of slavery. When hostilities closed at Appomattox, thousands of Virginians, who, for the moment, had no other means of livelihood, went back to the family farms and plantations. There they were compelled to face at once the change in the system of labor, but, happily, the bulk of the freedmen of mature years, accustomed to habits of industry, and devoted to their original cabin-homes, were willing to enter into the new relation of hired service.

During a period of at least fifteen years following the end of the War, the economic system of the rural districts was able to adapt itself to free labor with more success than had at one time been anticipated; and so long as that labor remained stable, the social system apparently preserved a definite degree of its old conservatism; but all this while the process of distintegration was working at its heart.

There were two powerful influences in action to complete in time the destructive effect of the abolution of slavery. First, the profits of agriculture, after a certain date, began to decline. Hired negro labor, even in the prosperous years just after the war, was not as lucrative as slave labor had been. The old tendency to the engrossment of the soil was no longer at play, but the reverse towards subdivision had not yet come fully into operation, although the surviving proprietors of advanced age found themselves "land poor" to a degree that they had never before known. Had they been younger men, they would have recognized their inability to meet the loss through taxes which this condition imposed inevitably, and saved themselves by selling at least a share of their holdings.

But before the reasons for subdivision could serve their full part, another influence, tending in the same direction, had arisen. By 1880, the greater proportion of the landowners who had inherited their properties before the war, had begun to die off. Their sons had come forward to take their place, but these young men, as a rule, were not willing to lead the lives which their fathers had done. Existence in the old rural homes no longer had the ease and comfort which it possessed in the days of slavery, when servants were numerous, and supplies were obtained in abundance from the soil of the plantation or farm, and when the returns from the fields brought in enough income to furnish the ready money that was currently needed.

But, above all, the social charm had disappeared. The falling off in the number of refined families in every neighborhood had left already many vacancies where once a warm and cultivated hospitality had extended its hand. The young men looked around them only to perceive a calling in which there was no pecuniary return unless they became common laborers and were willing to turn their backs on the social traditions of their respective families. Were they to give up all hope of success in life? Moreover, were they to remain satisfied with an environment which offered them few social advantages, and with such

advantages as survived showing a steady disappearance? From
year to year, the number of young men emigrating from the
country districts of Southside Virginia, Tidewater, and Middle
Piedmont, where the old economic and social system had once
prevailed in its greatest prosperity, grew larger and larger.
Many left before their fathers died in the old homes; and when
they in turn inherited the paternal acres, they quickly subdivided
and sold them to the highest bidder. The young men who remained were, as a rule, those who felt no ambition for improvement in their condition. On the other hand, those who went
away were the individuals who were most energetic, most resolute, and most aspiring.

By the time that one generation had passed, the old neighborhoods which had been occupied by proprietors of the highest
social position in the State could often not show a single representative of the families which had formerly been in possession
of the ancient mansions. These mansions had either fallen into
decay, in consequence of abandonment, or they belonged to men
who made no claim to any higher status than that of small landowners, and who were without any pretension to education or
even to refinement of manners, however industrious in habits
or however correct in conduct they might be. The Valley, for
the most part, had not changed socially, for there the inhabitants, outside the towns, had always cultivated their own soil
and continued to do so because they could make it profitable by
the use of their own hands, without the assistance of hired labor.
A remnant of the old social life continued to linger in the northern parts of Piedmont, where there had been few slaves, and
where the attention of the landowners had been directed chiefly
to the breeding of livestock. This was also partly true of the
counties lying to the west of the Blue Ridge in the angle of
West Virginia and the lower Shenandoah River.

When the young men deserted the farms and plantations in
the less fortunate divisions of the State, where did they go?
Some abandoned Virginia altogether, but the large majority

were satisfied to settle in the nearest towns and villages. Many adopted the various learned professions, but the bulk entered mercantile and industrial pursuits. It was a significant fact that those who accumulated fortunes were usually unwilling to repurchase their alienated ancestral homes, except possibly for recreation during the warm months of the year; but even such instances as the latter occurred with extreme rarity.

By the end of the nineteenth century, the social life which had given the older regions of Virginia so much social distinction in the past was practically defunct. The social life now in existence differs hardly at all from the one that has always prevailed in the affluent Northern States. It is the social life of cities based on wealth, without regard to family, and with little, if any, respect for social traditions. The social center has been shifted from the country,—except in small areas in Piedmont, and the Lower Valley,—to the towns, both large and small. The superiority of the new over the old lies in greater wealth alone, and in those special advantages which wealth has to offer: better highways, more extensive public education, a more practical outlook, a greater susceptibility to new ideas, a quicker responsiveness to community interests, a closer touch with mankind at large.

The old social civilization of Virginia, which was a rural civilization in its most cultured form, but necessarily more or less provincial, has passed, and with it have gone all those charming characteristics, all those imposing personal figures, which gave the Virginia of history so distinguished a place in the minds of men. Socially, the State no longer stands apart to itself. In the social province, as well as in every other, it has been merged in the broad stream which forms the general social life of America.

CHAPTER XIII

THE OLD FRAMEWORK OF GOVERNMENT

Before considering the actual or impending changes in the framework of the State Government (1928), it will be pertinent to give some description of the framework which was in existence during the years that preceded all thought of alteration. Let us take 1923, for instance, as a representative year. The agencies of Virginia's Government at that time fell into three divisions; namely, state, local, and national. The State functioned then as it does now, through the Constitutional Convention, the General Assembly, numerous commissions, the Governor, and the Courts. On the other hand, the city, town, and county, which constituted the local, operated through boards of supervisors, councils, committees, managers, electoral boards, school electoral boards, school trustee boards, and magistrate's courts. There were also the numerous subordinate local officers employed in the performance of separate public duties, such as the assessors, commissioners of the revenue, sheriffs, treasurers, road commissioners, superintendents of the poor, constables, and county surveyors.

Virginia, like all the other States, was, in 1823, as it is still, subject to the National Constitution. That instrument affirms that "all powers not delegated to the United States by the Constitution nor prohibited by it to the States," were reserved to the States respectively or to the people. This signifies that, within the scope of the powers delegated to it, the National Government was supreme; and these delegated powers have been so widened in their scope by the interpretation of the Supreme Court that

493

they today virtually cover most of the ground in every province of general authority.

Next in importance for Virginia in 1923 came its State Constitution. This document was supreme in all matters embraced in its terms, provided that they were not in conflict with the National Constitution.

Outside of the province of these two instruments, the Acts of the General Assembly were in 1923, as in 1928, the final rule, because that body represented the voice of the people as a whole. So soon as these Acts ran contrary to the fundamental law of the United States or of the State of Virginia, as incorporated in their respective Constitutions, they were deprived of all validity. An average citizen in 1923 as in 1928 knew, in his daily experience, little, if anything, of the operation of the Federal Constitution. It touched him rarely except in (1) the clause that reserved the distribution of the mails to the Federal Government; and (2) in the clause that validated the imposition of certain taxes. The Constitution of Virginia, on the other hand, touched constantly the immediate interests of every one of its people, although they were not all aware of that fact. There was not a sentence in this State Constitution which has not, in reality, the most direct bearing on the individual citizen's welfare.

One illustration is sufficient: the great public school system rested upon the provisions of this instrument. It was created by the Convention of 1868, and broadened by the Convention of 1902.

Though the work of a Constitutional Convention embodies the crystallized law, yet each Constitution in succession is a mere temporary record of the changes which have arisen in public sentiment, or public necessity, since the adjournment of the last Convention. The next Convention, in its turn, will reflect the changes of the like nature which have taken place in the course of the preceding interval. Sometimes, this call for alteration in the existing Constitution will be met simply by the passage of amendments.

The constitution of Virginia in 1923, as in 1928, followed the fundamental law of the United States by requiring a distinct separation of the legislative, executive, and judiciary departments of the State Government. The division was strictly enforced in the administration of these three great departments at the top, but it was not so scrupulously observed in the operations of the local boards, such as the supervisors and common councils, which managed the affairs of county or town, and, in doing so, assumed the right both to appropriate the public money and to disburse it also.

Let us consider the three great departments in turn as they stood in 1923. First, the Legislature or General Assembly. During the period which we are now covering, the Commonwealth consisted of 100 counties, twenty-two cities, and two hundred or more towns and villages. These communities, as a whole, were entitled to 100 delegates and forty senators. The delegates, who represented the counties or cities separately, were elected once in the course of every two years. On the other hand, the members of the Senate, who represented districts, were elected once in every four. They could sit for a period of only ninety days; but for the last thirty, they received no salary. The remuneration for the first sixty days was limited to $500. If a special session was held in obedience to the governor's proclamation, the remuneration was not allowed to exceed one-half of this amount. A regular session could only be called once in the course of two years. A special session, on the other hand, could be held as often as the State Executive thought the public interests demanded.

Every sane person over twenty-one years of age, whether male or female, was entitled to vote, provided that he or she had resided in the State for a period of at least two years, and in the county where he or she permanently lived, for a period of one. Previous to 1923, the poll tax was payable only by the male voter. The Confederate and Federal veterans were exempted from this requirement. The only individuals who were shut out of the enjoyment of the suffrage were idiots, insane persons, paupers, and persons disqualified by conviction of crime, or by having fought a duel, or even by having sent a challenge.

The acts which the General Assembly passed embraced the entire field of the people's interests. The variety was too great to be particularized here. It may be said of the statutes in general in 1923 that the title of each one had to express the object which the act had in view; and the act had to be limited to one object. If it included more than one, it was null on its face. No law could take effect under ninety days unless the contrary was expressly authorized by a four-fifths vote. The suspension of the writ of habeas corpus was forbidden; so was the establishment of lotteries; and so were appropriations for the benefit of charitable sectarian institutions not under the guardianship of the State.

The term of the Governor of the Commonwealth was, in 1923, restricted to four years. He was not permitted by law to become a candidate for a second term immediately in succession to his first. Another limitation prevented any person under thirty years of age from seeking the office. Both of these rules indicated an unnecessary degree of popular distrust—one, of the possible candidate's disinterested patriotism; the other of his experience and ability through immaturity.

The Governor possessed an official power that extended in very many directions. In a general way, it may be said of him that he was required to see that all the laws were faithfully carried out; to report to the General Assembly upon the condition of the State; and to recommend to their consideration such measures as he might judge to be necessary for the welfare of the community at large. He acted as commander in chief of the State troops; could suspend for misdemeanor any official of the Government below the rank of the Lieutenant-Governor; could

E. LEE TRINKLE
GOVERNOR 1922-1926

appoint temporary incumbents for vacant offices; could grant reprieves and pardons after conviction; and could also remove political disabilities. One of his most important functions was frequently exercised under his right to veto a bill; and his disapproval of such a bill was fatal, unless overriden by a two-thirds reaffirmative vote.

The officers who were subordinate to the Governor were the Lieutenant-Governor, the Treasurer, the Auditor of Public Accounts, the Second Auditor, and the Secretary of the Commonwealth. As the duties of these officials followed the conventional grooves which belong to positions of this nature, they require no extended notice here. An important feature of the Treasurership in 1923 was that no public revenue could be paid into or out of its depositories except upon the warrant of one or the other of the two Auditors. The books of all three had to be kept balanced to avoid confusion.

The money that belonged to the State Government was not placed in the Treasury itself, but in numerous banks, situated in different parts of the Commonwealth, which gave adequate security for its safety. They also paid interest upon the daily balance. The register of the land office had the custody of all the land patents; and he was also in charge of the public grounds and buildings. Like the public printer, he was not elected by the people, but by the General Assembly.

The judiciary department was the third great division of the State Government in 1923, just as it is today. It was composed of a series of courts, the first of which was the Supreme Court of Appeals. The jurisdiction of this body was appellate, except in three cases, namely, habeas corpus, mandamus, and prohibition. Prohibition, in this sense, means only an order forbidding on official to do some particular act. The appellate jurisdiction could be enlarged or contracted just as the General Assembly might consider necessary for the public welfare. Among the existing grounds of appeal in 1923 was the question whether a law passed by the Legislature was in conflict with the provisions of the State or National Constitution. Another was a case in which the life or liberty of a person was involved. In civil suits, the amount in dispute was not to be smaller than $300 unless the title or the boundaries of land entered into the controversy. There were also other exceptions. Some of these related to the condemnation of land, the probate of wills, and the qualification of guardians, personal represenatives, or curators. Certain questions touching the right of the State, county, or city, to levy a tax, or concerning the construction of statutes or ordinances imposing such burdens, also came up before the Court of Appeals.

Supplementary to the Court of Appeals was a Special Court of Appeals composed of a fixed number of circuit judges, judges of the large cities, and judges of the Supreme Court of Appeals. The judges of the latter court were elected by the General Assembly, and their respective terms extended to twelve years.

For every 40,000 persons in the State, there were required to be at least one circuit judge. His district was defined by the General Assembly, and he held his seat by the choice of that body. His term was restricted to eight years. Two other courts, besides the circuit court, were found in the cities. The most conspicuous was the Corporation Court. The Juvenile Court also played a useful part. Courts of Land Registration were erected in both city and county. Their jurisdiction related to the settlement, registration, transfer, or assurance of titles to real estate. All the judges were removable from office for malfeasance or neglect of duty by a vote of the General Assembly. Legal officers of importance were the Attorney-General of the State, the justices of the peace, and the grand juror.

Passing from the State Government to the county, we find that each of the 100 counties of Virginia in 1923, as mentioned at the beginning of this chapter, possessed its own officers for the performance of the various duties incident to the administration of its affairs. The functions of the treasurer, sheriff, commonwealth's attorney, county clerk, and commissioners of the revenue were those common everywhere to the respective positions which they held. It is not, therefore, necessary to describe them in detail. This is also true of the superintendent of the poor, and the surveyor. The principal boards were the county electoral board, the school electoral board, and the board of health. The county electoral board appointed the registrars, judges, and clerks of election. The school electoral board selected the school trustees. The county board of health, which was appointed by the State Board of Health, was engaged in preventing, checking, or curing all local contagious diseases. Every county enjoyed the services of an association of game-wardens, who were assigned, each to his own district.

From some points of view the most important of all these local officers were the county boards of supervisors. Each district elected a separate supervisor. Together they laid the county and district levies, and passed on the various claims which were made against the county's revenues. A constable and overseer of the poor were chosen in each district. The constable was the serving hand of the three justices of the peace, who administered the law in each of the several divisions of the county. Another officer was the coroner, who had to be a physician, and who sometimes performed the duties of a constable.

Legally in Virginia, in 1923, every incorporated community that numbered at least five thousand persons is a city, and if it could not count as many inhabitants as this, it was known as a town. The chief officers of a city or town were the mayor, the council, the treasurer, the sergeant, the commissioner of the revenue, and the city and commonwealth's attorneys. The duties of these officers did not vary from such as were performed by similar officers in other States. The cities, like the counties, were also subject to the guidance of numerous boards. These boards superintended the affairs of the schools and other departments of the community's life. Among these departments were those that directed the activities of the police, checked the spread of fires, or enforced the municipal building regulations.

The central administration of the State Government was also largely carried on through the agency of boards or commissioners. Some of these commissioners were really composed of one person, subject, it might be, to the supervision of a general board, like the commissioner of agriculture or the commissioner of education, for instance. Others were composed of several members, who were independent of oversight except by the Legislature or the Governor, to whom their annual reports were made. The law requiring a rigid separation between the three divisions of the Government were not always strictly followed in the practical operation of these commissions.

The commissioner of agriculture represented the Department of Agriculture and Immigration. We have, in previous chapters, described in some detail the duties of this officer. Suffice it to repeat briefly here that his principal functions in 1923 required him to enforce the careful execution of all regulations passed for the general protection of crops and the improvement of the soil; to suppress the improper sale of defective fertilizers; and to promote the immigration of a superior type of outsiders by exploiting the great advantages which the State had to offer to settlers, either from Europe or from the Northern States. It was his duty also to encourage the holding of farmers' institutes; to distribute valuable agricultural bulletins; and to make an annual report full of such information as would advance the usefulness of agriculture in the Commonwealth at large.

The State Board of Education had general supervision over the public school system. It was composed of the governor, the attorney-general, the superintendent of public instruction, and three educators of experience chosen by the State Senate from a list of persons submitted by a certain number of the State institutions of learning. In addition, two members of the board were selected from the ranks of the division superintendents of schools. The most important figure on the board was the superintendent of public instruction, who held his seat by popular election.

The duties of the board, of which the superintendent was the president, may be summarized as follows: it laid off the school divisions, each of which embraced not less than a county or a city; appointed the superintendent of each district; removed him for malfeasance or neglect of duty; invested the school funds; drafted the regulations for the management of the schools; selected the text-books; named the members of the library board, which had charge of the affairs of the State Library; chose the librarian; and, finally, acted as the custodian of the Literary Fund and the Samuel Miller School Fund.

The Literary Fund was established by an act of the General Assembly passed in February, 1810. It consisted of the money obtained by sales of public lands granted by Congress for the support of agricultural schools; by sales of escheated, unappropriated, or forfeited lands; by fines; and by such special sums as the State had appropriated for its increase. Only the interest from the Literary Fund could be used, but the principal could be loaned to the school districts.

The public schools were supported in two ways: first by State taxes, and second by local. The former consisted of the larger proportion of the head tax, and also a separate tax on property, not exceeding five mills on the dollar or falling below one mill. Local levies for the benefit of the public schools were laid by the boards of supervisors of the counties, and also by the councils of the cities and towns if either of the latter embraced a complete school district.

Under the provisions of the Constitution of 1902, as amended, a certain degree of discretion was allowed the General Assembly in prescribing the rules which related to compulsory education. In 1923, the limit was fixed at eight years of age on one direction and fourteen in the other; but this regulation was subject to numerous exceptions, which were carefully designated.

There were during that year about six hundred retired teachers on the pension roll, which had been established for the benefit of the instructors in the public schools. Under the provision then in operation, one per cent of the salary received from the State and locality jointly by each teacher in these schools was retained in the State treasury. The fund was known as the Retired Teachers Pension Fund; and to it annually the State contributed the sum of $10,000. Every teacher who was disabled, after serving twenty years in the school house, or who had completed a period of thirty years, whether disabled or not, was entitled to the pension. This apparently averaged then about four hundred dollars a year.

The State Corporation Commission exercised in 1923 powers of extraordinary importance. It was composed of three members, who served, respectively, during a term of six years. They were selected by the people, but might be impeached and removed by the General Assembly for cause. Their duties were prescribed by that body. These duties consisted chiefly of enforcing the laws relating to chartering, inspecting, overlooking, regulating and controlling corporations which were authorized to transact business in the State of Virginia. If the corporation was foreign, it had to obtain a license to do this from the commission. If domestic, it had to acquire a charter. The commission also supervised and regulated the transportation companies of the State in every department of their operations, such as the passenger and freight rates, traffic classification of goods, the maintenance of public service facilities and conveniences, preservation of the tracks to assure safety, and the avoidance of unjust discriminations against special localities. As to corporations in general, the commission was empowered to lay down and enforce rates of valuation where the assessment of their property, or the appraisement of their franchises, was involved. That body also passed upon protests by corporations against exorbitant or unfair taxation.   An appeal in such cases could be carried up to the Supreme Court of the State.

The State Highway Commission had, in the course of its later years, grown steadily in the scope and thoroughness of its work. Each of the five geographical divisions of Virginia was represented in this body by the governor's appointments, and the Senate's confirmation. An unusual feature of the commission, in the beginning, was the fact that its chairman could be selected from among citizens residing beyond the borders of the Commonwealth. The explanation of this provision lay in the necessity of obtaining a well-trained and competent officer, no matter where he was to be found. The commission was required to meet at least once in the course of every three months. It selected its own engineers and employees in general, and located the roads which were to belong to the State system. But it was necessary that the proposed highways should receive the approval of the local boards of county supervisors before they had been begun.

The commission let all the contracts for this road building; and it was also empowered, when a highway had been completed, to adopt rules for the regulation of the passing traffic in harmony with the general requirements of the existing State law. The commission was permitted most often to name the new highway included in the system. It was also authorized to act in cooperation with the National Government in laying off the beds and boundaries of post-roads in the rural districts. Virginia was, at this time, divided into eight construction districts, and as far as possible, the work done in each was kept on a parity. The funds accumulated by the State annually was apportioned fairly between these different divisions by the first day of each April. The decision, in no instance, was to be reached without a public hearing that had been publicly announced. All calls for bids were also to be advertised for a definite period of time.

The chairman has the right to exercise the power of eminent domain to a remarkable extent. This was often done by him in the appropriation of land in building a new road or in straightening an old one. The right was carried even further in the condemnation of quarries and woods containing material for application to the roadbeds. This condemnation, in some cases,

Courtesy of Norfolk-Portsmouth Chamber of Commerce

AIRPLANE AT NAVAL AIR STATION, NORFOLK

was by the act of the Highway Commission alone, without the intervention of formal proceedings. The roads were constructed and maintained by the levy of a gasoline tax, which rapidly increased in volume. The State of Virginia wisely refused to adopt a proposal which would have again saddled its people with an enormous public debt.

Subject to the Department of the Corporation Commission were the Bureau of Insurance and the Banking Division. The Bureau of Insurance was authorized to examine, at any time, the condition of any insurance company doing business in the State, if that step was considered necessary for the protection of its policy-holders, or of any town, city, or corporation interested in its solvency. One of the functions of the bureau was to grant licenses to Northern and foreign insurance companies, and certificates of authority to all home insurance companies organized to solicit patronage in Virginia. The reports of the commissioner, which were made to the Corporation Commission, were based on information acquired directly by his office through various agencies. The most important contained full descriptions of the fires that took place in the State at large. These he was required to investigate on request. He was also expected to inquire into all complaints as to excessive rates of insurance; and furthermore, to make such recommendations to the General Assembly in insurance matters as the existing conditions demanded.

The Banking Division was under the management of a chief examiner, who was assisted by numerous officers of subordinate importance. The province covered by their labors extended to State banks, savings banks, and saving societies. In short, to saving institutions of every kind. All these were chartered by the State Corporation Commission; and it was to that commission that the chief examiner had to report.

We have already dwelt very fully on the duties performed by the State Board of Health and the powers exercised by its commissioner. With equal fullness, the functions of the Prohibition Department, the Department of Game and Inland Fisheries, and the Commission of Fisheries, have been presented by us in previous chapters.

The Bureau of Labor and Industry was, in 1923, under the control of the commissioner of labor, who had received his appointment from the governor, with the consent of the State Senate. This officer was always one who, before his selection, had been personally identified with the interests of labor. The duty was imposed on him and his assistants to inspect factories, mills, mercantile establishments, workshops and the like, wherever situated in the State; and the information thus obtained had to be carefully recorded, sifted, and transmitted, in the form of a report, to the governor. In every case of violation of the factory laws, it was incumbent upon him to prosecute the offender. The provisions of these laws extended to many minute particulars, among which may be mentioned the regulations of hours of labor for women; the restrictions upon the employment of children; the protection of discharged operatives; and the maintenance of sanitary arrangements, safety appliances, and ventilation of factory premises. The commissioner was further required to keep a list of all persons seeking employment. The Department of Mines was also subject to his control; and this supervision was exercised by him through inspectors who had been thoroughly trained in the industry, and who were, therefore, practically informed as the nature of mine gases and the best methods of working and ventilating such properties.

The Industrial Commission was appointed in 1918 for the purpose of enforcing the Workmen's Compensation Act, which was adopted to prevent industrial accidents, and to fix rates of compensation whenever they occurred, in spite of precautions. The Dairy and Food Commissioner was subordinate to the Department of Agriculture. It was his duty to inspect the dairy and food and drink products which were manufactured in Virginia, or which were offered for sale in its markets, shops, and the like depositories. He was empowered to enter any place where these articles were stored, break open their coverings, and subtract specimens for chemical analysis. He had the right also to report for punishment all persons detected in selling improper imitations or substitutes for food, or who, in disposing of permitted food, allowed their premises to become unwholesome and unsanitary.

The State Veterinarian was subject to the direction of the Live Stock Sanitary Board, and the State Dairy and Food Commissioner. His principal duty was to apply the tuberculin test to breeding or dairy cows.

The State Board of Public Welfare, formerly known as the Board of Charities and Corrections, was required to inspect all State, county, municipal, and private institutions that partook of an eleemosynary, charitable, correctional, or reformatory character. The care or training of defective, dependent, neglected, or criminal classes also came within the scope of its duties The State Board was duplicated in local boards organized in different cities and counties.

Another State agency in 1923 was the Legislative Reference Bureau, which assisted in drafting bills to be submitted to the General Assembly; in collecting and classifying data for legislative use; and in preserving legislative files and documents. The State Tax Board, composed of the State treasurer and the two auditors, was required to supervise the tax officers of the counties and cities, and also to correct improper assessments. The Board was represented by examiners of records, whose chief occupation consisted of going over and reporting on fiduciary accounts.

The Purchasing Commission, which sat under the chairmanship of the Governor, bought the commodities needed for distribution by the State among the various hospitals. The State Fee Commission, also headed by the governor, regulated the compensation of the State's fee officers. The State Geological Commission was engaged in the development of the mineral resources of the Commonwealth. The Forestry Department was subject to the control of the state forester, who owed his appointment to the State Geological Commission. The Virginia War History Commission was erected by the governor for the preservation of the facts relating to Virginia's share at home and abroad in the events of the World war. Other Commissions in 1923 were the Virginia Board of Crop Pest, and the State Live Stock Sanitary Board. A commissioner was also in charge of the State Hospital. In addition, a board of commissioners had been appointed to promote uniformity of legislation in the United States.

In October, 1863, the Public Debt of Virginia amounted to $35,821,486.51. With the exception of $164,457.85 borrowed for State defense in the War then in progress, this obligation had been accumulated in the form of contributions to the construction of State plank-roads, turnpikes, bridges, railroads, canals, and river improvements. Had the War of 1861-65 not occurred, these investments would have proved highly profitable. Even if all had been retained after the close of hostilities, many of them would have made, as the State advanced in prosperity, as handsome a return as her interest in the present Richmond, Fredericksburg, and Potomac Railroad,—which she did not sell, —has done.

After passing through the furnace of a great political controversy the debt of the State, in the year 1923, amounted to $21,173,703.33, the difference being due to the passage of scaling acts. The share of the old debt assigned to West Virginia for settlement by the judgment of the Supreme Court of the United States was fixed at fourteen and a half millions of dollars. The two States thus assumed in the end, in unequal divisions, a public debt which, combined, approximated $35,700,000.

CHAPTER XIV

TAXATION AND REFORM

In beginning the previous chapter, we mentioned the fact that various changes in the organic law of the State, and in the agencies for its administration, had been proposed, and where requiring only the Legislature's approval, had been finally adopted. So far (December, 1927) the General Assembly's approval of the projected amendments to the Constitution, to which we will soon refer, has been obtained only in the first stage. A second vote is to be cast by that body in the winter of 1928, and if it is still favorable to the projected amendments, the latter are to be submitted in November of the same year to the ballots of the people at large for rejection or adoption, according to the attitude of the majority. The chances now point to adoption, although there exists a very decided sentiment in opposition to the concentration of the State offices in the hands of a comparatively few men, appointed, almost without exception, by the governor.

The initiative in proposing all these changes has been taken by Governor Byrd, a man who had won distinction in the province of business before he entered public life; who had enjoyed a long training as a member of the State Senate; and who, throughout his private and public career, has exhibited the possession of a constructive and far-visioned mind.

Before we consider the character and scope of the alterations which have been made or are yet to be made, it will be pertinent to inquire into the nature of the notable reform which has already been introduced into the incidence of the State taxes by the powerful direct influence of Governor Byrd.

Previous to 1927, there was a State tax of twenty-five cents on land and tangible personal property to the extent of every one hundred dollars of assessed value. In 1927, this tax was completely repealed. During many years, there had been complaint that many counties had not been carrying their just share of the burden of State taxation. It was pointed out that lands of the same quality of soil were assessed at a high rate in one county, and at a very low rate in another. Much bad feeling was aroused in the rest of Virginia because a horse or cow in the Southwest was valued at a far smaller figure than the same animal in the Southside or Tidewater. And this was equally true down the line of every form of personal property. A demand sprang up for the establishment of a board at Richmond which should forcibly reconcile all these differences. Fortunately, this suggestion made no headway, as no small body of men representing the whole State was competent to make the right adjustment, owing to the complete diversity of interests in the different geographical divisions of the Commonwealth. A regional board sitting in each of these divisions, laid off in conformity with identity of soil and crops and other interests, would be alone practicable in its actual working; but the cost of such a duplicated system was almost prohibitive of its adoption.

The opponents of equalization of assessments were, in some instances inclined to think that the suggestion of that measure had its origin, to some degree, in the extravagant borrowing which had distinguished some of the larger cities of the State. Saddled with heavy interest charges incurred through debts contracted for the erection of municipal public works, the cities which had gone too far had ground for expecting some relief if they could have forced a larger collection of State taxes by compelling the counties supposed to be delinquent in their assessments to make a more voluminous return to the State Treasury. It was asserted, too, that the proposed equalization would place a county lavish in its public expenses at no disadvantage with a county that had managed its affairs with strict economy. The prudent county would be indirectly driven by a general readjustment of its assessments from low to high to come to the rescue of the imprudent county, just as if it was an object of fraternal charity.

The element of unreasonableness in the respective attitudes of the two sides only made it more difficult to solve the problem with entire satisfaction to all the counties. Governor Byrd settled it by the stroke of a new Alexander's sword. He urged the adoption of the principle of segregation, which had already been tried in the State in another quarter with small success. Under the acceptance of this principle, the State tax on land and tangible property was abolished by the General Assembly. The relief obtained by the rural landowners particularly was acutely demanded by the unprofitableness of their calling in recent years. Had no other good been accomplished through the segregation law, the lessening of the farmer's heavy burden would have fully justified its enactment.

Accompanying the passage of this law, there was a marked reduction in taxes that had been exercising a bad effect on the expansion of manufactures as well as on the migration to Virginia of men of large fortune, who wished to change their residence. The tax on notes, bonds, and stock in foreign corporations, was lowered from 55 to 50 cents the $100; and on capital engaged in business in Virginia, from $1.15 to 85 cents on the same amount. A similar enlightened judgment was shown in segregating machinery to locality.

The loss that was incurred in making these changes in the taxation rates mentioned was almost covered contemporaneously by a small increase in the rate of taxation on incomes. That deficit, apart from this reimbursement, was justly considered to be compensated for by the impetus to be given to the introduction of new industrial enterprises into the state, from which it was known that every citizen would derive an advantage in one form or another; and this advantage was expected to be further augmented by the amount of money which would be placed in circulation by new residents of large means.

It is computed that the reduction, in 1927, in the amount of city land and personal property taxes, through the operation of the segregation law, reached a total of $255,823.92. On the other hand, the reduction in the amount of country land and personal property taxes was estimated at $1,314,059.15. Other tax reductions in the counties added $131,829.15 to this latter sum. Taking the entire degree of relief into consideration, it is perceived that the citizens of Virginia have already, under the new law of segregation, about $1,700,000 less to pay in taxes than under the regulation which preceded it.

In no particular is the income of the commonwealth growing more rapidly than through the imposition of a tax on every gallon of gasoline sold in the State. This tax will continue to increase with the rising prosperity of Virginia. Good roads and tourist travel go hand in hand. As the number of good roads enlarges, the number of tourists augments; and as the number of tourists augments, so the number of gallons of gasoline sold increases. The tax on gasoline is wisely reserved for the construction of new roadbeds and the preservation of old. In time, the volume of gasoline used will far exceed the most extravagant computation made in our own era.

Under the authority of an act of the General Assembly, passed at the session of 1926, Governor Byrd employed the Bureau of Municipal Research to examine the practical working of the state government, with a view to proposing alterations that would promote economy and efficiency. As far back as 1923, a report had been drafted by a commission on simplification and economy of state and local administration, which recommended the reorganization of the various state departments and the simplification of their processes. No action of importance followed until Governor Byrd had taken office. So soon as the report of the Bureau of Municipal Research was submitted to him, a commission, composed of Virginians well known in various business walks of life, was requested by him to consider its suggestions, and to inform him whether, in their opinion, these suggestions were feasible; and also to mention such further changes and additions as might appear to them to be advisable.

The report drawn up by the Commission adopted in the main the recommendations made by the Bureau of Municipal Research, and only discarded those which seemed to them to be of doubtful usefulness, in the light of conditions then prevailing in Virginia. In a general way, the attitude of the Commission was expressed in the preamble of their report. "Today, Government assumes the proportion of a great business enterprise. It should be equipped, as a great business enterprise must be, with a modern organization and up to date methods." Following out this principle, the Commission recommended that, of the eighty-five administrative agencies then in existence, all those which were essentially useless should be abolished; and that the remainder should be consolidated into the Governor's Office and a certain number of Administrative Departments.

First as to the Governor's Office. To that Office should be assigned the Budget, Records, Military Affairs, and Grounds and Buildings. These should constitute four Divisions. One of the duties of the Director of the Budget should be to reduce to the last degree of conciseness every State official report submitted to the Governor and Assembly. The object of this course of action would be to cut down the heavy bills for public printing. The Division of Records should be placed in the care of the Governor's secretary, while the office of Secretary of the Commonwealth, which, at this time, had the custody of these records, should be abolished. The duty of recording all charters now performed by that officer should be transferred to the State Corporation Commission; and his duty of selling and distributing the State publications should be turned over to the State Library Board. Here the object again was to subserve economy. The

Division of Military Affairs should remain intact.   One Director should be substituted for the Superintendent of Grounds and Buildings and the Superintendent of the State Office Building.

Secondly, the commission recommended that all the agencies of the State Government should, as far as possible, be consolidated into eleven administrative departments.   These should be embraced under the following heads: Taxation, Finance, Highway, Education, Corporations, Industrial Relations, Agriculture and Immigration, Conservation and Development, Health, Public Welfare, and Law.   First, as to taxation.   The State Tax Commission should be retained, but the State Taxation Commission should be abolished.   The tax on capital in business should be directly administered by the Department of Taxation; and that Department should also be intrusted with the duty now performed by the Auditor of Public Accounts in relation to the assessment of taxes.   The department of Finance should, in corresponding Divisions, under separate Directors, have charge of Accounts and Control, the Treasury, Purchase and Printing, and Motor Vehicle Licensing.

The Commission was especially urgent that the system of unified accounting and control should be established through the Department of Finance.   At present, they stated, collections of taxes running into millions of dollars were deposited with more than one Department of the State Government, and, in turn, disbursed by the same.   It was the opinion of the Commission that every dollar of revenue handed in should be placed to the credit of the Treasurer of the State; and when disbursed, should be disbursed through him, with the approval, however, of some selected State officer.   The major part of the work of the Auditor of Public Accounts and the Second Auditor should be transferred to the Director of the Division of Accounts and Control, to be known as the Comptroller.   The office of Auditor of Public Accounts should be retained; but its main duty should be to audit all the accounts kept in the Department of Finance, thus serving as the special agent of the General Assembly in checking the financial acts of the general administration. All transactions in public moneys should clear through the Comptroller's office; and he, in association with the Treasurer, should perform the duties now imposed upon the Commissioners of the Sinking Fund.

The Commission further recommended that the proposed Director of the Division of Purchase and Printing should exercise the powers, and perform the duties, hitherto assigned to the State Purchasing Commission, State Purchasing Agent, and Superintendent of Public Printing. Such director should be authorized to transfer surplus supplies from one department or institution to another, or to sell these supplies if not subsequently needed, thus removing the possibility of serious loss. The present office of Motor Vehicle Commissioner should be merged in the Division of Motor Vehicle Licensing, while general police powers should be conferred upon the men employed in enforcing the motor vehicle regulations. The only change in the laws governing the Department of Highways recommended by the Commission was that the appointment of the members of the Board in control should be made subject to the confirmation of the General Assembly, and not of the Senate alone.

As the Constitution of Virginia now stands, the State Board of Education can only be reorganized by an amendment by popular vote. Five members of the Board are at present practically independent of the creative power. This fact has occasioned general dissatisfaction. To remove this feeling, the Commission recommended that the Governor should be empowered to appoint the members of the Board, with the approval of the General Assembly; that their number should not exceed five; and that they should be kept under the strictest legislation supervision.

During some time, there had been in existence a State Board of Motion Picture Censors. It was recommended by the Commission that this Board should be converted into a Division of Motion Picture Censorship and made subject to the Department of Education. The Director should be appointed by this Department. To that Department also should be transferred the management of the four State Teachers' Colleges for white women, and the Virginia Normal and Industrial Institute for negroes, situated at Petersburg. The immediate charge of these schools should be assigned to a separate Board appointed by the Department. The Boards of the two Schools,—one white, the other black,—for the deaf and blind should be consolidated. All the other Boards, like those of the State library, those of the State institutions of learning, and those appointed to hold examinations for professional licenses, should be retained.

The Commission further recommended that the Bureau of Insurance and the Division of Banking should be merged under the name of the Bureau of Insurance and Banking, with an executive head, appointed by the State Corporation Commission, in control. The office of chief Examiner of Banks should, in their opinion, be abolished; and they also advised that the Industrial Commission and the Bureau of Labor should not be consolidated, but that the two should be brought under the supervision of one Department, in order to avoid the duplication of statistical and inspectional work. This Department should be known as the Bureau of Labor; and it should also embrace in its scope the functions of the State Board of Industrial Rehabilitation.

The recommendations of the Commission provided for the curtailment of the jurisdiction of the Department of Agriculture and Immigration by proposing that the inspection of food for human consumption, and the examination of the condition of dairies and cold-storage warehouses, should be transferred to the Department of Health; and furthermore that the educational and promotional work relating to dairies should be turned over to the State Agricultural College. As a substitute for these changes, the Department of Agriculture and Immigration should perform all the duties of the Convict Life Board, which organization should be abolished. The State Commission on Conser-

vation and Development, the Commission of Game and Inland
Fisheries, and the Commission of Fisheries, should be merged,—
without actual consolidation, however,—into the Department
of Conservation and Development. The object of this was to
avoid expensive duplication in their functions. This was to be
effected directly by semi-annual joint meetings, at which a full
description was to be given by each commission of what its
members had been able to accomplish, during the previous six
months, in the performance of the duties assigned to them.

The State Commission on Conservation and Development had
already been impowered by the General Assembly to assume
control over the Water Power and Development Commission, the
State Geological Commission, the State Geological Survey, the
office of State Geology, and the office of State Forestry.

No alteration in the functions of the Department of Health
was recommended by the Commission, beyond the transfer to it
of the food inspection work already mentioned. It was further
advised by the Commission that the Commission of Public Welfare should be appointed, not by the State Board of Public Welfare, but by the Governor, with the consent of the General Assembly; and that, until the office of the Commissioner of State
Hospitals for the Insane should be abolished by constitutional
amendment, the Commission of Public Welfare should serve in
place of the State Purchasing Agent. Under the law then in
existence, the Commissioner of State Hospitals was *ex officio*
the incumbent of this position.

There were four important reformatories or industrial
schools in Virginia, the affairs of which were administered by
separate boards, composed, in the aggregate, of thirty-eight
members. The commission recommended that these boards
should be reduced to five persons; and that these five should
have control over the four institutions combined. The latter
embraced the Home and Industrial School for White Girls, the
Virginia Industrial School for White Boys, the Virginia Manual
Labor School for Colored Boys, and the Virginia Industrial

School for Colored Girls. No change was recommended for the Prison Board, the State Hospital boards, or the Commission for the Blind. The attorney-general's office was now required to perform the principal administrative duties of the former Commissioner of Prohibition. No change was recommended in this province beyond the investment of the prohibition inspectors with the powers of general police. For the Department of Law proper, a Division of Legislative Drafting was suggested as a substitute for the Legislative Reference Bureau. This should function under the direction of a special officer of its own.

There was, at this time, a state obligation in the form of perpetual educational certificates of the commonwealth. This obligation amounted to the sum of $2,468,605.85, and it was not transferable. The commission recommended that the old certificates should be retired, and that new ones should be issued in their place, which should be subject to the payment of a lower rate of interest. At present, the rate was as high as six per cent. It was computed that not less than $48,300 would be saved by the state through this change.

The commission advised a radical revision of the automobile license law. They proposed that two-year automobile licenses for passenger cars should be issued in the place of the existing one-year licenses. This provision should become effective on January 1, 1928. The amount of the tax to be levied in this form was not to exceed $1.00 per 100 pounds for two years, divided between 70 cents for the first year, and 30 cents for the second. The advantage of the proposed alteration lay in the reduction for the second year. The income would be increased in the issuance of licenses during the first year, without any diminution during the second. At this time, it was calculated that the expense of issuing the licenses exceeded $220,000 a year. The commission also recommended that the gasoline tax should be raised from 4½ cents per gallon to 5 cents.

An undue amount was, in the judgment of the commission, paid by some of the state institutions in the form of architectural fees. They recommended that the governor should select some person who was particularly well qualified to make a survey, whenever such a step had to be taken.

In concluding their report on state reform in general, the commission computed that the alterations which they submitted would relieve the commonwealth ultimately of pecuniary burdens that now aggregated in amount $500,000 at least. This included the saving that would be effected by the adoption of those measures which required the passage of constitutional amendments. To these we will soon refer.

Turning lastly to the field of local government, the Commission recommended that the General Assembly should be authorized by constitutional provision to establish an optional form of Government in the case of every county which indicated, by a popular vote, that it desired to exercise this right, should it be granted. The commission further advised that the counties should be subjected to a certain degree of State supervision, so as to restrain the accumulation of heavy local obligations at high rates of interest. No city, in the Commission's judgment, should have more than one collector of taxes; and its comptroller should audit all its school funds and accounts. That body further recommended that, during a period of five years, the land, buildings, and machinery owned in any city by a new manufacturing plant should be exempted from local taxation.

A commission headed by the President of the Supreme Court of Appeals, Robert R. Prentis, was appointed by Governor Byrd to propose such amendments to the Constitution as the progress of time appeared to have made expedient. The demand for some of these amendments had become really acute, since many of the reforms, which, as we have already mentioned, had been submitted by the Simplification Commission, could not be adopted

unless the path had been cleared for them by the passage of
these new fundamental laws.

The normal course for the Governor of the Commonwealth
to pursue was to summon a Convention to overhaul the whole of
the existing Constitution by the deliberations of members selected
for that specific purpose. Perhaps, had this been done, a more
comprehensive popular understanding would have been obtained
of the work of alteration and addition that was so much desired.
The result too would, perhaps, have been more impressive to
the popular mind. But in opposition to this feeling, it was recalled that the expense of holding a general Convention would
be enormous; and that this could only be avoided by referring
the question of amendment to a body of able lawyers chosen for
their peculiar fitness for the performance of the duties of the
task. Such a body was chosen, and while their recommendations
may not carry as permanent weight as the conclusions of a
large Convention, composed of all the first citizens of Virginia,
instead of half a dozen, would have done, nevertheless those
recommendations, if finally adopted, will undoubtedly subserve
the purpose they had in view; namely, to bring the Commonwealth more directly abreast of the various needs of the present
hour.

The spirit which the Amendment Commission showed in
drafting their work was essentially conservative, although progressive too, because it assured a more elastic form of Government for the management of the affairs of the State. What was
the extent of their revision? There were fifty entire sections
in the existing Constitution which were materially changed, and
thirty-one sections which were not changed to a really important degree. Only seven sections were omitted altogether, as
they originally stood. The number of sections in the altered
Constitution submitted by the Amendment Commission aggregated one hundred and ninety-six. We propose now to refer to
those which the members pronounced to be the most weighty.

Let us begin with the first article. This permitted the accused in a criminal case to be tried by the judge and not as usual by the jury. The prisoner, under these circumstances, would be required to obtain the consent of the commonwealth's attorney, and also to plead not guilty. The second article reduced the voter's term of residence in the State from two years to one, and for the county, city, and town, from one year to six months. The restrictions on women voters were removed by the same article. Among the provisions of this article also was one which permitted the voter, as a prerequisite to exercising the privilege of the suffrage, to reduce the period of payment to two years. The fourth article made lawful the appointment of members of the General Assembly to office during their term, provided the Assembly assumed no right of election in that case. It allowed also a bill to be read by title as sufficient; but what was more important, it empowered adjacent counties to consolidate after a favorable vote. Article fifth advanced the date of the Governor's inauguration, removed the restriction on the amount of his salary, appointed a pardoning board to assure him personal relief, and authorized the Governor to nominate the Treasurer up to January 1, 1932, when the General Assembly was to decide upon the advisability of continuing this plan.

Article sixth provided for an increase in the number of judges occupying seats on the bench of the Supreme Court of Appeals. That Court was empowered to sit in two divisions, in order to afford its members ample leisure for the composition of their opinions. The session of these two divisions were not to coincide in time. The advantage of a divided court, in place of a single, would lie in the maintenance of uniformity of decisions through the close touch of the judges with each other. An important clause of this article authorized the Court of Appeals to end all litigation before it, and enter final judgment, whenever the case in controversy had been once fully developed in the trial court below.

Article seventh impowered the General Assembly to establish a different form of county organization and government, if the people interested had signified their approval of the proposed change by the ballot. Article ninth required that the Superintendent of Public Instruction should be appointed directly by the Governor, with the consent of the General Assembly, but this provision was not to be continued longer than January 1, 1932, should the latter body decide, for any reason, to the contrary. The principle upon which the Superintendent was to be chosen was the same as that illustrated in the case of the Treasurer already mentioned; namely, the Governor was responsible to the voters for the efficiency of his administration, and this could only be rightly demanded of him when his subordinates had been selected by himself. The Division Superintendents were to be chosen by the local boards from lists which had been approved by the State Board. The State Board was only to be permitted to make rules and regulations having the force of law, with the consent of the General Assembly.

By the terms of article eleven, owing to the constantly changing views respecting charitable and penal institutions, a broad authority was conferred on the General Assembly to adopt such methods for their administration as the demands of the time apparently made the most to be preferred.

The questions raised by the thirteenth article involving taxation and finance were, in one instance at least, of extraordinary perplexity. This related to the assessment of abutting lots and houses to defray the cost of street-bed improvements. The Constitution of 1902 had expressly forbidden such an imposition. The demand for the removal of this barrier was made with special urgency by municipal authorities, who had reached the limit of their legislative right to borrow. The imprudence of town councils, in some cases, in overdeveloping their towns in a spirit of ardent but shortsighted local patriotism, made it necessary, from time to time, to refill the municipal treasuries by some new means, unless the ordinary needs of a growing city were to be substantially neglected. But there was vigorous opposition from many sources to the alteration of the Constitution of 1902 in this respect, on the ground that the proposed change would be unjust to real estate in the urban centers, as that real estate already bore the largest burden proportionately to other interests. It was also asserted by these antagonists that, if this new power were conferred on the municipal authorities in general, there would be great danger of its constant abuse under the influence of the already top-heavy municipal projects. The members of the Amendment Commission were so impressed with the doubtful result of removing the obstruction created by the Constitution of 1902, that they left the question in an alternative shape.

In the same section, the Amendment Commission recommended the permanent adoption of tax segregation in the instance of certain kinds of property. This proposed change in a modified form the General Assembly had already passed upon favorably. Article thirteenth permits the issuance of bonds by the State only to the extent of one percent. of the assessed value of taxable realty. Even this cannot be carried so far without the approval of the people voting directly on the point. Finally, the same article permitted cities, towns, and counties to exempt manufacturing establishments from local taxation for a period not exceeding five years. The object of this measure was to encourage the introduction of manufacturing plants.

CONCLUSION

We have now completed our survey of the general conditions of every sort which prevailed in Virginia during the interval that lay between the year 1607 and the year 1927, nearly three centuries and one quarter of a century as a whole, a very long period as time is measured in the history of American communities. We have described the varied institutions the foundations of which the English colonists laid so broad and deep in the seventeenth century; the modifications which all those institutions underwent under the influence of the political separation from Great Britain in the eighteenth century; and, finally, the entire destruction of several of the most conspicuous of these institutions when the besom of the War of 1861-65 passed over them.

The progress which Virginia has made since 1876, when the wheels of her communities began to go forward with some speed again, has not been in the direction of readjustment in the sense of the substantial readoption of her antebellum status. It has rather been in the direction of a status that, when fully attained, will be essentially different from any that she has ever occupied before, even during the period of her greatest prosperity in the past. The abolition of the institution of slavery in 1865, and the increase in the means of locomotion by railway after 1876, tended to bring the State into touch with all the influences that were then moulding the destinies of the North and West. Every year after 1876 saw her draw nearer and nearer to the ideal of that civilization, which is so largely material, but is yet not altogether so. If there continued to be still a considerable degree of isolation, it was due chiefly to the fact that the surface of Virginia, during many years after the

war, remained agricultural, a mere map indeed, of farms, small
or great, with a dot, here and there, to represent a town. But
the towns went on expanding,—first by drawing to themselves so
many vigorous minds and hands from the rural districts; and
secondly, by encouraging the development of a great variety
of industries.

As the towns grew, the State dropped proportionately the
seclusion in which it had been so long wrapped. An ever increasing attention, in consequence, was paid to those means of
winning prosperity,—not simply one, as formerly, but many,—
which the most advanced countries of the world had always
used, and which they had never ceased to value. Nowhere was
this object lesson more impressively presented than in the North.
In the great State of Pennsylvania, for instance, mining, agriculture, manufactures,—in short every branch of the practical arts
had brought an incalculable wealth to its citizens. There the
farm and the city stood side by side. They were not mutually
antagonistic. Rather they were two undivided Siamese twins,
entirely dependent on each other for life. Virginia has not yet
reached so high a coigne of advantage. But, in recent years, as
we have shown in the previous text, she has laid the foundation
for a broad and permanent development of all her resources. She
stands as yet only at the dawn, but with good reason to thing
that so bright a beginning will be followed by a phenomenal degree of sunshine at midday.

In the State, there are now two perfectly homogeneous populations respectively,—the white descendants of the sturdiest
stock in Europe, the English, and the black descendants of the
most enduring stock in Africa. There is no permanent ground
for friction between the two. Each is capable of getting on
peacefully at the side of the other without mingling even partly;
and already the negro problem has been practically solved by
this searching test. In time, as the employments in Virginia
grow more varied and more numerous, additional white population will be drawn from other commonwealths to meet the needs

that will arise in local field, factory, and shop; but the introduction will, perhaps, be so gradual and so quiet as to occasion no disturbing influence upon the State's social or industrial life. With such an enormous mass of her citizens in these later times sprung from the original strain of Virginians, there is a strong probability that the conservative spirit of the community, inherited from a distant past, will outlive the stress even of this radically alien influx.

But it is not merely the new factories, the improved farms, and crops, and the expanding cities, that will advance the prosperity of the State. Already its romantic past, now that a system of good roads in very widely advertised, is exciting the increasing interest of the North and West. Even before the Highway Commission has really completed its work, tourists from these quarters of the compass are to be counted by tens of thousands on the Virginian roads. And they are certain to augment in number in the future, and thus conspicuously swell the income of each community as the years go by. The shrines to be found in every division of the commonwealth, by lending an unusual color to the localities where they are situated, will tempt visitors to the State to include them in their itinerary. Virginia lies in the middle ground between the North and the South. This fact alone will result in the traversal of its soil by thousands of persons, independently of those who are merely seeking a tour of pleasure. The beautiful scenery in the Valley, Piedmont, and Southwest, and along the great rivers of Tidewater, and on the seashore adjacent to Hampton Roads, will attract permanent settlers when the improved highways have made them fully accessible from every direction.

Men stand as yet on the mere edge of the diversified revolution which the motor-car has begun to produce. It is quite possible that the cities in time will become merely centers for the transaction of business during the day, without containing any area reserved, either in the day or the night, for residents of a higher social quality than the operatives in the factories.

The homes of people of means, large or moderate, will be scattred about within a radius of ten miles of the boundaries of the town. We already see the tendency to abandon city houses for these more healthy and more open spaces practically in the original country, which are, however, near enough to shop and counting-house to put no real obstruction on the daily pursuit of business under a town-roof.

The alteration in the general outlook now reflected in the extraordinary importance attached to success in business is producing a new type of Virginian,—the keen, shrewd, practical American, bent upon reaping those legitimate rewards which business sagacity and assiduity are sure to make possible. But this very man will cheerfully submit to any sacrifice of personal convenience or money to promote the welfare of the town in which he resides; and in this unselfish course, he is animated by a genuine feeling of patriotism. Under the influence of this fine civic spirit, all the towns are rapidly increasing, not simply in size, but also in beauty of aspect, and in solidity of construction.

The interest in education too is steadily expanding. The value in which the arts are held is also becoming keener as the people read and travel abroad more. The importance of good roads and all other forms of improvements are recognized with increasing clearness. In brief, the utilization of all the advantages of modern civilization is considered to be more and more imperative.

And yet behind this ardent progressive spirit, veneration for the great men of Virginia's past, and pride in the history of its great events, survive. This patriotic conservatism is revealed in the living Virginian at the very time that he is most eager to see his community crowned with all those material benefits that have already begun to flow to it through the development of the varied resources of the State. The old Commonwealth has, indeed, been reborn in recent years in a practical way; but her citizens are never likely to forget, or to allow their children to forget, the illustrious story of their forebears, beginning with the landing at Cape Henry in 1607, and coming down through the centuries to the World War, and from the World War, to the present day,—in which the living generation is making an industrial record not unworthy to be associated with the great achievements of Virginia's past in so many other departments of life.

BIBLIOGRAPHY

A full bibliography of the entire period covered by the first two volumes of this history of Virginia, namely, the interval of several centuries extending from 1607 to 1926, would embrace every book which has been written about the colony and state. The short list appended contains simply the works which throw a vivid light on certain sides of that history which appear to be of special significance from a social, political, or economic point of view.

Adams, Herbert B.—*The College of William and Mary*, 1887.

Ambler, Charles Henry—*Sectionalism in Virginia from 1776 to 1861*, 1910.

Anderson, D. K.—*Life of William B. Giles*, 1910.

Bagby, George W.—*The Old Virginia Gentleman*, 1910.

Ballagh, James C.—*History of Slavery in Virginia*, 1902.

Barton, Robert T.—*Virginia Colonial Decisions*, 1902.

Battles and Leaders of the Civil War.

Beverly, Robert—*History of Virginia*, 1722.

Bland, Richard—*Inquiry Into the Rights of the British Colonies*, 1766; *A Letter to the Clergy of Virginia*, 1760.

Bledsoe, Albert T.—*Is Davis a Traitor?*

Bradford, Gamaliel—*Lee, the American*, 1912.

Brown, Alexander—*Genesis of United States* and other works.

Bruce, Philip Alexander—*Life of Robert E. Lee; Social, Economic and Institutional Histories of Virginia*, 17th Century; *History of the University of Virginia*, 1921; *Rise of the New South.*

Bruce, William Cabell—*Life of John Randolph of Roanoke.*

Burk, John D.—*History of Virginia.*

Byrd, William—Writings of, Bassett Edition, 1901.

Campbell, Charles—*History of Virginia.*

530

Cooke, John Esten—*Wearing of the Gray*, 1867; *History of Virginia*.

Dabney, Robert L.—*A Defense of Virginia*, 1867.

Eggleston, Joseph D.—*Reports of Commissioner of Education, Virginia*.

Eckenrode, H. J.—*Separation of Church and State in Virginia*, 1910; *Political History of Virginia During Reconstruction Times*, 1904.

Fithian, Philip Vickers—*Journal and Letters, 1767-1774*.

Fontaine, James—*Memoirs of a Huguenot Family*, 1872.

Foote, W. H.—*Sketches of Virginia*, 1850.

Ford, W. C.—*Writings of George Washington*, 1893.

Gee, Professor Wilson—*Publications of School of Rural Social Economics*, West Virginia.

Gildersleeve, B. L.—*Creed of the Old South*, 1915.

Goode, G. B.—*Virginia Cousins*, 1887.

Gordon, Armistead C.—*Life of William F. Gordon*, 1909; *Life of W. Gordon McCabe*, 1926.

Green, B. W.—*Wordbook of Virginia Folk Speech*, 1912.

Grigsby, Hugh B.—*Discourses and Orations*.

Hoyt, Harris—*Reports as Commissioner of Education, Virginia*.

Hayden, Horace E.—*Virginia Genealogies*, 1891.

Henderson, Col. G. F. R.—*Life of Stonewall Jackson*, 1898.

Hening, W. W.—*Statutes of Virginia*.

Henry, William Wirt—*Life of Patrick Henry*, 1891.

Heatwole, Prof.—*History of Education in Virginia*.

Jefferson, Thomas—*Works*, Ford Edition.

Johnston, Mary—*Historical Novels*.

Jones, Prof. R. Chapin—*Monographs on Subject of Forest Resources of Virginia*.

Jones, Hugh—*Present State of Virginia*, 1724.

Kingsbury, Susan W.—*Records of Virginia Company of London*, 1905.

Koiner, G. W.—*Reports as Commissioner of Agriculture, Virginia*.

Lee, E. J.—*Lee of Virginia, 1642-1892.*

Long, Gen. A. L.—*Memoirs of General Robert E. Lee.*

McCabe, W. Gordon—*Virginia Schools Before and After the Revolution.*

McIlwaine, Richard—*Memoirs,* 1908.

Madison, James—*Works,* Hunt Edition.

Martin, Joseph—*The Virginia Gazetteer.*

Massey, John E.—*Autobiography.*

Minor, B. B.—*History of the Southern Literary Messenger,* 1905.

Mordicai, Samuel—*Richmond in Bygone Days,* 1860.

Morton, O. F.—*History of Rockbridge County,* 1920.

Morton, Richard Lee—*Virginia Since 1861,* 1923; *Virginia State Debt and Internal Improvements.*

Munford, B. B.—*Virginia's Attitude Towards Slavery and Secession,* 1907.

Neill, Edward D.—*English Colonization in America, 17th Century; Virginia Carolorum,* 1886; *Virginia Company of London,* 1869.

Page, Rosewell—*Government in Virginia,* 1924.

Page, Thomas Nelson—*In Ole Virginia,* 1887; *The Old Dominion, Her Making and Her Manners,* 1908; *The Old South,* 1892; *Robert E. Lee, the Southerner,* 1908; *Social Life in Old Virginia Before the War.*

Patton, John S.—*Jefferson, Cabell, and the University of Virginia,* 1906.

Pearson, C. C.—*The Readjuster Movement in Virginia,* 1917.

Randolph, John—*Letters and Speeches.*

Robertson, Alexander F.—*Life of Alexander H. H. Stuart,* 1926.

Rowland, Kate M.—*Life of George Mason,* 1892.

Royall, W. L.—*History of Virginia Banks and Banking Prior to the War,* 1907; *The Virginia State Debt Controversy.*

Ruffin, Edmund—*The Farmer's Register; Essay on Calcareous Manures.*

Sale, Edith Tunis—*Manors in Virginia in Colonial Times,* 1909.

Scott, W. W.—*History of Orange,* 1907.

Smith, Capt. John—*History of Virginia.*

Southern Literary Messenger—articles and poems.

Spotswood, Governor Alexander—*Letters,* Virginia Historical Society Publications.

Stanard, Mary Newton—*Story of Bacon's Rebellion; Colonial Virginia.*

Stith, William—*History of the First Discovery of Virginia.*

Strother, David H.—*Virginia Illustrated,* 1857.

Swem, Earl G.—*William and Mary College Quarterly,* New Series.

Taylor, John—*Arator,* 1813.

Taylor, Col. W. H.—*Four Years with General Lee,* 1877.

Thomas, R. S.—*Religious Element in Jamestown Settlement,* 1895.

Thompson, John R.—*Poems,* Patton's Edition.

Tyler, Lyon G.—*Cradle of the Republic,* 1906; *England in America,* 1904; *Williamsburg, the Old Colonial Capital; William and Mary College Quarterly,* First Series; *Tyler's Historical Magazine.*

Virginia Magazine of History and Biography.

Virginia Company of London, Abstracts of Proceedings, Virginia Historical Society Publications.

Virginia County Records for the Seventeenth Century.

Virginia Colonial Council, Minutes, State Publication.

Virginia Economic and Social County Surveys, University of Virginia Publications, Prof. Wilson Gee, Editor.

Virginia House of Burgesses, Minutes, State Publication.

Virginia Historical Register.

Virginia Reports of State Officers to Governor and General Assembly.

Virginia War History Commission Publications, edited by Prof. Arthur Kyle Davis, Sr.

Wayland, John W.—*German Element in Shenandoah Valley.*

Wertenbaker, T. J.—*Virginia Under the Stuarts,* 1914.

White, Henry A.—*Life of Stonewall Jackson.*

Wise, Jennings C.—*Military History of Virginia Military Institute*, 1915; *History of the Eastern Shore.*

Wise, John S.—*End of an Era.*

Wise, Barton H.—*Life of Henry A. Wise*, 1899.

Withers, Robert E.—*Autobiography of an Octogenarian*, 1907.